Playhouse Square and the Cleveland Renaissance

Playhouse Square and the Cleveland Renaissance

John Vacha

The Kent State University Press *Kent, Ohio*

ISBN 978-1-60635-474-2
Published in the United States of America

Cataloging information for this title is available at the Library of Congress.

28 27 26 25 24   5 4 3 2 1

To the memory of

Ray Shepardson

and

Elaine Hadden

Contents

Preface and Acknowledgments

In probably the first extended effort to tell its story, published in 1975 and fondly referred to afterward as "the Red Book," author Kathleen Kennedy managed in two sentences to encapsulate the sensation of Playhouse Square: "Of the few surviving movie palaces in the country, five of them are still standing in Cleveland; and four of these five (the Allen, the Ohio, the State and the Palace) stand side by side in one of the most unique complexes of theatres in the United States. These fabulous old buildings are not being torn down; instead they are being restored and preserved for a future greatness befitting their origins."[1] One might attach a couple of caveats to her summary. Absent is any reference to the Hanna Theatre, a legitimate theater, set apart from the four movie palaces on an adjacent side street but close enough to qualify as a part of Playhouse Square. Notice must also be taken of the use of the present tense in her second sentence, for in 1975 the fate of the four movie palaces, not only their restoration but their very preservation, was still far from guaranteed.

Nevertheless, Kennedy recognized the two singular sensations of Playhouse Square. First came the juxtaposition of the four Euclid Avenue theaters, their marquees extending practically shoulder to shoulder over the sidewalk on the north side of the street. Their unique concentration had been achieved through the legerdemain of a Cleveland realtor, and few American cities outside New York's Broadway could offer such a critical mass of entertainment choices.

Following World War II all four served as movie palaces, as the late Dick Feagler remembered:

> Suppose you wanted to see a movie that had just been released, *The Robe* for example. Well, you could wait until it came to your neighborhood theater, but it wouldn't get there for months. If you wanted to see it when people were still talking about it, you had to go Downtown to an area called Playhouse Square which was lined with fancy movie theaters with balconies and armies of ushers and splendid interiors that looked like the inside of a Paris opera house. The inside of places Downtown was awesome.[2]

But for various reasons, Clevelanders stopped going downtown for movies in the postwar era, and the four Playhouse Square marquees went dark half a century ago. That led to the second singular sensation of Playhouse Square, for they *weren't* torn down. Prompted by the mesmerism of a visionary from Seattle, all four plus the Hanna were saved for future generations of Clevelanders. Their survival and revival were all the more remarkable for bucking a national trend of decline and demolition. "Most of America's great movie palaces are gone, going or mutilated," declared architectural critic Wolf von Eckardt in 1980. "New York, where the first dream cathedrals were built, has virtually none left intact."[3] They aren't movie palaces anymore, but the four contiguous theaters saved in Cleveland, along with the nearby Hanna, survive as the second-largest performing arts center in America. It took fifty years for Playhouse Square to decline; it took another fifty years to bring it back to the milestone of its centennial.

A little more than a century ago, Cleveland went through possibly the most creative period in its history. The half dozen years from 1915 to 1920 saw the births of the Neighborhood Settlement (today's Karamu), the Cleveland Museum of Art, the Cleveland Play House, the Cleveland Orchestra, and the Cleveland Institute of Music. Julia McCune Flory, one of the Play House founders, likened it to an angel stirring the waters of the Cuyahoga River. Usually the list ends with the opening of the Cleveland Institute of Music in December 1920—only a few months before the opening of four of the Playhouse Square theaters. At the time, the theaters were regarded as more of a commercial than a cultural venture, but in its present reincarnation Playhouse Square takes its place alongside the Cleveland Orchestra and the Cleveland Museum of Art as one of Cleveland's world-class cultural assets. As many believe, its revival from the depths of the 1970s served as the lodestar for the comeback of an entire city.

My own experience of Playhouse Square began much as Dick Feagler recollected: being taken by my parents downtown to a movie. Later, I went with my wife to Playhouse Square not only to the movie palaces on Euclid Avenue but to Broadway plays and musicals at the Hanna. When I began writing about regional theater history, I covered several parts and periods of Playhouse Square in books and magazines and thought I might have been done with the subject, until I was asked to do an article on Ray Shepardson for the *Teaching Cleveland* website. Interviewing him and others involved in the campaign to save the theaters reignited my interest in Playhouse Square. With the centennial in mind, I began thinking of a comprehensive history of the district in the context of Cleveland's fluctuating fortunes. The result follows.

Like the history of Playhouse Square, the book is divided into two nearly equal sections covering forty-eight and fifty-four years. First comes the opening of the five theaters as vaudeville, silent film, and "legitimate" houses—an exuberant expression of Cleveland at the height of its national influence. Through the years vaudeville died, silents became talkies, and the two legitimate theaters dwindled to one. By World War II, the Euclid Avenue theaters had all become first-run movie houses, and postwar challenges to both movies and the urban environment resulted in the closing of all four by 1969.

Having covered what it was, the second half of *Playhouse Square and the Cleveland Renaissance* deals with what it has become. It opens with the dramatic story of how the two central movie houses were snatched from the orbit of the wrecking ball. Contrary to the generally compressed version, it was not a "one and done" deal. The Junior League's transformative gift of $25,000 was in the nature of seed money, followed by half a decade of individual and corporate and eventual government and foundation support before the theaters were secure. In the process, the preservation impulse spilled over from Playhouse Square to downtown Cleveland in general.

What Playhouse Square has become is a work in progress. From the reopening of the renovated movie palaces as an arts center second in size only to New York's Lincoln Center, it proceeded to the acquisition of neighboring real estate to provide an endowment for the theaters. Due to changing entertainment tastes, certain theaters were downsized and several smaller stages were added. The coming of the "megamusical" promoted the Broadway Series into the face of Playhouse Square. Its evolving success has made Playhouse Square a national urban planning model and a prime driver in the renaissance of Cleveland itself.

In compiling this history of Playhouse Square, I have made great use of newspaper sources, often extolled as the "first draft of history." They are especially valuable for a theater history: in their ads can be found verification of dates, programs, and popular appeals; their critics' reviews bring out eyewitness production details and original impressions of works that may in time become classics in their genre. Equally valuable for this account have been personal interviews with participants.

I am indebted to many people for assistance in gathering material for this history. Among them are Judith Cetina, Cuyahoga County archivist; Ruth Flannery, Playhouse Square archivist; Don Boozer and the Cleveland Public Library (CPL) literature department; Olivia Hoge and the CPL history and geography department; Brian Meggitt and the CPL photograph collection; Daniel Musson, Cleveland Landmarks Commission secretary; Beth Piwkowski, Cleveland State University Special Collections librarian; Kacey Shapiro, Great Lakes Theater marketing and communications director; as well as the staff of the Lakewood Public Library. I also greatly appreciated the assistance of Michael Baron, Bill Barrow, John Cimperman, Frank Dutton, Oliver Henkel, Betty Whitty Keeler, John Pyke, and Barbara Thatcher. Many people involved in the later history of Playhouse Square helpfully agreed to interviews.

Thanks are due to Susan Wadsworth-Booth and Kat Saunders of the Kent State University Press for publishing this valedictory volume. Mary Young, Erin Holman, Christine Brooks, Julia Wiesenberg, and Clara Totten all contributed greatly to seeing it in print. Special gratitude goes to Carter Ellison, Kelly Flanagan, and Kassidy Kovacik for converting my manuscript from hard copy to digital copy. Finally, I must express continued gratitude to my wife and soulmate, Ruta, for her lifelong encouragement, support, and companionship during countless nights at the theater.

PART I

• • • • • • • • • • •

The Way It Was

Another Op'nin'

Star Power

"A new theater and a new film star. A great combination," wrote movie critic W. Ward Marsh in the *Cleveland Plain Dealer*. Ina Claire was the new film star, miming her Broadway success in the silent screen production of *Polly with a Past*. "The theater—you will be right in saying is magnificent," said Marsh.[1]

More than three thousand Clevelanders undoubtedly shared Marsh's enthusiasm over the State Theatre's opening on February 5, 1921. Film mogul Marcus Loew had brought Metro Films stars to ballyhoo the latest in his chain of Loew's movie palaces. They included such now forgotten players of the silent screen as Bert Lytell, Zeena Keefe, Helene "Smiles" Davis, and Montagu Love.[2] (Only one, Anita Loos, would be remembered today—not as an actress but as the author of *Gentlemen Prefer Blondes*.)

At 7:00 P.M., the visitors joined an opening night audience at the new theater in the 1500 block of Euclid Avenue. They gathered beneath a marquee topped by a vertical fifty-foot blade sign extolled as "one of the largest in the middle west and the largest in Cleveland." Spelling out "Loew's State," it featured "a sunburst effect shooting from the base to crown augmented by a traveling border."[3] Up to four thousand Clevelanders paid fifty cents a head to see the new theater and the stars.

The company that lit up the Loew's State Theatre entrance claimed bragging rights as "The Largest Theatrical Sign in the Country." As depicted in this ad, the original State marquee was to be replicated in the theater's renovation some sixty years later. (*Cleveland Plain Dealer*, February 5, 1921)

They entered through a street vestibule with a coffered ceiling and a floor of white Vermont marble, which led through a set of doors to an outer lobby of ivory and gold, with high scagliola wainscoting. Even then, they were but halfway to the theater proper. Through another set of gleaming brass doors lay the grand lobby.[4] Crystal chandeliers hung from three octagonal saucer domes in the ceiling more than thirty feet above. A huge fireplace dominated one wall, flanked by four fluted columns, matched by a similar quartet on the opposite wall.

That still left a lot of blank space to fill, and the builders had turned that assignment over to a young muralist named James Daugherty. A native of Asheville, North Carolina, Daugherty had studied art in Philadelphia and London but developed his style of bold, sweeping lines and color while camouflaging the broadsides of ships for the US Navy during World War I. For the State lobby walls, he painted four ten-by-forty-foot murals on preapplied canvas, each devoted to images called to mind by the four principal continents: Asia—*The Spirit of Fantasy,* Africa–*The Spirit of*

Pageantry, Europe—*The Spirit of Drama,* and America—*The Spirit of Cinema.*

Henry Turner Bailey, director of the Cleveland School of Art, provided verbal descriptions of Daugherty's murals for *Cleveland Plain Dealer* readers. Comparing it with the European composition, he summarized *The Spirit of Cinema:* "Here the modern vamp supplants Helen of Troy; jazz drowns the pipes of Pan; an auto supersedes the chariot; a flying machine outsoars Pegasus; towering skyscrapers overtop the temple crowned Acropolis; Palm Beach bathers eclipse the nymphs; the boy scout takes the place of the shepherd boy. The totem pole of the north and the weirdly decorated Indian utensils of the south here take the place of Greek lovliness in common things. The composition is rush hour." Praising the artist's brilliant coloring and daring composition, Bailey suggested Daugherty might have achieved more refined results had the contractors, New York's Fleischmann Construction Company, allowed him more than sixty days for the job.[5]

At the far end of Daugherty's murals rose twin marble balustraded staircases to the balcony level, flanking a central passageway to the orchestra section. Either way, straight ahead lay not the auditorium and stage but a blank wall, turning the theatergoer ninety degrees rightward. Behind another set of doors on each level, patrons finally found themselves in the theater, though they couldn't see it directly through the doors. To view it, once inside theatergoers had to make another ninety-degree turn, to the left. Directly north, in the same bearing as their Euclid Avenue entrance, were the seating and stage.

Most would have agreed it was worth the long, zigzagging walk to get there. They were in an auditorium 120 feet wide and 180 deep, designed in what was originally described as "Italian Renaissance or middle period," though later called Roman, Greek, and European Baroque. Elements of all those styles probably figured in the overall effect. Black and gold draperies formed a backdrop for three step-staggered boxes on the side walls. Patrons sat in a claimed four thousand gray leather seats with red-velvet backs, facing a hundred-foot-wide stage. Glancing upward—or straight ahead from the balcony—they would have seen a large mural spread across the sounding board, *The Gods on Mt. Parnassus.*[6]

Following their eyepopping progress through the theater's regal anterooms and their arrival at last in the awesome audience chamber, first-nighters might have experienced the actual program as something of an anticlimax. One of Cleveland's three musical Spitalny brothers, Hyman, led the thirty-piece house orchestra in Sibelius's *Finlandia* by way of an overture.[7] *Neighbors*, a Buster Keaton two-reeler, was the featurette, followed by the feature, *Polly with a Past*. Of local interest was Claire's costar, a product of Cleveland's Glenville High School. Ralph Graves was described as having "'Gibson man' features and blonde wavy hair." He wasn't among the stars present "in person," but Mrs. J. H. Horsburgh, his mother, would be watching his performance from one of the State's boxes.[8] W. Ward Marsh summarized the film in the *Plain Dealer* as "the story of a girl who poses as a wicked French woman [so] that she may vamp the hero [Graves] so he will be 'saved' by his real sweetheart." Dismissive of the supporting players, including hometown boy Graves, he concluded, "Miss Claire is great enough to cover the deficiencies of the others."[9]

On Sunday, the day after the opening festivities, *Cleveland Press* critic George Davis returned for a closer look at "the colorful, playful modern mural paintings in the lobby of Loew's new State Theater." His hopes of overhearing some comments from other spectators were dashed, however, as all other eyes in the grand lobby were centered on movie actress Ruth Roland, one of the stars imported for the opening. "What does that mean?" he asked rhetorically and answered, "Perhaps that curiosity in no other object of art equals curiosity in a pretty gal."[10] Maybe so, but Roland is long gone and forgotten, while James Daugherty's murals would one day play a part in the State Theatre's salvation.

The State was one of some three hundred theaters designed by Ohio's own Thomas W. Lamb, easily America's most prolific theater architect. He had already opened three of New York City's most impressive movie palaces—the Rialto, the Rivoli, and the Capitol—and was finishing a Loew's State for Broadway concurrently with the Cleveland version.[11] Most of his movie houses were described as Adamesque, a style from which he evidently deviated in his plans for Cleveland's State. Lamb also designed "legitimate" theaters for live drama, with Broadway's Eltinge, Cort, and Candler theaters among his credits.[12] At the time he also happened to be finishing one in Cleveland next door to the Loew's State.

A "Legitimate" House

Only nine days after the State's debut, Loew's Ohio Theatre opened just two doors to the west. Its marquee and vestibule shared the same four-story facade of a narrow structure on Euclid Avenue, the Ohio Building. Once past the modest entrance to the offices above, the two theaters' lobbies abutted and extended side by side to the auditoriums beyond.

Like the State Theatre, the Ohio had a low-ceilinged outer lobby, eighty feet long and opening into a "grand foyer" every bit as impressive as its State counterpart on the other side of its eastern

A minstrel serenaded his muse on the covers of Ohio Theatre programs from opening night in 1921 to the end of the decade. During that period, manager Robert McLaughlin kept the theater's marquee lit for one stretch of 299 consecutive weeks. (Author's collection)

wall. Though narrower by ten feet than the State Lobby's forty-five, it was slightly longer, at around two hundred feet. "It may be compared best, perhaps, with the lobby of some metropolitan hotel," wrote *Plain Dealer* drama critic Harlowe R. Hoyt. "Rare antiques and furniture flank it," supplied largely by C. A. Selzer, an art dealer located just west of the theater.[13] On the foyer's eastern wall stood two fireplaces, each flanked by a pair of fluted columns, matched by two pairs on the opposite wall. Between each pair was a large painting in fresco, one titled *Venus, Her Birth from the Waves* and the other *Her Triumph*, both by an artist identified as R. D. Sampitrotti. Over the passage back into the outer lobby, his Venus group concluded with *Her Consecration*.[14]

Again hand-in-hand with the neighboring State, the Ohio's grand foyer culminated in a central passage to the orchestra between twin staircases to the balcony. Unlike the State, however, the staircases led directly to the auditorium, which opened straight ahead. (Few, if any, who had attended the Loew's State premiere the previous week would have realized that the zigzag route to the State's auditorium was necessary out of deference to the right rear corner of the Ohio's auditorium.) Inside, Lamb had provided decor described as "Italian renaissance" in style, finished in "shades of green and old ivory." A pair of large Arcadian murals by one P. Pitti covered the side walls of the balcony. Overhead hung a "rare crystal chandelier" recycled by Selzer from "an old estate near Milan." There were four side boxes arranged in two pairs on either wall of the orchestra, as well as a row of boxes in the rear of the balcony, where smoking by both men and women patrons was permitted.[15]

While just as ornate, the Ohio's auditorium was laid out on a much smaller scale than the State's, for this was to be a "legitimate" house, intended for live stage presentations. Its fourteen hundred seats were less than half the State's.[16] For those to whom it greatly mattered, the opening night's program was a revival of David Belasco's *The Return of Peter Grimm*, starring David Warfield. It was a typical pre–World War I melodrama, with Belasco's usual meticulous scenic effects. Critic Archie Bell summarized it for *Cleveland News* readers: "The crusty old bachelor [Grimm] dies in the first act and his spirit or ghost goes stalking through the play until the final scene"—where the plot satisfactorily untangled. Warfield, who had originated the title role in 1911, stepped out of character after the second act to address the audience. "I tell you it's the most beautiful theater in the world," he said of their surroundings.[17]

The 1920s were notable for not only the construction of opulent movie palaces but a quieter but no less noteworthy trend in the opening of playhouses. In New York, it was Broadway's last big building boom, as two dozen new houses raised their curtains during the decade. Five opened in 1921, led by the Ambassador Theatre only three days prior to the Ohio's debut in Cleveland. The Ambassador was followed on Broadway that year by the Ritz (later renamed the Walter Kerr), the National (later the Billy Rose), Jolson's 59th Street Theatre, and Irving Berlin's Music Box.[18] Cleveland also wasn't finished raising theaters that year: the Hanna Theatre opened its doors exactly six weeks after the Ohio.

A "Broadway-Style" House

In some ways the Hanna was the antithesis of the newly opened State and Ohio. Its marquee was located not on prestigious Euclid Avenue but around the corner of East Fourteenth, a side street. In that respect it shared a characteristic with Broadway houses, most of which were actually located just off the Great White Way on the cross streets of New York's West 40s. Location wasn't the only difference between the Hanna and the showcases of Euclid

The Hanna Theatre was ensconced on East Fourteenth Street in the eight-story Hanna Building Annex. The rear of the main Hanna Building can be seen in the background, on Euclid Avenue, beyond which were the four main theaters of Playhouse Square. (Author's collection)

Hanna Building looking North from Prospect, Cleveland, Ohio.

Avenue, however. In planning, dimensions, and ambiance, it was a Broadway-style house.

The Hanna Theatre was part of an acre-and-a-half office complex built in 1921 by Daniel Rhodes Hanna and dedicated to the memory of his father, the business and political leader Marcus A. Hanna. It was anchored by a sixteen-story office building on the southeast corner of Euclid and East Fourteenth Street. A seven-story pedestrian passageway over Brownell Court connected the main building with an eight-story annex on the northeast corner of Fourteenth and Prospect Avenue. The theater, in the Hanna Building Annex, had its entrance on East Fourteenth. Like the office complex, it was named after the late US senator, who was as passionate about theater as about politics. All was designed by New York architect Charles A. Platt in his idiomatic Florentine palazzo style. He had designed William G. Mather's Gwinn Estate and gardens in nearby Bratenahl and soon would plan the Freer Art Gallery in Washington, DC, but the Hanna was his first theater.

First-nighters entered the Hanna through a utilitarian lobby barely twenty feet square, with a box office window on the left-hand wall. An inner set of doors practically put them in the theater, separated from the outer lobby by only a narrow foyer leading to the orchestra, restrooms, and side stairways to the balcony. It was a far cry from the State's and Ohio's sumptuous grand lobbies but more suggestive of the entrances to many theaters on Broadway, where real estate values could mitigate against unnecessary frills.

Architect Platt and an interior decorator harmoniously named Faustino Sampietro compensated for the austerity of the front of the house with a truly elegant auditorium. Described as "Pompeiian in design and decoration," it was dominated by shades of green and gold in carpeting, seats, and stage curtain. Travertine side walls were overarched by a coffered ceiling of gold and aquamarine medallions containing such classical images as dragons and cupids. On the outer edge of the sounding board appeared the names of ten classic dramatists, from Aeschylus through "Shakspere" to Ibsen. Above the proscenium was a group of modest-sized classical landscapes, and each wall contained a single side box.[19] The theater's upper deck was divided by a crossover aisle into a four-row mezzanine and a larger balcony in the rear.

Although the Hanna's capacity of fourteen hundred playgoers roughly equaled that of the Ohio Theatre, observers then and later seemed to sense a heightened intimacy in the Hanna. Broadway's Lee Shubert and Crosby Gaige, who would lease the theater, were both in the opening-night audience. While there were many larger theaters in the world, none was more perfect for its intended use than the Hanna, observed Shubert. "It's large enough so its managers can afford to present in it the best plays offered; but it is 'intimate' enough to present the quietest comedy or drama to the best advantage," commented Gaige. "It's a gem."[20] It was a quality noted thirty years later by future critic James Damico, who remembered seeing some forty shows in the 1950s at the Hanna: "All from the last two rows in the balcony at $1.25 a pop—the only seats my student budget would allow—yet never missing a whisper or eyebrow lifting, because the Hanna in its original proscenium configuration, was by some measure the finest play venue in town."[21] What the opening night audience in 1921 saw was standard fare much in the vein of the Ohio's *The Return of Peter Grimm*. The Hanna's premiere offering was Amelie Rives's adaptation of *The Prince and the Pauper*. "It tells a delightful story, as all readers of Mark Twain's novel knows [*sic*], a satirical, stinging rebuke to the royal idea and a belief with proof that all men are created equals and that it is only circumstances that alter cases," explained Archie Bell to *News* readers.[22]

Both title roles in *The Prince and the Pauper* were not only played by the same person but by an actress, Ruth Findlay. Star billing, however, went to William Faversham, a veteran actor of David Warfield's generation who had once played Romeo to the Juliet of Maude Adams. Now he took on the avuncular role of Miles Hendon, the soldier of fortune who befriended the misidentified prince and helped restore him to his rightful place on the throne. Like Warfield at the Ohio, and contrary to the original plan, Faversham was compelled by audience demand to deliver some appropriate words for the occasion midway through the play's four acts. After paying tribute to the theater's namesake, Mark Hanna, as "a true friend (in time of need and at other times) to such actors as Lawrence Barrett and Edwin Booth," he congratulated Cleveland "upon the acquisition of this beautiful playhouse."[23]

One More Time

Still the show hadn't ended, as yet another opening waited in the wings. Eight weeks after the State's debut, theatergoers returned to Euclid Avenue, on April 1, 1921, to greet one more new theater, the Allen.

Several features set the Allen apart from its three other neighboring new theaters. Foremost was its purpose which was to be devoted exclusively to the showing of motion pictures. It was built for and named after brothers Jules and Jay Allen of Toronto, who were expanding their chain of Canadian movie theaters into the United States.

Like the Hanna, the Allen was incorporated into an office building, the eight-story Bulkley Building developed by Cleveland businessman, lawyer, and politician Robert J. Bulkley. Both building and theater were designed by Detroit architect C. Howard Crane, whose portfolio included numerous movie houses and Broadway's Music Box Theatre.[24]

Somewhere between the minimal lobby of the Hanna and the maximal ones of the State and Ohio, the Allen's outer lobby led to an imposing rotunda supported by sixteen Corinthian columns and topped with a thirty-three-foot-high dome. Reportedly modeled after the Villa Madonna outside Rome, it was centered by a "great chandelier, dancing with innumerable tiny balls of light" hanging above a fountain on the marble floor below. One of several amenities off the rotunda was the Allen Tea Room.[25]

Beyond its circular lobby the Allen's auditorium really set it apart from its theatrical neighbors. While the auditoria of the State, Ohio, and Hanna followed the traditional fan-shaped design of classical live theater, the Allen's conformed to the needs of the new twentieth-century art form of cinema. As screen images were much larger than live actors on a stage, it simply expanded the narrow shoebox shape of the early nickelodeon. Acoustics counted for little when films were silent, and the mezzanine lobby to the Allen's balcony circulated around an elliptical opening directly above the rear orchestra seats downstairs. There were no side boxes along the auditorium walls, decorated instead with faux windows backlit to suggest bright daylight outside. Adding to the atmospheric effect was a bright azure sky peeking through cumulus clouds painted on the ceiling.

Phil Spitalny, Hyman's brother, entered at 8:30 on opening night to lead the Allen's thirty-five–piece orchestra in "The Star-Spangled Banner" and Tchaikovsky's "Capriccio Italien." Then the lights dimmed for a series of "news, educational and scenic films" leading into the feature, *The Greatest Love*, starring Vera Gordon. Afterward, there was dancing in the rotunda until midnight. "An Appreciation" by the Allen's management ran in the next morning's *Plain Dealer*, thanking the public for its "spontaneous response . . . to the opening of Playhouse Square's newest theatre."[26]

Facing page: Faithfully restored after seventy-four years, the Allen Theatre's circular lobby, beneath a thirty-three-foot-high rotunda, set it apart from its Playhouse Square neighbors. The only thing missing from the original is the fountain that occupied the middle of the floor. (David M. Thum, Cleveland Landmarks Commission)

"Millionaires' Row"

Four spectacular new theaters opening within a block of one another in just two months! In the heady days following the Great War, Cleveland was bursting its seams. With a 1920 population of 796,841, it could style itself as the nation's Fifth City. Charles Brooks, a founder of the Cleveland Play House, took note of a sign in Public Square proclaiming a goal of 1 million Clevelanders by 1930. It was accompanied by a painted forty-foot thermometer to illustrate the city's progress.[27] Downtown Cleveland, which had begun in the blocks west of Public Square, then gathered around the square, was now reaching east. The logical route would have been to continue eastward along Superior Avenue, the city's main artery from the Cuyahoga River Flats to the square—but urban development doesn't always follow logic.

Like Broadway in Manhattan, Euclid Avenue deviated from the grid of early Cleveland. Extending east by southeast off the corner of Public Square, it originally followed the historic Lake Shore Trail of the region's Native Americans. Village officials surveyed it in 1816, after which it was called the Buffalo Road for a period, since it ultimately led to the principal city of western New York, but it acquired its permanent name from the nearer destination of Euclid Township.[28] After the Civil War, Euclid Avenue became Cleveland's most desirable address and assumed its local mystique as Millionaires' Row.

Visitors soon began extolling the splendor of Cleveland's Euclid Avenue. An early admirer was Edward Hingston, biographer of *Plain Dealer* humorist Charles F. ("Artemus Ward") Browne. "There is one street called Euclid Street," wrote Hingston, "which for its beauty, its leafy trees, its well-built villas, its stately aspect, and its cleanly condition, would be worthy of Paris, in the neighborhood of the Bois, or of Berlin, in the vicinity of the Brandenburg Gate."[29] Others such as the American journalist Bayard Taylor and English novelist Anthony Trollope added their encomiums. As contemporary historian Jan Cigliano sums it up,

> During the second half of the nineteenth century, Euclid Street— made an avenue in 1865—became one of the finest residential streets in America, distinguished for its architecture and the eminence of those who lived there. Extending four miles from downtown Public Square eastward to Ninetieth Street, the Avenue was a kind of linear roll call of the residences of Cleveland's business and cultural leaders. The houses lining the Avenue were stunning monuments to the city's and the country's growing prosperity. In their massive size, opulent style, and rich materials, the residences of Euclid Avenue symbolized the wealth and energy of the age.[30]

Like many other historical phenomena, Millionaires' Row was evolutionary rather than static in nature. Cigliano places the Avenue's great age in the 1890s, when some 260 homes lined the four miles between Erie Street (East 9th) and Doan's Corners (East 105th). John D. Rockefeller, Amasa Stone, and Stone's son-in-law John Hay may have been gone by 1890, but new mansions continued to be raised in the eighties and nineties for such as Sylvester Everett, William Chisholm, John L. Severance, David Norton, and Andrew Squire.[31]

By the turn of the twentieth century, the handwriting was on the wall for Euclid Avenue as a prime residential address. Creeping commercialization was the main culprit, as the cachet that had once made Euclid Avenue such a desirable residential address now made it an equally desirable business address. Cigliano notes that the blocks from Public Square to East Ninth Street were completely filled with retail and offices as early as the mid-1890s. By 1921 only 130 homes—half the total of the great age—were still standing.[32] Commerce crossed East Ninth (streets were numbered after 1906), then passed East Twelfth Street.

Department stores led the charge. Sterling & Welch moved from lower Euclid Avenue to a new building above Twelfth Street in 1909. The Halle Brothers Company followed the next year, opening a ten-story building across the street from Sterling & Welch. Halle's expanded that building in 1914 and by 1920 added a menswear annex at Twelfth and Huron Avenue. Meanwhile, the Higbee Company had built a new store designed by Abram Garfield on the old Amasa Stone estate at the northwest corner of Euclid and East Thirteenth Street.[33]

East of Thirteenth, the half block of Euclid between that side street and the Bulkley Building was filled with specialty retail. Kinney & Levan home furnishings opened a six-story building opposite Fourteenth Street in 1913. The Lindner Company built a women's apparel store next door to Kinney & Levan two years later. Its five-story baroque facade of white terracotta, in the words of one local landmarks historian, "provided the gateway to Playhouse Square as it was developed six years later in 1921."[34] Cowell & Hubbard jewelers epitomized the eastward drift of downtown Cleveland. Founded in 1849 at Superior and Bank (West Sixth) Street, they moved half a century later to Euclid and East Ninth; in 1920 they opened an elegant two-story establishment on the northeast corner of Thirteenth and Euclid.[35]

In the wake of retail, theaters also joined in the infringement on Millionaires' Row. Cleveland's earliest theaters appeared in the Warehouse District, notably "Uncle John" Ellsler's celebrated Academy of Music, where James O'Neill, Clara Morris, and John Wilkes Booth trod the boards and chewed the scenery. After the Civil War, and against the advice of well-wishers, Ellsler erected a grand new theater east of Public Square. This was the storied Euclid Avenue Opera House, actually located on Sheriff (East Fourth) Street. To justify the name, an alternate entrance was cut through a commercial block to the namesake avenue. As it turned out, Ellsler was overextended, which is why the opera house ended up in Mark Hanna's portfolio.

Other theaters were opened in the spreading downtown, such as the Lyric on Public Square and the Colonial across from the Hollenden Hotel on Superior Avenue, but the allure of Euclid Avenue proved irresistible. In 1907, the humongous Hippodrome was built at Euclid and East Sixth on what had been the estate of early settler Truman P. Handy and then the first quarters of the Union Club. The Hipp became home to gigantic stage spectacles as well as such leading artists as Al Jolson, Enrico Caruso, and the Metropolitan Opera.[36] Ten years later, the Stillman Theater was erected for the showing of motion pictures on the former estate of railroad builder Stillman Witt, alongside the thousand-room Hotel Statler at East Twelfth and Euclid.

The "Father of Playhouse Square"

While the forces of change on lower Euclid were largely economic and impersonal in nature, the agents of change took the highly human form of the real estate agent. In the development of Playhouse Square, the prime agent undoubtedly was a realtor named Joseph Laronge. Only thirty-four years old in 1921, a six-footer with a high forehead above rimless spectacles, Laronge looked like a high school English teacher. He displayed the energy and enterprise generally associated with his chosen profession at an early age, however, having begun selling real estate at nineteen and forming his own firm, the Joseph Laronge Company, only two years later. It was located on the seventh floor of the Williamson Building, at Euclid Avenue and Public Square.[37]

Where Laronge departed somewhat from the stereotypical real estate agent, however, was the special interest he took in the-

Realtor Joseph Laronge's determination to put his entrances on Euclid Avenue gave the State and Ohio Theatres reputedly the "longest lobbies in the world" and earned Laronge the honorific "Father of Playhouse Square." Only thirty-four in 1921, Laronge would live to within five years of the theaters' closing in 1969. (*Cleveland News,* February 5, 1921)

ater development. He began literally in the afternoon shadow of the Williamson Building with the Mall Theater on lower Euclid. Taking advantage of the difference in grade between Euclid and Superior Avenues, he put the orchestra on the Superior level and the balcony on the Euclid side, with an arcade lobby connecting entrances on either street.[38] (Later, the two levels would be operated as separate theaters, the Upper Mall and the Lower Mall.) The Mall was a motion-picture house, as was Laronge's next theatrical venture. That was the Euclid Theater, built on East Ninth Street in the block between Euclid and Chester Avenues. Its lifespan would be cut short, however, when Laronge included it in a parcel he assembled in 1923 for the construction of the capacious Union Trust (later Huntington) Building.[39] In the meantime, Laronge had merged his theatrical interests with those of Marcus Loew. Loew's Ohio Theatres, as the combination was known, operated the downtown Stillman as well as the Mall and the Euclid. On the east side, Loew's built the Park Theater, while on Detroit Avenue and West 117th Street they were constructing the Granada.[40]

But Laronge and Loew wanted a large downtown flagship theater. After World War I, real estate circles undoubtedly were buzzing about a new theatrical district taking form around East Fourteenth and Euclid. Laronge, according to a later summary of his career, "pledged himself very early to Euclid Ave. No one could convince him that any other downtown thorofare had its possibilities or its future."[41] If he were to get in on the new theatrical center, however, the property possibilities were quite limited.

Between the Bulkley Building and the northwest corner of Euclid and East Seventeenth, which was already reserved for construction of another office tower and theater, only one slim parcel was available. It was the former estate of Charles B. Parker at 1521 Euclid Avenue. A relative latecomer to Millionaires' Row, Parker occupied a comparatively restrained Georgian mansion built in 1892 and designed by Charles F. Schweinfurth, Cleveland's foremost architect of the late nineteenth century. Laronge obtained a ninety-nine–year lease on the property, giving him the desired outlet on Euclid Avenue. While some four hundred feet in depth, however, the parcel had a frontage of only eighty-five feet. This might suffice for a smaller theater Laronge had in mind, having secured the northern Ohio franchise for all shows from New York's Klaw and Erlanger on condition of building a suitable new house for them.[42] The Ohio Theatre would fulfill that obligation, but Laronge still needed a much larger movie house for Marcus Loew.

With the entire block on Euclid between East Thirteenth and East Seventeenth spoken for, Laronge looked down Seventeenth Street, past the corner preempted by somebody else's theater plans. Halfway down the western side of the block, he was able to lease some properties from the Samuel Dodge estate, giving him a large, inverted *L*-shaped holding from Euclid north to Dodge Court and from there east to Seventeenth Street.[43] Now he had enough room for two theaters, but he wanted them on Euclid Avenue, not East Seventeenth Street. That proved to be no problem for the man who had squeezed the Mall Theater into the no man's land behind the Williamson Building.

Consciously or not, Laronge borrowed a trick from the old Euclid Avenue Opera House, which had reached out from East Fourth Street to open an entrance on the avenue of its name. Laronge's solution was to use his Euclid Avenue frontage for entrances to both the Ohio and the State Theatres. Since both theaters were located midway into the block, it would take extraordinarily long lobbies to get there. Making a virtue of necessity, opening night publicity for the State claimed its lobby was long enough "to afford accommodation to waiting patrons in greater numbers than the theater itself will seat. . . . As a safeguard against the elements, this feature is one of the most commendable in the new building."[44] The real reason for the lobby's size, of course, was to get patrons from its Euclid Avenue entrance to a theater halfway down East

Seventeenth Street, which also accounted for that zigzag detour around the rear of the Ohio. Covering both theaters' side-by-side lobbies was an unimposing four-story office building, but it was built to support a potential height of sixteen floors.[45]

In time, Joseph Laronge would be called the "Father of Playhouse Square," although he doesn't appear to have coined the name itself.[46] With the opening of the Allen Theatre, the *Plain Dealer* had prepared a special insert for April 3, 1921, bearing the title "Playhouse Square Section." Drama critic Harlowe Hoyt stressed the name in the section's lead story. "Playhouse Square," he began, "Cleveland's newest theatrical center marks another step eastward in the growth of the municipality."[47] Nineteen months later, in another special Sunday section to mark the opening of yet another addition to the theater district, the *Plain Dealer* formally claimed credit for giving it its name. "William G. Vorpe, Sunday and feature editor of *The Plain Dealer*," the paper recalled, "believed that Playhouse Square exactly fitted the new district and suggested the name, which has stuck and doubtless will."[48]

While others may have christened it, however, Laronge might justifiably claim paternal credit. Not only was he responsible for two of the four marquees lining Euclid Avenue, but he had lit them before the others. Moreover, it was Laronge's determination to achieve a Euclid Avenue presence that was responsible for the unique concentration of marquees in Playhouse Square.

"Finest Theater in the World"

Before Cleveland's switch to numbered streets, East Seventeenth was Dodge Street. It was laid down by the sons of Samuel Dodge, who had arrived in Cleveland within two years after Moses Cleaveland stayed there briefly, in 1796. Dodge was a carpenter by trade, one greatly needed in the pioneer village. He was soon employed to build a barn on Superior Street for Samuel Huntington, Cleveland's most eminent citizen and a future governor of Ohio. It was supposed to be a $300 job, but money was scarce in the frontier community. Land, however, was in good supply, so Huntington paid off Dodge with 110 acres stretching on both sides of the future East Seventeenth Street, from the future Euclid Avenue all the way to Lake Erie.[49]

If he'd had his druthers, Dodge purportedly said later, he'd have taken the cash, but he took the land under duress. There he built

B. F. KEITH'S PALACE, CLEVELAND, OHIO.

Access to the Palace Theatre led through the twenty-one-story Keith Building, which would dominate Playhouse Square through its first century. It was crowned by an electric sign visible from the heights of the far east side. (Author's collection)

a log cabin for his young bride, the former Nancy Doan of East Cleveland ("Doan's Corners"), and dug one of the village's first wells. Samuel and Nancy had two sons and a daughter, whom they took to live in Euclid Township during the War of 1812. Dodge wisely held on to his land in Cleveland, to which they returned with their sons Henry and George around 1820. Both sons later raised substantial homes on the family property, Henry on the future site of the Bulkley Building and George on the northwest corner of Euclid Avenue and East Seventeenth, which he had cut through as Dodge Street. Behind George's twenty-room Italianate mansion, built in the earlier style of Millionaires' Row, was a field known as Strawberry Hill. "I remember many times in walking downtown of passing that home with its wide front porches and drive at the side," recalled one old timer many years after it was torn down to make way for the crowning glory of Playhouse Square.[50]

Someone else had his eye on that property, not for the house but for the land. Edward Albee, surviving partner of the Keith-Albee vaudeville circuit, was on a building binge. Starting from a somewhat derelict Boston variety house in 1885, Albee and B. F. Keith had assembled the dominant vaudeville circuit in the eastern United States. They entered the Cleveland scene early in the twentieth century, leasing the Prospect Theater on the downtown street of that name. A few years later they leased the much larger Hippodrome on Euclid Avenue, where the immortal Sarah Bernhardt headlined one of their programs.[51] Keith died in 1914, but Albee continued to expand the Keith-Albee chain, preferably by building its own theaters. "Building not only is my hobby; it is my job, primarily, in the Keith organization,"

Albee told Cleveland reporters. He had twenty-five new theaters under construction in 1921, six in Ohio. Cincinnati, Columbus, Dayton, and Toledo would each get one new Keith's theater, but Cleveland was earmarked for two. One, Keith's 105th Street Theater, would open that November on Euclid Avenue at the edge of University Circle; the other would join and complete the lineup at Playhouse Square. It would take a little longer, but Albee promised it would be "the finest theater in the world."[52]

In preparing his Playhouse Square theater, Albee must have enjoyed his hobby to the fullest. "He selected personally each of the fine pieces of Italian marble that decorate the lobby," wrote William McDermott in the *Plain Dealer*. He also went shopping for antique furniture and old master paintings to fill that lobby, paying as much as $27,000 (at 1922 prices) for a single oil by Joseph Israels, *Children Sailing Boat* ("An Israels in an American vaudeville theater!" marveled Archie Bell). In the newly independent country of Czechoslovakia, artisans in Maffersdorf were weaving to Albee's specifications a forty-by-sixty-seven-foot silver-gray rug with black and gold trimmings to carpet his lobby.[53]

Nothing could be too good for this theater, because Albee regarded it as a memorial to his late partner. In front and over the theater lobby was a twenty-one-story office building, the B. F. Keith Building, with a plaque in its lobby declaring, "This building was erected by Edward F. Albee in memory of his lifelong friend and associate Benjamin F. Keith." Both the building and its ensconced theater were designed by the Chicago firm of C. W. & George L. Rapp and built by Cleveland's Lundoff-Bicknell Company, at a reported combined cost of $5 million ($3.5 million for the office tower, the balance for the theater). For a few years, the white terracotta-faced building would be Cleveland's tallest skyscraper, heightened even further by what was ballyhooed as the world's largest electric sign, proclaiming "B. F. Keith Vaudeville" as far away as the eastside Heights.[54]

Officially, the playhouse, too, bore the name B. F. Keith Palace Theatre. Palace was also the name of the flagship theater of the Keith-Albee circuit on Broadway, the mecca of every vaudevillian in the nation. McDermott of the *Plain Dealer* guessed there were thousands of other Palace theaters in the country, but "here at 17th street is one that is a palace in more than name. Palatial, in fact, is the word that most accurately describes it." Late in October 1922, Albee donned overalls to inspect the last-minute progress. "I regard this as the master achievement of my life," he declared as he set opening night for November 6. "You know November has always been my lucky month," he told his theater manager. "Any deals I have entered into during November always have come out all right."[55]

Grand Finale

On the appointed Monday evening, several thousand entertainment seekers converged on the site of the old Dodge demesne at Euclid Avenue and East Seventeenth. Those without tickets came to gawk at the more privileged bearing entree, including several special railroad cars of New Yorkers. Entertainment royalty in attendance included the Martin Becks, the John Ringlings, the Adolph Zukors, William Brady, Max Gordon, Marcus Loew, Heywood Broun, and Julia Arthur. Other noted guests came from Washington, DC; Philadelphia; Detroit; Cincinnati; Louisville; and Pittsburgh.[56]

Ticket holders entered through a street vestibule into an outer foyer lined with some of Albee's Italian marble, including twelve columns topped with Doric capitals. (An architecture class might begin its study of the three principal Greek orders here, passing from the plain Doric columns of the Palace to the classical Ionic capitals of the State lobby and finally the sweeping Corinthian pillars of the restored Ohio lobby.) Through a set of doors, those first Palace patrons found themselves in another foyer, an anteroom to the main lobby. Before yet another set of bronze and glass doors, Archie Bell counseled theatergoers to pause and reflect prior to entering. "Here at this threshold, on the borderland between the street and the gorgeous Palace itself," wrote Bell of Cleveland's vaudeville shrine, "it is appropriate to pause for a moment and reflect that this marvelous structure has arisen as the result of and for the accommodation of vaudeville performances. Not opera. . . . Not for the classical drama."[57]

Once inside those doors, however, patrons may well have thought that they were inside the Paris Opera of Dick Feagler's imagination.[58] The "Great Hall" of the Palace wasn't elongated like the State and Ohio lobbies nor circular as the Allen's. It spread out broadly, 130 feet side to side, with a majestic staircase on either side and another in the center leading to the mezzanine level. Five chandeliers from Czechoslovakia were spaced across the ceiling, illuminating the carpet below from the same country. Off the ground floor were men's smoking and retiring rooms and a ladies' retiring suite. Ladies also had a separate, appropriately appointed

Egyptian smoking room located in an anteroom off an outer lobby. On the mezzanine level was a promenade circumambulating and overlooking the main level. Off the mezzanine were a music alcove and another ladies' suite. Louis XVI chairs and commodes furnished some of the retiring suites as well as the Great Hall itself. Thirty-two paintings embellished the walls of both levels, including a Nicolas Poussin, a Thomas Sully, and not one but two by Israels. Dominating the view from other levels, on the landing of the central staircase to the mezzanine, was a Numidean marble base bearing a large cobalt-blue Sevres vase. Obtained for Albee in Paris's Latin Quarter by C. A. Selzer, in time the great urn would serve as an iconic emblem for the Palace.[59]

Once past the Great Hall, the audience found itself in much the same atmosphere but on an even larger scale. In the auditorium, as in the lobby, Albee relieved the starkness of the white marble and ivory walls with panels of a rich brocade in a mulberry shade known as Albee red. There were skyboxes across the rear of the balcony, while tiered boxes, three to a side, descended gracefully down the side walls from the lower balcony to the edges of the proscenium. For all its size and 3,550 seats, Bell noted wonderful acoustics and an air of intimacy.[60] Behind the curtain was a proscenium opening of fifty-five feet and a stage forty-five feet deep.

Carrara marble from Italy, carpeting and chandeliers from Czechoslovakia, and bronze grillwork from Nuremberg gave the Great Hall of the Palace Theatre its palatial credentials. For the finishing touches to his "palace for the people," Edward Albee covered its brocaded walls with original oils by Corot and other masters. (Courtesy of Cleveland Public Library Photograph Collection)

Finished in green tile, the rear stage wall was back to back with the rear auditorium wall of the State Theatre.[61]

The backstage appointments were only slightly less luxurious than those visible to the audience. B. F. Keith had run his theaters in the tradition of Tony Pastor, the New York impresario who had turned vaudeville into an entertainment suitable for the entire family. Going a step further, Keith also insisted that his performers lead exemplary lives offstage. To that end, Albee honored Keith's standards by providing performers at the Cleveland Palace with all the amenities of a genteel existence. They entered the back of the house through a side entrance off East Seventeenth Street but walked into a marble wainscoted vestibule suggestive of a middle-class apartment house. Facing them was their own elevator, ready to lift them to far more than simple dressing rooms. As described in the opening night program,

> In this, as in the recently built theatres of the Keith circuit, the dressing rooms of the artists are supplied with modern bath rooms, social halls with billiard tables, a children's play room, laundries for the light work that the women artists wish to take care of in the theatre, a tailor shop and a sewing room. A remarkable innovation is the installation of a barber shop, manicure parlor and beauty shop and Golfers will have a large indoor golf cage. The orchestra musicians and even the stage hands have their own special rooms, well furnished and with shower baths and the finest toilet equipment.[62]

Breaking in those new digs that week was an inaugural vaudeville ticket of nine acts, including the opening rendition of the "Star-Spangled Banner" by the house orchestra under maestro W. F. Dugan. They included a pantomimist, a monologist, a male dance team billed as "Darktown's Beau Brummels," a "Saxophone Virtuoso," and a skit featuring that "Famous Italian Comedian" Harry Burns. About all that was missing was an animal act, though the Palace had facilities to handle those too, when needed. Diminutive Elsie Janis, known as the "Sweetheart of the A.E.F." for her efforts entertaining American troops in the World War, was the headline act that evening, with a "Recital of Typical Janis Hits." The closing act featured the Cansinos, a Spanish dancing troupe headed by Eduardo Cansino.[63] (It's possible that his three-year-old daughter—Margarita, later known as Rita Hayworth—was one of the first occupants of the Palace's backstage playroom.)

There were brief opening formalities before the show, including remarks by Mayor Fred Kohler and Governor Harry Davis, who considered the Palace "a source of pride to the entire state of Ohio." Albee remained quietly in his box, so former mayor Newton D. Baker, president of the Chamber of Commerce, presented the theater to the city on Albee's behalf. A bookish sort, Baker drew comparisons between the Palace and the theater of Shakespeare's time. "The idea seemed to be that the comparison was all in favor of Cleveland in 1922," observed George Davis in the *Cleveland Press*. Not to take anything away from Elsie Janis, the real hit of the evening may have been seen during intermission, when the souvenir program invited patrons "to promenade about the theatre and take advantage of its rare charm and artistic beauty."[64]

Palaces for the Masses

With the opening of the Palace in November 1922, the backbone of Playhouse Square was in place. There would be changes in the surrounding storefronts, but the five theaters would be the center of Cleveland's nightlife for decades. In his panegyric to the Palace Theatre, Archie Bell might have been speaking for all the theaters of Playhouse Square:

Being an American and being the president of the B. F. Keith circuit of theatres—he [Albee] erected his palace for the people. . . . And with tremendous capital at hand, he was as particular to make it a beautiful palace as was Chinese, Italian or German monarch. It was erected, decorated and furnished with the same good taste and el-

egance that a monarch would spend upon his residential palace. . . .

. . . A palace for the masses! Who ever heard of such a thing before E. F. Albee had his wonderful dream that came true?[65]

Millionaires' Row was already half gone when the Palace opened its doors, and its decline would continue at an accelerated pace. It would become an irretrievable loss, but most Clevelanders had never seen the inside of a Euclid Avenue mansion. In the Euclid Avenue theaters of Playhouse Square, they could experience much of the grandeur of what they had missed.

High Times,
Hard Times

Street Scenes

On the cusp of the Roaring Twenties, Playhouse Square had become not only Cleveland's entertainment center but also its premier shopping district. It was anchored at its western gateway by the big department stores, Higbee's and Halle's, facing one another across Euclid Avenue between East Twelfth and East Thirteenth Streets. Immediately to the west of Higbee's on the north side of Euclid were Sterling & Welch home furnishings and, facing Twelfth Street, the stately Union Club. Though smaller than the two department stores, Sterling & Welch would manage to siphon off some of their holiday traffic beginning in 1927, with its annual tradition of displaying the nation's largest indoor Christmas tree in its five-story atrium.[1]

But the retail anchor of Playhouse Square was Halle's, which seemed to grow like some exotic hothouse plant. Following the move uptown to its new quarters designed by Henry Bacon, architect of Washington's Lincoln Memorial, Halle's expanded four years later into an identical addition next door. In 1920, Halle's purchased the five-story Elks Club across East Twelfth Street on Huron Road, expanding the men's store into the first floor. Five years later, Halle's would vault over Huron Road to build a six-story addition between that street and Prospect Avenue.[2] Halle's

Champlin Press, Col's., O.   Hotel Euclid, Cleveland, O.

Entertainers could find lodgings right in the middle of the theater district at the Hotel Euclid. Dating from the turn of the century, it was razed in 1937 to make way for the widening of East Fourteenth Street. Nearly sixty years would pass before another hotel, the Wyndham, opened in Playhouse Square. (Author's collection)

became known for its quality as well as quantity, featuring exclusive goods that catered to the "carriage trade."

In the heady business expansion of the decade, Cleveland was becoming reconciled to the commercial infringement on Millionaires' Row. "Within as short a period as the last 10 years, the character of the Avenue in different sections has changed beyond belief," stated the first annual report of the Euclid Avenue Association in 1921. Organized only the previous year, the association's primary goal was to protect and improve property values along its namesake avenue. "Now that it is not only the main traffic artery of Cleveland, but its main business street, it is a matter of pride to the city that it shall become as famous as a handsome commercial street as it was a street of homes," noted the report.[3]

The backbone of the new Euclid Avenue was that spectacular block from Thirteenth to Seventeenth Streets containing four of the five theaters of Playhouse Square. It began modestly enough with a pair of two-story buildings housing a couple of oddly matched tenants. On the corner was Cowell & Hubbard Co., which offered a high-end selection of watches, silverware, fine jewelry, and notions. Should that prove a bit too pricey, one might stroll a few steps up the street to a Woolworth's five-and-dime. Continuing eastward past Kinney & Levan furnishings and Lindner's womenswear were the Allen Theatre and the Bulkley Building. In the basement of the Bulkley was the Colonnade Restaurant, while the law firm of Bulkley, Jamieson, & Sharpe occupied offices on the sixth floor.[4] On the ground floor, beyond the building lobby, the Bulkley Arcade led to the quarters of the original Cleveland Athletic Club.

First organized in 1885, the Cleveland Athletic Club had converted the former Millionaires' Row mansion of H. H. Dodge into their clubhouse in 1891. In the rear was a gymnasium where it sponsored boxing exhibitions featuring Kid McCoy and "Mouse" Siddons and wrestling matches with the likes of "Strangler" Lewis. By 1900 that original club had apparently become inactive. It was succeeded by a second Cleveland Athletic Club, which since 1911 had occupied its own building, just east of Halle's on Euclid.[5] Domiciled in the old lodgings of the original CAC was the antiquarian establishment of C. A. Selzer.

Charles A. Selzer was a native Clevelander who became an antiques dealer by accident when a shop he secured on lower Euclid Avenue to sell dental supplies came with the former tenant's stock of crockery and china. Selling off the china proved so profitable that Selzer changed trades and branched out into glassware, bronzes, and furniture. He made annual trips to Europe in search of objets d'art and moved the shop farther along Euclid to East Ninth Street.[6]

Lured by the development of Playhouse Square, Selzer made his final move to the old CAC lodgings at the terminus of the Bulkley Arcade. Cleveland arts reporter Grace V. Kelly recalled, "Visiting Selzer's seemed like going into a hospitable home," where "nobody was going to sell us anything unless we wanted to buy it and perhaps not then."[7] Among his wares Selzer advertised tapestries, painted wall panels, Old English and Sheffield silver, girandoles, and candelabra. "We direct attention to the exquisite Versailles Chandeliers and Sconces, in Crystal and Gilt, imported especially for the beautiful new B. F. Keith Palace Theatre," read his ad in that theater's opening night program.[8]

Back on Euclid Avenue, dwarfed between the Bulkley Building and the B. F. Keith Building was the four-story Loew's Ohio Building. There, atop the Ohio and State Theatre lobbies were the Carlton Terrace restaurant as well as a dancing and dramatic school. On the top two floors of the neighboring Keith Building were the offices of the American Fork and Hoe Company (later True Temper hardware).[9] For the time being, its employees could look down on all the rest of Cleveland.

On the south side of Euclid Avenue, across from the Palace Theatre, was a five-story building housing the Far East Restaurant. It advertised dancing to Howard Sands' Orchestra three times daily: for lunch, dinner, and after theater, Sundays excepted.[10] Moving back westward, Playhouse Square acquired a distinguished bookstore in 1924, when Korner & Wood moved to 1512 Euclid from its old store down the street.[11] On the corner of East Fourteenth Street stood the Hanna Building, nearly rivaling the Keith in height. Among its charter tenants was the Oglebay Norton iron ore company. A restaurant would traditionally occupy the building's Euclid Avenue frontage, originally managed by Henry Grebe of Grebe's Rathskeller but best remembered as the location of Monaco's Continental Restaurant.[12] The building's lobby cut diagonally across from Euclid to East Fourteenth Street, down which was the Hanna Theatre in the Hanna Building Annex.

Like New York's Times Square, Playhouse Square was not geometrically square. Just west of East Fourteenth, Huron Road destroyed any hope of symmetry by cutting into Euclid at an acute angle. At the intersection of the three roadways was the six-story Hotel Euclid, with its eastern facade, broken by bays on the middle four floors, extending back along East Fourteenth and its front entrance on Huron. Due to the sharpness of the angle, the hotel's frontage looked directly across to Euclid, thus justifying its name.[13] Since there was little depth in the nondescript two-story building squeezed into the angle between Euclid and Huron, the finer shops of this section of Playhouse Square were on the south side of Huron Road, from the Hotel Euclid to Halle's. They included Engel & Fetzer furriers, whose stock ranged from caracul jackets with fox trimming at $185 to wide Russian kolinsky wraps at $1175. Next door, one might spend even more in the downtown showroom of pioneer Cleveland automaker Alexander Winton. Befitting the high-end cars on display below, the three-story building flaunted a row of six Ionic columns in the setback of its two upper stories. Should shoppers still have balances left in their bank accounts, they might also visit two piano showrooms in the same block of Huron Road.[14]

Such were the early occupants of Playhouse Square. Notice might also be taken of two entertainment meccas on the neighborhood's fringes. At the intersection of Bolivar Road and Prospect Avenue, in sight of the Hanna Theatre, stood the crenelated tower of Grays Armory. Before the rise of the Playhouse Square theaters, its drill hall in the rear had hosted such cultural events as the Cleveland Orchestra's inaugural concert in 1918. The hall had recently burned down, but it would be rebuilt. On East Thirteenth Street, behind the Euclid Avenue facades of Playhouse Square, was the Wigmore Coliseum, a large exhibition hall that housed the Cleveland Electrical Exposition in 1914 and the city's first Flower Show five years later. Its functions would be assumed shortly by Cleveland Public Auditorium on the Mall, but the building would undergo several additions and be used for several functions in years to come.[15]

On with the Shows

On the Playhouse Square of 1922, the average Cleveland entertainment seeker gravitated toward the Allen, the State, or the Palace Theatre. These were the three largest houses on the block, their capacities averaging somewhat above three thousand seats apiece. While their ornate lobbies may have seemed befitting for royalty, the entertainment in their auditoriums was decidedly plebeian. It consisted largely of a mixture of silent films with live vaudeville and musical performances, with the Allen weighted toward film, the Palace vaudeville, and the State somewhere in between.

One of the Allen Theatre's stage prologues was tied to its showing of the expressionistic *The Cabinet of Dr. Caligari*. "The Futurist Ball" undertook to show what life in 1950 would look like if the Futurists or Cubists were to have their way (Courtesy of Cleveland Public Library Photograph Collection)

All three of the larger Playhouse Square theaters had satellites on the outlying fringes of the city. Only four days after the launch of their downtown flagship, the Allen brothers opened the Capital on West Sixty-Fifth Street in Gordon Square.[16] Naturally, the downtown Allen had first rights on movie releases for the Allen chain. During the first few months. its attractions included such titles as *Heart of Maryland, Straight from Paris, Private Scandal,* and *All's Fair in Love.* One-week runs were the rule, including for one provocatively titled *Why Girls Leave Home.* As reviewed in the *Plain Dealer,* "it tells why two girls leave home, tells the story emphatically in action if not in sub-titles. In fact, whatever weakness the film may have is in the theatrical flourishes of many of the sub-titles."[17]

If few of its photo plays were cinema classics, the Allen tried to give patrons their money's worth in the form of some impressive musical stage spectacles. With Phil Spitalny's orchestra in the pit, up to thirty elaborately costumed singers and dancers performed programs themed to holidays, exotic locations, and patriotic pageants. They were created and directed by S. Barret McCormick, who tied some to the movie on the screen that week. Called stage preludes or prologues, they put audiences in the mood for such feature films as *Dream Street, Tale of Two Worlds,* and *The Old Nest.*[18] Due to the shallowness of the original Allen stage, staging seemed to stress tableau-like scenes over action.[19]

Undoubtedly the most singular of McCormick's stage prologues was that prepared for the showing of the German expressionistic classic *The Cabinet of Dr. Caligari.* The movie easily is the best remembered of the Allen's screenings in its first year. It was advertised as "The Strangest Picture Ever Made! with 'Futuristic' & 'Cubist' Settings that has Startled the World." For its "Stage Prelude to 'Dr. Caligari,'" the Allen offered "The Futurist Ball": "What Will Happen by 1950 if the 'Futurists,' 'Cubists' and others have their way! Perhaps something like this 'Impressionistic' spectacle. 'The Futurist Ball' with the 'Orchestra From Mars,' 'The Follies Chorus of 1950,' 'The Crystalist Fashion Show,' and the other marvels in this glittering pageant of things to come! Produced by S. Barret McCormick. Color Impressions and Costumes by Zimmerer. Musical reactions by Philip Spitalny." Spitalny also provided an orchestral accompaniment for the film from scores by Stravinsky, Debussy, and Strauss, among others.[20]

Plain Dealer critic Ward Marsh found the prologue "in excellent keeping with the picture." As for the picture, he recommended seeing it once—but just once. "'The Cabinet' is different; awfully different!" he summarized in one succinct sentence. It was like watching a lunatic asylum with the inmates in charge, he thought. "The settings are, of course, the novelty," wrote Marsh. "But, if you want to see a horror story through a kaleidoscope try 'The Cabinet.'"[21]

One reason for McCormick's elaborate stage productions may have been the Allen's difficulty in booking some of the better films. The source of the problem was the rivalry between the Allen chain and the Loew interests, operators of the State Theatre half a block from the Allen. According to *Variety*, a tacit agreement between the two businesses had called for the Allen brothers to limit their operations to Canada and Loew's to confine itself to regions south of the northern border. When Loew's subsequently entered Toronto, the Allens had retaliated by descending into Cleveland. Loew, having prior call on the products of major studios such as Paramount, proceeded to freeze the Allen out of quality pictures.[22]

Loew's clearly had the upper hand in the dispute, and the Allens were forced to the wall by their creditors. In a June 1922 deal negotiated by Joseph Laronge on behalf of the Euclid–14th Theatre Co., the Loew's circuit secured a fifteen-year lease to operate the Allen Theatre.[23] A little more than a year after its opening, the only vestige of Jules and Jay Allen on Playhouse Square was the name on their theater's marquee. With its Loew's connection, the State had no problem in securing movies. Headquartered in the Loew's Ohio Building over the State's lobby was Fred Desberg, general manager for Marcus Loew in a midwestern district ranging from Rochester, New York, to Toledo. Besides the flagship State, Loew's theaters in the Cleveland area alone included the Stillman, Euclid, and Mall downtown, the Alhambra and Park near East 103rd and Euclid, and the Liberty at East 103rd and Superior Avenue.[24]

Veteran theater manager George Desmond came from Los Angeles to assume management of the Cleveland State Theatre. He relied on a formula of feature films in combination with stage programs to fill the huge house's seats. A typical bill during that first year coupled a personal appearance by silent star Theda Bara, a fall fashion show, and Constance Talmadge in the film *Dangerous Business*.[25] Several weeks later came a film that "broke all records at Loew's State." This was *The Sheik*, which may have pleased the ladies but failed to impress the *Press*'s George Davis. "What one sees is Rudolph Valentino, as the sheik, looking like a college boy dressed up for a masquerade in a tale by F. Scott Fitzgerald," he wrote. After boldly kidnapping the heroine, the hero then "abandons all masterful direct action and becomes an indecisive Hamlet."

Marion Davies, on screen at the State Theatre in 1925, shared billing with the vaudeville stage attraction of Balto and the canine sled team that had delivered lifesaving diphtheria serum to Nome, Alaska. Two years later, Balto and his surviving sledmates were rescued from a Los Angeles dime museum and given a permanent home in Cleveland's Brookside Zoo. (*Cleveland Plain Dealer*, November 15, 1925)

Davis did take note of the appearance in a featured role by a former Clevelander named Adolphe Menjou.[26]

Early in the decade, the State flirted with a vaudeville format. One reason Loew's leased the Allen may have been to free the State as a venue for the Shubert vaudeville circuit in fall 1922. That didn't last, and the State soon returned to its film-cum-stage programs, for example, Mary Murray in *Altars of Desire* on screen plus Guy Lombardo and His Royal Canadians Radio Band on stage. Another billing combined Marion Davies in *Lights of Old Broadway* on the screen with a stage act of nine Alaskan huskies. They were headed by Balto, the canine hero who had led them to deliver a lifesaving diphtheria serum to Nome, and introduced by their driver, Gunnar Kaasen. "While the act is not theatrical in nature," observed the *Plain Dealer*'s William McDermott, "it is made interesting by a talk describing the journey, the colorful northern setting, Kaasen's arctic costume and the barking huskies, and by Balto who remains singularly calm throughout the din."[27]

Little more than a year later, though they were no longer on the vaudeville circuit, the dogs had their pictures back on the walls of the State's lobby. A Cleveland businessman had discovered them in a seedy Los Angeles dime museum, reduced to seven in number, listless and seemingly neglected. Once-proud Balto lay his head between his paws. The Clevelander returned home and organized a Cleveland Balto Committee to raise $2,000 for the purchase of the dogs. Among the citywide appeals, Joseph Laronge, chairman of Loew's Ohio Theatres, not only posted pictures in the lobby but arranged for performers to address audiences from the State's stage. In days, the money was raised and the dogs brought to Cleveland. Before moving into special quarters at the Brookside Zoo, they were the featured attraction in a downtown parade that marched up East Fourteenth past Playhouse Square.[28]

The State was using its elongated lobby for more than simply a passageway from Euclid Avenue to its auditorium, as when Cleveland's Star Baking Company set up a counter there to distribute miniature loaves of bread to promote the showing of the MGM feature *Bread*.[29] Metro-Goldwyn-Mayer was the creature of Marcus Loew, who in 1924 had consolidated the studios of Metro Pictures, Samuel Goldwyn, and Louis B. Mayer.[30] Loew died in 1927, but MGM would remain the country's premier motion picture studio, and Loew's State would be its preferred showcase in Cleveland.

Booking movies was a nonissue for Keith's Palace Theatre, which maintained a straight vaudeville policy through most of its first decade. From an office off the Grand Hall, John F. Royal managed all the Keith interests in Cleveland.[31] That included the new Keith's 105th Theatre, which had opened a year ahead of the Palace. Like the Palace, the Keith's 105th seated about three thousand and designated its dressing rooms by the names of states rather than numbers, in an effort to forestall squabbling among its artists.[32]

Once it opened in November 1922, the Palace was unquestionably the Keith circuit's showcase in Cleveland. Its headliners in the early 1920s included Olsen and Johnson, Fannie Brice, Jack Benny, Wagnerian soprano Johanna Gadski, Bill "Bojangles" Robinson, Sophie Tucker, and Ethel Barrymore.[33] Lauded as "the consummate actress" by critic William McDermott, Barrymore appeared in *The Twelve Pound Look*, a one-acter by *Peter Pan* playwright James Barrie. Tap dancer Robinson, the "dancing demon of Georgia," was fully entitled to the accolade of "artist," in the opinion of Ward Marsh. "Jack Benny plays a little on a fiddle and takes a long, long time to tell a few good jokes," wrote McDermott.[34]

One of the most unconventional bookings at the Palace in this period was a one-week stand in 1926 by the Chicago Civic Opera Company. Its repertoire included single performances of *Tosca*, *Madame Butterfly*, *Martha*, *Hansel and Gretel*, and *Otello*. Russian bass Alexander Kipnis sang in Wagner's *Die Walküre*, while legendary soprano Mary Garden appeared in the title role of Bizet's *Carmen*. Quite likely this was the occasion manager John Royal gave a Palace usherette $125 to buy a black velvet gown and masquerade as a beautiful and mysterious first-nighter. She reportedly created a stir amid Cleveland society similar to that raised by the fictitious Eliza Doolittle at the embassy ball in Bernard Shaw's *Pygmalion*.[35]

Probably the most famous Palace legend of all, the marriage at the theater of George Burns and Gracie Allen, never happened—at least not at the Palace.[36] On tour early in 1926, they did stop in Cleveland to tie the knot but weren't even booked at the Palace that week. After checking in at the Hotel Statler, the couple went to the Cuyahoga County Courthouse on Lakeside Avenue to take out a marriage license. Dated January 7, 1926, the document states that Nathan Birnbaum (Burns) and Grace C. Allen were to be married by Justice of the Peace M. J. Penty of Warrensville, but the return at the bottom declares that they were hitched that same day by a JP named J. E. Chizek. Burns later related a story about how the couple collared a JP about to leave to go fishing, who married them in hip boots with a Bible in one hand and a fishing pole in the other. Maybe they didn't have the time or the cab fare to go out to Warrensville and instead found a JP closer to town; at any rate, they were married in Cleveland on January 7, 1926. A couple of months later, they returned to play the Palace, where Davis of the *Press* noted simply, "Grace Allen is cute and funny in 'Lamb Chops.'"[37] If he hadn't found out yet, that should have told Burns where he stood in that partnership.

In retrospect, it may not have been the best of times for newlyweds to break into vaudeville. First movies and then radio were making inroads on the mass audience that had belonged almost exclusively to vaudeville. In the summer of 1925, the Palace announced combination billings of movies with vaudeville, beginning with a showing of *The Iron Horse*. Although the theater reverted to a policy of straight vaudeville that fall, movies returned the following summer with Cecil B. De Mille's *The Volga Boatman* on May 23, 1926. This time films would remain throughout the year.[38]

The Houses Were Legit

While the larger Playhouse Square houses endeavored to strike a balance between vaudeville and movies, the more intimate Ohio and Hanna Theatres dominated what *Variety* classified as "legitimate" theater in Cleveland. Included in the term were performances of straight dramatic plays and musical productions with a unified plot or libretto, as opposed to vaudeville, burlesque, and movies. Two other downtown theaters qualified as "legit" at the beginning of the twenties. Mark Hanna's old Euclid Avenue Opera House was superseded by the new Hanna Theatre, however, and the venerable Opera House succumbed to the wrecking ball a year and six days after the opening of its successor in Playhouse Square. That left the Colonial Theater on Superior Avenue between East Sixth and Ninth Streets. That was a bit of a hike from Playhouse Square, and the Colonial led a sporadic existence during the decade on the leavings of the new theater district.[39]

So the Hanna and the Ohio became the venues of choice for Broadway road shows. Although the Hanna was considered an ideal home for drama, the Ohio enjoyed the advantage of Cleveland's most resourceful theater manager. Robert McLaughlin had been a dominant presence in Cleveland theater in the decade before the twenties, having managed the Metropolitan and the Colonial among other venues. Behind his fleshy face and thick-framed spectacles worked an inventive mind that kept theaters filled with such expedients as summer stock seasons and writing his own plays. (McLaughlin's *The Pearl of Great Price* would have its premiere at the Ohio in the summer of 1925.)[40] McLaughlin had had a part in planning the Ohio, in league with New York producer A[braham]. L[incoln]. Erlanger. A former Clevelander, Erlanger had worked for Mark Hanna as treasurer of the Opera House before going on to New York to organize the powerful Klaw-Erlanger booking syndicate.[41] Though the syndicate was no longer operative, Erlanger was still active as a Broadway producer.

Due to increased production costs, however, fewer road shows were coming out of New York. McLaughlin occasionally had to book nonlegitimate fare, such as a sixteen-week run of vaudeville in 1922. Movies such as the silent versions of *The Ten Commandments* and *Ben Hur* also filled in the gaps between roadshows. Veteran troupers still made the rounds, helping to maintain the Ohio's "legit" credentials. Robert Mantell came with weeklong runs of Shakespearean repertory, and Otis Skinner appeared with Minnie Maddern Fiske in *The Merry Wives of Windsor*. New York's Theatre Guild sent a younger generation of actors on tour, such as Alfred Lunt and Lynn Fontanne in Molnar's *The Guardsman*. "Mr. Lunt . . . and Miss Fontanne . . . take this play, which reads like a prize-winning drama by a high school youngster, and they raise it to something not only worth while but actually fascinating," wrote Archie Bell in the *News*. "It takes acting to do that."[42]

Other stars came who would in time become household names. Fred Astaire danced with his sister Adele in Gershwin's *Lady Be*

Good! W. C. Fields came with the *Ziegfeld Follies* and the Marx Brothers in *The Cocoanuts*. Helen Hayes came in *Bab* and Spencer Tracy in summer stock. One visitor who bridged the older and newer generations was Ethel Barrymore, who came to the Ohio to star in the world premiere of Somerset Maugham's *The Constant Wife*. It was not a highly auspicious opening for La Barrymore. "Obviously, Miss Barrymore was not just ready for the premiere," Bell politely noted in the *News*. "She was prompted frequently. Still, she gave a delicately chiselled personation of this wife and it was a joy, as usual, to see and hear her. She sparkles like a ten-carat diamond in such a role."[43] In the *Plain Dealer*, McDermott was less forgiving:

> I remember once writing that Miss Barrymore could be touching and exciting if she were put to reading nothing more dramatic than the names out of the telephone book. Well, being apparently in a state of great vagueness about Mr. Maugham's lines last night, very many of them were read to her by a gentleman who sat, like Santa Claus, in a stage fireplace, turning Mr. Maugham's precious leaves with considerable audibility in plain sight of the somewhat startled circle in which I sat. . . .
>
> If this report seems harsh and unchivalrous because the defects it emphasizes are temporary and may be ironed out in a day or two, one can only say that it is an affront to open a play that is not ready to open and to add that, not being a genius, the reviewer is unable to predict with any exactitude what a performance might be and can only describe what it is.[44]

Fortunately the defects were ironed out, and Miss Barrymore's ultimate triumph in the play amply repaid Mr. Maugham for the opening night ordeal.

Around the corner on East Fourteenth Street, the Hanna proceeded through the twenties under the management of New York's Shubert organization, the principal successor of the defunct Klaw-Erlanger syndicate. Like the Ohio, the Hanna occasionally covered booking holes with such movies as *Orphans of the Storm* and *The Big Parade*. Legitimate fare at the Hanna was dominated during the decade by a Shubert specialty: operetta. The Shuberts opened the Hanna's 1923–24 season with *Blossom Time*, a musical biography of composer Franz Schubert. It ran two weeks, returned in midseason for two more, and closed the season with a three-week run. *Blossom Time* returned the following season for what was billed as a "Farewell Appearance," but it proved to a very drawn-out goodbye. Eventually the show racked up twenty-six weeks over a period of twenty-eight years at the Hanna. Nearly as ubiquitous was Sigmund Romberg's *The Student Prince*, which after a five-week debut would eventually play a total of seventeen weeks at the Hanna. Romberg came to the Hanna in 1928 to conduct the premiere of his revised and highly successful *The New Moon*.[45]

Drama was also given its due at the Hanna, with Shakespearean repertory by E. H. Sothern and Julia Marlowe and visits by the New York Theatre Guild and even the Moscow Art Theatre—in Russian yet! Cleveland-born producer Arthur Hopkins brought John Barrymore to the Hanna in his final American performances of *Hamlet*, an interpretation generally held to be the gold standard for Shakespeare's most complex character. A young actress named Katharine Cornell made her Hanna debut on Christmas Day in 1926, in a play titled *The Green Hat*. Over the years she would register twenty-two appearances at the Hanna, twice as many as any other actor.[46]

One show in particular amusingly exemplified the rivalry between the Hanna and the Ohio on Playhouse Square. *No, No, Nanette* was one of the decade's biggest musical comedies. It came to the Ohio on its way from Chicago to New York in 1925, and McDermott found it "something miraculous." Its big showstopper wasn't "Tea for Two" but "I Want to Be Happy." "They sang it dancing, they sang it jumping, they sang it sitting," reported McDermott. "They sang it eighteen more times and the audience kept yelling for more." They got more, as *Nanette* returned to the Ohio three more times. A week before its final visit, however, the Hanna finally had an answer to *No, No, Nanette* in a musical comedy titled *Yes, Yes, Yvette*. Admitting up front that the Hanna's contender didn't measure up to *No, No, Nanette*, *Plain Dealer* reviewer Glenn Pullen did see one redeeming feature: "Jeanette MacDonald virtually runs away with the show, playing the title role."[47] So Hanna patrons that week got a sneak preview of one of the movies' biggest musical stars of the 1930s.

Between the musical comedies and star turns, however, 1920s audiences at both the Ohio and the Hanna might also witness the birth of serious American drama. To the Hanna came Maxwell Anderson and Laurence Stallings's *What Price Glory?*, Robert E. Sherwood's *The Road to Rome*, and Eugene O'Neill's *The Hairy Ape*. O'Neill emerged as America's leading playwright, and the Ohio Theatre booked his *Desire under the Elms*, *Marco Millions*,

No, No, Nanette, with its toe-tapping songs and chorus line, was the stage epitome of the Roaring Twenties. By the time the musical was due for its final visit to the Ohio Theatre, the Hanna Theatre responded with *Yes, Yes, Yvette*. *Yvette* went nowhere, but its star, Jeanette MacDonald, would enjoy immortality on the silver screen. (*Cleveland Plain Dealer*, November 7, 1926)

and *Strange Interlude*. The latter was a nine-act marathon, and theatergoers could use the dinner break to refuel at the Music Box above the Ohio, the Clark's Restaurant next door, or the Far East or Monaco's across the street. As for the play, Bell of the *News* judged it "a great drama by a great American dramatist, perhaps as fine as anything ever written by a native of this country, which produces many second, third, and fourth-rate playwrights, but mighty few outstanding dramatists." As Nina Leeds, the main character, Judith Anderson "makes you believe that Nina is not only possible, but that she is the eternal feminine."[48]

There were some intimations of future things to come on Playhouse Square. A melodrama called *Chicago* came to the Hanna; it would return to Playhouse Square after a half century with a score by Kander and Ebb. *Porgy,* a folk drama, played the Ohio, as did *Green Grow the Lilacs;* they would enjoy second lives as the opera *Porgy and Bess* and the musical *Oklahoma!* One musical already perfect in itself floated into the Ohio on its pre-Broadway voyage. This was the soon-to-be immortal *Show Boat,* with its score by Jerome Kern and Oscar Hammerstein II. McDermott's only complaint was "there is too much of it and too much of it is good." It "didn't seem too long" to Davis of the *Press,* who described it as similar to such European romantic operettas as *Blossom Time* and *The Student Prince,* but with one significant difference: "The United States is the scene of 'The Show Boat.' . . . The music is American in style."[49]

Davis was on to something. It would take fifteen years to come to fruition, but he had just witnessed the harbinger of the modern American musical theater.

Towering Moments

As the twenties roared to their climax, Cleveland shared in the general national prosperity. The rise of the Great Bull Market was reflected in the growth of the urban skyline and the abundance of the theatrical season. In New York, Broadway enjoyed its greatest season, quantitatively at least, in 1927–28 with a total of 280 productions.[50] On Cleveland's Playhouse Square that season, the Ohio offered fifty weeks of shows including summer stock, while the Hanna enjoyed a forty-week season before going dark for the summer. The decade also saw Broadway's last boom in theater construction, as seven new houses opened their doors in 1927 alone. There were no new commercial legitimate houses in Cleveland after the Hanna, although the noncommercial Cleveland Play House, the Gilpin Players (later Karamu), and the drama department of Western Reserve University all launched new stages during the twenties.[51]

One new marquee did light up on Playhouse Square during the decade, albeit for a comparatively modest movie house. Originally called the Cinema, it was built on the south side of Euclid Avenue, east of the Hanna Building and across from the Palace Theatre and East Seventeenth Street. It opened on October 14, 1928, under the management of Louis Israel, with a showing of *The Patent*

Leather Kid starring Richard Barthelmess. There were a thousand seats in the blue-and-gold auditorium. Indirect ceiling and wall lighting and a "Mighty Wurlitzer" organ apparently sufficed for atmosphere. By the first of the following year, the Cinema was running *The Road to Ruin,* a "Flaming Drama of This Jazz-Crazed Pleasure-Made Age."[52]

Better things were in store for the Cinema, however, thanks to the Warner Brothers, once of Youngstown, Ohio, and then of Hollywood. They were flush with funds due to their success with the first "talkie," *The Jazz Singer,* and investing in theater ownership across the country. After buying out the Philadelphia-based Stanley chain, they cast their eyes on Cleveland. With the Uptown on the east side and the Variety on the west side under their belts, they then sought a downtown showcase. Taking over the Cinema on Playhouse Square, they gutted it to the walls and invested $200,000 in improvements. These included new seats, carpets, drapes, decorations, lights, and, of course, sound equipment. "It's in the style called modernistic," reported Sidney Andorn in the *Press.* "The coloring is copper, sand and blue, with this color scheme carried out even to the backs of the seats." Outside, glittering over a new marquee was a blade sign seventy feet in height, illuminating with more than seven thousand electric bulbs the theater's new name: the Lake.[53]

In conspicuous newspaper ads, Warner's touted its acquisition as a "Jewel Box of Entertainment," and a "further testimonial of Warner Bros. Faith in Cleveland."[54] Scheduled to officially open to the public on Christmas Day 1930, the Lake hosted an invitational preview two nights earlier. Some overzealous press agent, apparently, invited twice as many guests as the theater had seats—even if they were all installed, which they weren't. As a result some one thousand Clevelanders were forced to cool their heels on the Playhouse Square sidewalks for better than an hour, until manager Willett Warren could appease them with a second screening of the Lake's initial offering, *Kismet.* It starred Otis Skinner, who frequently acted in person at Playhouse Square's Ohio Theatre in the 1920s.[55]

Another newcomer to Playhouse Square, though not a theater, was filled with theater lovers. The Hermit Club had been organized in 1904 by Frank Bell Meade, an architect with theater proclivities. Modeled on New York's Lambs Club, it was open to professional men with an interest in the performing arts. Meade designed their first clubhouse, called an "abbey," on East Third Street in Cleveland's former theater district, within hailing distance of the old Prospect Theatre, the Hippodrome, and the Euclid Avenue Opera House. To pay for the abbey and indulge their artistic bents, members began to stage annual musical comedies at the Opera House.[56]

In 1928, with the Opera House gone and the theater district relocated to Playhouse Square, the Hermits packed their trunks and followed suit. Meade drew up the plans for a new $75,000 abbey at the end of Dodge Court, in the shadows of the Allen and Ohio stage houses. Described as an "outstanding example of 'Olde Englishe eclectic whimsey,'" the exterior was faced in dark-red brick with a half-timbered second floor, diamond-shaped windows, and a main gable with scalloped bargeboard. Interior amenities included a restaurant on the first floor and meeting and game rooms on the third. A spacious lounge dominated the second floor, with a dining room at one end and a stage on the other.[57] A larger venue was needed for the club's annual revues, and the nearby Hanna Theatre proved convenient for this. There, in conjunction with Cleveland's Junior League, the Hermits presented *Stepping Out* in May 1929.

As the 1920s wound down, the Cleveland skyline surged upward. In 1927, the Ohio Bell Telephone Company moved into its new headquarters on lower Huron Road. "A Temple to Telephony," as denominated in one of the company's promotional pamphlets, it rose from a site formerly occupied by the Huron Road Hospital and the Empire Theatre burlesque house. At 365 feet and twenty-two stories, it surpassed the twenty-one-story B. F. Keith Building on Playhouse Square as Cleveland's tallest structure.[58]

Bragging rights became moot anyway, when the fifty-two-story Terminal Tower opened the same year on Public Square. Not only did its 708 feet make it Cleveland's tallest building by far, but for nearly four decades it would be the tallest in the world outside New York City. Its name came from the fact that it was constructed above the city's new railroad station, the Union Terminal, which was slated to replace the old Union Depot on the lakefront. Besides the railroad depot, the new terminal would also accommodate the downtown stop of the Shaker Heights Rapid Transit.[59]

There was much more to it than the tower and the terminal, however. They were the centerpiece of a seven-building complex spread over seventeen acres—nearly twice the footprint of the adjoining Public Square. As glowingly envisioned in a *Plain Dealer* special section,

Public Square has been rejuvenated. The center of Cleveland becomes the gateway of continental travel, the hub of the city's street railway transportation and the center of the rapid transit system soon to be established. . . .

All buildings in the terminal area are inter-connected by underground streets and passageways. The traveler arriving in Cleveland at the new station will be able to visit hundreds of stores, shops and offices without stepping into the outdoors.[60]

As exciting as this must have sounded to Clevelanders in general, it likely sent tremors of apprehension across Playhouse Square. They were soon justified, when Higbee's department store vacated its building across from Halle's to move into new quarters in the Terminal group. "This shifting of the downtown axis toward the [Public] Square resulted in a tug-of-war between upper Euclid and lower Euclid," noted Cleveland newspaperman and historian Philip Porter. Playhouse Square responded to the challenge by forming its own promotional group in 1931, Euclid Ave. Fine Shops and Theaters, Inc.[61] As far as shopping was concerned, however, Public Square and Playhouse Square would soon have more serious things to worry about than location.

Down and Out

Fall of 1934 found William McDermott in a reminiscent mood. "In the matter of the touring stage we have sunk to the level of a country village," wrote the *Plain Dealer*'s drama critic. "Not a stage show in town, except in the cabarets, burlesque, or at the Play House, and here it is late September. Not even a vaudeville show." It didn't used to be that way:

I notice the difference on Euclid Avenue. In the old days, no longer than a season ago, the players were leaving their imprints on the Avenue. You couldn't walk down the street at noon without seeing evidence of them.

A group of dancers, maybe, from the vaudeville theaters, hurrying toward the stage door in their paint and furs and the excited animation that young women have when they are in a strange city. Or you could see some of the orchestra men from the theaters grouped in conversation on the sidewalks, taking the air.

When the shows were in town you were pretty certain to run into some visitor who you knew, or whose face and name was famous. I have met George Arliss on Euclid Avenue and Ethel Barrymore and

Groucho Marx and John Barrymore and Eddie Cantor and George M. Cohan and Ruth Chatterton and a hundred others of the aristocracy of players.[62]

McDermott had actually been chronicling the malaise of the theatrical road for much longer than "a season ago." Nearly five years earlier, he had recorded his disturbing recognition that for the first time in memory the city's legitimate theaters were all dark that week. He attributed the phenomenon to the dearth of enough good theater towns left on the road to make touring profitable.[63] A couple of years later, he extended blame to Broadway producers for trying to cut their losses by closing shows before they had a chance to find an audience.[64] Hollywood also came in for a share of culpability for draining actors from the live stage to the sound stages of the talkies. Within the previous three years, McDermott noted in 1933, "no less than 197" of the "315 stars, or featured players" in Hollywood had come from the living stage. "What is Hollywood to do when, to put it colloquially, the cow dries up and no more milk is forthcoming?" he asked rhetorically. "I think I have said before that if the stage did not exist it would be necessary for Hollywood to invent it."[65]

Unmentioned by McDermott, though he had to be aware of it, was the elephant in the room. He was writing during the first few years of the Great Depression, when a lot more than legitimate theater and vaudeville were undergoing hard times. The economic catastrophe is generally dated from the last week of October 1929, when Wall Street laid an egg, in the showbiz vernacular of *Variety*, the entertainment weekly. By the time the economic freefall bottomed out, in the winter of 1933, nearly one out of three in the Cuyahoga County labor force was out of work. Homeless down-and-outers built makeshift shantytowns dubbed "Hoovervilles" in insult to the President blamed, justly or not, for the depression. One of several such encampments in Cleveland was in prominent view on the downtown lakefront.[66]

Playhouse Square came in for its share of collateral damage. Charles A. Selzer, the antiques dealer behind the Bulkley Building, died of pneumonia in 1931, and the contents of the establishment that had furnished the lobbies of Playhouse Square went under the auctioneer's hammer. "Heels clattered loudly on the bare floors where the footsteps of the city's wealthy were wont to fall silently on deep carpets in the old days," wrote Robert Bordner in the *Press*.[67] The old H. H. Dodge mansion he had occupied

Nikolai Semenoff, fleeing the Russian Revolution in the 1920s, set up a dance studio in Playhouse Square. He thrived until the Depression and modern dance did him in. (Hanna Theatre program, author's collection)

was leveled for parking. Another Millionaires' Row landmark, the home of Western Union founder Jeptha Wade, fell a victim to the wrecker's ax in 1934. Described as "once the core of Cleveland's social whirl," its demise marked another milestone in the transition of Euclid Avenue from an elite residential address to a commercial thoroughfare.[68]

Yet another departure from Playhouse Square was made by a refugee from the Russian Revolution named Nikolai Semenoff. He had come to Cleveland in 1920s to open the Imperial Russian School of Dance in Cleveland's Carnegie Hall, an office building across from Halle's on Huron Road. His ads in local play and concert programs offered classical ballet training for "boys and girls of aristocratic and noble families." Unfortunately, by the 1930s many of Cleveland's "aristocratic and noble" families were feeling the pinch; those who weren't were enrolling their children in the currently voguish modern dance, a free form of discipline disdained by Semenoff as a slander on the ballet. Closing his studio, he took a train to Niagara Falls and was last seen wading into the rapids above the falls.[69]

Theaters fell victims to both the Depression and the competition of talking motion pictures. No major legitimate theater was to open on Broadway after the Craig in 1928; instead, many existing theaters were being converted into movie houses.[70] On lower Euclid Avenue in Cleveland, the Star Theater reinvented itself as the Cameo movie house (later the Embassy) in 1926, and the mighty Hippodrome removed its stage trappings in favor of the silver screen in 1931. The following year saw the destruction on Superior Avenue of the Colonial Theater, just short of its thirtieth anniversary. A highlight in its distinguished career was the 252-performance run in 1923–24 of *Abie's Irish Rose*, which remained a Cleveland record for half a century.[71] The Colonial's demise left Playhouse Square's Ohio and Hanna as the only commercial legitimate shows in town.

But not for long. By the second year of the Depression, even the state-of-the-art Hanna and Ohio found it difficult to fill their seasons. In New York, the Shubert organization went into receivership, and in Cleveland, Carl Hanna assumed personal control of the Hanna Theatre. Abe Erlanger died in 1930, and his heirs took over management of the Ohio from Robert McLaughlin. In the 1930–31, season the Hanna was dark for thirteen weeks and the Ohio for twenty-nine. Over the following seasons, both theaters averaged around thirty dark weeks despite an increased booking of movies. McLaughlin briefly returned to the Ohio but wasn't able to keep it lit for much more than a couple of seasons of summer stock. From 1923 to 1928, he had kept the Ohio's marquee ablaze for some three hundred consecutive weeks; except for half a dozen movies, a few weeks of summer stock, and a one-night stand of legit, it was dark for seventy-six weeks between the fall of 1932 and the fall of 1934.[72]

Then, George Davis announced in the *Cleveland Press* on October 23, 1934, "Ohio Theater tonight opens what once, in a snooty day, was called the legitimate theater in Cleveland." It was a two-night and single matinee stand of Marc Connelly's *The Green Pastures* and was close to a sellout.[73] A retelling of the Old Testament from the perspective of a rural Black Southern congregation, it had played two years on Broadway and toured for two years since, including a week at the Hanna in 1933. Most of the Black original cast was still intact, headed by a septuagenarian former Chautauqua reader named Richard B. Harrison as "De Lawd." Though its racial naivety would hardly suit today's sensibilities, in its day it was regarded as a landmark in the pursuit of interracial bridge building.

In the *Plain Dealer*, McDermott described it as "tricky and dangerous stuff. Outwardly the play is expressed in comical terms and its effect is often irresistibly droll," he wrote. "But beneath its superficial comedy there had to be a reverent spirit and a feeling of beauty and awe." Though the play conveyed that delicate balance, McDermott wondered whether it was the novelty of the play or simply the playgoing experience that moved Clevelanders the most. "Indeed, the size of the audience and its manifest eagerness at the prospect of seeing a play has been so unusual a spectacle of

After fifteen years as a legitimate house, the Ohio Theatre went dark on October 24, 1934, with this production of *The Green Pastures*. Richard B. Harrison, who had created the role of "De Lawd" on Broadway, was still admonishing sinners nearly two thousand performances later. (*Cleveland Plain Dealer*, October 21, 1934)

late months that it all gave the impression of something slightly and pleasantly antique."[74]

It would become more than slightly antique. Half a century would pass before the Ohio stage saw a legitimate production again, but at least it went dark with dignity. A year later, McDermott delivered its eulogy. "As a house for the drama, the Ohio is gone," he wrote. "Warfield played there and George Arliss and all the Barrymores. It was not an old theater, but it has memories."[75]

Dancing in the Dark

By any measure, New Year's 1933 was the worst of times. America seemed stuck in the interregnum between the outgoing Hoover administration and the recently elected Franklin Delano Roosevelt. Unemployment had reached a peak of nearly 13 million. Wages in Ohio the previous year had been less than half of what they were in 1929. Broadway productions were plunging from a peak of 240 in 1929 to only a quarter of that number a decade later.

All that aside, on the second day of 1933 the Hanna Theatre staff members might have been singing the theme song of FDR's winning campaign—"Happy Days Are Here Again." They were opening a new play that night by Noel Coward. Not only was Coward himself to appear in it, but his costars were America's leading acting team, Alfred Lunt and Lynn Fontanne. The play, *Design for Living*, was not coming from Broadway; it was headed for Broadway. Its world premiere would take place that night on the Hanna stage.[76]

Despite an increase in its top ticket price from two to three dollars, the Hanna sold out the week's run before opening night. Two hundred additional gilt chairs were placed in the orchestra aisles to meet the demand, perhaps fanned by the revelation that "the plot is very, very daring" by Noel Francis (aka Winsor French) in the *Cleveland News*. "Never before was quite so much interest centered in a play opening in Cleveland," observed Davis in the *Press*. Stringers from the Associated Press and United Press joined a dozen local newspaper writers assigned to cover the event. "Nearly every smart gown has fur trimming," noted the *Plain Dealer*'s fashion editor of feminine first-nighters. Fire marshals evidently overlooked the seats in the aisles, perhaps because one of them was occupied by former city manager William Hopkins.[77]

The curtain rose at 8:45, only fifteen minutes behind schedule. Coward, who would later count *Design for Living* as his favorite among his plays, had written it for himself and his two friends, the Lunts. They played the three main characters: Otto (Lunt), Leo (Coward), and Gilda (Fontanne). "Three for one and one for three" is how Bell described their ménage à trois in the *News*. Audience and critics took it all in stride. "The three of them have a forgiving indulgence for their own unconventionalities," wrote McDermott in the *Plain Dealer*, "and the feeling they leave at the last is that they belong, by right of their difference from [the] herd, together." Scholars have since noted a gay subtext to the plot, which audiences apparently didn't get and critics chose not to notice. Coward and friends took eight curtain calls at the Hanna that night. "It is a charming and gracious thing to us that we could play together," said Coward in a curtain speech. "We are glad you like it."[78]

As *Design for Living* went on to Pittsburgh, Washington, and Broadway success, the Hanna remained lit for two and a half weeks and then went dark for eight. The Ohio, meanwhile, would be dark but for three movies all that season and bring down its final curtain the following year. Ten years earlier, the Ohio had seemed the more successful of Playhouse Square's two legitimate houses, until the coming of the Depression and the departures of Erlanger and McLaughlin. Fortunately for the Hanna, the senator's heirs, especially grandson Carl, felt ties to his namesake theater.

The Hanna also enjoyed one other potentially decisive advantage over the Ohio. It rested behind and under eight stories of rentable stores and offices, connected to another sixteen floors of the same—the block-long Hanna Building and Annex. Even in the absence of records, one might assume that the offices and storefronts served to subsidize the theater, a hedge that may be traced back to such nineteenth-century theatrical ventures as Cleveland's Academy of Music on Bank (West Sixth) Street. All the Ohio Theatre had in that respect was the narrow, shallow four-story Loew's Ohio Building over its and the neighboring State's lobbies. There was a foundation underneath that modest structure capable of supporting sixteen stories, but the additional dozen floors had never been built.[79]

While the Ohio was dark, however, it didn't remain quiet for long. The silence was broken not by the sounds of a play in rehearsal but by those of carpenters preparing the former legitimate house for an entirely different production. Below the stage they installed a kitchen, from which a tunnel opened to the middle of the auditorium, now stripped of its theater seats. From the old orchestra section, a staircase was installed along the auditorium wall leading to the balcony, similarly cleared of its rows of seats. Overhead, the ceilings were lowered six feet in the auditorium and eight feet in the grand lobby.[80] As with the original theater, workers rushed feverishly right up to the eve of its scheduled reopening on October 22, 1935, two days less than a year since the Ohio's curtain had fallen for the last time.[81]

Crowds of curiosity-seekers gathered on the Euclid Avenue sidewalk to see such local royalty as Mayor Harry Davis, Leonard Hanna, and Edward Grasselli and their parties, all in evening attire, enter the doors of what was the Ohio Theatre but now styled itself the Mayfair Casino. "More dress suits and formal gowns were worn—more ermine and more jewelry flashed—last night than Cleveland had seen since pre-depression days," wrote Charles Schneider in the *Press*.[82] The Depression may not have been over yet, but Prohibition was, and with its end, the speakeasy doors opened to the nightclub era. A model for Cleveland's Mayfair was New York's French Casino, which opened in 1931 in the redesigned Earl Carroll Theatre on Seventh Avenue. Cleveland's version attracted a crowd of twelve hundred on opening night, which was sold out weeks in advance.[83]

First-nighters were greeted by veteran showman George Fox, whose theatric resume included managerial duties at the Ohio and the old Euclid Avenue Opera House. Inside the doors, what had been one of the longest theater lobbies in the country now housed one of the world's longest bars, "said to be bigger than the Jockey Club bar in Shanghai," reported McDermott. Oblong-shaped and hollow inside with stools all around, it was built by a Cleveland concern now back in the cocktail bar business after a decade building soda bars during Prohibition. In the middle, sixteen bartenders, "looking sad in a businesslike way," served mixed drinks and $12-a-bottle champagne. Harry Propper, Mayfair manager, let the crowd enjoy a preshow cocktail hour before opening the inner doors to the casino.[84]

In place of the Ohio's rows of theater seats were ranks of dining tables and chairs in the old orchestra and the balcony. Masking the former classical decor of the Ohio was an inner shell done in modern art deco style with tones designer Jac Lessman described as "a tomato red, velour background, relieved by peach, champagne, and chartreuse," which McDermott interpreted as "dull red broken by white and silver." The *Plain Dealer* drama critic confessed to feeling nonplussed at seeing patrons dancing on a platform "consecrated in its original state by Warfield, Arliss and the Barrymores." Nonetheless, the operators had been under bond to leave the original trappings intact under their $125,000 makeover, so McDermott might still nurse "an idea that the theater might come back into its own."[85] (He was no older than forty-four at the time, but he wouldn't live to see the day.)

In the meantime, in place of drama the Mayfair purveyed drinks, dinners, dancing, and floorshows, the last with no cover charge. Dinners went for $1.50, which seems reasonable even by Depression standards, so the profit margin must have come from the drinks. More than a hundred waiters kept the meals coming out of the tunnel to diners on the main floor and up the stairway to those in the balcony. Imbibers in the balcony had their own sky bar in the upper reaches. Between courses or drinks, patrons might dance to the rhythms of three orchestras, including one in the lobby lounge. Between sets they could rest their feet watching a two-hour floorshow featuring twenty acts by a cast of sixty, including a chorus line of "30 voluptuous so-and-so's hand-picked from the rose gardens of Broadway."[86]

Despite its spectacular debut, the subsequent career of the Mayfair Casino proved anticlimactic. Early warning signals included a request from a local iron company that the restaurant be thrown into receivership for nonpayment of $3500 owed on ornamental work for renovations. Its request was denied on a legal technicality.[87] For the summer of 1936, Propper closed the auditorium restaurant but kept the lobby lounge in operation. He reopened the Casino in the fall and celebrated its first birthday in October with a "Broadway after Dark" revue headlined by exotic dancer Faith Bacon. Even seminudity didn't help, as the Casino filed for bankruptcy the next month.[88]

Though it managed to limp along for another year, the Mayfair Casino never really recovered. New York's French Casino was said to be interested in purchasing the Cleveland property but declined to follow through. From the beginning, there had been rumors of gambling at the Mayfair. A month after its opening, a squad of Cleveland detectives showed up for a spot inspection in search of gambling rooms and equipment and turned up nothing. "The fix was on, supposedly, and they were going to have gambling in the basement," recalled Don Grogan, whose father managed several downtown properties. "Then, apparently, the fix was not on and they didn't get gambling and it closed."[89] The Mayfair went into bankruptcy a second and final time in November 1937, little more than two years after its ostentatious opening.

The Mayfair's closing didn't leave Playhouse Square entirely bereft of nightlife, however. Around the time of the casino's arrival, an Austrian immigrant named Herman Pirchner opened the Alpine Village nightclub in the former home of the Far East Restaurant, opposite the Palace Theatre. Still in his teens when he immigrated to Cleveland after World War I, Pirchner eked out a living with jobs in a pretzel factory and brewing illegal beer in the cellars of German clubs. He then purchased an eastside café, which he renamed the Alpine Shore Club, serving drinks in an upstairs speakeasy and thence openly after the repeal of Prohibition. In 1935, he was ready to test his fortunes in downtown Cleveland.[90]

Located within shouting distance of one another on either side of Euclid Avenue, the swank Mayfair Casino and Bavarian-themed Alpine Village couldn't have presented a sharper contrast in ambiance. It was like stepping from glamour into gemütlichkeit. Instead of a maître d' in evening wear, one was liable to be greeted by the tall, blond proprietor decked out in lederhosen and other Tyrolean gear. Pirchner circulated freely among his tables, encouraging his patrons to get into the act with a song, dance, or other bit of improv. His own contribution to the entertainment was an attempt to see how many full beer steins he could schlep, unsupported, across the dance floor. Grasping a base of seven steins by their handles in each hand, he piled on two more layers to a total of thirty-seven. Though he lost one along the way, Pirchner managed to reach his goal with a claimed record of three dozen.[91] What it lacked in sophistication, the Alpine Village possessed in longevity, remaining as a Playhouse Square fixture long after the Mayfair Casino had vanished.

There were other signs of revived prosperity on Playhouse Square in the mid-1930s. Early in 1936, a link in the growing Stouffer restaurant chain opened in the Kinney & Levan Building on Euclid opposite East Fourteenth Street. Stouffer's had begun as a stand-up milk counter in Cleveland's Old Arcade in 1922. By 1931, its headquarters and flagship restaurant were located in the Citizens Building at East Ninth and Euclid. Though the company subsequently opened offshoots in Detroit, Pittsburgh, and Philadelphia, the Playhouse Square outlet marked its first expansion in its home city.[92] Stouffer's, too, became a Playhouse Square destination, especially popular for lunch on matinee Wednesdays at the Hanna Theatre.

Another sign of neighborhood revival came with the opening that year of the new home of Engel & Fetzer's on Huron Road. It wasn't a big move for the furrier, which had occupied two neighboring storefronts to the west. The new home had been built for the Winton Motor Carriage Company and was occupied in the interim by a Lyon & Healy piano outlet. It was a three-story building with storage vaults for seven thousand fur coats on the third floor and employee workrooms and lunchrooms on the second. On the main floor and mezzanine were fitting rooms and a custom-made salon. Outside it may have been July, but at an opening reception in the former automobile showroom, to music provided by Johnson's Society Orchestra, four New York models demonstrated the latest in winter fur fashions.[93]

Hollywood Gold

One of the few businesses to survive the Depression relatively unscathed was the movie industry. For one thing, among the day's entertainment options, movies offered probably the biggest bang for the rare discretionary buck. Even at the downtown first-run houses, cinema tickets made a smaller dent in the family budget than live theater. In addition, movies entered the 1930s with something new to see—or make that hear. Sound had finally entered the picture.

Playhouse Square just missed hosting Cleveland's first exposure to the new cinematic technology when *The Jazz Singer* opened at the Loew's Stillman, just on the other side of East Twelfth Street, on February 5, 1928. "Al's In the Movies Now!" trumpeted the theater's ad, "See and Hear Him!" He was heard in no more than a few songs and a couple lines of dialogue, but that was good enough for a five-week run at the Stillman.[94] By year's end, the Playhouse Square houses were also preparing to show the talkies. Fanny Brice opened 1929 at the Allen in *My Man* and outdid even the great Jolson in that theater's publicity: "Fannie Sings! Talks! Laughs! Cries!" Nancy Carroll sang "Gotta Be Good" in *Manhattan Cocktail* at the State. Though the Palace had announced plans to be wired for sound in August, it was apparently still working on it in December.[95] A year later, Warner Brothers had added the redesigned and wired Lake to the Square's cinema showcases.[96]

The larger houses sought to achieve the right balance between stage and screen. No longer under lease to Loew's, the Allen in 1934 sought briefly to resuscitate its stage with a revue called *Spices of 1934*, billed with the film *Masters of Men* starring Fay Wray of *King Kong* fame. "It is not a show with much of what the trade calls 'class,'" wrote McDermott of the revue, noting that the Allen was "crowded with flesh-hunters" who "found plenty of it exposed." Soon the Allen passed under the aegis of the newly formed RKO studios, which also assumed control of downtown Cleveland's Hippodrome and Lake theaters. It became studio policy to open films at the "Hipp," still the city's largest house, then move them over to the Allen and finally to the Lake before their release to neighborhood theaters. Warner Brothers later took over those theaters and followed the same plan.[97]

Early in the decade, the State laid big plans for its stage component. In the summer of 1932. the Loew's flagship closed for nearly four months for installation of new stage equipment as well as innovations in the front of the house. Among other plans of H. M. Addison, the State's new manager, were the hiring of a sixteen-piece orchestra and weekly lobby exhibitions by Cleveland civic organizations.[98]

Evidently, the State's stage hopes were short-lived. When Judy Garland appeared there in 1939, the State was said to have "resumed the combined stage and screen policy for the first time in several seasons." MGM's teenaged singing star had the crowd "hanging from the chandelier." Screen stars also made special appearances to promote their movies, as when Cleveland son Bob Hope took the State's stage at 11:30 one Saturday night in 1941 to plug his latest film, *Nothing but the Truth*. A week later, the State arranged a unique film tie-in for the showing of Paramount Studio's animated version of the popular comic strip "Superman." Since Superman's creators happened to be Clevelanders, the State brought Jerry Siegel and Joe Shuster to its lobby for two days, where they demonstrated the art of cartooning and autographed strips for youthful fans. Lobby displays also continued, such as a 1938 garden sponsored by Halle's department store.[99]

True to its birth as a vaudeville house, the Palace next door maintained a fair balance between live acts and film. By 1930 vaudeville was in terminal decline due to the competition from radio and movies. Edward Albee, builder of the Cleveland Palace, lost the Keith circuit in 1928 to the Radio-Keith-Orpheum combination (RKO) engineered by Joseph P. Kennedy, father of the future president. RKO would later become a major Hollywood studio, and the Palace would premiere some of its films in Cleveland. The Palace's live acts, too, were increasingly headlined by stars of the silver screen. They included the Three Stooges (Moe, Larry, and Curly), who brought their *Revue de la Nutts* to the Palace in 1937. "They fracture each other's skulls . . . and behave generally in the idiotic manner that has elevated them into the higher income brackets," wrote Winsor French in the *Press*. A couple of years later, Mae West, "slick as a wet seal in her black sequins," in the words of Ward Marsh, sashayed across the Palace stage.[100]

Big bands also played the Palace, such as Benny Goodman's the week prior to Mae West. To swing specialties such as "One O'Clock Jump" and "Sing, Sing, Sing," the "younger generation . . . stamped their feet in time, clapping hands, whistling and shouting 'Yeah, man!' until the stage machinery rattled," reported Glenn Pullen in the *Plain Dealer*. When guest bands didn't occupy the stage, the Palace's house orchestra was under the direction of the third of the musical Spitalny brothers, Maurice. Joel Grey, whose father, Mickey Katz, played clarinet under Spitalny, remembered Maurice as known for "the tight white flannel pants he wore to show off his 'manhood' while conducting."[101]

But movies increasingly dominated the Playhouse Square marquees in what many consider to have been Hollywood's golden age. Early in the decade, such Warner Brothers classics as *Little Caesar*, *Public Enemy*, and *I Am a Fugitive from a Chain Gang* played the

Lake.[102] Two of the biggest hits arrived in 1934. Claudette Colbert was Queen of the Nile at the State in the title role of the Cecil B. DeMille spectacle *Cleopatra*. At the Palace, Colbert was teamed with Clark Gable in the screwball comedy *It Happened One Night*. It wasn't the story itself, wrote Marsh, but "the excellent direction, and also the snappy way Director Frank Capra has made this tale move and the honest way he convinces you [it] might easily have happened—but more important, the sincere way he makes you hope it did happen."[103]

This parade of features rose in a crescendo culminating in the legendary crop of 1939, year of cinema classics. On Playhouse Square, the Palace premiered *You Can't Cheat an Honest Man* with W. C. Fields and *Confessions of a Nazi Spy* with Edward G. Robinson. The Allen screened a few secondhand after they moved over

Hollywood's most legendary year was 1939, with its bumper crop of movies. Although Playhouse Square missed *Gone with the Wind*, which appeared two blocks west at the Stillman, the State Theatre was the first in Cleveland to screen *The Wizard of Oz*. (*Cleveland Plain Dealer*, August 18, 1939)

from the Hipp, including *Gunga Din, Dodge City, Dark Victory,* and *Mr. Smith Goes to Washington.* It was the State, however, with its Loew's–MGM connection, that reaped the cream of the crop. They included *Goodbye, Mr. Chips,* premiered on a reserved-seat basis, and *Stagecoach,* which Marsh viewed as approaching "a degree of perfection seldom attained by the American native screen story, the Western." Perhaps the State's biggest coup was the eagerly awaited *The Wizard of Oz,* "In Gorgeous Technicolor!" starring Judy Garland, Bert Lahr, Ray Bolger, Cleveland's Margaret Hamilton, and a host of Munchkins. If that weren't enough, *Wuthering Heights, Beau Geste, Intermezzo,* and *Ninotchka* ("Garbo Laughs and Laughs!") also opened at the State.[104]

Unfortunately, the biggest picture of that year, *Gone with the Wind,* didn't hit Cleveland until January 1940, and when it came it didn't open on Playhouse Square but at the neighboring Stillman on a reserved-seat basis.[105] It remained there until April—a ten-week run. While Playhouse Square missed out on the decade's most successful film, two years later the Palace snagged many critics' choice for the era's greatest artistic success. Marsh, however, demurred from the general critical acclaim for RKO's *Citizen Kane.* While lauding Gregg Toland's cinematography and Orson Welles's pyrotechnical title performance, Marsh deplored the general villainy of the characters: "There is no one in the entire production to whom the spectator can point and say . . . 'I want to be like that.'"[106]

The Hanna's New Deal

Talking pictures may have proved to be the salvation of the movies during the Depression, but they posed a near mortal threat to legitimate theater. It went back even further than sound, as noted by Hallie Flanagan, who would direct the New Deal's Federal Theatre Project. "As far as actors were concerned," she wrote, "they had suffered their own particular depression ever since 1914, when the Strand Theatre, seating 3,000, opened on Broadway for exclusive showing of motion pictures."[107] The coming of sound exacerbated the problem, especially for Broadway and the road. Playwrights who could string a few lines of dialogue together and actors who were trained to give them voice boarded the train from New York to Southern California.

The ebbing of the Broadway pipeline was bound to have a ripple effect on the Hanna Theatre, now Cleveland's sole outlet for road shows. New York's dominant Shubert Organization, managers of the Hanna since its beginning, was thrown into receivership in 1931 and began divesting itself of many of its theaters around the country. They had never owned the Hanna, but Carl Hanna found it a propitious time to take over his theater's management. At the same time, Hanna, who had managed all the family's real estate, turned over operation of the Hanna Building to the T. W. Grogan Company.[108] The 1933–34 theatrical season marked ebb tide for the Hanna, which offered only four weeks of road shows, seven weeks of films, and eight of springtime stock.

Fortunately for live theater, it still had Katharine Cornell. Hardly anyone alive today has a memory of her acting art, for she never sold out to Hollywood. In the words of critic Alexander Woollcott, "it would still be true to say that Katharine Cornell had reminded the people of her day that there once had been and still was a vast and inviting province called 'the road.'"[109] He was referring to "Miss Kitty's" epic sixteen-thousand-mile tour of three plays in 1933–34, which played in seventy-three cities across America.

As it happened, the Hanna wasn't on that tour, but Cornell was no stranger to its patrons in the 1930s. If she couldn't open a show in her native Buffalo, Cleveland was her next favorite venue, and she had given the American premiere of what became her signature role in *The Barretts of Wimpole Street* at the Hanna on January 29, 1931. "The house was sold to capacity and there were standees," reported Bell in the *News*. "The same thing is certain for the three remaining performances; and Miss Cornell leaves Cleveland with a production that is likely to serve her as a stellar vehicle for two years, if she cares to remain in it that long."[110] (She did; it was on the bill for that legendary tour two years later.) Cornell would return to the Hanna in half a dozen plays during the decade, including Shakespeare's *Romeo and Juliet*, Shaw's *Saint Joan*, and S. N. Behrman's *No Time for Comedy*. Davis in the *Press* noted "three kinds of orchids and three kinds of ermines" in *Romeo and Juliet*'s opening-night audience. "Funny about dressing up for shows," he observed, "how distinctions are made between business suits being all right for the art of George Cohan and the Theater Guild, but only tailed coats being quite adequate for the art of Katharine Cornell."[111]

Where Cornell led the way, other theater royalty followed. The Lunts, who had premiered *Design for Living* with Noel Coward at the Hanna in 1933, returned in Shakespeare's *The Taming of the Shrew* in 1935 and Robert E. Sherwood's *Idiot's Delight* in 1937.

In the latter, Davis saw Lynn Fontanne, playing the mistress of a munitions maker, "in the best Garbo mood." Alfred Lunt as a vaudeville hoofer "gives the play its vivacity and lusty humor."[112] Like Cornell, the Lunts never went to Hollywood. Ethel Barrymore came to the Hanna in a 1935 revival of the play she had nearly capsized in its world premiere at the Ohio, Maugham's *The Constant Wife*. Helen Hayes brought portrayals of two dissimilar queens to Cleveland during the decade, the doomed *Mary of Scotland* and the long-lived *Victoria Regina*.

New faces also began to appear at the Hanna, both on stage and in the front of the house. Carl Hanna hired William Blair as manager in 1934. Two refugees from the darkened Ohio took up duties at the Hanna: Russell Harris in the box office and Don Carlos at the door.[113] A new playwright appeared in Clifford Odets, whose early work was forged in the crucible of the Depression. New York's Group Theatre brought his first full-length play, *Awake and Sing*, to the Hanna in 1936. Marsh called it "a play of power and magnetism," which "leaves with you the impression that you have studied a small and unhappy lot of humanity through a microscope." Directed by Harold Clurman, the acting company included Stella and Luther Adler, Morris Carnovsky, and Jules "John" Garfield.[114]

President Roosevelt's New Deal brought renewed hope and confidence not only to the country but to the theater. FDR could be seen in the musical comedy *I'd Rather Be Right*, which hit the Hanna in 1938. As McDermott explained,

> Credit George M. Cohan with an assist in this respect. Mr. Cohan, as everybody should know by this time, impersonates the president of the United States. . . .
>
> Mr. Cohan's song-and-dance in this piece is a sheer triumph of nostalgic sentimentality. It is ludicrous to see the president of the United States shuffling and hotfooting it to the jaunty rhythms of a swinging cane, but it is touching and heart-warming to see Cohan doing it again, for while he is about it your mind brings up a crowded panorama of the old theater and George M. Cohan is in the center of it, young, nimble, electric, compact of all the delights the old theater knew.[115]

That audiences accepted the idea of a polio-afflicted president breaking into dance may have been as much a tribute to the acting ability of "That Man in the White House" as to the old trouper at the Hanna.

A couple of weeks later, the Hanna hosted a show that Mc-Dermott called "a direct offspring of the New Deal." The show was called *Pins and Needles,* a musical revue "presented entirely by working folk who, in this case, are exclusively members of the International Ladies Garment Workers Union." McDermott credited a section of the New Deal's National Industrial Recovery Act with reviving the American labor movement to the point where it could put on a hit show on Broadway. "They do not make social consciousness, or political progress incompatible with fun and tolerance," said McDermott of the cast, all of whom were on leave from their day jobs in New York's garment district. "Maybe what the professional stage needs are a few good amateurs."[116]

As the country continued to pull itself out of the Depression, so did the American theater. Playwrights such as George Kaufman and Moss Hart, Thornton Wilder, Maxwell Anderson, S. N. Behrman, Robert E. Sherwood, and Lillian Hellman rose to the occasion with their best work. Kaufman and Hart's classic comedy *You Can't Take It with You* was good for three stands at the Hanna within the space of a year. More modest hits often sent their original casts on the road following respectable Broadway runs. Frank Craven came as the Stage Manager for Wilder's *Our Town;* Walter Huston sang Kurt Weill's "September Song" in Anderson and Weill's *Knickerbocker Holiday;* Raymond Massey took the title role in Sherwood's *Abe Lincoln in Illinois.* When Tallulah Bankhead opened in Hellman's *The Little Foxes, Press* artist Jim Herron caricatured some of the Hanna's first-nighters including Playhouse Square stalwarts Samuel Halle and wife, Mr. and Mrs. Carl and Gertrude Hanna, and the Vernon Stouffers.[117]

One play that reversed the usual pattern and went from the Hanna to Broadway rather than vice versa was Maxwell Anderson's *High Tor.* Its world premiere took place at the Hanna on December 30, 1936. It starred Burgess Meredith, a native Clevelander who had appeared at the Hanna earlier that year in Anderson's *Winterset,* and British actress Peggy Ashcroft, who was making her American debut on the Hanna's stage. Written partly in blank verse, *High Tor* was like an American *Midsummer Night's Dream,* with three sets of characters—the romantic leads, land speculators and bank robbers, and the ghostly crew from an old Dutch trading ship. While pursuing their disparate goals, their paths cross and collide with one another. Some of the action takes place in the maw of a large steam shovel, while stagehands literally had to move the mountain of the title around the set. Local opinion on Anderson's fantasy was mixed, but the play went on to win the New York Drama Critics' Circle Prize for 1937. It may well be the most eminent play ever to have premiered in Cleveland.[118]

As the 1940–41 season drew to a close, Carl Hanna faced a problem. William Blair having submitted his resignation, he needed a new manager for the Hanna Theatre. Hanna took his problem to Marcus Heiman, head of New York's United Booking Office, which had absorbed both the old Erlanger and Shubert booking operations. Heiman thought of a young protégé from his experience with the Orpheum Circuit in Chicago: Milton Krantz, who in the interim had served as manager or assistant manager of several Chicago theaters. "I was married March 15, 1941," recalled Krantz. "I got a call in late March from Heiman—would you consider going out to Cleveland for about a year. Tim Grogan came to talk to me. I made a deal for a year with Grogan, beginning September 1st." So Krantz brought his bride, Helen, to Cleveland, where he set to work cleaning up the Hanna Theatre, putting a crew together, signing unions to three-year contracts, and bringing the theater its first quarterly profit in years.[119]

"They said he won't stay, because he's New York material," commented Tim Grogan's son Don. "Well, he stayed fifty years."[120]

Timeline of 1921–1941

November 27, 1921
Rudolph Valentino appears as *The Sheik* at the State Theatre

June 28, 1925
The Iron Horse becomes the first movie shown at Keith's Palace

January 7, 1926
George Burns and Gracie Allen tie the knot in Cleveland, but not at the Palace

December 25, 1926
Katharine Cornell makes her first of an eventual twenty-two appearances at the Hanna Theatre

November 28, 1927
Show Boat docks at the Ohio Theatre on its way to Broadway

October 14, 1928
Cinema Theatre opens in Playhouse Square

December 25, 1930
Warner's reopens former Cinema as the Lake Theatre with *Kismet*

January 2, 1933
World premiere of Noel Coward's *Design for Living* plays at Hanna

October 24, 1934
Ohio Theatre goes dark as a legitimate house

October 22, 1935
Ohio Theatre reopens as the Mayfair Casino nightclub, which closes after two years

December 30, 1936
British actress Peggy Ashcroft makes her American debut in world premiere of *High Tor* at Hanna

August 18, 1939
The Wizard of Oz comes to the State Theatre

Backing the Home Front

"We Are All in It"

It wasn't a bad Sunday morning for early December—clear if cold, with temperatures hovering just above or below the freezing point. On Playhouse Square the movie theaters opened between 11:00 and 11:30. Gene Tierney emoted in *Sundown* at the State, while Abbott and Costello clowned around in *Keep 'Em Flying* at the Allen. A future screen classic, *The Maltese Falcon*, with Humphrey Bogart, was in its first run at the Palace. Alfred Hitchcock's *Suspicion* was in its third week across the street at the Lake, with Cary Grant and Joan Fontanne. The Hanna was dark, preparing for Monday's opening of Velez and Yolanda in their dance recital, *Dancopation*.[1] The Ohio was dark indefinitely, with no sign of relighting.

Sometime during the second showing in the movie houses, between 2:00 and 3:00 P.M., the news came to Cleveland. Some managers relayed it to patrons on loudspeakers between features; others turned on radio broadcasts in their lobbies. It was December 7, 1941, and Japan had just attacked the US naval base at Pearl Harbor.[2] There was a crowd of young men at the Keith Building the following morning, but they weren't there to get into the Palace. It was the US Coast Guard recruiting office on the premises that had attracted them on the day after Pearl Harbor. On Tuesday, President Roosevelt was scheduled to broadcast to the nation at 10:00 P.M., and Playhouse Square planned to tune in. It would be heard from the stage at the State, on the mezzanine of the Palace, and in the lobby of the Allen.[3] "We are now in this war," came FDR's familial, confiding voice. "We are all in it—all the way. Every single man, woman and child is a partner in the most tremendous undertaking of our American history. We must share together the bad news and the good news, the defeats and the victories—the changing fortunes of war."[4]

One showman in Playhouse Square was caught as off guard by the Japanese as was the US Navy in Hawaii. Herman Pirchner was a survivor. His Alpine Village had outlasted the far tonier Mayfair Casino, and Pirchner was rebounding from bankruptcy incurred in an ill-fated nightclub called the Show Boat in Cleveland's 1937 Great Lakes Exposition. A key to his survival was his ability to pinch pennies when necessary, especially in producing the floor shows for the Alpine Village. A frequent resort was to prepare a mini version of a popular musical comedy or European operetta. For the week of December 7, 1941, he had come up with what must have seemed a pretty safe bet: a streamlined production of *The Mikado*. Overnight, on December 8, Gilbert and Sullivan's Japanese themed satire had lost its humorous appeal. Pirchner abruptly pulled the plug on the show, a move that even attracted the attention of *Time* magazine. In its place, the Alpine's company would be singing "a medley of familiar tunes that arranger Cliff Barnes cooked up."[5]

Around the corner from the Alpine Village, the Hanna Theatre had far better luck. Following the run of Velez and Yolanda's *Dancopation* the week of Pearl Harbor, the Hanna had booked the movie *Kukan*, advertised as "The Story Japan Never Wanted the World to Know." Sponsored by the China Relief Organization, the film was a documentary portrait of a China under attack by Japan for the previous four years. "If there was nothing else in 'Kukan' save that awful bombing of Chungking, the picture's horrendously stirring climax, it would be something every American should see," wrote Arthur Spaeth in the *News*. "Here is what Pearl Harbor and Honolulu underwent at the bloody hands of Japan only a week ago." He would have been ready to recommend it regardless, said the critic; "Now I want to insist that 'Kukan' demands your attention."[6]

The Hanna caught another break at that time, just as unpremeditated as and even more fortuitous than the booking of *Kukan*. "After Pearl Harbor I got a call from a Colonel Donlevy in the Union Commerce Building," recalled the theater's new manager, Milton Krantz. The colonel was looking for experienced theater people to take shows over to Europe and other military venues and commissioned Krantz as a first lieutenant. "Then one morning I woke up with a swollen leg," Krantz continued. "It was diagnosed as thrombosis phlebitis, and I got an honorable discharge."[7] As disappointing as it may have seemed to Krantz, were it not for that medical incident the history of the Hanna Theatre might have been very different.

Meanwhile, Cleveland geared up for life on the home front. A temporary War Service Center was built downtown to accommodate recruiting offices and such agencies as the Red Cross and the War Housing Service. Like the Terminal group of the late 1920s, however, it was located on Public Square, more than half a mile from Playhouse Square. William A. Stinchcomb, director of the Metropolitan Parks, was appointed civilian defense director and scheduled a countywide blackout at 8:40 on the night of September 24.[8] "Playhouse Square presented a strange spectacle as all traffic came to a halt and lights went out one by one," observed the *News*. Marquees dimmed on *Panama Hattie* at the State, *The Gay Sisters* at the Allen, *Sherlock Holmes and The Voice of Terror* at the Palace, and the Lunts in *The Pirate* at the Hanna. Taillights on a stopped car outside the Hanna Building continued to glow until some pedestrians shouted, "Take your foot off the brakes." Then, in the words of the *Plain Dealer,* Playhouse Square became "a tunnel of darkness, with only the bright moonlight as illumination."[9]

Hollywood Goes to War

But the lights would come back on those marquees for the duration. "The American motion picture is one of our most effective mediums in informing and entertaining our citizens," President Roosevelt had said in December, when the wreckage of the Pacific Fleet still littered Pearl Harbor. Detroit's assembly lines would begin turning out tanks and bombers in place of automobiles, but it would be business for the most part as usual on Hollywood sound stages. "We are hoping that most of you and your fellow workers will stay right here in Hollywood and keep on doing what you're doing," Lowell Mellott told the studio chiefs in January, "because your motion pictures are a vital contribution to the total defense effort." Mellott was the government's coordinator of motion pictures, so in effect he had declared movies an essential war industry.[10]

One way Hollywood could attempt to fulfill FDR's mandate to both inform and entertain the citizenry was through war movies.

According to one estimate, 28 percent of the more than thirteen hundred feature films turned out from 1942 through 1944 dealt with some aspect of the war. Early examples of the genre necessarily dealt vicariously with the war experiences of countries before Pearl Harbor, such as the stiff upper British lips of *Mrs. Miniver.* Previewing its showing at Loew's State, Ward Marsh noted that despite the absence of battle scenes, the movie's "real greatness lies not only in its careful revelation of war-time life but in the heart-gripping nobility which war brings out in the souls of the ordinary civilian." One of the first films to deal with Americans at war was *Wake Island,* the story of a valiant but doomed stand by beleaguered Marines against a superior Japanese invasion force. "It'll Make You Fighting Mad!" bellowed the ad of the State, which screened it in the fall of 1942. Marsh considered it "a straightforward, factual, stand-up-and-cheer story of Americans who could take it—and ask for more Japs!"[11]

War films became regular fare on the Playhouse Square screens. The Allen showed *Hitler's Children, Casablanca,* and the Irving Berlin revue *This Is the Army,* generally a week after their local premieres down the street at the Hippodrome. Those at the State were always Cleveland first-runs, including *In Which We Serve,*

Wake Island brought an early American defeat in World War II to the State Theatre screen in the fall of 1942. "Owl Shows," shown at midnight, were designed to accommodate late-night-shift workers from Cleveland's defense plants. (*Cleveland Plain Dealer,* October 3, 1942)

Noel Coward's salute to the Royal Navy; *Hangmen Also Die,* a story of the Czech resistance; and *The Human Comedy,* William Saroyan's slice of life on the home front. Marsh gave the latter a curmudgeonly review, deeming its Pollyanna-like attitude toward life to be as outdated as the Horatio Alger stories of his youth. Nonetheless, stellar performances by Mickey Rooney and Frank Morgan managed to sway the critic in favor of *The Human Comedy:* "Unquestionably the greatest 'audience picture' I have ever seen. As such, my recommendation for it is boundless."[12]

Destination Tokyo came to the State early in 1944, with Cary Grant guiding an American sub right into the harbor of the enemy's capital. That was largely fiction; *Thirty Seconds over Tokyo,* which arrived at the State at the end of that year, was a loosely factual account of General Jimmy Doolittle's bombing raid over Japan early in the war. Though Marsh had little patience for the picture's "love sop to a public that likes to gurgle over the Hollywood type of saccharine love," he thought "this love pap" more than redeemed by the film's accurately detailed depiction of the training and preparation for the morale-boosting mission. "The take-offs are superbly well photographed and each plane leaving the [aircraft] carrier furnishes the film with a fresh climax," he wrote.[13]

Despite such occasional peaks as *Thirty Seconds,* run-of-the-mill war pictures lost some of their box-office appeal after a while. Theater managers began to call for more pure entertainment, a commodity Hollywood always had on tap and needed little persuasion to supply.[14] An early response to that demand was *Holiday Inn,* which arrived at the State just before Labor Day 1942. It so happened that Labor Day was the only major holiday the titular hostelry did not celebrate, but *Holiday Inn* had every other reason to sing, including Bing Crosby, Fred Astaire, and songs by Irving Berlin. "Crosby's singing is still the best," said Peter Bellamy in the *News.* "The best song he has to sing is Berlin['s] tender and wistful 'White Christmas.'"[15] The song, fated to become a seasonal standard, had probably been already heard on the radio, but the State Theatre formally introduced it to Cleveland.

Additional servings of lighter fare at the State included *The Miracle of Morgan's Creek, Star Spangled Rhythm,* and *Meet Me in St. Louis.* One of the biggest attractions at the Allen, following its run at the Hipp, was *Arsenic and Old Lace.* Few big celluloid hits came to the Palace, which subordinated films in its ads to such live acts as Woody Herman, Duke Ellington, and Count Basie and His Orchestra ("A Harlem Jive Jamboree!").[16] Perhaps the biggest movie hit of the war years was *Going My Way*, which was screened at the State as Allied forces advanced through France in the summer of 1944. Bing Crosby and Barry Fitzgerald played two Irish priests who reconciled their generational differences for the good of a threatened urban parish.[17] Both Bing and the picture would get Oscars that year.

Going strictly by box office receipts, it didn't seem to matter what Hollywood sent to the theaters. "From 1941 through 1945 movie exhibitors experienced a golden age, one never since repeated," stated movie scholar Douglas Gomery.[18] One reason for the surge was the rise in employment due to the demands of war production. Manufacturing employment in Cleveland leaped from 191,000 in 1940 to 340,000 in 1944. On the other side of the coin, with gasoline rationing and automobile and home appliance production suspended in favor of armaments, there was little for war workers to spend their earnings on other than evenings at the movies. According to a report in *Film Daily,* Cleveland's downtown first-run movie houses enjoyed their "biggest week's business on record" over Labor Day week of 1943.[19] With box offices booming, Loew's Cleveland & Toledo Theatres decided to open another downtown screen in Cleveland. They didn't have far to look, with the Ohio Theatre lying dark right downstairs.

The former legitimate house had seen dark days indeed during the past decade. After the glitz of the short-lived Mayfair Casino, it sat empty for three years until 1940, when a pair of Chicago promoters booked a "World's Fair Museum" in its lobby. Zaza the Alligator Girl headlined its twenty-two acts, bringing complaints from the managers of the Palace and the Allen against the "cheapening" of Playhouse Square. Following the run of Zaza and company, talk of converting the Ohio into a burlesque house raised similar opposition but turned out to be just talk. Reluctant to turn the theater over to a competing movie chain, Loew's saw the wartime boom as an opportunity to run it profitably itself.[20]

The company brought back Phil Garbo, who had worked on the house's decorations in 1921, to convert the faded casino back into a theater. Out went the art deco shell masking the original classical decor; in were theater seats replacing the night club's tables and chairs. Loew's imported Gertrude Tracy from one of its Massachusetts theaters to manage the Ohio, making her the first woman to run a major Cleveland movie house. The resuscitated Ohio opened its doors on September 23, 1943, with the northeast Ohio premiere of Paramount's *For Whom the Bell Tolls.* Adapted from the Ernest

Hemingway novel, the story set in the Spanish Civil War starred Gary Cooper and Ingrid Bergman. Marsh considered it to be not only "one of the great films of our day," but worthy of taking its place among some of the "great films of all time," from *Birth of a Nation* to *Gone with the Wind*.[21] It gave the Ohio a nine-week run. More importantly, with the Ohio back in line, Playhouse Square was once again fully aglow.

Playhouse Square Does Its Bit

Movie theaters across America sought to do more for the war effort than merely show the films turned out by Hollywood, and those on Playhouse Square were no exception. They expressed their patriotism in many media, among them large display ads in Cleveland newspapers. In 1942, Loew's Theatres ads adopted a format around a large *V* for victory filling the two-column width. Within the arms of the *V* appeared the feature appearing at the State; outside on the left was the film playing at the Stillman, while to the right appeared what was showing at the Park and Granada. A line urging "Buy War Bonds and Stamps Regularly!" marched across the bottom of the ad. For the Third War Loan in 1943, the Allen and Palace ads contained boxes commanding: "Back the Attack with War Bonds."[22]

Hollywood, Playhouse Square, and fifteen thousand movie theaters everywhere were enlisted for a billion-dollar war bond drive in September 1942, designated as "Salute to Our Heroes" month. On the first of that month, movie houses across the city interrupted their programs at 9:00 P.M. for bond sales talks. "When you buy War Bonds you, in effect, put your money into

Moviegoing became so popular during World War II that Loew's took the Ohio Theatre, closed since 1937, out of mothballs for the screening of films. It reopened in 1943 with the film version of Ernest Hemingway's novel of the Spanish Civil War, *For Whom the Bell Tolls*. (*Cleveland Plain Dealer,* September 21, 1943)

Displays and stands for the sale of war bonds became fixtures in the State Theatre lobby for the duration of World War II. Playhouse Square theater lobbies also served as recruiting centers for the armed services. (Courtesy of Playhouse Square Archives, Cleveland Memory Project, Michael Schwartz Library, Cleveland State University)

the savings bank of your government at interest, and at the same time you help your government to secure what it needs to win the war," Cleveland attorney Harry F. Peyer told the audience at the Palace Theatre. Outside, a twenty-four-hour-a-day war bond booth opened on Playhouse Square.[23]

Hollywood did its part by dispatching 337 actors and actresses across the country in a Stars over America "bond blitz." At mid-month, Cleveland came in for its share with the arrival of Hungarian American actress Ilona Massey, actor Hugh Herbert, and actor-dancer Fred Astaire. They appeared at a Public Hall rally, admission to which was the purchase of a minimum $18.75 war bond. Playhouse Square got into the act by sending some of that week's performers, including singer Judy Canova from the Palace and a troupe from the Alpine Village.[24]

Following the departure of the stars, Playhouse Square continued to push bonds. "Buy U. S. Government War Bonds and Stamps at Loew's Theatres," read an ad for the Ohio Theatre in 1944. At the Allen in 1945, bond buyers were offered premiums of nylon parachute silk handkerchiefs. Alpine Village Haushofmeister Pirchner and Palace clarinetist Mickey Katz earned recognition for the sale of nearly half a million dollars' worth of war bonds. Bond displays and sales counters were a permanent fixture in the State Theatre lobby, where $5.5 million of bonds were sold in a two-year period. The State's vast lobby was also put to use for more ambitious war promotions. At various times, it served as a recruiting station for Marines, the Coast Guard, the Red Cross, and war workers. It was a collection center for a drive to send old phonograph records to servicemen overseas. There were informational displays for the Merchant Marine, Army war artists, and bombing runs over Japan. They even drove a jeep into the lobby for a Spar (women's Coast Guard) recruiting campaign.[25]

Probably the most ambitious wartime lobby promotion at the State was the *Women at War* exhibit, mounted in conjunction with the *Cleveland Press* in January 1943. Its purpose was to recruit women—not for the armed services but for work in the area's war plants, which needed an estimated sixty thousand additional operatives. Eight Cleveland companies participated in the sprawling display, including Thompson Products, Eaton Manufacturing, Cleveland Graphite Bronze, and Parker Appliance. They set up work stations and provided female employees "to show by demonstration what women can do in war plants." In the *Press*'s words:

> You'll see a girl writing on a shiny metal bearing with an electric needle and a woman finishing an airplane propeller on a little polisher revolving 180 times a minute. . . .
>
> You'll see girls inspecting aircraft parts with the fine steel "stop and go gauges" and see them assembling electrical instrument parts so tiny you'll think they must be jewelers, and you can watch the woman lathe operator as she starts her machine, and watch the thin metal peeling shaved from the metal part coil and twist like confetti.

Free and open to the public from 1:00 to 10:00 P.M. daily, the exhibit was originally scheduled to run for two weeks but extended for two more at the request of William P. Edmunds, area director of the War Manpower Commission.[26]

Many war workers, male and female, had to work on the night shift as factories geared up to full production. Movie theaters regularly accommodated them with midnight screenings, as did the State with *A Guy Named Joe,* "Beginning with War Workers' Midnight to

Dawn Show, Wednesday Midnight Feb. 16th, Doors Open 11:45 P.M."
Even the Hanna scheduled a midnight showing for the Czech film
Ecstasy, which exposed Hedy Lamarr to the world.[27]

Troupes for the Troops

A few months after Pearl Harbor, Helen and Nicki Burnett were
on a mission—in downtown Cleveland. Helen had been a steward
at the Hollenden Hotel and Nicki a radio announcer for station
WHK. Their self-given assignment was to organize a Stage Door
Canteen in Cleveland, following a precedent set on Broadway.[28]
As the chief American embarkation point for the European Theater of Operations, New York City had a substantial population of
transient soldiers and sailors at any given time. The Stage Door
Canteen was established to provide a place where they might find
some free hospitality, refreshment, and entertainment. Under
the aegis of the American Theatre Wing of the United Service
Organization (USO), playwright Rachel Crothers and actresses
Gertrude Lawrence and Helen Hayes organized it. Located in a
former rathskeller in the basement of the 44th Street Theatre, it
opened its doors on March 2, 1942. Before long there were coun-
terparts in eight other American cities, among them Washington,
DC, New Orleans, and Hollywood.[29]

In Cleveland, the Burnetts first looked for a site on lower Euclid
Avenue near Public Square, convenient to the city's Union Terminal
railroad station. Negotiations for the former Hofbrau, operated by
restauranteur Herman Pirchner at 315 Euclid, fell through. When
Loew's Theatres then offered a space on the second floor above
its State Theatre lobby at 1515 Euclid, the Burnetts grabbed it. It
may have been nearly a mile from Public Square, but it was in the
heart of Playhouse Square, Cleveland's mini Broadway. Like its
New York prototype, Cleveland's Stage Door Canteen would live
up to its name.[30]

Broadway producer Brock Pemberton came on behalf of the
American Theatre Wing to inspect the future canteen quarters.
Originally occupied by the Carlton Terrace Restaurant, the space
had more recently housed the Music Box Cafe. "This must have
been quite a glamorous cafe during the early 1920s," he mused. "I
understand Guy Lombardo's Royal Canadians started their ca-
reers here 15 years ago and that Sophie Tucker once operated it,

too." Pemberton was especially impressed by the surviving murals, which the Burnetts planned to retain amid other necessary renovations and redecoration.[31]

Work was soon under way, with materials and labor donated by local companies and trade unions. Aided by a volunteer staff, the Burnetts scrambled to equip the canteen's kitchen, dining room, and game rooms. While the American Stove Company supplied just what one might have expected, a steam table came from the unlikely source of the Ohio Bell Telephone Company. The Phonograph Operators' Association of Cleveland installed music boxes. Two bottling companies were enlisted to supply soft drinks. (Alcoholic beverages were not solicited, as these were non grata in all USO facilities.) Even area artists offered their services, in the form of caricatures and portraits to be drawn on the spot and presented to servicemen as souvenirs of their visits. Such Cleveland School luminaries as Paul Travis, Kalman Kubinyi, Jim Herron, and Joseph Jicha signed on.[32]

The canteen would greatly need junior hostesses to serve as waitresses, dancing partners, and simply conversationalists for the guests. Recruited from local theater groups and schools, some four thousand volunteers were assigned working shifts and supplied with red, white, and blue aprons to wear while on duty. An eight-page pocket-sized booklet used light verse and sketches to make expectations clear:

So, now you are a hostess at the famous Stage Door Canteen!
And you're more frightened than in all your life you've ever been.
Well, pull yourself together and learn this from all the rest
That once you get the hang of it, you'll work with fun and zest.
The thing you must remember is to be a happy gal—
An able conversationalist, a dancer and a pal.
Also keep it in your mind your petticoat to hide,
For skirts these days are very short and when you dance they ride.

It went on for five more verses, including a couple of more serious precepts. Hostesses were reminded of "the rule on dating," which was officially frowned upon, "for your protection, dear." Another stricture was that "talk of war must be taboo," evidently out of fear that spies might be listening.[33]

By the final weeks of 1942, the Burnetts had enlisted an impressive roster of civic support. As codirectors, they headed an

Actress Dorothy McGuire, starring that week in *Claudia* at the Hanna Theatre, showed up on January 14, 1943, to help open Playhouse Square's Stage Door Canteen in the Loew's Building. Guests from the armed services responded to her and the free turkey sandwiches. (Photo by Clayton Knipper, Courtesy of *Cleveland Press* Collection, Michael Schwartz Library, Cleveland State University)

executive committee that included Milton Krantz, manager of the Hanna Theatre; Nadine Miles of Western Reserve University's drama department; Glenn Pullen of the *Cleveland Plain Dealer;* advertising executive Fred Stashower; and Al Sutphin, owner of the Cleveland Arena. Choosing an honorary chairman must have been a no-brainer: hometown movie star Bob Hope's name was raised to the top of the letterhead.

A week before the opening, the public was invited to a Package Party, with a package of sugar, canned goods, or other staples as the only price of admission. To pay for expenses not covered by donations or volunteers, the Phonograph Merchants' Association organized a "Swing Shift Jamboree" at Public Hall. The marathon fundraiser was scheduled to last from 9:00 P.M. Saturday to 4:30 Sunday morning, allowing both day- and night-shift war workers to attend. Ten thousand did, raising an estimated $5,000 for the Cleveland canteen.[34]

At 5:00 P.M. on January 14, 1943, Cleveland's Stage Door Canteen opened in Playhouse Square. Within two hours, two hundred servicemen were scarfing down turkey sandwiches from the buffet and jitterbugging with junior hostesses. Five orchestras took turns providing the music. Dorothy McGuire and Frances Starr mingled with early arrivals before walking up East Fourteenth Street to play in *Claudia* at the Hanna. Brock Pemberton was there, judging Cleveland's canteen "even more attractive than New York's." A private in attendance testified, "This place beats the Hollywood Canteen by a mile for size." At 9:30, the new Cleveland branch was saluted on the CBS *Stage Door Canteen* radio program. Ohio governor John Bricker spoke from Columbus and Bob Hope from Hollywood.[35]

Favorite Son

Although he couldn't make it to the canteen's Cleveland opening, Hope was no stranger to the USO or to Playhouse Square. Born Leslie Townes Hope in England in 1903, he was brought to Cleveland at the age of five and raised on the east side, near the city's "second downtown" at Doan's Corners. There, his mother took him to see vaudevillian Frank Fay at Keith's 105th Street Theatre. In hopes of breaking into show business himself, Hope dropped out of East High School and took dancing lessons. The closest he got to Playhouse Square in those days was Halle's department store, where he developed a lunch-hour crush on Mildred Rosequist, a girl at the cosmetics counter. One of his first gigs was at the Band Box Theater on East Ninth Street.[36]

By 1931, Bob Hope (as he now billed himself) had worked his way up the vaudeville circuit to an appearance at his hometown's showcase, the Palace Theatre on Playhouse Square, where his act was hyped as "A Glimpse of Tomorrow's Fun." From vaudeville, Hope moved into Broadway musical comedies, his breakout appearance coming in Kern and Hammerstein's *Roberta* in 1933. In Cole Porter's *Red, Hot and Blue* he shared billing with Ethel Merman and Jimmy Durante. A radio show followed, which led to his first Hollywood feature, *The Big Broadcast of 1938*, where he introduced what would become his sign-off song, "Thanks for the Memory." By 1943, Hope had sixteen movies to his credit, including the first three "Road" films with Dorothy Lamour and Bing Crosby. For two years he had been taking his radio show to army bases, and by the summer of 1943 he was planning to take it to American troops overseas.[37] Before taking off to England, however, Hope put in an appearance at a place where he enjoyed the distinction of honorary chairman: Cleveland's Stage Door Canteen.

Four WAACs (members of the Women's Army Auxiliary Corps) escorted Hope and his troupe in a jeep caravan up Euclid Avenue to Playhouse Square. Up to two thousand servicemen and women overflowed the five-hundred-seat canteen, even standing on the tables for a better view. "When Hope and [Jerry] Colonna began exchanging staccato wisecracks there was so much enthusiastic foot-stomping that one table promptly collapsed," reported Pullen in the *Plain Dealer*. Bob Alexander's Orchestra backed vocalists Vera Vogue and Frances Langford. Uniformed guests rushed the stage when Langford asked for a dancing partner and quickly unburdened the lunch counters of food, some of which had been prepared by Hope's wife, Dolores. Hope was ready with a racially disparaging ad lib following the explosion of a photographer's bulb: "Those Japs!" As the *Cleveland Press* summarized the evening, "it probably was one of the few times on record that the honorary chairman of anything took an active part."[38]

Hope was only one of a galaxy of stars who appeared on the second floor of the Loew's Ohio Building. Prominent among them were Louis Armstrong, Count Basie, Perry Como, Tommy Dorsey, Lena Horne, Stan Kenton, Guy Lombardo, Martha Raye, and Frank Sinatra. Once a week, performers from shows playing the Palace Theatre would step next door to go through their acts on their normal off days. Performers from the Alpine Village, Herman Pirchner's Playhouse Square nightclub, also made regular appearances. Actors from the Hanna Theatre showed up from time to time, among them Katharine Cornell and Raymond Massey during their week's run of *Lovers and Friends*.[39]

Local talent was also recruited to supplement visits from more renowned performers. Ann Carroll, just out of John Hay High School, was singing on a local radio show over WHK, Nicki Burnett's station. She recalled, "People on the show kept saying, 'Why don't you go to the Stage Door Canteen?'" and so she did. There she joined a variety of volunteer performers including magicians, dancers, and other solo singers. Her repertoire consisted mainly of standard ballads such as "It Had to Be You" and "You'll Never Know"—in her words, "songs pertaining to when the boys were coming back."[40]

There were other USO facilities in town, too. Lounges for service personnel in transit could be found in the Terminal Tower, the bus terminal on East Ninth Street, the airport, Prospect Avenue, and St. John's Cathedral. One contained clean beds for a night's rest, another facilities for laundering uniforms, and most offered snacks and refreshments. Food, coffee, and soft drinks were always free.[41]

Ann Carroll sometimes performed at the St. John's Cathedral lounge, but emphasized, "The one above the State had all the famous people such as Artie Shaw, Dolores and Bob Hope. They never made a big fanfare for the stars that appeared. It's amazing how humble they were," she said. "I was just new in the business and learned a lot from them." She had especially fond memories of Dolores Hope, also a singer. "She was a lovely lady." The stage was just a corner of the dance floor: "I remember the audience just standing around the performers. The servicemen always wanted to talk to show people. There was a rule that you never left with any of them."[42]

From 6:00 P.M. to midnight, the Cleveland canteen held daily open house, staffed entirely by volunteers who did the cooking, serving, and housekeeping chores. These included businessmen, lawyers, and other professionals who rolled up their sleeves to bus tables and wash dishes. Most visible were the junior hostesses in their distinctive aprons, greeting the visitors, keeping them company, and serving as dance partners. A *Press* reporter who became a hostess for an evening revealed, "Giving last names, phone numbers or addresses is taboo." Leaving the canteen in the company of a serviceman may have been verboten, but love evidently found ways. "The number of romances developed on the canteen dance floor is unrecorded," noted a *Plain Dealer* reporter at the end of the canteen's run, "but the consensus is 'plenty.'"[43]

While older, senior hostesses generally worked in the kitchen or served as chaperones, the face of the canteen was predominantly one of spirited, youthful femininity. Dancing with a guest from the RAF one evening, a junior hostess heard kibitzers on the sidelines calling "Snow's falling," and "You're slipping." Finally getting the message, she glanced down to discover her petticoat cascading toward her ankles. Not all experiences were that light, however. "The canteen has had more than one case of shellshock," wrote one junior hostess in the *Plain Dealer:* "more than one hostess struck wordless for a moment when a plastic leg or arm was revealed— more than one shock to the homefronters working in the canteen who had never come face to face with so much reality of the war."[44]

Some of the canteen's clients were brought in from the Crile Hospital, which the Army had newly opened in Parma. Hostesses operated the elevator to take them to the second floor. Some of them went beyond the call of duty to take nursing courses on dealing with cases of what was then called battle fatigue and now posttraumatic stress disorder. As the *Plain Dealer*'s guest writer put it, "suddenly the canteen has found that it plays host to more and more boys with somber steps and faces painted with memories—boys with Guadalcanal in their eyes and the south Pacific in their hearts." In such cases she saw the canteen as "a place of rebuilding—not bones or limbs—but a place for rebuilding the heart."[45]

For nearly three years, men and women of America's armed services found a home away from home in Playhouse Square's Stage Door Canteen. An estimated 200,000 had come by the end of 1943, when the Cleveland canteen prepared to celebrate its first birthday. Another 850 showed up for the festivities, which featured four hours of continuous entertainment. Louis Gina's continental trio, which had performed at the canteen's opening, led off the anniversary show. Local radio personality Gene Carroll turned up with his popular "Jake and Lena" radio act from WTAM. Brock Pemberton of the American Theatre Wing came to help award sil-

Other than food, dancing with the red, white, and blue aproned junior hostesses was probably the greatest attraction at the Playhouse Square Stage Door Canteen. Murals from a previous nightclub in the Canteen's quarters are faintly visible in the background. (Photo by Clayton Knipper, Courtesy of *Cleveland Press* Collection, Michael Schwartz Library, Cleveland State University)

ver and gold pins to one-year volunteers. Bob Hope couldn't come but wired greetings and promised to return the next time he was back "in your territory."[46]

While area merchants, performers, and service organizations donated most of the entertainment and refreshments at Cleveland's canteen, some expenses called for fund-raising. On the national level, Hollywood released the feature film *Stage Door Canteen*, profits from which were earmarked for Stage Door Canteens across the nation. It played the State, just below the Cleveland canteen, in June 1943. Many faces familiar to the Hanna Theatre—such as Tallulah Bankhead, Katharine Hepburn, Alfred Lunt and Lynn Fontanne, Ethel Waters, and Ed Wynn—made cameo appearances. Locally, the Cleveland Barons had a benefit hockey game and fifteen hundred guests attended a Labor Day fund-raising excursion aboard the *City of Detroit II.* An after-cruise open house took place back at the canteen. Bob Hope returned as promised and, following another show at the canteen, performed in a midnight benefit at the Palace which raised $12,000 for the cause. Helen Burnett also borrowed the idea of an "Angel Table" from New York's canteen, which allowed non-service outsiders to come and share in the canteen festivities for a contribution of $25.[47]

Midway through the Cleveland canteen's second year, the Burnetts relinquished its directorship. Nicki Burnett had taken a producing job at CBS, and Helen, pleading poor health, followed her husband to New York. The American Theatre Wing promoted the canteen's office manager, Lucille Boaeuf, to executive secretary of the Cleveland branch. To assist her in day-to-day operation, they enlisted a group of codirectors to share operational responsibilities on a revolving monthly basis. Ten codirectors were appointed, including Norman Siegel and Franklin Lewis of the *Press*.[48]

So Cleveland's Stage Door Canteen carried on for the duration of World War II. After two years, nine months, and an estimated one hundred tons of food, the canteen hosted its final open house on October 26, 1945. Fourteen hundred guests enjoyed entertainment from the Palace and the Alpine Village and a smorgasbord from Stowe's Corner before the doors closed at midnight. "To hundreds of volunteers who faithfully came downtown after a hard day at the office to wash dishes, prepare and serve food, or jitterbug with the boys, Cleveland owes a vote of thanks for giving the town a nationwide reputation for hospitality and friendliness," wrote Marjorie Johnson in the *Plain Dealer*. "The measure of their success," editorialized the *Press*, "lies in the appreciation and thanks of more than 750,000 servicemen and women, some stationed here, others only passing through, who found at Cleveland's Stage Door Canteen free food, entertainment, service and a generous welcome."[49]

Beautiful Mornin'

Early in 1942, Milton Krantz was approached by "this little girl," on behalf of her cast appearing that week at the Hanna Theatre. She wanted to draw a logo of their presentation on the beige duck backing of the theater's curtain and have it signed by the entire company. "Would you mind?" she asked with the innocence of an ingénue. Most property managers would have dismissed such a proposal out of hand, but this was show business, and Krantz was a born showman: "I said sure, I thought it was a good idea."[50] So was born the Hanna curtain tradition. Krantz gave at least one variant account of its origin, in which he had come across an actor penning his unauthorized autograph on the curtain and given it his approval ex post facto. Either version may contain an element of truth, but both dated it from 1942. As the curtain accumulated signatures, it helped set the Hanna apart from Pittsburgh's Nixon, Columbus's Hartman, and other road houses. "Word got around, and every show said, 'You've got to see the Hanna curtain,'" recalled Krantz.[51]

One of the lingering signs of the Depression had been three-night stands at the Hanna, in which a show would open the week at the Hartman Theater in Columbus and then come up to the Hanna for the weekend. Krantz convinced Carl Hanna and Tim Grogan to notify the New York booking office "Cleveland is no longer a split-week city," and three-day runs soon became history at the Hanna. With fifteen hundred seats, Krantz found himself in charge of a larger house than most Broadway theaters. "I was ready to leave Cleveland at the end of the year, when Carl Hanna offered me a permanent job," he remembered. "It was a long-term contract with a percentage of the profits. I was released by Marcus Heiman."[52] Milton Krantz had found his place in the theater.

Working in Krantz's favor was a revival of the Broadway road. He was only a few weeks into the job when *Life with Father* paid its first visit to the Hanna. Already completing its second year in New York, the comedy by Howard Lindsay and Russel Crouse was on its way to setting a record for straight plays of 3,224 performances. It gave the Hanna its first two-week run in five years and returned on the first anniversary of Pearl Harbor for another two-week run. "Father is back. And that is something we are very happy to report," wrote Omar Ranney in the *Press*. "He's a character, that man. A blustering, ranting old fellow. But through it all—or, rather, over it all—he's a man of good humor." Percy Waram played Father, and Margalo Gilmore was "charmingly convincing as the sheltered spouse of those days when wives weren't supposed to think, but still, in some mysterious manner, were able to get around their husbands."[53] The play would return for three additional one-week stands.

Another cash cow was still going strong after eight visits to the Hanna. In nine years on Broadway, *Tobacco Road* would rack up a record run later to be eclipsed by *Life with Father*. Critics had universally panned *Tobacco Road*, but playgoers continued to wallow in its trough of assumed southern depravity. As it arrived at the Hanna for the ninth time early in 1944, Pullen neatly capsulized it in the *Plain Dealer:* "Once more you have the white-haired [John] Barton [as Jeeter Lester], a master of timing and shrewdly droll bits of business shouting ribald quips at his brood of dirty-faced Georgia crackers with his usual gusty manner. He is still a pow'ful sinner, selling his 12-year-old daughter for $7, cheating his son-in-law out of turnips and hatching ways to avoid unpleasant work." Interspersed among the usual Hanna first-nighters were war workers in leather jackets, some of whom had dumbfounded manager Krantz with inquiries on when the third evening performance would begin and whether there would be any newsreels between features.[54] *Tobacco Road* became the *Blossom Time* of its day, giving the Hanna eleven one-week stands.

Lesser successes included Joseph Kesselring's black comedy, *Arsenic and Old Lace*. In its second call at the Hanna, Ranney found Boris Karloff "properly menacing" as Jonathan Brewster. When Mae West brought *Catherine Was Great* to the Hanna, however, Ranney saw it as an "overstuffed turkey." The "buxom Mae" not only wrote it but appeared in the title role: the Empress Catherine of Russia. In Ranney's eyes, her portrayal was merely West's "old character, Diamond Lil, in royal robes and a crown. . . . As a piece of theater, it is cheap, vulgar and trashy—a play that is poorly written, slow and, except for Miss West's occasional spicy lines, very dull." Not everyone in the audience saw it that way. One World War II veteran who had been stationed at the Crile Hospital remembered how Krantz would send a bus to bring patients and staff downtown for dinner, a show at the Hanna, and after-theater beer and sandwiches at Otto Moser's on East Fourth Street. "One of the shows that made an impression on me was Mae West in 'Catherine Was Great,'" he reminisced. "This exposure made me a regular theatergoer ever since."[55]

Not everything at the Hanna was played for laughs. Though not as action-oriented as the war movies on the screens of Euclid Avenue, more didactic versions of the anti-Axis struggle appeared on the East Fourteenth stage. One of the best was Lillian Hellman's *Watch on the Rhine,* in which the argument against fascism played out under the roof of a comfortable American home. It was more than "the best of the anti-Nazi plays," wrote William McDermott in the *Plain Dealer.* "It is simply a fine and moving play which stands for human decency and human integrity." Less successful were two plays by Maxwell Anderson that at least partially depicted scenes of soldiers in harm's way. *The Eve of St. Mark* alternated scenes of an American soldier in camp and then the Philippines, and his family and girl back home. *Storm Operation* was set entirely in North Africa with the American invasion force.[56]

The most sensational war-themed play to hit the Hanna boards was *Tomorrow the World,* which came in October 1943. It dealt with an American professor's adoption of a German nephew whose father had been killed by the Nazis—but not before they had indoctrinated the child in the dogmas of the master race. The orphan proceeds to spew Nazi propaganda, play one member of the family against another, and nearly break his uncle's engagement to a Jewish woman before finally realizing the values of freedom and democracy. "When the thought strikes you that there are somewhere around 12,000,000 of these youths in Germany, trained to believe in the same things he does—notably force, blind obedience and ruthlessness—you get quite a jolt," commented Ranney. "This lad is a terror."[57]

All was not comedy or war at the Hanna, however, and its audiences might also view some of the leading luminaries of the stage in acknowledged classics by such masters of the drama as Chekhov. "There is nothing in the story. There is everything in the atmosphere," said McDermott of *The Cherry Orchard.* Eva Le Gallienne's performance was "beautifully done in the spirit of Chekhov's play," and her costar Joseph Schildkraut "similarly subordinates himself for the sake of the play in the role of the dreaming, futile brother." Katharine Cornell returned to one of her preferred road houses and brought a dream cast for Chekhov's *The Three Sisters.* Ruth Gordon and Judith Anderson joined her, supported by Dennis King, Edmund Gwenn, and Alexander Knox. "The rhythm is perfect," wrote McDermott. "A performance of this sort has the quality of symphonic music." Later he reported that a week of all but full houses had produced a box office take of $28,000—with only one exception "the best week at the Hanna in a year, or longer."[58]

Margaret Webster's production of Shakespeare's *Othello* gave the Hanna an opening-night sellout audience. "Miss Webster cannot be commended too highly for her insistence that a Negro be cast in the role of Othello," wrote Peter Bellamy in the *News*. "It is well-nigh incredible that [Paul] Robeson is the first Negro Othello that the United States has ever seen, for put a white man in the role and the play loses most of its point."[59] Othello's nemesis, Iago, was enacted by Jose Ferrer, whose real-life wife, Uta Hagen, portrayed Othello's wife, Desdemona.

As America ended its second year at war, the Hanna Theatre reflected the nation's rebound from the Depression. During the last three seasons before the war, its marquee had been lit for only an average of seventeen weeks of live theater annually. Some of those were three-night stands; by far the longest run in that period was recorded by a movie—Walt Disney's *Fantasia*, which stayed for nine weeks. During Krantz's first two years, the live theater seasons expanded to an average of twenty-four weeks. There were no three-day runs in his second year, which also enjoyed a six-week summer season in addition to twenty-three weeks of road shows.

Recovery took a quantum leap for the Hanna in the fall of 1943. Krantz dated it from the October morning when he entered the theater to be greeted by ten sacks of mail in the theater's small lobby. He had run an ad in the Sunday *Plain Dealer* for the road company of a new Broadway musical hit that opened the previous spring. He and his wife, Helen, had been there for the legendary premiere of *Oklahoma!* as guests of Lawrence Langer, an official of the show's producer, New York's Theatre Guild. On opening night, the show's prospects had seemed so dicey that Celeste Holm led other cast members to New York's Stage Door Canteen up the street from the St. James Theatre, to paper the house with guests from the armed services.[60]

Now, six months later, *Oklahoma!* became the Hanna's first show to be entirely sold out by mail. That presented Krantz with some sticky problems, but undoubtedly not ones he wasn't happy to solve. For one thing, he had several hundred thousand dollars' worth of orders for only $32,500 worth of seats. It cost him $2,000 for extra help and postage to return the checks for orders he couldn't fill. And then, to assure those unsatisfied customers that he hadn't played favorites, he called in reporters from all three

Cleveland dailies to bear witness to the impartiality with which orders were filled. Critics from all three papers gave the show a thumbs up. "The fact is, 'Oklahoma!' makes you feel good," wrote Ranney in the *Press*. A lot of other shows had given their audiences a lift, he admitted,

> But with this Rodgers-Hammerstein musical the lift is simply bigger, and better, and at a time when the human heart, weighed down with war, is more receptive to bits of theatrical magic that can cast a light, buoyant spell.
>
> People who go see "Oklahoma!" not only come out of the theater humming—"Oh, what a beautiful mornin',
>
> "Oh, what a beautiful day,
>
> "I got a wonderful feelin',
>
> "Everything's going my way."
>
> But they are still humming it the next morning, and the morning after that.[61]

Ranney was perceptive in attributing the show's appeal to its uplifting effect on a war-weary country. What most critics were slower to perceive was *Oklahoma!*'s game-changing effect on American musical comedy. Music would become increasingly tied to the stories, and stories would become more serious. Wartime audiences at the Hanna could have seen other attempts to break the conventional musical mold. A year prior to *Oklahoma!* Moss Hart and Kurt Weill's *Lady in the Dark* had psychoanalysis as its storyline and a score of three extended musical sequences portraying the heroine's dreams. Its heroine was portrayed by Gertrude Lawrence, who won more plaudits from local critics than the show's innovations did. Weill teamed up with poet Ogden Nash for *One Touch of Venus*, which, like *Oklahoma!* featured a dream ballet choreographed by Agnes de Mille. Venus happened to be played by Mary Martin, however, who once again stole the show. *Oklahoma!* lyricist Oscar Hammerstein II wrote new lyrics to Bizet's opera *Carmen* and set it in the American South as *Carmen Jones*. The "biggest, best and last show of the Hanna season," in Ranney's words, came with an all-Black cast in May 1945.[62]

While all these shows displayed innovations, none was to be as influential as *Oklahoma!* It was scheduled to return to the Hanna for two weeks at the end of 1945.

All Clear

Unless they had gold stars in their window or loved ones still in harm's way, Clevelanders may well have been inclined to celebrate New Year 1945. With the climactic Battle of the Bulge in December, Nazi Germany had clearly spent its last hope for victory. On December 31 in Playhouse Square there were ads for "New Year's Eve Midnight Shows at all Loew's Theatres Tonight!!" At the Palace, "Cleveland's Own Bob Hope" was appearing on screen in *The Princess and the Pirate*, while *Earl Carroll's Vanities of 1945*, "with the most beautiful girls in the world," cavorted on stage. Across Euclid Avenue, the Lake interrupted a four-week run of *Laura* for a one-night-only showing of *Hollywood Canteen*.[63]

Yet there was still a war on, as State Theatre revelers were reminded by the feature *Thirty Seconds over Tokyo*. As if to drive that point home, a coal shortage occasioned the citywide closure of all theaters and nightclubs and most retail stores and restaurants on the first Monday in February. "Due to the Critical Fuel Shortage All LOEW'S THEATRES Will Be Closed Today," read the State's ad for *Meet Me at St. Louis*. "Re-opening Tomorrow with Our Regular Attractions." Apparently there had been talk of making all Mondays dark days, but the following Monday the RKO Palace ad assured moviegoers, "All RKO Theatres Open Today."[64] Instead, the lights of Playhouse Square were merely dimmed by a nightly brownout.

There would be one additional theater closure that spring, occasioned by the death of President Franklin Delano Roosevelt. On Saturday, April 15, the day of the funeral services, the city's movie theaters remained closed until 6:00 P.M. On Playhouse Square, that included Loew's State and Ohio and RKO's Palace and Allen. The Hanna cancelled its matinee performance of Cornelia Otis Skinner in *The Searching Wind*, and the Warner Brothers' Lake remained closed all day. Most retail stores and restaurants, including Halle's department store and Stouffers Playhouse Square, closed at 2:00 P.M.[65]

Despite dimmed marquees and mourning observances, the overall mood on Playhouse Square that spring was buoyant. One benefit of the war was the occupancy of the former Higbee Building at Thirteenth and Euclid, vacant since the department store's move to Public Square in the late 1920s. In late 1942, the War Assets Administration leased the property for the Navy Bureau of Supplies and Accounts. As part of a government decentralization program, eight hundred Navy employees moved in from Washington, and

North Side of Euclid Ave., from East 13th St., Cleveland, Ohio.

Years after Higbee's left its Playhouse Square building at Euclid and East Thirteenth Street, the US Navy moved in with its Bureau of Supplies and Accounts during World War II. The slightly taller façade next to the former department store belonged to Sterling & Welch, home of the annual five-story Christmas tree. (Author's collection)

four hundred Cleveland women were wanted as clerical workers. They would be occupied in making payments to dependents of naval enlisted men and officers and would provide potential patronage to neighborhood shops and theaters.[66]

News from the battlefronts gave increasing cause for optimism. Less than a month after FDR's death, word came of Germany's surrender. V-E (Victory in Europe) Day saw the lifting of the brownout, as the marquees of Playhouse Square glowed at full strength after a hundred days of twilight. "The city began to look like a city again," observed Alvin Silverman in the *Plain Dealer*.[67]

That was just a warmup for the headline on August 15, 1945: "WAR IS OVER, TRUMAN ANNOUNCES," reverberated the banner across the front page of the *Plain Dealer*. "A city which had taken V-E Day in almost complete silence blew its top," wrote the paper's Roelif Loveland. Confetti and shredded paper poured out of windows of Public Square and up Euclid Avenue. People streamed out of offices and shops and from neighborhoods to pack Euclid from sidewalk to sidewalk, unfazed by a mid-evening shower. Soldiers and sailors kissed their girlfriends to the cheers of thousands of onlookers. "By 8:10 the crowd in the vicinity of Playhouse Square was dense, and theater managers were faced with the astounding fact that the streets of downtown Cleveland offered a better show than they had indoors," reported Loveland.[68]

Timeline of 1941–1945

December 7, 1941
Movie matinee-goers on Playhouse Square learn of Japan's attack on Pearl Harbor

December 9, 1941
Herman Pirchner cancels *The Mikado* at the Alpine Village

August 28, 1942
Bing Crosby croons "White Christmas" in film *Holiday Inn* at the State Theatre

September 24, 1942
Playhouse Square goes dark in trial countywide blackout

January 14, 1943
Cleveland's Stage Door Canteen opens in Loew's Building on Playhouse Square

January 25, 1943
Women at War exhibit in State Theatre lobby demonstrates employment opportunities for women in defense industries

June 13, 1943
Honorary chairman Bob Hope appears at the Playhouse Square Stage Door Canteen

September 23, 1943
Ohio Theatre reopens as movie house with *For Whom the Bell Tolls*

November 8, 1943
Oklahoma! opens at Hanna Theatre

April 15, 1945
Playhouse Square theaters remain closed until 6:00 P.M. on day of President Roosevelt's funeral

October 26, 1945
Stage Door Canteen closes its doors on Playhouse Square

Postwar Peak to Pits

Back to Business

Although peace had broken out in between, there was little visible change in Playhouse Square from New Year 1945 to New Year 1946. Street vendors along Euclid Avenue were especially thick on Playhouse Square, selling paper hats and assorted horns, rattlers, whistlers, balloons, and "what have you." Business wasn't that great, they complained, due to the competition from other hawkers and the special midnight shows in the theaters.[1] "Make Up a Party— Come early . . . stay late!" ballyhooed the Palace for its late showing of Errol Flynn in *San Antonio*. Next door, the State advertised a "Gala New Year's Eve Show" for the war film *They Were Expendable* with Robert Montgomery and John Wayne. Across the street, the Lake offered a late New Year's Eve screening of the World War II–themed comedy *SNAFU* (they didn't spell out the acronym).[2]

Around the corner on East Fourteenth Street, on Christmas Eve, the Hanna had begun a two-week run of *Oklahoma!*—the musical sensation making its second visit to Cleveland. After the show, playgoers might drop in for a late supper at the Continental in the Hanna Building, which also offered "The Celebrated Irish Tenor Peter Higgins." Jerry Ganson's Hanna Grill enticed New Year's celebrants with Ruby and His Orchestra, including singer Ginger Jones.[3]

Cleveland had good reason to celebrate the coming of 1946. It could look back with pride to its contribution, as the nation's fifth largest industrial center, to America's victory in World War II. America's defense efforts had not only won the war but ended the Depression. Now, with wartime rationing out and peacetime production in, it was time for pent-up wartime buying power to explode.[4]

During the 1940s, the Cleveland Electric Illuminating Company (CEI, today Centerior Energy) began promoting Cleveland as "The Best Location in the Nation." It published newspaper and magazine ads showing the city in the middle of a map of the northeastern United States and southern Canada. Within a five-hundred-mile radius (or a day's drive) of the mouth of the Cuyahoga River were most of the major population centers of North America, from St. Louis to New York City.[5] Even then, however, CEI's product was beginning to power air-conditioning in the South and West. Cleveland's population was holding steady, from 900,429 in 1930 to a peak of 914,808 in 1950, but its relative national rank was slipping, from fifth to seventh.[6] The Sun Belt was starting to play catch-up.

That was scarcely evident in the afterglow of World War II, however, and no part of Cleveland glowed brighter with CEI power than Playhouse Square. Six theater marquees dominated its streets by night, dozens of upscale shops by day. Gone from the corner of Huron Avenue and East Fourteenth Street was the Hotel Euclid, razed in 1937 to accommodate the widening of East Fourteenth. Since the turn of the century, it had provided lodgings for touring entertainments such as Texas Guinan, a Kokoon Arts Club ball, and one of Cleveland s first cabarets.[7] Though somewhat shabby of late, its passing left Playhouse Square proper without a suitable hostelry, though there were accommodations nearby in the Hotel Statler at East Twelfth and Euclid, the Hotel Winton on Prospect Avenue and Huron Road, and the Allerton Hotel at East Thirteenth Street and Chester Avenue.

While Playhouse Square may have lost a hotel, it soon regained a major department store. In 1950 the Lindner women's apparel shop and W. B. Davis men's furnishings merged with the Sterling & Welch Company. Lindner & Davis moved into the old Higbee building on Thirteenth and Euclid, next door to Sterling & Welch. Walls between the two buildings were opened up for what became the Sterling-Lindner-Davis department store. Besides home furnishings, the contribution of Sterling & Welch to the combination was the five-story Sterling Christmas tree in its atrium, a downtown holiday tradition since 1927.[8] The Navy Bureau of Supplies and Accounts, which had reopened the Higbee building during the war, was displaced but remained in downtown Cleveland.

On the south side of Euclid Avenue, Halle Brothers department store remained the linchpin of Playhouse Square retail. Like the rest of the country, Halle's greeted peace in an expansive mood. Feeling a need for more sales space, it demolished the old Elks Club on Huron Road and broke ground for an eleven-story West Wing to its main Euclid Avenue store. It was faced with identical white terracotta and connected to it above East Twelfth Street by a ten-story bridge. Playhouse Square denizens thereafter often referred to East Twelfth from Euclid to Huron as "Halle's Alley." Another addition went up on Prospect Avenue adjoining the 1926 Huron-Prospect Building, most of it to house service workers. The additions gave Halle's a total floor space of nine hundred thousand square feet, nearly equal to its Public Square rival, Higbee's.[9]

During the first full year of peace, Halle's sales were 29 percent higher than in 1945. Long after the disappearance of carriages, the store supplemented its "carriage trade" goods with growing lines of mid-priced wares for the growing ranks of the war-enriched middle class. In another nod to changing demographics, Halle's began opening suburban branches, beginning in 1949 with a mid-century modern building at Shaker Square.[10]

Midsized and smaller shops lined the sidewalks of Euclid, Huron, and East Fourteenth Streets. Women's apparel dominated the show windows in such establishments as Wm. Kitt, Peck & Peck, and Milgrim's. When Lindner's merged into the Sterling-Lindner-Davis operation in 1951, Bonwit-Teller moved in behind the white rococo facade of the recently vacated Lindner building. Luxury goods were readily available at Cowell & Hubbard jewelers, the Travellers Shoppes, Chandler & Rudd gourmet grocers, and Marcel Pick imported wines. For the intellectual, Burrows stocked books along with its stationery, while browsers at Korner & Wood might rub elbows with visiting authors such as Sinclair Lewis. More corporeal appetites had a range of restaurants from which to choose, including Clark's, Stouffer's, and the Continental. Lined up on the south side of Euclid, from the Lake Theater to the Hanna Building, were Boukair's SeeSweets, Herman Pirchner's Alpine Village, and Pierre's. Operated by Clevelander Hector Boiardi (Chef Boy-Ar-Dee), Pierre's was a favorite gathering spot for actors at the Hanna Theatre, whose stage door was convenient to the restaurant's rear

Traffic on Euclid Avenue in the 1950s passes the Playhouse Square movie marquees on the right. Behind the Georgian façade covering the closed Lake Theatre at far left were the studios of a new competitor—WJW-TV. (Author's collection)

entrance. The Alpine Village became a destination for out-of-town visitors, none higher than General Dwight D. Eisenhower, who came to Cleveland to lead a World War II victory parade.[11]

On Dodge Court, half a block north of Playhouse Square, members of the Hermit Club began their second half century of music and amateur theatrics in 1954. Jake Hines led them in singing "The Hermit Hymn":

> I pledge thee in this glass I hold
> For what ye are and were of old
> I've shared the best of all life's span—
> True fellowship of man to man.

If any had shed tears at the razing of their original quarters on East Third Place six years earlier, they would soon be cheered by the burning of the mortgage on their present home, modeled after the first.[12] Looking eastward down Dodge Court, the cowled Hermits might have espied a novel newcomer across East Thirteenth Street. There, in a nondescript two-story building on December 17, 1947, Cleveland's (and Ohio's) first television station had begun broadcasting its flickering black-and-white pictures to the area's few receiving sets. It was owned by the publishers of the *Cleveland Press*, the E. W. Scripps Company, and identified by the call letters

WEWS.[13] Whether the large movie palaces around the corner were aware of it, an adversary had arrived.

Silver Screenings

"Grandeur of the Palace lobby and the many reception rooms remains undimmed," noted Jack Warfel in the *Cleveland Press*. "A quarter-century ago today American vaudeville achieved its greatest glory at E. 17th St. and Euclid Ave." It was November 6, 1947, and the Palace Theatre was celebrating its silver anniversary. While the backstage appointments for vaudeville performers were frequently dark, all but one of the original oils in the front of the house were still in place. Only two of the theater's original crew were still in place after twenty-five years: stagehand Harry "Red" Goldman and Peter Zicarelli, who had worked his way up from electrician to maintenance superintendent. Former usher Lew Wasserman was in Hollywood as head of the Music Corporation of America.[14]

Many members of that November 6, 1922. opening-night audience would still have been on hand. Palace manager Max Mink said that if they had saved their ticket stubs, they might produce them for free admission to the theater's official birthday celebration the following week. The delay was due to Mink's desire to evoke the theater's vaudeville roots with a live show starring former vaudevillian Danny Kaye. Singer Gloria Gibbs, dancers Tip, Tap and Toe, and the Bunin Puppets backed the headliner. "Kaye pulled out all the stops and gave everything he had to the crowd," wrote *Plain Dealer* movie critic Ward Marsh. "It was unquestionably the most amusing and certainly the most intimate show the Palace has offered in the 25 years of its existence." Rounding out the program was *The Crime Doctor's Gamble*, a movie March dismissed as "just about an average 'Crime Doctor' story with plenty of herrings across the trail of three deaths before the crime is solved."[15]

That pretty much was the story at the Palace in the first postwar decade: dismissible movies relieved by what remained of vaudeville; for what was once B. F. Keith's Palace was now the RKO Palace. Regular vaudeville programs at the Palace were discontinued a few months after the war, though occasionally agents booked shows for a week at a time, according to former Stage Door Canteen performer Ann Carroll. For the most part, these were variety shows with no star performers.[16] Major attractions such as Cab Calloway at times emblazoned the theater's marquee. Probably the highlight of the postwar Palace stage was the legendary Josephine Baker's show in 1951. The dancer and chanteuse first won notice in the chorus of Sissle and Blake's *Shuffle Along* and *The Chocolate Dandies* in the early 1920s. She stepped out of the chorus and became a star in Paris, exposing most of her svelte form in the *Revue Negre* at the Folies Bergère.

La Baker (or La "Bahkair," as she was known in Paris) arrived at the postwar Palace with sixteen trunks and forty-four pieces of luggage packed with her Parisian costumes and wardrobe and "enough diamonds to set up a jewelry store." For her week's run plus a day held over, the Palace would pay her $22,000, worth every dollar in view of a box office rivaling the record Jack Benny had set three years earlier. The *Plain Dealer* billed her as "The Provocative, Exotic Rage of Paris," and the paper's Glenn C. Pullen judged her fully worthy of the often overworked adjective *fabulous:*

> Her underpinnings are still shapely and vigorous but not unveiled so frankly. Generally they are artfully hidden by eye-stunning gowns from the Dior, Rochas, and Balenciaga ateliers. . . .
>
> Many better voices can be found in vaudeville but not all of them possess this star's vocal vibrancy or her quite special theatrical talent.
>
> Singing in five languages, she sounds particularly appealing in her American blues medley. There is calculated art and high exuberance of spirits in all her work, from her strutting, hip-shaking steps to her more politely delivered "Merci Beaucoup."

Exotic it was, but the show couldn't have been too provocative. Part of Baker's act was inviting children in the audience to join her on the stage in a dance, for which they were rewarded with candy bars.[17]

For the few who may have come for the movie, Baker shared the bill with a radio-derived detective flick, *Fat Man*. With the RKO studios in freefall, the Palace got few smash hits from Hollywood. One notable exception was 1954's Universal-International's *Magnificent Obsession,* with Jane Wyman and Rock Hudson. Produced by native Clevelander Ross Hunter, it had its world premiere at the Palace.[18]

Good and bad alike, movies were doing well in the first years after the war. According to movie historian Douglas Gomery, in the spring of 1946, box office revenues peaked "at the highest per capita levels in history."[19] Metro-Goldwyn-Mayer (MGM) was the bellwether of Hollywood's movie industry; it was the nation's "Biggest Movie-Making Machine," according to a wartime article in *Life*

magazine: "Its prestige and its profits are higher than any other studio's. Its collection of stars has a more genuine shine than any other studio's." Illustrating the point in typical *Life* fashion was a two-page spread showing studio head Louis B. Mayer surrounded by sixty-four MGM stars, from boyish Mickey Rooney to venerable Lionel Barrymore. In between were such familiar faces as Katharine Hepburn, James Stewart, Esther Williams, Red Skelton, Lucille Ball, and William Powell.[20]

If MGM dominated Hollywood, the State Theatre, with its Loew's connection, dominated Playhouse Square. As the first theater to have opened on the block, the State celebrated its twenty-fifth anniversary on February 2, 1946, which also marked the silver anniversary of Playhouse Square. It happened to come during a three-week Cleveland newspaper strike, however, so any special festivities marking the occasion went unrecorded. The State contented itself with Cleveland premieres of major movies every week, as fast as MGM and other major studios produced them. To keep new films coming to the State's huge auditorium, Loew's generally consigned special attractions likely to enjoy longer runs to the

Record movie attendance during World War II carried over into the early postwar years—at least until television made inroads into the audience. Ticket buyers are lined up in front of the Palace Theatre, which still occasionally paired its movies with vaudeville programs. (Courtesy of Cleveland Public Library Photograph Collection) smaller Ohio and Stillman theaters. In January 1957, for example, while the blockbuster hit *The Ten Commandments* was starting its third month at the Ohio, and with *Teahouse of the August Moon* in its fifth week at the Stillman, the State gave one-week Cleveland first runs to Clark Gable in *The King and Four Queens* and Bob Hope with Katharine Hepburn in *The Iron Petticoat*.[21]

At times, the displays in the State's immense lobby overshadowed its screen. To complement a film billed as a "big look at the new-look peacetime Army," the State invited the Army to set up an eighteen-foot Nike missile in its 180-foot main lobby. Part of the nation's air defense system during the Cold War, the missiles were in the process of deployment at seven sites scattered across Cuyahoga County. It left more than enough room in the lobby for a 105 mm recoilless cannon. As for the movie, despite the efforts of Tab Hunter and Natalie Wood, Ward Marsh couldn't rate *The Girl He Left Behind* as "much more than military old hat."[22]

Occasionally movies shared billing at the State with stage shows, as when "The nation's most talked-about singer . . . Johnnie Ray" headlined a program that also included the Four Lads. Hundreds of bobbysoxers in poodle skirts queued along the sidewalk of Playhouse Square for admission to the noon show. "My ears are still ringing. Not from Ray, but those teenagers," wrote Omar Ranney in the *Press*. "They practically drowned him out with screams, and that's some screaming." Yet, Ranney noted some empty seats downstairs at the first show, even with the balcony closed. "Perry Como used to draw absolute capacity, both upstairs and down, on opening day when he played theater dates here."[23]

Alongside the State, the Ohio was in the third year of its resuscitation as a movie house. In its former life as a legitimate house it had hosted Robert Mantell, playing Hamlet in four separate stands of Shakespearean repertory. If Mantell's ghost still haunted the theater, it might have been mollified by the Ohio's 1948 showing of Laurence Olivier's film of *Hamlet*. William McDermott, the *Plain Dealer*'s drama critic, couldn't resist penning a crossover column on the screen version and found it "magnificent. In some ways it is better than any stage 'Hamlet' I have ever seen, and I have sat through several dozens of them. . . . This film version of the play is the clearest, the simplest, the most moving for large audiences that I can recall." McDermott's main quibble was over Olivier's extensive textual cuts.[24]

Shown on a reserved-seat basis ($1.20–$2.40 evenings; $.90–$1.80 matinees), *Hamlet* gave the Ohio a ten-week run. A few years later, Cecil B. de Mille's epic *The Ten Commandments* was good for twenty-nine weeks at the Ohio. Marsh felt "sure I will not ever see a greater motion picture."[25] Loew's continued to steer reserved-seat long runs to the Ohio while opening more standard fare at the State. While Michael Todd's *Around the World in 80 Days* followed *The Ten Commandments* at the Ohio, the State opened the one-week wonder *Tarzan and the Lost Safari*. "A Tarzan film is of the old school," wrote the *Press*'s Stan Anderson, but "Todd's dramatization of the famed Jules Verne yarn will bring out of hiding many who have not attended movies for months." With the added bonus of forty-four stars in brief cameo appearances (Frank Sinatra, Marlene Dietrich, Noel Coward, Bea Lillie, and more), *Eighty Days* stayed at the Ohio for forty-two weeks.[26]

Major releases also brought postwar prosperity to the Allen Theatre, which acquired first-run features from Warner Brothers and Columbia. In 1951 *David and Bathsheba* took in a record one-week Allen box office of $32,000, a mark Marilyn Monroe in *How to Marry a Millionaire* eclipsed by $10,000 two years later. Other hits to play there in the 1950s included the World War II dramas *Mister Roberts*, *The Caine Mutiny*, and David Lean's *Bridge over the River Kwai*. The Allen hosted a rare personal appearance when television pianist Liberace came to publicize his film *Sincerely Yours*. Some of the Allen's prosperity was reinvested in the theater. In 1961, extensive renovations included redecoration of both lobby and auditorium, installation of a fifty-foot-wide movie screen, a new sound system, and improved heating and air-conditioning.[27]

Tale of Two Theaters

Across from Euclid Avenue's movie house row, the two smaller Playhouse Square theaters experienced divergent fortunes. It was to prove the best of times for the Hanna, but for the Lake, time ran out.

At the Hanna it soon became clear that *Oklahoma!* was no flash in the pan. Having welcomed in 1946 on its second visit there, the musical demonstrated its legs (its durability, that is, not the chorus line variety) with four more calls to East Fourteenth Street by 1952. First of the megamusicals (2,212 performances on Broadway), *Oklahoma!* set off a chain reaction of imitative or innovative musicals, sometimes both at the same time. *Bloomer Girl* arrived in 1947 with Celeste Holm (*Oklahoma!*'s Ado Annie) as bloomer-wearing proto-feminist Evelina Applegate. It also shared the same theme (early Americana) and choreographer (Agnes de Mille) with its predecessor. Also cast in the *Oklahoma!* mold, with more justice, was Rodgers and Hammerstein's *Carousel,* which followed *Bloomer Girl* a few months later. It featured not only the same composer and lyricist but the same producer (Theatre Guild), director (Rouben Mamoulian), and choreographer (de Mille again).[28]

But *Carousel* was much more than an *Oklahoma!* clone. "'Carousel' is entirely different outwardly but it has some of the same style and spirit," observed McDermott in the *Plain Dealer.*[29] The chief difference lay in its darker theme (the hero dies early in the second act) and its use of fantasy (he is allowed to return for a day to try to patch up the botch he had made of his previous existence). *Carousel* made only one visit to the Hanna, and four Rodgers and Hammerstein shows achieved longer Broadway runs. Frequently asked to name his personal favorite of all his musicals, however, Rodgers never equivocated. "My answer is *Carousel.*"[30]

Carousel's use of fantasy also inspired imitators. In *Brigadoon,* the Hanna would see a Scottish village that came to life only one day every hundred years. Omar Ranney described how an opening offstage chorus set the mood: "As the last strains of the voices trailed off in the highland hills, there was a feeling that if we followed them we would eventually go beyond earthly limits into fields of fantasy. And that is exactly what happened." Alan Jay Lerner and Frederick Loewe, the show's creators, would be heard from again at the Hanna. Two months later it hosted a musical about a leprechaun who follows an Irishman and his daughter to Kentucky in pursuit of a pot of gold the colleen's father had misappropriated. "This difficult material is handled with a nice touch for humorous fantasy," wrote McDermott, who gave *Finian's Rainbow* a slight edge over *Brigadoon.*[31] The score by Burton Lane and E. Y. Harburg contained a number of standards, headed by "How Are Things in Glocca Morra?"

One of the most innovative and least imitative of the new musicals had come early in the game, within three years of *Oklahoma!*'s first visit. This was *On the Town,* an impetuous tale of the activities of three sailors on a twenty-four-hour leave in wartime New York City. It featured two members of the original cast, Adolph Green (also a co-lyricist) and Nancy Walker, "an extremely funny comedienne" who stole the show, in McDermott's view. "As for the music, the show is not one that is long on hit tunes," commented Ranney on composer Leonard Bernstein's maiden score. "Nevertheless it has an outstandingly good score, a score that expresses the moods and the spirit of New York, which, after all, is the important thing in 'On the Town.'" Both critics were impressed with the balletic choreography of Jerome Robbins, also making his Broadway debut.[32]

The Hanna's patrons saw more than innovative musicals in the postwar era, and after 1947, they saw those shows in a renovated theater. The new look began over the East Fourteenth Street sidewalk outside the lobby, with a rectangular marquee topped by a colonial-style pediment. Changes in the auditorium were equally notable. "Why, you would hardly know the old place," one first-nighter was overheard exclaiming. The original straw-colored walls were now a dramatic jade green, and the old dark-green seats now a contrasting burgundy. Carpeting of a "striking floral design" replaced the former green-and-gold pattern. More drinking fountains, better ventilation, and improved acoustics attended to audience comfort. Performers enjoyed a new pulley system to lift their baggage to five floors of redecorated dressing rooms.[33] Ina Claire didn't need this new system, however, when she occupied the star dressing room on the ground floor, inaugurating the new digs in *The Fatal Weakness* on September 22, 1947. (Coincidentally, Claire's screen image had inaugurated the opening of the State Theatre twenty-six years earlier.)

Carl Hanna invested $150,000 in his theater's refurbishment. Tallulah Bankhead came the following spring in Noel Coward's *Private Lives*. Not long afterward, she recalled an old theater witticism about the two worst box office weeks in the year: Holy Week and Cleveland. "So we played Cleveland in Holy Week and defied the lightning," she wrote. "Well, Cleveland has been slandered. Bill Veeck's parish romped to our theater in droves."[34] The 1948–49 season saw the Hanna's new marquee lit for a total of twenty-six weeks. Besides *Brigadoon* and *Finian's Rainbow,* there were Rodgers and Hammerstein's *Allegro,* Irving Berlin's *Annie Get Your Gun,* and a revival of Jerome Kern's *Show Boat.* Straight plays included Terrence Rattigan's *The Winslow Boy,* Garson Kanin's *Born Yesterday,* and two of Tennessee Williams' best: *Summer and Smoke* and *A Streetcar Named Desire,* the latter with Uta Hagen and Anthony Quinn.

Ironically, one of the greatest highlights in the Hanna's history involved a show ultimately judged a failure. It was a musical titled *Me and Juliet,* whose world premiere the Hanna hosted on April 20, 1953. What made it so special was its creation by Rodgers and Hammerstein. That was also what made it a perceived failure, as it fell far short of the smash hits the pair generally enjoyed.

Among the Hanna Theatre's proudest moments was the world premiere of Rodgers and Hammerstein's *Me and Juliet* in 1953. Buried in its credits was the name of a dancer who before long would step out of the chorus to movie stardom: Shirley MacLaine. (Cleveland Public Library Literature Department)

PROGRAM — Continued

DANCING ENSEMBLE: Francine Bond, Betty Buday, Penny Ann Green, Lorraine Havercroft, Patty Ann Jackson, Helene Keller, Lucia Lambert, Harriet Leigh, Sonya Lindgren, Elizabeth Logue, Shirley MacLaine, Cheryl Parker, Dorothy Silverherz, Thelma Tadlock, Norma Thornton, Janyce Ann Wagner, Rosemary Williams.

Lance Avant, Grant Delaney, John George, Jack Konzal, Ralph Linn, Eddie Pfeiffer, Augustine Rodriguez, Bob St. Clair, Bill Weber.

SINGING ENSEMBLE: Adele Castle, Gwen Harmon, Susan Lovell, Theresa Mari, Georgia Reed, Deborah Remsen, Thelma Scott, Barbara Lee Smith.

John Ford, Jack Drummond, Richard Hermany, Henry Hamilton, Michael King, Larry Laurence, Jack Rains, Warren Kemmerling.

Most Rodgers and Hammerstein shows tried out on the East Coast (usually New Haven), within an easy commute for show doctors from New York. But *Me and Juliet* was a backstage story with complicated scenery designed to allow audiences to see what was happening onstage and backstage simultaneously. A couple of scenes were even set in the orchestra pit. Thanks to its recent facelift, which included an enlarged orchestra pit, the Hanna was up to the show's requirements. The authors also stated that they were coming to Cleveland "because of our desire to help 'the road' and to stimulate the theater outside New York."[35]

Excitement mounted as seven baggage cars of scenery and a company of seventy arrived in Playhouse Square. Twenty-two stagehands began to maneuver eighty-five tons of scenery from Brownell Court onto the Hanna's reinforced stage.[36] "It will be the most important theatrical opening Cleveland has had in years," wrote McDermott. "Indeed, I don't remember any previous occasion when a musical show of this promise and magnitude had its first tryout performance in our precincts."[37]

A standing-room crowd filled the Hanna on opening night. Hammerstein took his usual seat in the eighth row, while Rodgers watched from the last row of the orchestra. So keyed up was the audience that it broke into spontaneous applause at the lowering of the house lights even before the raising of the curtain, a moment Rodgers afterward confessed to have found "electrifying. . . . I don't remember such a clear demonstration ever happening before at the opening of a show I was connected with." By the time of the intermission, however, Rodgers was getting a different message. "Whatever flickering optimism any one of us may have had about *Me and Juliet* was quickly doused when we heard people raving about the sets, without a word being said about the rest of the show."[38]

Eager to put a positive spin on the event, Cleveland critics found more to praise in the show's parts than in the whole. Ranney acclaimed it "theatrical razzle-dazzle," and McDermott singled out Hammerstein's lyrics and George Abbott's direction.[39] Unfortunately, neither was perceptive enough to single out from the chorus a young dancer named Shirley MacLaine, thereby forfeiting a footnote in theatrical history. Though not a big hit, *Me and Juliet* was a respectable success, achieving a run of 358 Broadway performances. Milton Krantz had had the prestige of a Rodgers and Hammerstein premiere and a solid two-week run.

On another side of the block, the story of the Lake Theatre was short and bittersweet. Warner Brothers divested themselves of the modest-sized house in 1948, selling it to a local group that reopened it as the Esquire Theatre. In its brief career, the 714-seat Esquire scored at least a couple of notable runs. First, opening on Christmas Day 1948 came *The Red Shoes,* the classic ballet film. It was shown on a reserved-seat basis, with tickets priced from $.90 to $1.80 for matinees, $1.20 to $2.40 evenings (the same as for *Hamlet,* then playing the Ohio).[40]

All three Cleveland critics raved about *The Red Shoes,* especially the *Plain Dealer*'s Ward Marsh, who called it "an emotional, artistic and at times breathlessly exciting film, so beautiful and often of such delicate charm that it seems like a lovely dream. . . . It is positively a must-see picture." He was especially impressed by newcomer Moira Shearer as "a girl who not only wanted to dance but also wanted to become the greatest ballerina the world had ever known." She danced on the Esquire's screen for a first run of eighteen weeks, then returned two years later at popular prices for another eight weeks.[41]

Singer Al Jolson, who had flopped in his last appearance on the Hanna's stage, made a triumphant comeback on screen five years later in *The Jolson Story*. Actually, he was played by a young actor named Larry Parks, who lip-synched to the inimitable Jolson voice on the film's soundtrack. It played the Hippodrome in 1947, but two years later a sequel, *Jolson Sings Again*, came to the Esquire. Marsh, who had panned the original film as "sickeningly saccharine," thought the epilogue "at least twice as good as the original film." It gave the Esquire a twelve-week run, which, in retrospect, was something of a last hurrah. A year and a half later, on May 28, 1951, the Esquire dimmed its marquee for good.[42] In what might have served as a metaphor for the sci-fi film classic *Invasion of the Body Snatchers*, five years later WJW—a television station—occupied the building.

Double Whammy

Television was only half of the one-two punch absorbed by the nation's downtown movie houses in the postwar period. The first had come in 1948 in the unlikely guise of a landmark Supreme Court decision. Since the 1920s, the biggest Hollywood studios had dominated the distribution of all motion pictures through their nationwide ownership of thousands of theaters, from downtown firstrun movie palaces to smaller neighborhood houses. Hollywood's Big Five studios were generally regarded to be Paramount, MGM, Warner Brothers, Twentieth Century-Fox, and Radio-Keith-Orpheum (RKO). Foremost in Cleveland was Loew's/MGM, which controlled the State, Stillman, and Ohio; and Stanley/Warner, which booked the Hippodrome, Allen, and Lake. "The Big Five company first booked their own films; for example, Loew's, Inc. scheduled MGM films," explained one movie historian. "Then the firm worked in the best films offered by the other four."[43]

In the 1930s, under the Roosevelt administration, the Justice Department had invoked the Anti-Trust Act to force the studios to divest their theater chains. The studios fought the issue in the courts, but after the war the Supreme Court ruled in the Paramount case that the studios did indeed constitute a monopoly. Under the terms of a subsequent series of consent decrees, the studios began selling off the better part of their theater holdings. Warner's sale of the Lake Theatre in 1948 may have been an instance of reading the handwriting on the wall. Actually, divestiture proved a drawn-out process, but downtown theaters eventually did lose their prior rights to first-run features. Officials from Loew's Theaters came to Cleveland in 1964 to reopen the recently fire-gutted Ohio Theatre. While expressing faith in downtowns generally, they were hedging their bets. "We plan a new theater for Cleveland," said general manager Bernard Diamond, "but it will not be downtown." Loew's West opened soon afterward in Fairview Park's Rockport Shopping Center.[44]

The potential threat of television, which soon proved a more formidable adversary than the Supreme Court, had been long foreseen. "In another fifty years—or ten, I am willing to bet, moving pictures will no longer be the central medium," film critic James Agee had predicted in 1943. "Radio will have taken their place; television, very likely, will have taken the place of both." Agee would have won the bet on his shorter estimate of ten years. When WEWS went on air in December 1947, there were only seven commercial television stations and fourteen thousand families with television sets in the entire United States. Two years later, Cleveland had acquired two more television stations, WNBK and WXEL (now WKYC and WJW); the country had fifty stations and nearly a million families with sets.[45]

By 1952, there were more than a hundred stations and 15 million families with television sets nationwide. A *Cleveland Press* story stated, "One by one, screens of old, familiar neighborhood movie houses are dying." Of eighty-six Cleveland movie marquees flickering in 1947, more than twenty-five were dark five years later. Among the casualty list were the Corlett, Denison, Gordon Square, Memphis, Superior, and the downtown Lake. From managers of the failed or failing houses "discouraging references to the competition of television screens [were] unguarded." When WJW finally occupied the former Lake on Playhouse Square in 1956, 35 million American families were plugged into television.[46]

Hollywood responded to the challenge of the new medium with a technological counterattack. "Third dimension—depth—is the big news in Playhouse Square this week," wrote Ward Marsh in January 1953. Ads for the Allen Theatre the day before had promised "A lion in your lap! . . . A lover in your arms! The flat screen is gone. You—not a camera—but you are there!" The film, an African adventure titled *Bwana Devil*, was "incredibly bad," said the *Plain Dealer* critic, despite Robert Stack's efforts heading a cast whose

Three-dimensional (3-D) films were among Hollywood's first attempts to entice patrons from their small, two-dimensional television screens. They were first seen locally at the Allen Theatre, which screened *House of Wax* shortly after *Bwana Devil*. Among its amazing novelties," said one reviewer of *House of Wax*, "are a bevy of Can-Can dancers who threaten to kick you in the face." (*Cleveland Plain Dealer,* April 22, 1953)

"single claim to distinction and to fame is that they have appeared in the first third-dimension film." The process seemed an instance of back to the future: "You will find that the super-imposed twin pictures projected on the screen and then seen through the polaroid [and disposable] glasses given you at the door will remind you—if you are old enough to be so reminded—of the stereoscope through which you looked at the turn of the century."[47]

Three months later, the Allen screened another 3-D picture, billed as the first to be released by a major studio (Warner Brothers). Glenn Pullen described *House of Wax* as "the macabre tale of a mad sculptor and his creepy museum of wax-dipped cadavers." Among the film's special effects were "eerie stereophonic sounds which come from every direction" and "a bevy of Can-Can dancers who threaten to kick you in the face." Both 3-D movies did well at the Allen's box office, but the novelty soon wore off. Moviegoers didn't view them as worth the discomfort of the awkward glasses, nor did the returns justify the investment in special equipment for studios.[48]

Moviemakers continued to search for a decisive technological edge over television. Their initial advantage of color was even then coming to the small screen. 3-D having failed to turn the trick, they experimented with another, older dimension—the size and shape of the screen. From the beginning, screen dimensions had held to the relatively narrow rectangle dictated by the shoebox shape of the early nickelodeons. In the early 1950s, Hollywood began to shoot movies on wider-framed film to take advantage of the peripheral vision of the human eye. One of the first was Twentieth Century-Fox's CinemaScope, designed to be shown on a wide, slightly curved screen. CinemaScope made its debut in September 1953 with the biblical epic *The Robe*. The Hippodrome introduced it to Cleveland, but by the end of the year the Allen and the State brought CinemaScope to Playhouse Square. Other variants such as Paramount's VistaVision and Todd-AO made their appearance within another year.[49]

But it took more than four years for the original widescreen process, Cinerama, to reach Cleveland. Even as 3-D drew audiences into the picture at the Allen, Ward Marsh reported on his viewing of *This Is Cinerama* in New York. It opened with an introduction on the old small screen by Lowell Thomas. Then two more projection booths, one on either side, went into action, "projecting a sight on the screen I shall not forget." The image on the huge, deeply curved screen widened to 146 degrees, and "a new screen world opened that very instant." It wasn't three-dimensional so much as, in the words of its creators, a "new dimension." Ward correctly predicted that its cost would prevent Cinerama from becoming the industry's standard; nevertheless, he believed "every major city should have at least one Cinerama theater."[50]

Eighteen cities later, Cleveland was finally ready for Cinerama. It would make its debut in the crown jewel of Playhouse Square, the Palace Theatre, whose marquee shed the letters RKO. The Palace would also have to shed more than fifteen hundred seats, half its capacity, to make room for three projection booths in the rear of the orchestra and keep viewers within the desired sightlines of the seventy-five-foot-wide curved screen. Seven speakers would be installed to surround viewers with "high-fidelity cineramasound." There would be thirteen showings weekly (evenings nightly, matinees Wednesday through Sunday) with a price range of $1.20 to $2.40. It was scheduled to open on Wednesday, November 8, 1956.[51]

By that time, Marsh had already seen Cinerama four times in venues from New York to Hollywood and was yet to become jaded. "There is nothing to compare with Cinerama because this revolutionary process of film making and film exhibition is in a class by itself." He assured Clevelanders that the projection and sound reproduction at the Palace showed improvement over the New York original. There was still that dramatic opening when the screen suddenly widened and the audience found itself in a roller coaster on the cusp of a breathtaking plunge. As for what followed, Marsh admitted, "Cinerama has no story to tell. . . . None is necessary as yet." Essentially, it was a glorified travelogue taking viewers to the military tattoo in Edinburgh, a regatta at Venice, *Aida* at La Scala,

A promotional postcard distributed by the Palace Theatre showed how *This Is Cinerama* would take its audience on a breathtaking plunge down a roller coaster. (Courtesy of Cleveland Public Library Photograph Collection)

"The biggest new entertainment event of the year." - LIFE

the Vienna Boys' Choir at Schönbrunn Palace, and other exotic locales. It was enough for a thirty-two-week run at the Palace, a house record.[52]

This Is Cinerama was followed by the second Cinerama production, *Cinerama Holiday*. That carried the process past its one-year anniversary at the Palace, which brought a "special citation of merit" from the Cleveland Convention and Visitors Bureau. Over the next two years, other travelogues followed. Still later came a few Cinerama story features, including *The Wonderful World of the Brothers Grimm* and *It's a Mad Mad Mad Mad World.* Those later films survive only in conventional formats; as of 2018, the original Cinerama features could be viewed in only three locales, all far from Cleveland. Overall, in the words of one critic, it was just "one of the gimmicks developed to help movies compete with television in the 1950s."[53] While they may have provided some life support for downtown movie theaters, other problems loomed that were beyond the capabilities of the movie industry to solve.

Greener Pastures

In the summer of 1960, a Willard Combes cartoon in the *Cleveland Press* depicted a slight man of advanced middle age confronted by a hefty, grinning young man towering over the fence from the neighboring backyard. The elder figure doesn't look threatened, only bemused. "The little boy next door," he says to himself. Across the stripling's shirt is the label "Suburbs," while the older neighbor represents "Cleveland."[54]

In place of bemusement, Combes might have drawn a look of concern. Preliminary 1960 census returns had been released, showing a population increase of 47 percent in the nation's suburbs against only 8 percent in its cities. Cleveland fared even worse: final returns would show a loss of 38,758 residents over the previous decade, dropping it from seventh to eighth place among American cities. Cuyahoga County, however, would gain more than a quarter million denizens. Its total population of 1,647,895 was now nearly double that of the central city; in other words, the suburbs had a combined population nearly equal to Cleveland's.[55]

It was a seismic demographic shift, accelerated by developments on the World War II home front. New war plants needed large allotments of land, and little was available in Cleveland's constricted area of seventy-eight square miles. Of necessity, they were built in the suburbs. Cleveland's Post-War Planning Council accordingly predicted a peacetime "splurge of home-building in the suburbs," along with "wholesale abandonment of older areas and catastrophic losses in investments and tax values" for the city.[56] The 1960 census returns ratified its prediction.

There was another largely unmentioned motive behind the exodus. "Whites began to move away, fleeing the Negroes," chronicled Dick Feagler, who came of age in the postwar period. "They moved out past the bus lines to the new suburbs." He went on to describe the new suburban lifestyle: "Shopping centers, then shopping malls rose from vacant lots to fill the needs of these exiles. Mothers learned how to drive automobiles. Families now had two cars. You could park in a shopping center lot even if your parking skills weren't so hot. . . . If you wanted a dress or a pair of shoes, you could go to the new May Company or the Higbee store out there in the suburbs— you didn't have to go Downtown. First-run movies began booking into the little movie theaters in the malls and Playhouse Square (which was really Moviehouse Square) withered and died."[57]

Suburbanites developed a certain smugness about their new communities and a corresponding snobbishness toward the city they had left behind. In 1960, *Press* columnist Julian Krawcheck pitted the loyalties of Greater Clevelanders to their central city against those of people from comparable cities toward theirs. Leafing through guest books in a couple of recent vacation stays, he and his wife found plenty of entries from Chicago, Detroit, Toronto, and other cities, but only two or three from Cleveland. Instead, they found names from numerous Greater Cleveland suburbs, from Fairview Park through Parma to South Euclid. It was hardly a scientific survey, but enough to convince Krawcheck "that Cleveland suburbanites, on evidence, strive to disassociate themselves from the central city more than suburbanites do from other metropolitan centers." Krawcheck wasn't sure of the reasons for that attitude, but thought, "It helps explain why Toronto, a city of similar size and industrial makeup, has a fine, efficient subway . . . while Cleveland has none."[58]

Subways touched a sore spot with many Clevelanders in 1960. Much of the previous decade had been occupied on the question of whether to build one in downtown Cleveland. Construction of a rapid transit system to connect the city's east and west sides was under way, and the Cleveland Transit System wanted to include a downtown subway loop in the plan. Instead of a single stop at Public Square, a subway would give passengers the option of several stops through the downtown area. It would be financed by a proposed $35 million bond issue on the ballot in November 1953.[59]

Public opinion, led by the three daily newspapers, was largely in favor of the idea. The retail establishments of Playhouse Square especially supported it. Halle's department store ran an ad in the *Press* listing "4 good reasons *for* voting for the subway," one of which was "The subway will make *all* downtown easy to reach . . . and add to the prosperity of *everybody*." Opposition centered around the formidable and outspoken figure of Cuyahoga County engineer Albert S. Porter, who never saw a freeway he didn't love nor a railway he didn't disdain. From an engineering standpoint, he claimed that digging for the subway would endanger many buildings on the route; fiscally, he claimed that the final cost of Toronto's subway would be nearly double the original estimates. Voters apparently were unimpressed, as they approved the proposed bond issue by a nearly two-thirds majority.[60]

Studies and arguments, however, continued for several years. The most likely route would run from the Union Terminal on Public Square, under Huron Road to Playhouse Square, then under East Thirteenth Street to Superior Avenue and thence back to the Terminal. Cars from the west side would follow the same route in reverse.[61] Cleveland mayor Anthony J. Celebrezze finally called for action in 1957, saying that the question had been settled by the people's vote and that "the most costly item in government is delay." Though the mayor pushed for immediate construction of the subway, the decision lay in the hands of the three Cuyahoga County commissioners. They, in turn, paid due deference to the professional advice of engineer Porter, who stressed such collateral construction costs as the moving and replacement of utility lines. His arguments swayed two of the three commissioners, who voted against the subway.[62]

Still, the dream refused to die, and proponents made one final effort to revive the subway before the bond issue expired in 1960. While Playhouse Square continued to lobby for the tube, opposition forces had added strength through the long debate. Porter supplied fresh stories of the hidden costs uncovered by Toronto's subway experience. His brother Philip W. Porter, managing editor of the *Plain Dealer*, wrote a column critical of Playhouse Square's self-serving support for the project. Mail mostly in opposition to the project flooded the office of the county commissioners, who again voted it down, two to one. Frank M. Gorman, the lone dissenter, correctly observed, "If it is not built now, there will never be a subway."[63]

Gorman placed the blame for the defeat on City Hall. "The mayor could have had the subway if he'd pushed hard enough," he charged. Asked years later to name the worst mistake during his mayoralty, Celebrezze answered: "That's easy. Not building the downtown subway." He told T. W. Grogan, owner of the Hanna Building complex, "Tim, for a long time the pressure was tremendous on me not to do or say anything about it." According to Grogan's son Don, who witnessed the exchange, "that pressure came from the Public Square group: Society Bank, Terminal Tower, May Company, Higbee's, et cetera. The business community was pretty much split by East Ninth, those west of Ninth were against it, those east, for it."[64]

If Celebrezze had been tardy in his support for the subway, he wasted little time in regrets and announced that he would seek federal funds for a multi-million-dollar downtown urban renewal project.[65] Announced and adopted in 1961, Erieview would largely extend along the bluff above the lakefront, from East Sixth Street to East Seventeenth, with an "ell" extension southward within the East Ninth to East Thirteenth corridor to Chester Avenue. Its eastern portion would largely be devoted to residential development, while that from around East Ninth to Thirteenth was envisioned as commercial. Developed by architect I. M. Pei & Associates, Erieview would be the largest downtown renewal project in the nation.[66] Erieview was steamrolled through with the support of the federal government, City Hall, and the *Cleveland Press*. City officials contrasted the dead nightlife of Cleveland with that of comparable cities as a reason for the need of downtown revitalization. The *Press*, at the apex of its influence under editor Louis

B. Seltzer, had just opened its shining new editorial and printing plant on Lakeside Avenue, right across East Ninth Street from City Hall. (A popular rumor of the day claimed that a secret tunnel ran under East Ninth from City Hall to Seltzer's office for mayors to come for their instructions.) Its key location at the project's northwestern corner, as Philip Porter would later observe, made the *Press* building the "fulcrum of Erieview."[67]

Opposition to the project came mainly from older sections of downtown. For once, Public Square and Playhouse Square were united in defense of Euclid Avenue as the "Main Street" of downtown Cleveland. Erieview workers would have to use up much of their lunch hours to cross the Mall to reach the stores and restaurants of Public Square or hike several blocks to those of Playhouse Square. Both Tim Grogan and Henry H. Eccles of the Cleveland Building Owners and Managers Association warned that Euclid Avenue, once the "Showcase of America," might deteriorate into a backwater of downtown.[68]

During its first decade, Erieview showed promise of fulfilling its planners' dreams of downtown revitalization. Its centerpiece, the forty-story Erieview Tower (second only to the Terminal Tower in the Cleveland skyline), opened in 1964, followed by the Federal Building on East Ninth Street. Over the next twenty years, several buildings of varying size were added, but even as early as 1976 Philip Porter could appraise Erieview as "one of the city's biggest mistakes." He saw its new office buildings as pulling renters out of older ones on Euclid Avenue and accelerating the street's "degeneration . . . which was already under way."[69] The planned Erieview II residential section didn't happen. It was "probably a bad mistake," according to Don Grogan, "because there hasn't been a market for that kind of housing."[70] Eventually there was, but when residents finally came, they settled everywhere but in Erieview II. A harbinger of downtown living, the Chesterfield Apartments, opened in 1967. The twenty-story building was raised on East Twelfth Street and Chester Avenue, at the southern extent of Erieview and on the fringes of Playhouse Square.

The Playhouse Square theaters didn't have to worry about competition from Erieview, as theaters weren't in the project's plans. Their main competitors lay elsewhere. In 1964, Ward Marsh took note of an increase in "saturation bookings; that is a dozen or a score of theaters playing a picture entirely new to this area, ignoring the downtown." It was happening at the Detroit in Lakewood, the Mayland in Mayfield Heights, the Colony in Shaker Square, and soon in a new theater being built in Cleveland Heights. "When theaters begin moving from the downtown area, the heart of the city goes too," observed the *Plain Dealer* movie critic.[71]

Bucking the Trend

Its off-center location on East Fourteenth Street and its unpretentious front of the house had always set the Hanna Theatre apart from its opulent Euclid Avenue neighbors. With the coming of the 1960s it also enjoyed another distinction from moviehouse row: it didn't have to worry about television or suburbanization. Live theater had survived the challenge from Hollywood "talkies" in the thirties and experienced rejuvenation with the advent of musical plays in the forties. True, there was live theater in the suburbs, with up to fifty "little theaters" of varied ambition and quality from Bay Village through North Royalton to Willoughby.[72] None, however, could approach the Broadway cachet of the Hanna, which might have regarded them not as rivals but rather as schools for serious theatergoers and future subscribers.

Building and maintaining a dependable subscription base was always the key to Milton Krantz's strategy for keeping the Hanna viable. "At one time I had the largest Theatre Guild subscription list in the country—9,837 seats sold in advance out of 12,000 [weekly] capacity," recalled Krantz. From the 1920s through the 1940s, the guild had kept the road, including the Hanna, supplied with a steady and distinguished string of its own productions, from *Liliom* to *Oklahoma!* By the 1960s, it was beginning to withdraw from the production business but used its pioneering experience in theater subscriptions to organize audiences for road seasons of touring Broadway shows.[73]

Krantz, who began working in theaters at the age of fifteen, cultivated his audiences with liberal examples of "the personal touch." "I always thought that people who came to legitimate theater should be your friends," he said. He took lessons in first aid, CPR, and on at least one occasion restored a man's heartbeat before the arrival of paramedics.[74] Don Grogan vividly recalled Krantz's traditional opening-night ritual: just before curtain time the tuxedoed manager would walk down the orchestra aisle to the edge of the orchestra pit, turn around and survey the house with a proprietary air, then slowly walk up to the back of the house, nodding to and greeting subscribers right and left along the way.

Hanna Theatre manager Milton Krantz (*right*) supervised the handling of ticket orders for *South Pacific* in 1950. Demand was so great that he leased the much larger Cleveland Music Hall for the two-week run. (Courtesy of *Cleveland Press* Collection, Michael Schwartz Library, Cleveland State University)

Krantz admitted to doing his homework, memorizing the names and seat locations of subscribers and keeping abreast of their affairs in the Sunday paper.[75]

In 1958, Grogan and his father, T.W., managers of the Hanna Building since the 1930s, became outright owners of the building, including the Hanna Theatre. Heavily in debt, the Hanna heirs, including Carl, had been forced to sell. Daniel R. Hanna Jr., was the only family member to retain a stake in the properties, as a minor investor. His father, Daniel Rhodes Hanna, had built the theater as a monument to *his* father, the theater buff Senator Mark Hanna. Orchestra seats D-101 to D-104 had traditionally remained in the family, their few inches of extra leg room personally dictated by the six-foot-four-inches-tall Dan Rhodes Sr. "It was a beautiful theater—and well taken care of," said Don Grogan. "The Hanna brought Broadway to Cleveland."[76]

Like Mark Hanna with the old Euclid Avenue Opera House, the Grogans had no illusions about running a theater themselves, especially with a savvy manager such as Milton Krantz in place. "I had 1,512 seats—more than the largest theater in New York—when I came here," declared Krantz, who was charged with filling them.[77] In 1960–61, he put together a twenty-eight-week season. It included stints of such golden-age musicals as four weeks of *The Sound of Music* with Florence Henderson, three weeks of *My Fair Lady,* and two of *Fiorello!; Once upon a Mattress* with Buster Keaton and a return visit of *The Pajama Game* were good for a week apiece, as was *Gypsy*, which the Hanna booked in the larger Music Hall. Straight plays included *A Raisin in the Sun* with Claudia McNeil, *Five-Finger Exercise* with Jessica Tandy, and *A Majority of One* with Gertrude Berg and Cedric Hardwicke.

One offering that season came not from Broadway but from Lawrence Langer's American Shakespeare Festival in Stratford, Connecticut. The company had first visited the Hanna in 1957, with a production of *Much Ado About Nothing* headed by Katharine Hepburn and Alfred Drake. This time it would offer the Bard's *A Midsummer Night's Dream* and *A Winter's Tale*, both featuring the former burlesque comedian, Bert Lahr. Their appearances were underwritten by a score of local sponsors headed by philanthropist Kenyon C. Bolton. Manager Krantz arranged a gala opening night complete with floodlights, searchlights, and a reception committee of civic dignitaries, though assuring playgoers that the delegation would forego "the traditional speeches."[78]

One young *Midsummer* playgoer was future actor John Lithgow, whose father, Arthur Lithgow, was artistic director of the Great Lakes Shakespeare Festival in suburban Lakewood. His father went primarily because of a couple of cast members he knew, but John remembered "witnessing one of the greatest comic performances I had ever seen, or have seen since," by Bert Lahr in the choice role of Bottom the Weaver. Young Lithgow later learned from Lahr's son that the elder Lahr had a special piece of schtick stored up for the part. It came in the mock tragedy put on by the rustics in the last act, in which Bottom draws a sword to commit suicide. As related by Lithgow, Lahr drew his sword with a flourish—and his pants fell down! The audience laughed so hard and long that it infected the actors onstage, who included Mariette Hartley, Will Geer, and William Hickey. [79] After an act like that, *A Winter's Tale* proved anticlimactic, despite the appearance of Lahr as Autolycus. *Press* critic Stan Anderson, however, made a revealing comment on current production trends. "The festival company is playing without a sound system, except for incidental music," he wrote. "It is good to hear stage actors in an earnest effort to project without electronic assistance."[80]

Lahr would make only one more appearance at the Hanna, starring in the world premiere of an unsuccessful musical called *Foxy*. Other representatives of the grand tradition took their final bows on East Fourteenth Street. Katharine Cornell made the last of her record twenty-two stops at the Hanna in the American premiere of Christopher Fry's *The Firstborn* in 1958. That year also saw the final appearance there of Katharine Hepburn, though she would later appear in *Coco* at Music Hall, under Hanna auspices. Tallulah Bankhead had already made her farewell in *Dear Charles* in 1955. The Lunts made *The Visit* their final visit in 1959. Cornelia Otis Skinner bowed out the following year in *The Pleasure of His Company.* Maurice Evans, who had twice trod the Hanna boards as Hamlet, made his final stop in *A Program for Two Players* in 1962. His costar in that production, Helen Hayes, made her tenth and last Hanna curtain call six years later in *The Show-Off.*[81]

Plays and musicals from Broadway were beginning to move in new directions. The late 1950s brought two widely divergent takes on Shakespeare's *Romeo and Juliet* to the Hanna, the first being Peter Ustinov's *Romanoff and Juliet.* Hoyt found it an entertaining mixture of satire, burlesque, and lengthy speeches with "clever epigrams." "I wonder if they have considered this play for a musical," he observed in conclusion. "It would make a fine one." Leonard Bernstein and Jerome Robbins took him up on that with *West Side Story,* which updated the tragedy of Shakespeare's lovers to the modern Manhattan slums. It came to Cleveland in 1960 with its Broadway cast headed by Larry Kert. Anderson of the *Press* found Bernstein's score "wild, tortured, protesting," but "entirely suitable" to the grim story and setting. "Out of the grimness, out of the agony comes something of such moving significance that it surely may be called beauty," he wrote. "If there is truth in the contention that the American musical theater, unique within itself, now needs to venture into fresh forms, then 'West Side' is on the right path."[82]

Even the British were catching on, as exemplified in the avant-garde musical import *Stop the World—I Want to Get Off.* Anthony Newley wrote it and starred in it on Broadway, but the road company that stopped at the Hanna was headed by a diminutive native Clevelander named Joel Grey. *Plain Dealer* critic Peter Bellamy recalled having last seen Grey in the title role of the Cleveland Play House children's theater production of *Little Black Sambo.* It was "not the Curtain Pullers' finest moment," remembered Grey, who had played the role in blackface makeup and a "Topsy" wig.[83] For *Stop the World* twenty-five years later, he wore the whiteface and baggy pants of a circus clown to impersonate the life of a cockney Everyman named Littlechap, from birth to hollow success and final disillusionment.

Bellamy reported that "the cast headed by Joel Grey and Julie Newmar, perform most ably, and with nonstop singing, dancing, acting and pantomime. I found the show sometimes maddening, but never dull." Anderson informed *Press* readers that Grey had developed into "a vital and versatile performer. He is on stage almost every minute of the long evening and is as energetic about it all as Sammy Davis Jr. in a one-man performance." While Anderson's engagement began to flag around two-thirds into the show, he nevertheless found it "quite refreshing . . . that it calls upon us to use our imaginations. That is an asset in these days of formula shows."[84]

Near the end of the 1960s, two musicals came to the Hanna from Off Broadway, where even musicals hewed to the mantra of "smaller is better." When *The Fantastics* rolled into Cleveland, it was still playing in Greenwich Village after more than six years, and one member of the Hanna cast had racked up eighteen hundred performances in his role. The company of nine, in Emerson Batdorff's opinion, did "a delightful job of bouncing a soap bubble." A couple of years later, a cast of six came for a seven-week run at the Hanna in *You're a Good Man, Charlie Brown,* a musical based on the popular "Peanuts" comic strip. "Any show this deceptively simple is the product of skill and artistry," observed Tony Mastroianni in the *Press*. "The company is out there walking on eggs and getting away with it."[85]

Despite the dominance of musicals, Broadway was still sending straight plays on the road. Comedy was always popular, and *Come Blow Your Horn* and *The Odd Couple* introduced Neil Simon to the Hanna. The mystery genre offered Shirley Jones in *Wait until Dark.* More serious drama included Edward Albee's *A Delicate Balance* with Hume Cronyn and Jessica Tandy and Arthur Miller's autobiographical *After the Fall.* Bellamy considered the latter "one of the finest plays written by America's greatest living playwright." He cautioned audiences, however: "It is no play for those seeking gay, casual escapist entertainment. It demands intense concentration."[86]

Dramas of sexuality also came to the Hanna's stage. In the 1950s, Deborah Kerr in *Tea and Sympathy* had used her seductive skills to reassure a confused young man that he was conformably heterosexual. Fourteen years later, the characters in *The Killing of Sister George* were unapologetically lesbian. Bellamy admitted prejudice against the play: "I find the parading of compulsive sexual aberrations on stage personally repellent." Even actress Claire Trevor expressed a hardly enlightened attitude toward her character. "They are human beings and are cursed with an affliction or psychological illness for which they are not to blame," she told Bellamy in a phone interview. The critic overcame his scruples and actually went to review the show. "There are several scenes of sadistic lesbianism," he reported, "but no love scenes, thank the Lord."[87]

To paraphrase a popular anthem of the day, the times, if not general prejudices, indeed were changing.

Decline . . .

According to historian Jan Cigliano, the last family to live on Millionaires' Row moved out in 1950, presumably headed for the green hills of suburbia. Of the 260 houses on Euclid Avenue at the turn of the twentieth century, fewer than half a dozen would remain, none for residential use, at the turn of the twenty-first. Residents had successfully kept streetcars off the most exclusive stretch of the "Row" until 1915; trollies made their final trip down the avenue in 1952, when none of the old dwellers were around either to celebrate or mourn their passing. Not even the businesses that had crowded out the avenue's residences were immune to changing demographics. Halfway between Public Square and Playhouse Square, Taylor's department store closed its doors in 1961.[88]

There were a few positive signs on the eastern edge of Playhouse Square, outside the traditional gateway formed by the Keith and Hanna buildings. Although most of Cleveland's Jews had moved to the eastern suburbs, the Jewish Community Federation dedicated a new building on the southwestern corner of East Eighteenth Street and Euclid Avenue in 1965. The four-story modernistic structure, designed by Edward Durell Stone, was intended as a demonstration of Jewish commitment to downtown Cleveland. Across East Eighteenth from the Federation building, the five-story Downtown Motor Inn opened that same year, with 150 rooms and a heated swimming pool. Further up Euclid Avenue, in mid-decade newly established Cleveland State University opened on the former campus of Fenn College at East Twenty-Fourth Street.[89] It would be a few years before the university began filling in the acres between Fenn Tower and Playhouse Square.

Those few visible signs of progress, however, were undercut by a vaguer but widely perceived image of the central city. Crime became endemic in most American cities, and Playhouse Square was not immune. One particularly audacious example occurred in 1953 when the State Theatre promoted a crime film with an exhibit of guns and other crime apparatus—and a .32 automatic pistol was lifted from the display. Ushers at the Allen were attacked by a teenage gang and the theater's manager shot and injured in a holdup. An actress appearing at the Hanna was assaulted and robbed at knifepoint. Outside a Euclid Avenue jewelry store in 1963, a Cleveland detective stopped two men on suspicion, discovering a concealed gun on one. The arrest was challenged all the way to the US Supreme Court, which upheld the detective's action.[90]

Such cases, multiplied and highly publicized, especially when occurring downtown, were particularly injurious to nighttime activities like theatergoing. The nationwide riots of the long, hot summer of 1966 exacerbated urban crime fears. Cleveland's share came in the Hough neighborhood, midway between downtown and University Circle. Over the course of several days, four people were killed, dozens injured, and some 250 fires turned a once vibrant neighborhood into a desolate ruin. While Hough was dozens of blocks removed from downtown, the riots had a ripple effect on Playhouse Square. "One of the almost insuperable obstacles to bringing people downtown was that the main east side arteries, Chester, Euclid, and Carnegie avenues, ran through the city's biggest slum, and citizens disliked driving back through them at night," stated Philip Porter, who reported that "several motorists had been held up and robbed when they stopped at traffic lights, on their way to and from the Heights." The Hanna offered those intrepid enough to risk the trip "the only all-weather garage attached to a legitimate theater in the United States" in the season following Hough. Patrons could walk from their cars straight into a special new "lounge lobby" with its own ticket taker.[91]

Playhouse Square's movie palaces had more to worry about than suburbanites' anxieties about crime. Both of Loew's downtown theaters, the State and the Ohio, were closed in January 1968, reported Emerson Batdorff, the *Plain Dealer*'s entertainment editor. While the Ohio was slated to reopen that week with the movie musical *Dr. Doolittle*, the State would remain dark until June, when *2001: A Space Odyssey* relighted its marquee. "Thus it appears that Loew's theaters downtown will remain closed unless they can get exclusive runs of big pictures," wrote Batdorff. He quoted a Loew's spokesman to the effect that in the future downtown theaters would play movies on a roadshow basis. "And there aren't enough big pictures these days," he observed.[92]

Ever since *Hamlet* in the 1940s, the Ohio had specialized in exclusive showings of first-run movies on a reserved-seat basis. For most of the following two decades, there had been enough big pictures to keep the Ohio's box office busy. *South Pacific* was good for a run of forty-seven weeks, soon topped by *Ben-Hur* with forty-eight. Even *Gone with the Wind,* reedited for the wide screen, returned after thirty years for a run of fourteen weeks—four more than its original run at the Stillman. But the high point of the Ohio's career came in 1965 with its screening of Rodgers and Hammerstein's *The Sound of Music,* which became the only movie in Cleveland history to achieve a run of an entire year and finished with an incredible ninety-one weeks.[93]

Road-show bookings brought long runs to the other three Playhouse Square movie houses. Besides *2001,* the State got decent runs from *Grand Prix* and *Far from the Madding Crowd.* At the Allen, *The Great Race, Those Magnificent Men in Their Flying Machines,* and *The Sand Pebbles* enjoyed runs of thirteen to seventeen weeks. Once Cinerama had exhausted its vogue, road-show runs at the Palace included *Porgy and Bess, Spartacus, The Agony and the Ecstasy, Is Paris Burning?,* and *Judgment at Nuremberg.*[94]

But first-run films such as Jules Dassin's *Topkaki* and Billy Wilder's *Kiss Me, Stupid* were opening in the suburbs, as Ward Marsh had noted. "Who is going to go home from work, driving about 15 tortuous miles, gulp down dinner, and then drive back downtown just to see a film he can see at his shopping center next door or maybe 5 miles away?" Batdorff asked. "Worriers about a deteriorating downtown can get an added edge to their blues when they consider that shopping-market theaters on the edge of plowed ground are thriving." If there was any hope for downtown, Batdorff saw it as a return to downtown living. "What's needed is a built-in audience from apartments filled with, one hopes, people who go out dining and to shows every night of the week," he concluded. "They will keep downtown going for us free riders who want to live like that only one night every couple of weeks." The hands of the downtown clock, however, were approaching midnight.[95]

... and Fall

After six decades of dealing in Cleveland real estate, Joseph Laronge died at the age of eighty-two on October 10, 1964. His many professional honors included the presidency of the National Institute of Real Estate Brokers and a directorship on the National Association of Real Estate Boards. He had assembled the sites for downtown's Union Trust (later Union Commerce, still later

Huntington) and Ohio Bell Telephone buildings. He had created more than twenty residential subdivisions containing fifty miles of streets. He had been instrumental in the building of fourteen theaters in and around downtown. Most of all, forty-three years after the State Theatre's opening, he was remembered as "the father of Playhouse Square."[96]

In his career, Laronge had been a master of location; his death might be viewed as an unintentional stroke of timeliness. In 1921 he had been described as a visionary who "looked over the street [Euclid Avenue] of fading memories and saw something besides old houses, fast passing to decay." Looking over Playhouse Square in 1964, Laronge would have been hard put to see little beyond "fading memories" and "old houses, fast passing to decay." Just west of East Twelfth Street, its marquee visible from Playhouse Square, the Stillman Theater dimmed its lights for good on July 28, 1963. It was demolished and replaced by a parking garage, entered through the faded pilasters of the theater's former lobby.[97]

Playhouse Square was beginning to lose some of its éclat. "The exodus from downtown Cleveland was continuing," Philip Porter observed. Stouffer's restaurant at Playhouse Square, a fixture for forty years, stopped serving at night and soon would close entirely. Herman Pirchner made his final "auf Wiedersehen" at the Alpine Village in 1961; Korner & Wood, after losing $5,000 in a robbery, closed its downtown bookstore in 1963. One of the most noticeable

From 1934 to 1961, Herman Pirchner's Alpine Village was the mainstay of nightlife on Playhouse Square. Entertainers such as Cab Calloway and Sophie Tucker performed there for guests who once included General Dwight D. Eisenhower. Its closure was the harbinger of the darkening of Playhouse Square by the end of the 1960s. (Courtesy of *Cleveland Press* Collection, Michael Schwartz Library, Cleveland State University)

Cleveland's version of "The Last Picture Show" was the disaster movie *Krakatoa: East of Java*, which showed at the Palace Theatre until an air-conditioning failure forced the theater to close on July 20, 1969. The State and Ohio had shuttered earlier that year, the Allen a year earlier. Except for the Hanna on East Fourteenth, Playhouse Square was dark for the first time since 1921. (Courtesy of *Cleveland Press* Collection, Michael Schwartz Library, Cleveland State University)

losses came in 1968 with the shuttering of the Sterling-Lindner-Davis department store opposite Halle's on Euclid Avenue.[98] There would be no more Sterling Christmas tree, and the old Sterling building (but not the modernized former Higbee building) would soon be razed.

Even fortune seemed to be working against the district. Early on July 5, 1964, a janitor in the State Theatre smelled smoke and called the fire department, which found the lobby of the adjacent Ohio Theatre ablaze. Before fire fighters could put it out, it had destroyed most of the lobby decor and spread to the mezzanine ceiling. Damage to the recently renovated theater was estimated at $50,000 to $100,000, and Loew's at first was noncommittal as to whether the Ohio would reopen or close permanently.[99] It finally masked most of the damage with a coat of red paint and reopened. Shorn of much of its original splendor, the Ohio wasn't much more impressive than the utilitarian movie houses opening in the suburbs.

Some years previously, Stan Anderson had written a feature in the *Press* about the State Theatre's lobby. "When opened 36 years ago amidst great fanfare Loew's State boasted of the world's largest theater lobby," he wrote. "Today probably only two houses exceed it in lobby space, New York's Roxy and St. Louis' Fox." Anderson consulted a real estate broker to appraise the value of the land that the State's lobby occupied and reported an estimate of $1.5 million, nearly as much as the original $2 million cost of the entire theater. "Today the battle is to keep a house from going out of business," he concluded. "It is to fill a theater with a drawing card like 'Around the World in 80 Days,' not with impressive but unfunctional lobby space."[100]

The Allen, however, would become the first Playhouse Square theater to succumb to the economic realities of downtown decay. Ward Marsh, who had been there at the theater's opening in 1921, thought he was witnessing its demise when he attended a showing of *Bonnie and Clyde* on March 5, 1968. Rumors of its death, as Mark Twain might have put it, were only slightly exaggerated. Two months later, when the *Plain Dealer* printed a Marsh column charging the increasing prevalence of "Sexy Films" with alienating traditional movie audiences, an ad for the Allen on the same page touted an adult double bill of *My Third Wife, George* and *A Taste of Flesh*. On that ignominious note, the Allen finally called it quits on May 7, 1968.[101]

"Just west of the two Loew's theaters," Tony Mastroianni noted in the *Press* early in 1969, "the darkened Allen gathers refuse, old newspapers and empty wine bottles in its doorway." He was reporting that those two Loew's theaters, the Ohio and the State, would probably be next on the chopping block, as soon as their current roadshow attractions of *Star* at the Ohio and *Ice Station Zebra* at the State ended their runs on February 2. As it happened, both films were held over for another week, delaying their final curtains until February 9, 1969.[102]

So the dominos fell in sequence, west to east, until only the Palace was left standing—but not for long. A couple of years earlier, *Press* columnist Winsor French had answered a reader who lamented the passing of the Palace's glory days of vaudeville. Vaudeville "has not died but simply moved from the theaters to the television studios," French observed. As for the Palace, he wrote, "My guess is that one day it will cease to be even a movie house. It was built with no regard to costs and there are acres of empty space that are far too valuable to be left unused."[103]

Half a year following the demise of the State and the Ohio, the Palace's exclusive engagement of the disaster film *Krakatoa, East of Java* was expected to be the theater's last picture show. Despite a record box office in its first week, the film's run was foreshortened after the air-conditioning system failed. Rather than repair it, the Palace closed its doors on July 20, 1969.[104]

For the first time in nearly half a century, save for the one-night trial blackout of World War II, the Euclid Avenue marquees of Playhouse Square were dark. "Indeed, for all practical purposes," Peter Bellamy would observe, "Playhouse Square might as well now be called Hanna Square."[105]

Timeline of 1945–1969

November 13, 1947
Danny Kaye helps the Palace Theatre celebrate its twenty-fifth anniversary

December 17, 1947
Cleveland's first television station, WEWS, signs on

May 28, 1951
Esquire Theatre (formerly the Lake) goes dark on Playhouse Square

June 7, 1951
Josephine Baker appears at the Palace

January 22, 1953
Bwana Devil, the first 3-D movie, screens at the Allen Theatre

April 20, 1953
Rodgers and Hammerstein's *Me and Juliet* has its world premiere at the Hanna Theatre

November 8, 1956
This Is Cinerama opens at the Palace

December 20, 1959
Cuyahoga County Commissioners vote against building a downtown subway

January 26, 1960
Ben-Hur begins forty-eight-week run at the Ohio Theatre

July 5, 1964
Ohio Theatre is gutted by fire

October 10, 1964
Joseph Laronge, the "Father of Playhouse Square," dies at 82

May 7, 1968
Allen Theatre goes dark

February 9, 1969
State and Ohio Theatres go dark

July 20, 1969
Palace Theatre closes its doors

PART II

• • • • • • • • • • •

What It's Become

"It Was Those Murals"

Déjà vu

At the onset of the 1970s, school employees still were expected to appear well groomed. So a twenty-six-year-old personal assistant to Cleveland Public Schools superintendent Paul Briggs named Raymond K. Shepardson visited the barber shop, probably early in March 1970, for a haircut. We can roughly date his visit because he remembered picking up the February 27, 1970, issue of *Life* magazine while waiting his turn in the chair. On the cover, under the head "Goodby to the Glory Days," was a colorful painting of a movie director and cameraman shooting a scene for a Hollywood film. It produced a déjà vu moment in Shepardson: where had he seen that picture? It was a foldout cover, and opening the inside flap he would have discovered not only the rest of the painting but its source: *The Spirit of Cinema America,* a 1920 mural by James H. Daugherty in Loew's State Theatre, Cleveland.

That was it! Only a few weeks earlier he had seen the original, along with three companion pieces, in the State's once palatial lobby. As part of his job, he was scouting possible venues for Cleveland teachers to gather and socialize. He had needed special arrangements to gain access, as the theater had gone dark a year earlier and was already partially stripped for presumable demolition.

Inside that copy of *Life* was a cover story titled "The Day the Dream Factory Woke Up." It was about not the closing of downtown movie houses but the sell-off of Hollywood movie studios, such as Paramount. Had he scanned that article, he would have read, "Ended forever is the studio-centered, glamor-glossed, lotus-land Hollywood that has been celebrating itself for 50 years" and transferred that sentiment from Hollywood studios to the faded splendor he had seen in a fifty-year-old Cleveland theater. That likely was Ray Shepardson's epiphanic moment. The State Theatre, along with its neighbors in Playhouse Square, needed to be saved. Somebody ought to do something—even if he was that somebody.[1]

"What did it was those wonderful murals," said Elaine "Lainie" Hadden, who would become one of Shepardson's earliest and staunchest disciples. "Ray took that as a message from heaven."[2] In particular it was the *Spirit of America* on that *Life* cover, once floridly described by Cleveland School of Art director Henry Turner Bailey: "Here the modern vamp supplants Helen of Troy . . . an auto supersedes the chariot. . . . Palm Beach bathers eclipse the nymphs." Daugherty had painted many murals in the 1920s, notably in hotels and Loew's theaters.[3] What drew *Life* photographer Henry Groskinsky to the State's lobby in 1970 undoubtedly was Daugherty's *The Spirit of Cinema*, perfect for a cover story on Hollywood's faded "glory days." Before the artist's death in 1974, Playhouse Square wrote to inform him of efforts to save and restore the theater housing his murals. Daugherty replied that their campaign to rescue his works from their "entombment" put him in mind of "something out of the Arabian Nights," and he conjectured, "Perhaps you have started a Cleveland renaissance—a new cultural era of the Middle West."[4]

If James Daugherty sounded like a visionary, he had a kindred spirit in Ray Shepardson. John Hemsath, another of his disciples, described Shepardson as "probably the most intense character I've ever met. . . . He had the personality of a pioneer, the self-confidence and perhaps the naiveté to do what couldn't be done." Shepardson once cited the futuristic architect Buckminster Fuller as "a major influence on me. . . . He said, 'Do something big enough to make a difference.'"[5] Fuller made his difference with the geodesic dome; Shepardson would make his with the salvation of endangered, irreplaceable theaters.

There being no instruction manual for saving old theaters, Shepardson had to make up his own on the job. Historic preservation in America had as yet paid little attention to theaters, except for successful efforts in the 1960s to reclaim such nineteenth-century opera houses as the Goodspeed in East Haddam, Connecticut, and the Fulton in Lancaster, Pennsylvania. These were standalone efforts to restore quaint relics of a distant age, however; Shepardson would be dealing with up to four massive and outmoded remnants of a more recent, often disparaged era. A British historian writing in 1966 of the rise of movies in the 1920s concluded, "The buildings themselves in which films were shown displayed mass architecture of the worst kind; none is ever likely to attract support from even the most zealous preservationist." It's unlikely Shepardson ever read that sentence—or that it would have given him pause even if he had. "Well, I'm a farm kid from Seattle," he recalled of his first impression of the Playhouse Square theaters. "I thought they were spectacular."[6]

There had been talk and even plans for the restoration of Playhouse Square before Shepardson had ever seen the State lobby. Even as the theaters were going dark in early 1969, a group of about three hundred merchants and businesses in the district bounded by East Ninth to Eighteenth Streets between Chester and Prospect Avenues formed the 9–18 Corporation to promote its revitalization. Halle's department store commissioned a $50 million plan by Cleveland architect Robert A. Little that envisioned a pedestrian mall on Huron Road, more parking facilities around Playhouse Square, renovation of existing buildings, and new residential construction. Not much was said about the future of the four closed theaters. Halle's denied reports that they wanted to buy the Loew's Building, and Donald Grogan, manager of the Hanna Building, speculated that the theaters might be converted into office buildings. Kenyon C. Bolton, board president of the Cleveland Play House, raised the possibility that if 9–18 could provide a site, the resident east side theater might move downtown.[7]

The Halle-Little project failed to materialize, which left the future of Playhouse Square's movie palaces uncertain. Their fate ultimately rested in Ray Shepardson's hands. Lacking the resources and clout of the 9–18 Corporation, Shepardson nonetheless was committed enough to do what none other dared: quit his day job. He left the Board of Education on May 15, apparently with the blessing of Briggs, who Shepardson said "was very respectful of what I wanted to do" and "helped enormously with the press."[8]

Spreading the Word

Like a latter-day Don Quixote, Shepardson set out on his quest against the windmill of neglect and decay. In order to be closer to the theaters, he moved from East Boulevard to the Chesterfield Apartments downtown. Shepardson had established good press relations through his school position, in which he had directed the highly publicized Visiting Scholars program.[9]

By June, Shepardson was getting feature coverage in the *Cleveland Press*. His original plans, as told to Bob Kitchel of the *Press*, involved the State and Ohio theaters. He envisioned the State converted into what sounded like a reincarnation of the erstwhile Mayfair Casino: a large nightclub on the main floor of the auditorium, a restaurant on the balcony, and a lunchroom by day and nightclub by evening in the lengthy lobby. The Ohio, which had been briefly transformed into the Mayfair in the 1930s, would revert to its original status as a legitimate theater. Shepardson thought it would take around $2 million to realize his plan. He hoped to raise it by selling subscriptions at $120 apiece, setting a goal of 24,000 subscribers. An article in the *Parma Sun-Press* three days later announced that Shepardson hoped to open all facilities—State, Ohio, and Allen—at the same time in order to attract national coverage. A small private security force would be hired to protect patrons "until the area becomes well populated with night people."[10]

By the following month, Shepardson had incorporated the Playhouse Square Association (PSA) and began collecting members. One of his first converts was his landlady, Alice Drummond, manager of the Chesterfield Apartments. When she became the Chesterfield's first tenant in 1967, a *Plain Dealer* reporter would recall, the building "sat in the middle of a deteriorated neighborhood with sleazy barrooms, strip joints, flop hotels and an ancient fire station that matched the neighborhood decor." That was barely a block away from Playhouse Square. "Ray Shepardson was a great idealist who got many of us working for what was a project that caught nearly everyone's imagination and helped save the downtown," recalled Drummond, who became not only a charter member but a worker and promoter.[11]

Besides cultivating the press, Shepardson began networking with influential civic leaders. "Lainie Hadden was huge," he said. He also mentioned Kay Williams and Kay Halle as "people who really made a difference." Katherine Withrow Williams and her husband had helped found the Brush Development Corporation, a producer

Kay Halle (*left*) exchanges greetings with Shirley Stokes, wife of Cleveland's Mayor Carl B. Stokes, at a Supersesquicentennial event. A daughter of the Halle's department store owners, Halle took Ray Shepardson under her wing and introduced him to some of the city's movers and shakers. (Photo by Frank Reed, Courtesy of *Cleveland Press* Collection, Michael Schwartz Library, Cleveland State University)

of radio and recording equipment. She became one of Cleveland's leading arts promoters. "Kay Williams kept inviting [Shepardson] to her wonderful parties, which were really more like the old fashioned salons of Europe, and introducing him to people," recalled Hadden. One of her introductions undoubtedly was to Kay Halle, daughter of the department store owners, who divided her time between Cleveland and Washington. Halle was back in Cleveland in 1971 to help the city celebrate its 175th anniversary, when she introduced Shepardson to members of the Intown Club. This group of women shared an interest in the arts and met for luncheon in quarters in Playhouse Square's Kinney & Levan Building.[12]

Shepardson reviewed his evolving plans for the theaters to around seventy-five Intown members. In addition to the State and Ohio, the undertaking now encompassed the Allen, as a multiscreen movie theater and museum, and a future reopening of the Palace. The price tag had risen to $4.5 million, although his association as yet had only a hundred members. Time may have been running out for the State and Ohio, which were up for sale. "I think more of this project than of the John F. Kennedy Center for the Performing Arts in Washington," commented Halle. "I never stop dreaming about revitalizing Cleveland and I hope none of you ever do." Following the presentation, members were given a guided tour of the theaters. *Press* reporter Marjorie Alge recorded the consensus reaction: "I had forgotten how big and beautiful they were."[13]

Halle then enlisted Shepardson to help with her contribution to the Cleveland Supersesquicentennial, as the 175th anniversary festivities were called. It was to be a civic reception and dinner for 175 "eminent Clevelanders," and it would take place amid the marble and Albee red splendor of the Palace Theatre's Grand Hall. Among those on the guest list were Congressman Charles Vanik, former congresswoman Frances P. Bolton, Metropolitan Opera soprano Rose Bampton, Cleveland Orchestra Chorus founder Robert Shaw, Cleveland Browns immortal Lou "The Toe" Groza, and sundry judges, college presidents, and writers. Shepardson's main assignment was to spiff up the lobby, shuttered for a year. "It was the first event in which I had anything to do with the theaters," he recalled.[14]

On the appointed Saturday night, June 24, guests were serenaded under the Palace marquee by a five-piece Cleveland polka band. Once in the Grand Hall, they enjoyed cocktails and canapés before sitting down to dine on prime rib, Ohio corn, and local wines. They had nearly worked their way to dessert before the belated arrival of the guest of honor, Cleveland son Bob Hope. He entered to his theme song, "Thanks for the Memory," rendered by fiddler Rab Joska and his Gypsy Cellar band. "I've played the Palace Theater many times. But never in the lobby," wisecracked Hope. "I'm really happy to be here. But why didn't you get [Bing] Crosby?—he knew Moses Cleveland [*sic*] personally." Hostess Halle then proposed a toast to city founder Cleaveland, and another to a "Greater, Greater Cleveland."[15]

Halle and Shepardson were lucky their event went as smoothly as it did. Two days earlier, a reenactment of the city's actual founding met some unanticipated opposition on the banks of the Cuyahoga. Clay Herrick, president of the Early Settlers Association, prepared to disembark from the *Goodtime III* costumed as Moses Cleaveland, when he was confronted by a score of hostile Native Americans ordering him, "Go back!" Russell Means of the American Indian Movement led them, relenting only after being allowed to read a protest against the white man's destruction of the environment and to demand that money being spent on the Supersesquicentennial be reallocated toward "cleaning up the pollution brought to this virgin paradise by Moses Cleaveland and his followers." Mayor Carl B. Stokes tried to smooth over the disruption: "While it may be true that we all came here on different ships, you can be sure that we're all in the same boat now."[16]

Underneath the Supersesquicentennial hoopla lay the reality that Cleveland had little to feel complacent about in 1971. It was two years since the Cuyahoga River's burning had brought the city considerable unfavorable national attention and provided fuel for Russell Means's protest against pollution. The subsequent election of Stokes, the first African American mayor of a major American city, had briefly rehabilitated Cleveland as an exemplar of progress in racial relations. That distinction was short-lived, however, as the Glenville shootout the following year undercut the racial progress at City Hall. It left seven dead, including three policemen and three Black militants.[17]

Kay Halle went from the Supersesquicentennial back to Washington, while Ray Shepardson returned to his campaign to save Cleveland's downtown theaters. August found him making his pitch to the Rotary Club of Cleveland at the Hotel Statler Hilton. Noting that the theaters had opened on Cleveland's 125th birthday fifty years earlier, he foresaw a redeveloped Playhouse Square as a Cleveland version of New York's Lincoln Center or Washington's Kennedy Center. He reviewed his plans for the four theaters, which he was convinced would bring people downtown again "if there is something unique offered to them." Association membership was up to 250, still but a fraction of his original objective. He ended on a note of urgency: "We must act soon."[18]

Shepardson was faced with a chicken-or-the-egg conundrum: What was the point of restoring the theaters, if Clevelanders weren't coming downtown anymore? "By 1980, to most Americans going to the movies meant going to the mall," wrote movie historian Douglas Gomery. They were going to suburban shopping malls for most of their other needs, too. Even Lainie Hadden was skeptical at first.

"When I first met Ray and heard his pitch, I said: 'Mr. Shepardson, you are out of your mind. Nothing can be done for downtown Cleveland. It's too far gone,'" she recalled. "But eventually the spark caught in me." She became the first PSA president.[19]

Shepardson's networking began to bring in key volunteers, workers, and allies. That fall, he took a call from a part-time business student who had seen an interview he had given on WKYC. Cecilia Hartman was twenty-four, old enough to remember the pictures shown on the program from her teenage dates at the theaters. She told Shepardson she wanted to help save them, and he invited her to come down the following Saturday to his office in the Bulkley Building. There he put her to work on that and following Saturdays sending thank-you notes to new PSA members.[20]

When, after several weeks, Hartman asked Shepardson who did his books, he gave her a blank look as much as to say "What books?" The "books" consisted of a checkbook with a record of deposits and withdrawals. She volunteered to put the association's records in bookkeeping form and keep them up to date. In the words of lawyer Oliver Henkel, another early supporter, Shepardson "had the good sense to hire Ceil as the initial business manager." Like Shepardson with the Board of Education, Hartman quit her job as business manager for an auto dealer to work, full-time at far less pay and no benefits, for a rescue mission. "My employer thought I was out of my mind," she said, but "I was there because of my interest in saving the theaters." When Shepardson put her on the PSA payroll he asked, "How much do you need?"—not want, but *need*.[21]

No one sacrificed more in the early days of the movement than Shepardson. Hartman estimates that he took out only from $2,000 to $3,000 during the first year. He fell behind in his rent, but Chesterfield manager Drummond was understanding. He fell behind on payments for the Mercedes he had purchased while selling cars in Seattle, and it was repossessed. He called the dealer and evidently made his case, because he was told that he could reclaim it and pay when he could. One of his Chesterfield neighbors, Hungarian publisher Zoltan Gombos, would call and in his thick Magyar accent say, "Let's do dinner." Shepardson and Hartman would join him at Pat Joyce's, a popular restaurant and watering hole on Chester Avenue near East Twelfth. "When we would meet with Zoltan at P.J.'s it was the only time we had a decent meal during those early days," recalled Hartman.[22]

Born in Hungary, Gombos had emigrated to the United States in 1925. Having been an all-star high school soccer player in his native country, he became captain of the soccer team at Cleveland's Western Reserve University. He paid for his tuition by writing stories for Hungarian newspapers, and after graduation he became sportswriter and later night editor of *Szabadsag*, a Hungarian daily founded in Cleveland in 1890. Gombos purchased *Szabadsag* in 1939 and added other papers, Hungarian and English, to his portfolio. For a time, he also operated some of Cleveland's first foreign movie theaters, showing Hungarian, German, and Russian films on the east side, west side, and downtown. A silver-haired, European-style cosmopolite, he maintained that a "city cannot be sustained without cultural and entertainment events downtown."[23]

Testing the Waters

Gombos provided Shepardson with much more than a good meal. A charter PSA member, he was willing to sponsor an opportunity to see whether Clevelanders were ready to return to Playhouse Square. He proposed bringing in the touring Budapest Symphony for a concert and asked if Shepardson could provide a venue. The only one of the four theaters available and presentable enough at the time was the Allen, then under the control of the real estate partnership of Michael L. Miller and Benjamin F. Cappadora, or Millcap Corporation, owners of the Bulkley Building. They leased the theater to Shepardson on a per-event basis, and Gombos agreed to underwrite the cost of the concert.[24]

In little more than a year, the PSA was prepared to demonstrate the viability of its vision. Shepardson transitioned from promoter to producer. He was not a complete novice to show business, having initiated a series of cultural programs at his alma mater, Seattle Pacific College. His experience encompassed everything from renting halls and booking presenters to selling tickets. In preparation for his Cleveland debut, he moved the PSA office from the Bulkley Building's fourth floor down to the former manager's office in the Allen, off the lobby's Romanesque rotunda.[25]

The prospect of something happening again in the dark theaters piqued community interest. William F. Miller announced the concert in the *Plain Dealer*, describing Gombos's role and Shepardson's plans. While Shepardson expressed hopes of converting the Allen into a three-screen cinema within a year, he intended to use it over the next ten months for a variety of events, from classical music to rock, to see if Clevelanders would come downtown. Two weeks before the concert, and only four hours after being sworn in at City Hall to succeed Carl Stokes, Mayor Ralph Perk showed up in front of the Allen Theatre on Euclid Avenue. Awaiting him under the marquee were a stepladder, a bucket of paint, and a brush. Clad in blue suit and blue overcoat, the mayor mounted the ladder and applied a few ceremonial dabs of white paint to the weathered marquee, along with a few drops on his coat and a couple of spectators below.[26] It may have been a foretaste of the accident-prone mayor's administration, noted for a photo-op in which, wielding a blowtorch, he set his own hair on fire.

Perk returned on November 21 for a pre-concert reception at Stouffer's Playhouse Square restaurant, a few doors from the Allen's marquee. Most of the three hundred invited guests were PSA members. Magyar violinists provided appropriate mood music, and Hungarian delicacies added ethnic flavor to the buffet dinner. "There were furs, swept-up coiffures and hats on the ladies and hand-kissing was de rigueur amid the punch cups," noted Marjorie Alge in the *Press*. "I remember these theaters when I was courting Mrs. Perk," said the mayor. "We would come once a week and it was a big event."[27]

Straight from his inauguration at City Hall, Mayor Ralph Perk showed up at Playhouse Square to apply a few strokes of paint to the Allen Theatre marquee (and a few drops to his coat as well) in advance of the Budapest Symphony concert. (Photo by Timothy Culek, Courtesy of *Cleveland Press* Collection, Michael Schwartz Library, Cleveland State University)

Nearly three thousand Clevelanders ventured out on a blustery evening to fill the Allen for the concert, though Ceil Hartman suspects that Gombos liberally "papered the house." Hungarian Girl Scouts in traditional dress passed out programs. Robert Finn, music critic for the *Plain Dealer*, found the acoustics dry, the theater cold and drafty, and the program notes disastrous. Applause between movements indicated that it was not your usual classical music audience. "But none of these things really matter. The important thing is that the concert took place at all," he wrote. Finn paid chief credit for the evening's success to a man whose name wasn't even listed in the program:

> Shepardson has worked long and hard against all kinds of obstacles, but principally against two: pervasive community apathy and lack of money. He is still a long way from his objective. One symphony concert does not make a downtown Renaissance. But a successful start has been made. Shepardson has been dismissed as an impractical kid, a brash, wet-behind-the-ears outsider, by many who have never lifted a finger to help rescue Playhouse Square from decline. If that is so, it seems we could use a couple dozen more impractical kids like him, and maybe things could get done in this city's cultural life that have sadly needed doing for years. I take my hat off to the man.[28]

For the time being there was only one Shepardson, joined by a handful of like-minded zealots. Over the following half year, they managed to light up the Allen with more than a dozen events. At the end of the year, with a grant from the 9–18 Corporation, they brought in the Sierra Leone Dance Company, which drew in ten thousand people for ten performances. Gombos put Shepardson in touch with a Czech film producer, who booked the movie *Adrift* for a twelve-day run. It drew poorly, however, despite an outlay of several thousand dollars for new projection equipment. In March, a failure in the theater's heating system forced cancellation of a concert by the Prague Symphony Orchestra. "What is really needed is major financial support from the business community," said Shepardson in frustration. "We are still awaiting that and can't understand why we don't get it." The desired businessmen were reported to believe Shepardson was too visionary about the theaters.[29]

One segment of the community beginning to line up behind Shepardson was the media. Finn followed his Budapest Symphony review with a full-page spread in the Sunday *Plain Dealer* under a head stylized as a theater marquee: "Will the Lights Go on Again in Playhouse Square?" It reviewed Shepardson's plans for the four theaters, with the aid of a diagram juxtaposing their locations within the city block of Playhouse Square. Assisting Shepardson was a staff of five, supported by 438 PSA members, including doctors, lawyers, dentists, architects, newspapermen, a cocktail waitress, several suburban mayors, and a visiting photographer from San Francisco who "saw the theaters and got interested in what we were doing." Finn noted that other cities—such as Pittsburgh, Akron, and St. Louis—had recently converted old theaters into concert halls. "If sheer willpower could revive Playhouse Square, Ray Shepardson would have accomplished it long ago," Finn wrote. "He is still hanging in there, hoping for eventual recognition from those who have more than willpower to offer."[30]

Those with more than willpower still held back, while those with nothing more continued to respond. A teenager named Frank Dutton read Finn's article on Sunday and on the following Friday went downtown after school and reported for service to Ceil Hartman in the Allen Theatre. She told him to return Saturday morning, when he joined a small band of workers, some on a volunteer basis and others for varied forms of compensation. Ralph "Smitty" Smith was a thirty-nine-year-old general handyman actually living in an old office on the Allen mezzanine. Weldon Carpenter was a collector of theater memorabilia and former chef who had moved from Columbus to become part of the Playhouse Square restoration.[31]

Dutton's first day on the job proved to be a baptism under fire, as it was the morning of a concert appearance by the Irish actor and singer Richard Harris. "I dusted seats and filled popcorn boxes that day," said Dutton. His first encounter with Shepardson was brief, as the impresario "was running around like crazy." That evening, "just before the doors opened, Ray shoves a cash box into my hands, says 'You're in charge,' and quickly disappears." He found himself in control of the concession stand without a clue even of what prices to charge. Fortunately Gordon Bell, a college friend who had followed Shepardson from Seattle to Cleveland, passed by and told Dutton simply to charge twenty-five cents for everything. "Ray at first seemed kinetic, [I] hardly saw him the first couple of days I was there," recalled Dutton, "he usually flew by in a blur."[32]

As for the concert, a "near-capacity audience" undoubtedly released Gombos from another commitment to underwrite any loss. "Playhouse Square and the Allen Theater got another shot in the arm Saturday night," wrote *Plain Dealer* drama critic Peter Bellamy. "The size of the audience was even more impressive because the

Allen's attraction was competing against the Sportsmen's Show at Public Auditorium and 'Jesus Christ Superstar' at the Music Hall." Supported by a thirty-two-piece orchestra, the multitalented Harris sang popular ballads, recited his own poetry, told stories, and showed a clip from his appearance as King Arthur in the movie version of *Camelot*. Bellamy thought he was "one of the most relaxed performers one will ever see. . . . He sings and talks sometimes while sitting down or lying flat on his back on the stage."[33]

Ten days later, an act, and presumably an audience, of a different nature came to the Allen. Sally Rand was the headliner for a "Senior Frolic" that drew twenty-two hundred golden agers to a special matinee. Rand, who had first gained notoriety at Chicago's Century of Progress nearly forty years earlier, was now a sixty-eight-year-old senior herself but could still display a reported 35–23–34 figure. She reprised her historic act clad in blue light and two deftly manipulated ostrich feathers. "Does she or doesn't she?" asked Jane Scott in the *Plain Dealer*. "Wear a body-stocking that is." Her question went unanswered.[34]

Mayor Perk made an onstage appearance to present Miss Rand with the key to the city. He also serenaded her with two off-key verses of "Till We Meet Again." Rand recalled playing in Cleveland at the Palace Theatre, whose lobby she compared favorably with those of La Scala in Italy and New York's recently demolished Roxy Theater. "I wish we would keep the buildings we have, instead of tearing them down," she told the audience. "Let's save what we've got."[35] There was a second performance that evening for the general public.

Some of the other attractions in Shepardson's Allen Theatre series included an Up With People concert and a children's program based on the Yogi Bear and Flintstones cartoon characters. There were rock concerts, some provided by Belkin Productions. These included appearances by Dave Mason, JoJo Gunn, and Jeff Beck. "Usually for Allen shows I worked the candy stand," said Dutton. "We would get big bags of pre-popped [popcorn] for $2 a bag, we'd get about 50 boxes per bag, and sell them at 25¢ a box. . . . We'd sell a lot of stuff before the show, especially if it was a rock show, intermissions were absolutely crazy."[36] Concessions usually provided the profit margins for events in the early days.

Cleveland State University (CSU) also provided speakers. Catholic bishop Fulton J. Sheen was scheduled one afternoon, followed the same evening by radical Black activist Angela Davis. Some of the Bulkley Building tenants protested against the controversy surrounding the Davis appearance. "Millcap wasn't happy about

Angela; they said that's it," said Hartman.[37] That soon brought the Allen Theatre experiment to an end, but Shepardson was confronted with a far more existential crisis.

Sounding the Alarm

It was the headline that galvanized Cleveland. For most Clevelanders, seeing it spread across the front page of a newspaper was analogous to Ray Shepardson's spotting that mural from the State Theater on the front cover of *Life* magazine. It was a wake-up call.

Right below the nameplate of the *Cleveland Plain Dealer*, datelined Thursday, May 25, 1972, italic letters announced: *"Loew's Ohio and State Theaters to Be Razed."* According to Ceil Hartman, Shepardson had orchestrated the story, written by William F. Miller. "He was pleased as can be about the banner head." Evidently the story had leaked out of a meeting of the Fine Arts Advisory Committee to the City Planning Commission, when an architect appeared with plans for a parking lot at East Fourteenth and Euclid. "We drew out that the idea was to tear down the theaters" recalled architect Peter van Dijk, a committee member. "The guy was ashamed to mention this, of course." Telling the architect to come back with a better looking plan, the committee bought the theaters a couple of more weeks.[38]

Miller's story reported that the two theaters, as well as the Loew's Building linking their elongated lobbies to Euclid Avenue, would shortly be demolished to make way for an eighty-eight-thousand-square-foot parking lot. One of the Loew's Building's two remaining tenants, an Arthur Murray Dance Studio occupying the space that had once quartered the Stage Door Canteen, had already been given its marching orders. "I have a very good business here and I don't want to leave," said manager Victor Dominic. "But I was told to find other quarters." The property was under the ownership of the Millcap Corporation, owner of the neighboring Bulkley Building. "We just can't go on forever keeping those buildings empty," said partner Michael Miller of the Loew's complex. "We'd like to do something to save them, but nothing has happened."[39]

Millcap had originally acquired the Loew properties as junior partners of Halle's department store. At the urging of Shepardson and two other Clevelanders, Chisholm Halle had formed Cleveland Downtown Properties, Inc., with Miller and Cappadora to purchase the two theaters. Halle's not only put up 75 percent of the $200,000 purchase price but advanced Millcap its share of the down payment. The department store would sink an additional $300,000 into the properties just to maintain them. In the meantime, Halle's was merged into Marshall Field & Co. of Chicago, and in March 1972 Field's instructed Chisholm Halle to liquidate the store's interest in the two theaters. That left Millcap in full ownership and in need of realizing a return on its investment.[40]

Miller described Halle's original motivation in buying the properties as having been one of maintaining the Playhouse Square neighborhood. "It's now a horrible eyesore," Chisholm Halle told the reporter. "I see the demolition and future development as a positive move for everybody's benefit." Halle's "everybody" wouldn't have included Shepardson and PSA, who were reported to "have resorted to patching holes in the Loew's Building roof to prevent water damage in the theaters." They had been unsuccessful, however, in attracting investors to support their preservation plans, and Shepardson described matters as a "crisis situation."[41]

Shepardson shifted into crisis mode to stave off the wrecking ball. On the day following the *Plain Dealer* article, he appeared on the Alan Douglas show over WEWS-TV to review the history of Playhouse Square and his plans for its revival. He was thinking of another season at the Allen, explaining that "using the Allen keeps interest alive in the area." If the State and Ohio were torn down, however, he told Tony Mastroianni of the *Press*, he would be left with only a film center in the Allen and concert hall in the Palace. There would be no restaurant or nightclub in between. With his attention focused on the endangered Loew's theaters, the Allen would be relegated to a back burner.[42]

Even as Shepardson worked to save the State and Ohio from complete demolition, his volunteers were working to preserve what still remained. Frank Dutton and Ralph Smith would ask the elevator attendant in the Bulkley Building for the keys to the Ohio so they could continue work on the roof. "Helen would always tell me I was wasting my time working on buildings that would soon be torn down," remembered Dutton. "Stuff started disappearing out of both Loew houses." He and Smitty took the precaution of removing the leaded glass exit signs from the two theaters.[43]

"It must be admitted, the plan to save the Ohio and State is something of a long shot," editorialized the *Plain Dealer*. But it made little sense to replace them with parking lots in the absence of attractions to bring in traffic. "No one comes downtown just to patronize a parking lot," it concluded. A letter from a tenant in the

Hanna Building echoed that reasoning. "If we persist in tearing the heart out of Cleveland no one will have any need or desire to drive into the city," he wrote. A writer from Euclid made the point with heavy irony, calling for the razing of Public Square, the Soldiers' and Sailors' Monument, the Arcade, and the Terminal Tower. "Let's raze Cleveland!" he fulminated. "Let's make it the largest parking lot in the world."[44]

It was only a month since the closing of Bonwit Teller, the upscale ladies' apparel store just west of the Bulkley Building in Playhouse Square. "We just couldn't beat the downtown situation," said Bonwit Teller's president, William Fine. "After 4 P.M. we might as well have been closed. Our shoppers, the fashionable women, weren't venturing downtown." Women from out of town, he noted, also were no longer accompanying their husbands for business trips or conventions. As the letter writer from the Hanna Building had lamented, "Why must we perpetuate the half-truth that the only excitement after dark in Cleveland is the fear of being mugged?"[45]

One positive and potentially weighty response to the demolition threat was the reorganization of the PSA's board of directors. The new board included such business and professional leaders as Lee Howley of the Cleveland Electric Illuminating Company and Hugh Calkins, a partner in the Jones, Day, Gockley & Revals law firm. Other directors were John E. Porta, president of Union Commerce Bank; Willis M. McFarlane, president of Associated Inns & Restaurants Corp. of America; and Mrs. Scott R. "Gwill" York, past president of the Junior League. Speaking for the group were Osborne C. Dodson Jr., property manager with Ostendorf-Morris Co., and Edward H. deConingh Jr., vice president of Mueller Electric Co. Dodson announced that the board was working on an economically sound plan to save the theaters. If a business arrangement proved unfeasible, however, deConingh held out the prospect of the theaters' surrender to the wreckers.[46]

Woman Power

Behind the predominantly male face of the new board lay a determined female backbone. Gwill York of the Junior League was far from a token appointment. League members were credited with having worked with the PSA to recruit members of the business community for its board. Many of the league's members had been among the earliest PSA members. Lainie Hadden was not only its first president but a past president of the Junior League as well.[47]

Founded in 1912, the Junior League of Cleveland was dedicated to developing the potential of women by promoting volunteerism. Through the years, its programs of community improvement had included maintaining a low-rent residence for working women, providing milk stations during the Depression, and conducting savings bond drives during World War II. Early in 1972, the league launched its first Decorators' Showhouse, in which local interior decorators were invited to practice their craft in the rooms of an area home. The showhouse that first year had been the Eells residence on Denton Drive in Cleveland Heights. It was opened to the public, which contributed $65,000 to the league's coffers.[48] Not inclined to nurse their nest egg, the women were now poised to break out of the box.

On the morning the *Plain Dealer* announced the impending doom of the State and Ohio theaters, Lainie Hadden met Virginia Felderman at the airport with a copy of William Miller's front-page article. Felderman was succeeding Hadden as president of the Junior League, which would be having its annual meeting within a few days. Nine days after his first story, Miller had another front-page scoop: "Junior League Pledges Cash to Save Theaters."[49]

Learning at their annual meeting that the recent Decorators' Showcase had increased their treasury so substantially, the league voted almost unanimously to make a $25,000 grant to the PSA's efforts to save the State and Ohio theaters. It was the largest single grant the local league had ever made and well outside the usual pursuits of any Junior League chapter. As Lainie Hadden would testify, however, it wasn't in any way a spur-of-the-moment decision. Shepardson had been proselytizing among its members for months, and they had given his campaign considerable research. "We knew that the buildings contained irreplaceable coffered ceilings, marvelous murals, marble mantelpieces, staircases, columns and woodwork fashioned by European artisans no longer available," she said. In contrast to the previous indifference of business support, Hadden saw the league's action as an example of "the growing power of women. We could see that what Ray was trying to do was a valid idea."[50]

Mrs. Hadden's feminism never strayed far from the Junior League idea of civic involvement. Even as late as 1972, newspaper accounts of the league's gift referred to its leaders as Mrs.

Elaine "Lainie" Hadden (pictured with Ray Shepardson) cited the campaign to save Playhouse Square as an example of "the growing power of women." The Junior League's $25,000 grant was a seminal contribution to the cause. (Photo by Frank Reed, Courtesy of *Cleveland Press* Collection, Michael Schwartz Library, Cleveland State University)

Kenneth I. Felderman and Mrs. John A. Hadden Jr. Born Elaine Dowling Grasselli into Cleveland's Grasselli Chemical Company family, Elaine, "Lainie," majored in English at Vassar College and joined the league shortly after her graduation. In 1955, she married John Hadden, a distinguished child psychiatrist affiliated with University Hospitals. Lainie Hadden would become a major supporter of the Hanna Perkins Center, a therapeutic preschool in Shaker Heights. She would also become the first female director of a Cleveland bank, the Union Commerce, and chair the Board of Overseers at Case Western Reserve University. Above all, however, she would be recognized for her unflinching support of Ray Shepardson. "There are some mobilizing forces that all of a sudden blend people together into an irresistible force, and that's what happened with the Junior League at that point," she observed.[51] Much of that force was due to Lainie Hadden.

Hartman believed Shepardson had been working with Hadden to secure the league's intervention. His reaction to the news at least showed signs of prior thought. "It looks like the ball has started to roll rather than to swing," he said. To the best of Hartman's recollection, the league's gift was probably largely applied to a rental payment for the two theaters to keep Millcap's head above water. Actually, the wrecking ball was neither swinging nor rolling as yet, but in suspension. In announcing the action taken by the league, president Felderman stressed the need for at least an additional $75,000 to be raised in order to save the theaters.[52] The league's $25,000 was more a morale booster than an actual turning point. The wrecking ball would remain in a state of suspension for the remainder of that year.

A two-page spread in the *Press Showtime* supplement of July 21 examined the past, present, and future of Playhouse Square. Feature writer Dick McLaughlin reviewed the storied history, beginning with the "golden bloom" of theater openings half a century in the past. Outside the theaters he remembered Korner & Wood's book store, Beattie jewelers, Huyler's confectionary shop, and Frank Monaco's restaurant in the Hanna Building. McLaughlin closed with the depressing news that Stouffer's Playhouse Square restaurant would close at the end of the month. Drama critic Mastroianni reported that PSA membership had reached 500, but the estimated price tag for Shepardson's plans had also increased to $7 million. PSA board member Osborne Dodson said that the association would have to be restructured from a social club into a charitable or educational institution in order to qualify for foundation grants. Shepardson figured they had only thirty to sixty days left to save the State and Ohio.

Saving them made no sense to *Press* real estate writer Ray De Crane, however. "The long-range future of the area is believed to be in first-rate office buildings, plush apartment buildings and specialty stores," he wrote. "But not entertainment centers. The once bright era of stage shows, name bands, and first-run movies is over." De Crane saw the two partners of Millcap as representative of "a new breed in downtown building ownership." Bids had been taken on demolition of the two theaters at a cost of $175,000, he reported. The land would then be paved to provide parking for 260 cars, the revenue from which would end the owners' "current cash drain." The land itself could "only increase in value as time goes on."[53]

De Crane's newspaper wasn't so ready to pave Playhouse Square. Four days later the *Press* editorialized that "Those who see downtown's future entirely in terms of office buildings and apartments are missing the fact that night-time entertainment is a vital ingredient, too. If that is missing, Cleveland gets the reputation of being Dullsville." Recalling Shepardson's hopeful discussion of his plans at the Rotary Club the previous summer, the *Press* soberly observed that "Today Playhouse Square is much closer to being Parking Lot Square than it was a year ago." Shepardson and the Junior League needed more support in their efforts to save the theaters, said the *Press*. Mayor Perk and his administration needed to give more than lip service; they needed to become "deeply involved." And perhaps above all, "At this point some wealthy backers must come forward."[54]

Shepardson and his Junior League allies were already working on that last point. A major tennis tournament coming to Cleveland gave them an opportunity to widen their network by sponsoring a "Classic Finale" party at the Allen Theatre in August. The tournament itself was part of the World Championship Tennis tour, which would bring thirty-two professionals to Public Hall for the seven-day Cleveland Classic. Locally it was sponsored by the Junior Woman's Committee of the Cleveland Orchestra for the benefit of the orchestra. The "Classic Finale" party was undertaken by the Junior League working in tandem with PSA. Scheduled for the Saturday night between the tournament's semifinals and finals, its three-fold purpose was described as "to entertain the tennis champions and propel people to the Playhouse Square area as well as promote downtown." Speaking on behalf of the league was party cochair Barbara deConingh. "We pledged time and effort as well as $25,000," she said.[55]

Dutton, Smitty, and their fellow volunteers got to work getting the Allen in shape for the event. The stage was converted into a dance floor with the aid of stage lights "scrounged up" from the State. A cooking area was improvised out of lumber and heavy plastic in the alleyway between the Allen and the Seltzer Building. Tickets were priced at $6 at the door, and refreshments included beer, wine, and a Chinese buffet. The pop group Woodsmoke with M. Melinda Myer provided music for dancing on the stage, while a local society band, "Trevor Guys and Doll," played Dixieland in the rotunda.[56]

Guests on August 12 began trickling in at 9 P.M., though most of the five hundred guests arrived around 11:30 following the semifinals at Public Hall. One disappointment was the scarcity of tennis players, most of whom had left town after being eliminated. More important, however, was the presence of many of the town's movers and shakers, who, after talking tennis, turned their attention to "the lively Allen Theater, which was decorated in red, white and blue, and the lighted Playhouse Square, reminiscent of past years." In retrospect, Dutton saw the "Classic Finale" as a turning point. "The event was a rousing success and was a pivotal moment in which the Junior League started to lobby on our behalf," he said. "The fruits of this event would be apparent in the months and years ahead."[57]

The immediate weeks ahead didn't appear too fruitful, however. Just days prior to the party a secretary walking along Playhouse Square had been struck by a crumbling piece from the Loew's Ohio marquee. She suffered minor injuries, the sidewalk in front of the theater was barricaded, and the building's owners were said to be expecting "to raze the movie theater eventually and operate a parking lot there." At the end of August another Playhouse Square restaurant, the Colonnade, served its last meal after forty-one years in the Bulkley Building. Its closing came a month after Stouffer's had called it quits. "We don't see any way that the business can come back," commented Carroll H. Chapin, president of the Colonnade chain. "There just aren't the people there anymore."[58]

Messrs. Miller and Cappadora were becoming impatient to turn their theaters into a parking lot. A lawyer from Jones, Day, Reavis & Pogue, on behalf of the Junior League, worked to put roadblocks in their path. Oliver "Pudge" Henkel had been involved in efforts to save the theaters almost from the beginning. He had seconded Shepardson in persuading Chis Halle to purchase the theaters following their closing. Between buying and moving into the Eells house in Cleveland Heights, he and his wife Sally had turned it over to the Junior League for the Decorators' Showcase that raised the money the league granted to Playhouse Square. Soon after the *Plain Dealer*'s story on the theaters' threatened destruction, Henkel went to City Hall to seek a delay in the granting of a permit for a Euclid Avenue curb cut allowing cars to drive into the proposed parking lot. "It seemed like a flimsy kind of argument, but he made it seem like the Grand Canyon," recalled Lainie Hadden. And it bought time.[59]

But the countdown to D-Day continued. In September Henkel went before the City Planning Commission seeking a forty-five-day delay on Millcap's demolition permit on behalf of the PSA. "We are trying to put together a financial package, and renderings of what we intend to do," said Henkel. "Demolition would be premature, and the existence of the theaters is very important to the long-range rejuvenation of the Playhouse Square area." A report submitted by the PSA planning board raised the possibility of converting the theaters into a "complex of performing arts, film and popular entertainment and dining facilities." Speaking for Millcap, Michael Miller agreed to a thirty-day reprieve and said negotiations with PSA to see if the theaters could be used economically would continue.[60]

While Pudge Henkel fenced with Millcap, the Junior League continued to drum up support for the theaters. "After the tennis party, things did start to move," said Dutton, who recalled "more parties over the next several months, all in the Palace lobby that fall, for a number of different organizations." If the league's original gift was intended to be a "trigger mechanism," in Lainie Hadden's words, in time it had the desired effect. "Gwill York and I asked for matching funds," she recalled. Six donors, or angels, in show business terms, stepped up to match the league's $25,000 commitment. John and Lainie Hadden did more than match it. "My husband said, 'Let's give $50,000,'" said Lainie. The list of $25,000 angels included Dick Baker of Ernst & Young; Ray Armington, board chairman of the Cleveland Foundation; Alfred Rankin, president of the Cleveland Orchestra's Musical Arts Association; and R. Livingston Ireland, retired chairman of Hanna Coal.[61]

One final match came from an outwardly unlikely source. A couple of years earlier, Don Grogan had seen nothing amiss about converting the Ohio and State theaters into office buildings. As owner of the Hanna Building complex, his Hanna Theatre had the last remaining lighted marquee on Playhouse Square. Nonetheless, the genial Irishman was sincerely devoted to the entire neighborhood, earning him the sobriquet of "Mayor of Playhouse Square." He just didn't see much hope in reviving mass entertainment downtown, his usual reference to Ray Shepardson being "He's mad as a hatter." Lainie Hadden recalled that it took "a certain amount of urging" to enlist his support as an angel. "I still think you're mad as a hatter," said Grogan to Shepardson as he turned over his check for $25,000.[62]

Six members of the PSA board formed a Playhouse Square Operating Company to formulate a long-range plan for the theaters. Headed by Willis McFarlane, the group included Hugh Calkins, Gwill York, John Porta, Edward deConingh, and Lainie Hadden. Armed now with a war chest and the prospect of loans, they returned to the negotiating table to work out a deal with Cleveland Downtown Properties Inc., as the theater owners were now constituted. They emerged with a five-year lease for the Loew's Building and the State and Ohio theaters at an estimated cost of $50,000 a year. "We are just as uncertain now as we were six months ago whether there is any plan that will be economically sound," said Calkins. "All that we have done is to buy time in which we can try to decide whether something constructive can be done." DeConingh added, "The important thing is that they [the State and Ohio] will not be torn down."[63] Not for the next five years, anyway.

Following seven tension-filled months, 1973 opened without the shadow of the wrecking ball looming over Playhouse Square. Members of the PSA board set about devising a plan to keep it away. Ray Shepardson and Ceil Hartman took in a show.

"Didn't Know You Had a Cabaret"

In the long-winded titular style of that day, the show was *Jacques Brel Is Alive and Well and Living in Paris*. While Oliver Henkel was squeezing a thirty-day demolition reprieve out of Michael Miller the previous September, *Jacques Brel* was closing the Berea Summer Theater's season with a two-week run. It was directed by CSU's Joseph J. Garry Jr. and featured a cast of four singers. "The production has no plot, consisting of a little dialogue and many songs," wrote Peter Bellamy in the *Plain Dealer*. "They treat of angels and devils, of dreams and hope, of despair and the hell of war. They also deal with youth, old age, drunks, prostitutes, dogs, rainbows, cotton candy, carousels, and calliopes." Bellamy "urgently recommended" Clevelanders see *Jacques Brel*.[64]

Those who missed it in Berea were soon given a second chance when Garry revived *Brel* the following winter at CSU. Under the aegis of the school's theater department, it was presented in the Main Classroom Building's five-hundred-seat lecture hall by the original Berea cast: Providence Hollander, David O. Frazier, Cliff Bemis, and Theresa Piteo—a quartet fated to be legendary in Cleveland theater lore. Garry recalled that he hadn't liked the show after first seeing it in London, "and only after hearing David [Frazier] play the recording for five years did I consent to direct the musical. Then I grew to love it." Bemis, however, guaranteed the production's local immortality with a telephone call to Ray Shepardson. "Cliff Bemis called Ray and asked him to come see the show," said Cecilia Hartman, "with the idea of continuing the show in Playhouse Square."[65]

Shepardson took Hartman to see *Jacques Brel* on its final night at CSU and, according to Lainie Hadden, was "blown away" by it. Instead of going home, he walked with Hartman, half a dozen blocks through the frigid winter night, straight to the State Theatre. Hartman remembered him pacing back and forth in the cavernous lobby and having "it" figured out within half an hour. "That's where Ray's genius was—finding space and using space," she said. He called Joe Garry the following day and said he wanted Garry to come and do *Brel* in his cabaret. "I didn't know you had a cabaret," said Garry, to which Shepardson responded: "We will."[66]

Garry's first reaction to the future cabaret site was far from encouraging. "It has to be one of two things: a gambling casino or a brothel," he said of the stripped down State lobby. Dutton recalled six weeks of steadily intensifying labor to turn the space into the Playhouse Square Cabaret. He and another volunteer spent weeks removing up to eight coats of black paint from the lobby's marble baseboards. Five hundred yards of carpeting were purchased to cover the 180-foot grand lobby. Since this was to be a dinner theater, new kitchen equipment was installed in a former restaurant adjacent to the outer lobby.[67]

The loftier regions of the inner lobby also required considerable work. Dust and dirt had to be vacuumed from the lighting troughs just below the ceiling. The theater's engineer, on duty since the 1920s, restored the overhead steam heating system. A team of artists climbed scaffolding to touch up or restore faded and peeling sections of the ceiling. Missing from the original vault were three large chandeliers, believed to have been sold off to "somewhere in Akron." Shepardson found suitable replacements serendipitously when looking for a piano on Mayfield Road. Composed of polished crystal and burnished brass, the trio had once illuminated Toledo's former Commodore Perry Hotel, and the keyboard dealer had purchased them along with some pianos and had stored them since 1938.[68]

That left the problem of a stage, which the lobby naturally had never needed. An old theater saying goes that all that's needed to put on a play are a platform and a passion. Shepardson may have had the passion, but it fell to Garry and Ralph Smith to devise the platform. They constructed a stage in the center of the lobby's eastern wall. Viewed to the north, the audience would form a large capital *C* around the performing area, seated at tables largely scrounged from the closed Black Angus restaurant on Huron Road. Smitty cannibalized the scaffolding of the State's old Cinerama screen to support the base of the new stage. Framing for the stage was fashioned from the aluminum framing of the Ohio's screen. On a frigid Sunday, Smitty and Dutton hammered the stage together. "It was so cold in both the Loew houses that winter," said Dutton, "cold enough to see your breath."[69]

Garry now had a stage on which to freshen up his show. The former ladies room on the State mezzanine served as a unisex dressing room for the tried-and-true cast: Piteo, Hollander, Frazier, and Bemis. Workers continued sprucing up the State lobby, mopping floors and polishing the brass railings on the twin marble staircases. All the activity piqued the curiosity of Euclid Avenue passersby, who would press their noses against the glass on the outer lobby doors to see what was going on in the long-dark theater.[70]

Four weeks before opening, Shepardson and Hartman took a break to get married. The wedding took place on March 22 in the west side residence of Paul Briggs, the man responsible for bringing Shepardson to Cleveland. *Brel* was scheduled to open on Wednesday, April 18, for two preview performances attended by PSA members and "other wheels." (It was in the middle of Holy Week, traditionally not a good theater week.) Hartman recalled Ray running around to neighboring restaurants on opening night to borrow ashtrays. "We didn't really know what we were doing—just flying by the seat of our pants," she said.[71] Nonetheless, Shepardson had succeeded in conjuring up his cabaret.

Bellamy wrote a preview in the *Plain Dealer* the day before the public opening on April 20, in which he took note of the one stretch of the 180-foot lobby that hadn't needed replacement or repair, namely the four 10-by-40-foot murals of James Daugherty. He mentioned that *The Spirit of Cinema America*, pictured below his article, had appeared on the cover of *Life* three years earlier.[72] Unmentioned was that if it weren't for that mural, the State lobby might well have been gone by 1973.

A Palpable Hit

Cleveland's critics unanimously bestowed what can only be described as rave reviews on *Jacques Brel*. "A show that is truly good is one that is filled with moments you take away with you," wrote Mastroianni in the *Press*. "This one has more than its share." Praising the "fluidity

Providence Hollander and Theresa Piteo comprised the feminine half of *Jacques Brel's* four-member cast. Hollander (*left*) stopped the show "not once, but several times," in the words of one critic; Piteo was singled out for her "look of innocence that can turn momentarily wicked with a toss of . . . her waist-length hair," to quote *Press* critic Tony Mastroianni. (Courtesy of *Cleveland Press* Collection, Michael Schwartz Library, Cleveland State University)

and excellent timing" of Garry's direction, the *Plain Dealer's* Bellamy avowed that "a musical with more intelligent, civilized comment on life, love, tragedy and the sins and woes of this planet will seldom be encountered."[73]

All four of the troubadours came in for their share of the kudos. Theresa Piteo won Mastroianni's notice as "a lady with a lilting voice" and a "look of innocence that can turn momentarily wicked with a toss of her head and her waist-length hair." Bellamy praised Cliff Bemis for his "fast-developing, warm voice and youthful magnetism" and compared David Frazier with Alfred Drake as "a take-charge man."[74]

Both critics, however, saved their highest accolades for Providence Hollander. "She stops the show not once, but several times," noted Mastroianni. Calling her the "long-time queen of community singers in Greater Cleveland," Bellamy stated she had "reached her zenith in this show." She possessed "the most moving, heartbreaking catch in her throat this side of Barbra Streisand and the late Judy Garland," he wrote. "She is so small, so eternally feminine and so vulnerable. She tears herself apart even as she does the audience."[75]

Besides the cast and show, the critics gave due notice to the venue. "Consider the setting—the inner lobby of old Loews State, now filled with tables and people who have just dined and are still sipping a drink," said Mastroianni. "The air is smoky, sometimes a little too much so." Bellamy outdid his *Press* colleague in scene painting:

> With a room as spacious and spectacular as almost any palace in Europe and a musical as good as any to be found off Broadway, the new Playhouse Square Cabaret Theater has opened in a blaze of glory.
>
> Located in the lobby of the old Loew's State Theater, one of the largest lobbies in the world, the vast room is so stately and royal one expects a liveried footman to appear at any moment at the top of the grand double staircase to announce the arrival of royalty.
>
> It is probably the only dinner theater extant with a marble fireplace large enough for a table for two.[76]

Cabaret-goers entered the State not through the traditional Euclid Avenue doors but via the East Seventeenth Street exit, across the street from the Playhouse Square garage, which offered free parking for the show. Traversing the rear of the auditorium, they passed between the two mezzanine staircases into the grand lobby. There were five shows a week, with tickets for dinner and the show priced from $7.75 to $9.75 on Wednesday, Thursday, and Sunday, and $9.75 to $11.75 for Friday and Saturday. Paul Hom's Chinese catering business prepared dinner. Admittedly no gourmet, Bellamy judged the food "satisfactorily palatable with plenty of meat in it." Acoustics were problematic on the extreme ends of the long lobby, however, leading to the cancellation of Wednesday and Thursday shows the second week for improvements to be made.[77]

Critical acclaim continued to come in from commentators such as Pat Jenkins in *Scene* and Howard Wertheimer on radio station WERE. Perhaps the most influential plaudit came a week after the opening from Cleveland novelist Don Robertson, who also did television commentary and had a regular column in the *Press*. In the latter, he described how, "on a small black stage that had been constructed on one side of the old lobby, four perfectly lovely people . . . made perhaps the most powerful contact with an audience I have ever experienced." He found the acoustics fine, at least from his table, the food "more than adequate," and "a sort of panache" to the entire evening that gave him thoughts of Playhouse Square rising from its ruins. "I go to a lot of shows, and sometimes I become quite jaded," he confessed. "But this production of 'Jacques Brel' hit me smack in the gut. If you care anything about theater, you absolutely cannot afford to miss it."[78]

According to Oliver Henkel, *Brel* was produced on a budget of $30,000 and booked for a three-week run. Reaction to the reviews and perhaps word-of-mouth swiftly caused a change of plans. Weekends began selling out two weeks in advance, and even weekday attendance was pronounced "excellent" for "a downtown area that generally is asleep after 6 P.M." By June, nearly eight thousand Clevelanders had returned to the State Theatre lobby, and the run had been extended to June 24. "The Playhouse Square Cabaret is alive and well in Cleveland and doing a smashing business in a lo-

An army of volunteers transformed a somewhat shabby State Theatre lobby into the swank Playhouse Square Cabaret. Guests enjoyed a preshow dinner on tables surrounding the playing area. (Courtesy of Cleveland Public Library Photograph Collection)

Ray Shepardson took to an improvised stage on April 18, 1973, to introduce the first State Theatre Cabaret performance of *Jacques Brel Is Alive and Well and Living in Paris*. He would happily repeat the job more than five hundred times. (Courtesy of *Cleveland Press* Collection, Michael Schwartz Library, Cleveland State University)

cation the demolition boys wanted to turn into a parking lot last year," wrote William Miller in the *Plain Dealer*. It appeared that the only thing that might stop it was the summer heat in the uncooled lobby. To keep the cast comfortable under the stage lights, Shepardson placed dry ice in buckets on the edge of the stage, with fans to blow cool air on the performers. At the end of June, he cancelled shows for a few days to install an air-conditioning system. It took a helicopter to lower the two-ton unit to the roof of the State lobby. Shepardson justified the $30,000 investment by the cabaret's unexpected success. *Jacques Brel* was in it for the long haul.[79]

"He was hands-on and involved," said Henkel of Shepardson and *Brel*. "It was his passion—every day and night." He squeezed extra tables into the lobby, raising seating capacity from the original 250 to 370 seats. If he could squeeze two fingers between one table and the next, in his mind they qualified as private tables. "They'll just be happy to be here," he'd say. While patrons continued to fill the cabaret by night, Shepardson was spreading buckets of tar over the theater's roof by day. When it leaked, he would place linens and bus pans between the roof and the interior ceiling to preserve the plaster work. According to Hartman, restoration of the State began during the *Brel* run, when Shepard employed Theresa Piteo's husband, an unemployed painter, in the theater's auditorium.[80]

Garry and his players remained as committed as Shepardson. "It was an extraordinary moment of the right people coming together at the right time," said the director. Three of the four opened as professionals, and Theresa Piteo would earn her Equity card before the Playhouse Square run was over. Cliff Bemis, a product of the Baldwin Wallace College music department, would later pursue an acting career in movies and television. Usually the last to show up for performances, after preparing one of her daughters for her role in a community production of *Gypsy*, Providence Hollander invariably stopped the show with a standing ovation for her rendition of "Marieke." David Frazier, a seven-year veteran of the Cleveland Play House, was so involved with the show that some patrons assumed he was Brel himself.[81]

"Almost the entire run, we were so concerned about making budget and keeping the theaters open," said Garry, "there was never any ego." Frazer confirmed, "The play works because all of us work so well together." Since Brel was a cabaret singer, Frazier saw the Playhouse Square Cabaret as an "ideal setting. People are tired of the suburbs," he said. "They want something more exciting."[82]

What surprised Garry and the cast was "how much the audience became involved with the actors, "lingering afterward to share memories of Playhouse Square in its heyday. One audience member told Frazier they had broken his heart and made him laugh and think—and he was going to return to have his heart broken "all over again."[83]

It soon became obvious that *Jacques Brel* was developing a cult following. By August, Sally and Bernard Bergman had come to a total of fifteen performances. Sally, an artist, began bringing her sketch pad to capture impressions of the show and present them to the cast. Bill Rudman, future founder of the Musical Theater Project, would recall that he and his girlfriend saw it six times. "It was our show," he said. Many undoubtedly were returning for more than a show, no matter how good; they were also coming to recover pieces of their past.[84]

"Some who had not been downtown in twenty years came for what a lot of people described as a religious experience," remembered Lainie Hadden. "It was a common thing to have people see that show twenty-five times. I think I saw it twenty-four; I took hundreds of people to it." Not all were from the east side upper economic and cultural strata, either. A Parma steelworker told the cast after the show that he "must be all right," because he had the same reaction as all the rest of the audience. "People who were there shared in something and felt themselves spiritually bonded for the time they were there," said Hadden. "It was my favorite experience in Cleveland."[85]

With all the activity and traffic passing through after the theater's three-year hiatus, even the State's ghosts seemed to become aroused. Four life-sized photo cutouts of the cast had been placed on the stage in sight of entering audiences. Shepardson entered alone one night, in time to see two of the figures unaccountably fall on their faces. One of the cast members reported seeing Judy Garland as a child standing at the top of a staircase, probably one leading from the main floor to their mezzanine dressing rooms. "I used to live in one of the dressing rooms," said theater buff Weldon Carpenter, "and one night I went in and Judy was standing there with her mother and her mother was saying, 'You are going on.'"[86] (For the record, Garland indeed had "gone on" at the State in 1939.)

Such paranormal activity evidently failed to scare away audiences. What originally had been planned as a three-week run almost imperceptibly developed legs. "As long as we were selling tickets, we just kept going," said Hartman. Along the way, the show began to pass milestones. On September 15, *Brel* reached its hundredth performance. On October 31, a party marked not the Halloween holiday but the twenty-ninth week of *Brel*'s run, the longest in Cleveland's theatrical history. The ethnic comedy *Abie's Irish Rose* had set the old record, twenty-eight weeks, nearly fifty years earlier at the Colonial Theater on Superior Avenue, long since reduced to rubble. One could quibble with *Brel*'s claim, since *Abie* gave nine shows a week against *Brel*'s five, for a total of 252 performances. The distinction became academic, however, as *Brel* would keep rolling along for a final run of 522 performances when it closed after more than two years on June 29, 1975. It had been seen by over two hundred thousand people and earned more than $1.75 million. There had been nights, according to Garry, when the company had to count the take to make sure it could pay the waiters and barmen, but the show ultimately finished in the black, with a profit of $239,000.[87]

Booked originally for only a three-week run, *Jacques Brel* soon settled in for the long haul in the State Theatre lobby. Rave reviews in the local media got it started, but word of mouth kept it going for more than *500* performances. (*Cleveland Plain Dealer Action Tab,* June 1, 1973)

Early in the run, Peter Bellamy described the *Brel* phenomenon as a "Playhouse Square miracle." Forty years later, Oliver Henkel marveled at the audacity of "staging a musical in the cavernous, marble-floored, largest theater lobby in the United States." During the run, Frederik Smith, a drama professor at Case Western Reserve University, noted that Shepardson and his PSA were "getting people back downtown at night in droves. . . . It's hard to escape the fact that it is theater which is selling so well in downtown Cleveland and making the restoration of the theaters themselves financially feasible." Lainie Hadden would summarize the show's long-term effect more succinctly: "That brought people in, who saw what we would be losing."[88]

Afterward, *Jacques Brel Is Alive and Well and Living in Paris* would take on a mystique, setting it apart from any other show that ever played Playhouse Square. It ended its run at the halfway mark of the Playhouse Square Operating Company's five-year reprieve from the wrecking ball. In the trials to come, *Jacques Brel* would serve as a reminder that miracles were possible.

Timeline of 1970–1975

February 5, 1970
Ray Shepardson enters State Theatre lobby

February 27, 1970
State Theatre mural appears on cover
of *Life*

May 15, 1970
Shepardson quits his Board of Education job

July 20, 1970
Playhouse Square Association incorporated

June 24, 1971
Supersesquicentennial dinner is served in Grand
Hall of Palace Theatre

November 21, 1971
Budapest Symphony gives concert in Allen
Theatre

May 25, 1972
Plain Dealer reports imminent razing of Ohio and
State Theatres

June 3, 1972
Junior League announces $25,000 grant to save
theaters

July 31, 1972
Stouffer's Playhouse Square restaurant closes

August 12, 1972
Junior League "Classic Finale" tennis party given
in Allen Theatre

September 8, 1972
Owners agree to thirty-day delay in demolition of
State and Ohio

November 1972
Playhouse Square Operating Company formed

December 22, 1972
Playhouse Square Operating Company leases
State and Ohio for five years

April 18, 1973
Jacques Brel Is Alive and Well and Living in Paris
opens in State Theatre lobby

October 31, 1973
Brel begins twenty-ninth week, to become
longest running show in Cleveland's theatrical
history

June 29, 1975
Jacques Brel ends record local run after 520
performances

In Search of a Plan

Behind the Scenes

Outside of the spotlight focused on the *Jacques Brel* phenomenon, others were working more quietly to ensure the future of Playhouse Square. Described by one writer as "an unlikely coalition of businessmen, bankers, attorneys, real estate developers and Junior Leaguers," their nucleus consisted of the Playhouse Square Operating Company organized at the end of 1972: Willis McFarlane, Hugh Calkins, John Porta, Edward deConingh, Gwill York, and Elaine Hadden. Early the following year they reorganized as Playhouse Square Associates bringing in realtor Osborne C. Dodson Jr. as general partner of the company's board of directors.[1] Here was the business and community backing for which Ray Shepardson had been waiting for two years.

Dodson had foreseen the need for redirecting the purpose of the Playhouse Square Association from its original social to more eleemosynary ends. Accordingly, the Playhouse Square Foundation (PSF) was incorporated on August 6, 1973, as an Ohio nonprofit corporation. As stated in the articles of incorporation, its purpose was "to combat the deterioration of the portion of downtown Cleveland known as 'Playhouse Square' and its environs." That would encompass restoring both public and privately owned portions of the area and "presenting to the public productions of artistic or cultural value." As later summarized on a Playhouse

Square organizational chart, the foundation would "Receive and administer charitable funds to preserve art and architecture, and support arts-oriented activities," while the Playhouse Square Associates were responsible for "general planning and policy, finance, administration, [and] real estate management."[2]

These new entities were intended to supplement rather than replace Shepardson's Playhouse Square Association. That particular organization's articles of incorporation needed to be amended after the Internal Revenue Service notified PSA that it was operating not as a social club "primarily for the benefit of its members," as originally incorporated, but as a civic and social welfare organization. As such, it needed to qualify as a nonprofit, which it did by amending the articles to state that the organization's purpose was to establish a center for cultural activities for the benefit not only of its members but "of the community." PSA's functions on the Playhouse Square organizational chart were described as "theater use concepts, renovation, programming and promotion." Shepardson was listed as executive director and his wife, Cecilia, as business manager. Its board included such stalwarts as Lainie Hadden as chair, Zoltan Gombos, Jules Belkin, and Gwill York. Newer faces included Oliver Henkel's wife, Sally; attorney John Lewis of Squire, Sanders & Dempsey; and Pat Modell, wife of the Cleveland Browns' owner.[3]

As the seventies progressed, other entities were added to the organizational chart. A Playhouse Square Advisory Board comprised business and professional leaders such as William Bryant of the Greater Cleveland Growth Association and William West of Ostendorf-Morris Company. Neighborhood stakeholders such as Don Grogan and Halle's also had seats on the board. Formed to organize volunteer services was the Playhouse Square Cabinet, chaired by Sally Henkel. By the end of the decade, Playhouse Square Associates would become the Playhouse Square Development Corporation.[4]

Beyond Playhouse Square, others were engaged in creating plans to revitalize the city. One was Herbert E. Strawbridge, chairman of Higbee's, the Public Square department store, who was motivated by a 1972 *Plain Dealer* story that someone was trying to buy the section of the Cuyahoga riverbank in the Flats where Moses Cleaveland had disembarked in 1796. The would-be buyer of what came to be known as Settlers Landing seemed to be planning to use the spot as a junkyard. Strawbridge moved fast, buying up Flats proprieties with the support of his board until Higbee's had assembled a four-acre parcel stretching from the riverfront to West Ninth Street. It was anchored by the eight-story Western Reserve Building on the bluff edging the Flats, an 1892 Burnham & Root–designed building.[5]

Soon afterward came the arrival from San Francisco of urban planner Lawrence Halprin for an inspection tour of the city on behalf of the Greater Cleveland Associated Foundation. The Higbee's chief must have been elated by the visitor's enthusiasm over the Cuyahoga River. "Cities have turned their back on areas like this," said Halprin. "If I had an office in Cleveland, this is where it would be." Playhouse Square was also on the consultant's agenda. He told Gwill York and Willis McFarland that restoration of the area seemed "a valid idea" but that "youth downtown is one of the keys to revival. . . . The worst thing to do is build up a situation where just the middle-aged people are involved. If you do you're dead." Halprin associate Barry Wasserman offered a gloomy overall impression of Cleveland: "one of the darkest cities I've ever seen."[6]

Halprin and company were brought back three months later by the Cleveland Foundation to conduct a three-day Take Part Workshop. Three dozen Clevelanders brainstormed ideas for downtown improvement in a social room at the Chesterfield apartments. Four more workshops were conducted over the following two years, directed to downtown stakeholders. They set up shop in Playhouse Square's Point Building, a two-story structure forming an isosceles triangle between the junction of Euclid Avenue and Huron Road, its base anchored against the side of the Halle Building. From the nondescript location would issue the much-anticipated Halprin plan for Cleveland's revival.[7]

Concurrently with the Playhouse Square Associates' deliberations and the Halprin workshops came the first local stirrings of the historic preservation movement. Nationally, the movement was galvanized by the Historic Preservation Act of 1966, which authorized the Secretary of the Interior to compile and maintain a National Register of Historic Places. Locally, the Cleveland City Council created a Cleveland Landmarks Commission in 1971 on a motion first introduced by John D. Cimperman. Mayor Ralph Perk appointed the commission's original members, who included Cimperman, Bob Gaede, Tom Campbell, Maxine Levin, and John Pyke Jr. Two years later, Cimperman resigned from council to become the commission's first director.[8]

Pyke, a Hanna Mining Company lawyer, had attended Columbia Law School in New York, where he became interested in the preservation movement and authored a handbook titled *Landmark Preservation*. In it he described some of the impulses leading to a burgeoning interest in preservation:

> Our lives are enriched by reminders, personal and public, of our past. Those grand old buildings which we call landmarks are an important part of our public past. . . .
>
> A city's landmarks, by and large, are structures. To qualify as a landmark the structure must be endowed with a special value to the community that transcends function. This value may exist for any number of reasons: an accident of history, felicity of style, unusualness in structure, materials or workmanship, attractiveness of setting, or nostalgia. . . .
>
> . . . Today, however, preservationists are widening their scope to include . . . buildings which reflect a particular period or style of living and assorted buildings which, while not important historically or representative of a period, are worth saving for the extravagance, humor or eccentricity that went into their creation.[9]

Pyke remembers that Playhouse Square was among the early subjects to come up in Landmarks Commission deliberations. "The problem was that the ordinance only covered exteriors, and the magic of the theaters was their interiors."[10]

Whether eligible for landmark designation or not, theaters obviously met many of Pyke's criteria for preservation. It was already too late for some of the nation's most cherished examples. One writer in 1971 listed several that had recently been turned into rubble: Grauman's Metropolitan in Hollywood, San Francisco's Fox, Philadelphia's Mastbaum, Kansas City's Midland, and "the greatest of them all and the greatest loss," New York's Roxy. There was a countermovement, however, and the author found one in Cleveland, where "a group of interested citizens" was trying to save "one of the old Babylonian-Aztec palaces, unused and empty . . . along with two neighboring theaters, with very little success." [11]

In the spring of 1973, Playhouse Square Associates announced the retaining of architect Peter van Dijk of Dalton, van Dijk, Johnson & Partners to devise a plan for the district. A self-described "Shell Oil company brat" from Indonesia via Holland and other stops, van Dijk was esteemed in Cleveland as the main designer of the music shell at Blossom Music Center. With the aid of architecture students from Kent State University, he prepared a Playhouse Square design showing how its theaters might be connected. Shepardson previously had plans done for nothing by architect Robert Geary of Geary, Moore & Ahrens and had hoped to steer him some business. However, "when people got involved in Playhouse Square they wanted the blue-blood people's architect [van Dijk]," said Hartman.[12] Playhouse Square was no longer a one-man show.

After *Brel*

Shepardson was at no loss for ideas. What to do after the triumph of *Jacques Brel* was obvious: produce more shows! He had an artistic director in Joe Garry. With *Brel* going strong in the State lobby, he surveyed his premises for another venue. The Ohio was in a deplorable condition, but in July 1973 the boards were removed from the Palace's outer lobby windows. "Because Ray wanted all of the theaters to come alive, he immediately began to program creatively in the Palace Theatre, using the auditorium and the marvelous Grand Lobby in combination, for a Cole Porter musical revue," said Oliver Henkel.[13]

One problem with moving into the Palace was the matter of a liquor license: Shepardson had one for the State but couldn't afford a second one for the Palace. With a benevolent wink from city inspectors, he cut a tunnel walkway from the State lobby into the palace auditorium, and his single license did double duty in two theaters for years to come. Later, the passage was given official designation as Exit 85. "Ray knew that much of what we were doing in the early years would violate the City of Cleveland building and occupancy codes," remarked Henkel. "So he purposely became good friends with the City Building Inspectors. They became enthusiastic about the project and were soon co-opted by Ray to become our informal consultants on such matters."[14]

Garry's new Palace production outdid even *Brel* in titular verbosity: *Ben Bagley's Decline and Fall of the Entire World as Seen through the Eyes of Cole Porter*. It kicked off with a black-tie first-night gala on November 5, 1973, just a day short of the glamorous theater's fifty-first birthday. "Cleveland doesn't have too many splendid evenings but last night's Palace Theater opening was one of them," wrote Marjorie Alge in the *Press*. In the *Plain Dealer*, Mary Strassmeyer was more succinct: "BEST PARTY OF THE YEAR." Tickets for the preview ran for $50, and a full house of 366 showed up. Prices thereafter were scaled from $6 to $15, depending on day, time, and bill of fare. Wednesday matinees included tea and pastries; Wednesday through Saturday evenings, buffet dinners; Saturday midnight shows, hors d'oeuvres.[15]

"Where else in the world can one have cocktails in the orchestra pit, dine in a garden setting on the great stage of the Palace and then retire to the magnificent lobby of the theater to watch the production?" William Miller described the evening's experience in the *Plain Dealer*. The show consisted of Cole Porter songs

Following the success of *Jacques Brel* at the State, Ray Shepardson, Joe Garry, and company shifted attention to the Grand Lobby of the Palace Theatre with a Cole Porter revue. C. C. Connor and David O. Fraser (both standing far right) headed the cast. (Courtesy of *Cleveland Press* Collection, Michael Schwartz Library, Cleveland State University)

strung together in a narrative set in the 1930s, climaxed with a medley of the composer-lyricist's standards including "Begin the Beguine" and "Night and Day," sung by a cast of six, five of them veterans of community theater and the Cleveland Play House.[16] The sixth was a veteran of various road gigs named C. C. (Cathy) Connor, native of Canton, Ohio. The daughter of a vaudevillian billed as "Ukelele Jake," she had toured as a vocalist with Harry James and with her own musical trio. Called back to Ohio due to a family illness, she auditioned for Joe Garry and was hired for the Porter revue almost on the spot.[17]

Ben Bagley's Decline and Fall was good for almost half a year in the Palace. During the run, Shepardson picked up another dedicated worker when John Hemsath showed up for a coffee shop interview. "Before I got married and got a real job, I wanted to do something for Cleveland," recalled Hemsath. "These theaters were part of my growing up." He had tried acting at Lutheran West High School in Rocky River but decided he was more suited to working behind the scenes. Shepardson offered him a job handling group sales and special events but in lieu of a salary gave him the coat-checking concession at the Palace. "I was Johnny Coat-Check and made my way in tips," he said. "But that was OK. The whole place was surviving on popcorn and beer sales, and nobody was getting paid, including Ray." Thanks to *Brel*, he was soon put on salary and within a few years had his "real job" as Playhouse Square's director of theater operations.[18]

Following the Porter revue, Shepardson kept the Palace lit with a show appropriately named *Alice! At the Palace.* Garry directed his own adaptation of characters and events from Lewis Carroll's *Alice in Wonderland* stories, using a cast of six and "only the suggestion of a set." An oversold house of more than four hundred showed up for opening night on October 3, 1974. *Press* reviewer Tony Mastroianni thought it "a stage version that retains the mixture of wit and sophistication that makes the work appealing to adults yet one that seldom loses the crazy, topsy turvey stories and characters that have made it loved by children." The critic saved his highest kudos for the only female in the cast, Yolande Bevan, "an amazing bundle of talent with an amazing way with a song."[19]

"Every time we wanted to save another space, we created a show to put in that space," Joe Garry once told a Playhouse Square touring group. While not strictly applicable to every post-*Brel* production, that generalization certainly fit the next show, which moved from the Palace lobby to State Theatre's main auditorium. Like its predecessors, it was financed from the profits of *Brel*, which had been mounted on the grants from the Junior League and its matching angels. "Ray Armington said it was used over and over again," recalled Lainie Hadden, quoting one of the original donors. What made this production uniquely apropos was that it took place in a venue currently under restoration. Looking up from their tables, members of the audience could see scaffolding along the auditorium's upper reaches. Painter Rick Trela, Terry Piteo's husband, was up there at work before the show and during intermission, providing a graphic example of work in progress.[20]

Playhouse Square described the show, *El Grande de Coca-Cola*, as a "slapstick farce set in a dilapidated section of Honduras in which a third-rate impresario presents his family of amateur acts under the pretense that they are international celebrities." Don Robertson of the *Press* had recommended the production, which had lately played at Cuyahoga Community College under Fran Soeder's direction. Seeing it at the State, Dick Wootten described it for the *Press* as "a new rundown hot-spot in downtown Cleveland putting on a madcap, wacky, zany, nutty and crazy kind of show." It took talent, he concluded, for Soeder's cast to "pull off the illusion of no-talent." Coke, among stronger libations, was among the liquid refreshment, and Shepardson got Coca-Cola to pay for his ads by allowing people to bring in bags of Coke bottle caps for admission.[21]

Halfway through the four-month run of *El Grande*, *Jacques Brel* finally ended its record-setting run in the State Cabaret. Garry didn't have to look far for its replacement. David Frazier, his life partner, had been working on a one-man show based on the life and writings of the late Irish poet and writer Brendan Behan. One of Garry's English students at CSU had written it some years earlier. "Joe assigned us to put together a dramatic script from non-dramatic material," recalled Kathleen Kennedy. "I had read Behan's 'The Hostage' and 'The Quare Fellow' and although I'm not a professional Irish person, I was really taken with the colorful nature of the writing. It had a natural kind of dramatic quality to it." Her script came to the notice of Frazier, who enlisted Garry to direct him in it and worked with Kennedy to make it stage-ready. "David would find a line in Behan's writings that he loved and I would find a way to work it into the script," said the budding playwright.[22]

She was raised in suburban Brooklyn and Parma, the oldest in a family of five girls. As a child, she dreamed of being a dancer or actress, practicing dance steps from a book in her basement. She gave up her acting ambitions with no regrets, reflecting that only two percent of Equity actors were steadily employed. Instead, she channeled her talents into writing and went from Nazareth Academy to earn a bachelor's degree in English at Cleveland State, followed by a couple of years doing public relations for the Cleveland Play House. She was working on her master's at CSU, where Garry successfully produced her dramatic adaptation of Dante's *Inferno*.[23]

Described by one reporter as "willowy and winsome," Kennedy impressed those who knew her with deeper qualities. She struck John Hemsath as "very bright, articulate"; to Ceil Hartman she was "a very intelligent woman with a great sense of humor who loved theater in all its forms." Inevitably, she showed up at Playhouse Square, hoping for a job in public relations. "At the time we weren't hiring anyone in that area (mostly because we couldn't afford to)," said Hartman. "So Kathy started with us as a waitress in the Cabaret during 'Jacques Brel.'" After *Brel* turned into a cash cow, however, Kennedy got her public relations director position.[24]

It must have seemed like her dream job, and Kennedy threw herself into it with abandon. Besides normal PR work and revisions on her Behan script, she had taken on the writing and publication of a soft-bound book on Playhouse Square. She did it despite the debilitating effects of bronchial asthma, a disease that had plagued her since birth. "She had a tendency to work longer hours than her health would allow," observed Hartman. In fact, her doctor had recommended that she quit work and go on welfare to save her life—advice she ignored.[25]

Kennedy's *Playhouse Square: Cleveland, Ohio*, a sixty-eight-page souvenir book, came out in July 1975. On the cover was

As *Brel* ended its record run in the State Theatre lobby, Playhouse Square kept the marquee lit with a satiric revue, *El Grande de Coca-Cola*, in the main auditorium. Ads like this one were paid for by the eponymous soft-drink company, in return for which patrons were granted free admission in exchange for bags of Coke bottle caps. (*Cleveland Plain Dealer*, May 11, 1975)

Aspiring author Kathleen Kennedy's "Red Book" was the first volume to tell a comprehensive history of Playhouse Square. (Photo by Larry D. Nighswander, Courtesy of *Cleveland Press* Collection, Michael Schwartz Library, Cleveland State University)

the great Sevres vase of the Palace lobby, outlined in gold against a textured background in the "Albee red" of the theater's furnishings (hence the designation "Red Book," to distinguish it from two later editions). It opened with pictures and descriptions of the Playhouse Square theaters and restoration work. Then came an extensively researched chronicle of entertainment in Cleveland, from the first professional performance in 1820 to the melodramas and vaudeville of the early twentieth century and from John Ellsler's Academy of Music to Mark Hanna's Euclid Avenue Opera House. The Playhouse Square era continued the pageant from the openings of 1921 to the closings of 1969, followed by an account of

the Playhouse Square Association's first five years. In the center of the book were stunning color photographs of the four theaters' interiors, along with a reproduction of the *Life* magazine cover instrumental in saving them from destruction.[26]

A week or two after the book came the premiere of Kennedy and Frazier's *Conversations with an Irish Rascal* in the Playhouse Square Cabaret. Impersonating the freewheeling and hard-drinking Behan, Frazier convincingly appeared to consume two-and-a-half fifths of whiskey and two beers during his unbroken time on stage, supported only by a red-haired local folk singer singularly named Gusti. Irish folk songs and drinking songs, rendered by Gusti, Frazier, or both, relieved the stream of Behan's stories and talk. "They are of the foot-stomping, hand-clapping kind and every Irish person in the audience knew just when to stomp and clap," wrote Wootten in the *Press*, adding that Frazier "may just be turning in the best performance of his career to date." In the *Plain Dealer*, Bellamy singled out Kennedy and Frazier's script as "a brilliant and theatrical choice of selections from Behan's books, poems and plays."[27]

Seven days later, returning from a visit with family in Baltimore, Shepardson and Hartman called Kennedy to see if she wanted to go to dinner after the show. "Ray couldn't get hold of her," remembered Hartman. Concerned, they went to check at her apartment in the Chesterfield. "We got her keys and found her dead, the phone off the hook." In front of her was the script of *Conversations,* on which she had been making minor revisions. She was taken to St. Vincent de Paul Hospital, where the cause of death was determined to be an asthma attack.[28]

"She had just begun to realize her potential," said Shepardson. In that single month of July, Kathleen Kennedy had seen her first book published and her first professional play premiered, then died, aged twenty-eight. Her family requested that contributions in her memory be directed to the PSF. Shepardson converted an unused storage space under the Ohio Theatre into Kennedy's, an intimate cabaret. Cleveland State University, accepting *Conversations* in lieu of her unfinished thesis on Virginia Woolf, awarded her a posthumous master's degree.[29]

Conversations with an Irish Rascal enjoyed a brief afterlife following its ninety-day run at Playhouse Square. Frazier went on to portray Behan at the Edinburgh Festival in Scotland and then Off Broadway in New York at the Gate (later Village Gate) Theater. He and Garry brought it back for an encore appearance at Playhouse Square. Shepardson's next, post-*Conversations* productions, unfortunately, proved briefer and far less distinguished. *Bullshot Crummond* closed after only a two-day run, while a Kurt Weill revue, *Berlin to Broadway,* was judged insufficiently polished to even open. *Oh Coward!* Did somewhat better, running for five weeks in Kennedy's. Of the dozen productions to follow *Brel,* none had produced a profit.[30]

The brightest financial return of 1975 came not from a Playhouse Square production but a benefit appearance by Broadway composer Marvin Hamlisch. It came through the efforts of Sally Henkel, who approached the Academy Award winner through a mutual acquaintance. "She didn't tell me until later that this Palace was in Cleveland," quipped Hamlisch from the Cleveland Palace stage on July 12. "Then, she added, 'And you're going to donate your services.'" He gave two performances, accompanying himself on the piano and backed by the Hal Lynn Orchestra. The weekend added $30,000 to the Playhouse Square restoration efforts.[31]

Lights on East Fourteenth

Euclid Avenue remained dark on the night of March 9, 1971. Two years had passed since the movie marquees of Playhouse Square had dimmed their lights. Ray Shepardson was preparing to take his pitch to save them to the Intown Club some three weeks later. *Jacques Brel* was still two years in the future.

Lights burned as brightly as ever on East Fourteenth Street, however. Just two and a half weeks short of its fiftieth birthday, the Hanna Theatre was keyed up for one of its most anticipated openings. Milton Krantz had to rent a separate office in the Hanna Building to handle ticket orders for the show's expected five-week run. Ten days before opening, he had five thousand more orders for Saturday night tickets than seats, leading the *Plain Dealer*'s Peter Bellamy to speculate that the demand was not generated by the Hanna's customary audience. "It's inconceivable that sophisticated, veteran theater goers would send mail orders for Saturday nights to the number of 13,000," he opined.[32]

It was no ordinary Hanna show that aroused such enthusiasm, but the self-styled "tribal love-rock" musical *Hair*. The novelty of a rock score in a Broadway book musical created much of the enthusiasm. A certain amount of prurient interest might also be attributed to a well-publicized, if brief, nude scene in the finale of the first act. Accordingly, opening night became more of a media spectacle than theatrical event. The rock radio station that had bought out the house generated much of the publicity. Bright lights illuminated the sidewalk under the Hanna's marquee that Tuesday night. A pair of go-go girls dancing to a soundtrack from a parked WIXY-1260 vehicle greeted arriving playgoers. A buttoned-down young protester waved a sign charging "Sheman scum" with scorning the American flag while young men were dying for it in Vietnam. A smiling Mayor Carl Stokes, undeterred by prior protests from religious groups, arrived in the company of Virginia Graham, hostess of a nationally syndicated television talk show. Keeping out of the spotlight were representatives of both the city and county prosecutors' offices, coming to check whether the show violated any obscenity statutes. This had troubled Bellamy, who worried that any attempt to close the show "would make the city a laughing stock and add to the ammunition of comedians who are already making it the butt of acid jibes."[33]

Bellamy needn't have worried. An assistant county prosecutor, while offering his personal opinion of *Hair* as "vulgar, tasteless and an artistic failure," ruled that it wasn't obscene by current court rulings, and no attempt would be made to shut it down. Flashing strobe lighting made it problematic for a city prosecutor's eyes to determine whether the nude scene was indecent. As for the professional critics, Tony Mastroianni in the *Press* echoed the prosecutors by judging *Hair* "the most over-rated and over-amplified show in the history of musicals." For good measure, he added, "It is also over-sexed." Bellamy was more evenhanded, balancing the show's "animal zest and joy of living" with "its near monotonous preoccupation with four-letter words." Overall, he observed, "It's much pleasanter to see these kids cavorting on stage than to see them as war casualties."[34]

Reviews, good or bad, didn't count for much in this instance, anyway. *Hair* had sold out its first three weeks before opening night. It sailed through the anticipated five-week run, after which it planned to stay on a week-to-week basis for up to ten weeks. As the cast members began their sixth week, however, a phone call during intermission sent them into a panic. A fire had been reported at the Pick Carter Hotel on Prospect Avenue, where many of them were staying. Stage manager Russell Carlson and actor Jonathan Johnson had left young wives and infant daughters at the hotel. Later, they learned that all four were among the seven fatalities in what was called the worst downtown hotel fire in Cleveland history. The following night's performance was cancelled, then the show went on again.[35]

Fire wasn't the only hazard the controversial production faced. As in other cities on the *Hair* tour, there were bomb threats. During the first week of the Hanna run, a bag containing dynamite was found in front of the theater during the day, and the house was evacuated the same night following a telephoned bomb threat. There were other threats by telephone and postcard. Finally, on the morning of the show's final performance, a car pulled up on East Fourteenth Street and a man got out to hurl a package under the theater marquee. In addition to breaking windows in the Hanna's doors and neighboring shops, the ensuing explosion knocked three letters from the theater's name on the marquee. A near full house of twelve hundred braved the farewell performance that night. *Hair* had compiled a seven-week run and might have done eight, but Krantz granted the cast's request for a release in order to give them a rest and "to get away from the daily reminder of that burned-out hotel."[36]

That bomb-damaged marquee was less than a year old. Earlier that year Krantz had unveiled a $100,000 overhaul of the legitimate gem, the Hanna's first extensive facelift since 1947. It began with that new, streamlined marquee over the sidewalk. Just inside the street doors, a new chandelier and newly installed carpeting brightened the small outer lobby, making it, in Krantz's words, "the only carpeted outer lobby of a legitimate theater in the country." Stairways to the balcony and mezzanine levels, as well as the upper foyer, were carpeted for the first time, while the main foyer and auditorium were recarpeted in a bright cardinal red. The old, dark-green walls gave way to goldbeige upholstered, sound-absorbing wall covering. Unseen, but hopefully heard, was a new sound system, which so far seemed to have quelled audience complaints about inaudible lines. "That's right, not one complaint," reported Krantz.[37]

Of Playhouse Square's original five theaters, only the Hanna had remained in business by its fiftieth birthday. Technically that had occurred during *Hair*'s run in late March, but Krantz decided to wait for the ensuing 1971–72 season to celebrate the golden anniversary season. He planned to kick it off on October 17 with a prestigious world premiere of *W.C.*, a biographical musical based on the life of the comedian W. C. Fields, with Mickey Rooney in the title role. Golden souvenir programs would pay homage to the theater's anniversary. Rounding out the first half of the season would be another four musicals and four plays. The plays included Moliere's *The School for Wives*, the thriller *Sleuth*, Julie Harris in *And Miss Reardon Drinks Little*, and the British comedy *How the Other Half Loves* with Phil Silvers. The musicals were all products of established creators: Stephen Sondheim's *Company*, Bert Bacharach's *Promises, Promises*, Ossie Davis's *Purlie*, and Harold Rome's new musicalization of *Gone with the Wind*. For the latter half of the season, Krantz was negotiating for the plays *The Me Nobody Knows* and *The Gingerbread Lady*, as well as more musicals: *No, No, Nanette, Applause*, and *Dames at Sea*.[38]

Unfortunately, not everything worked according to plan. Krantz's biggest disappointment had to be the nonappearance of *W.C.*—just one more of many shows that never left the starting gate. It had to put a damper on the opening of the Hanna's anniversary season, which kicked off instead with Moliere's three-hundred-year-old *School for Wives*. Other no-shows that season included *Promises, Promises, Applause, Dames at Sea*, and *How the Other Half Loves. Gone with the Wind* would undergo endless years of tryouts in locales ranging from London to Tokyo, but Scarlett O'Hara would never sing in Cleveland or on Broadway.

One show that did come through for the Hanna that season was *No, No, Nanette*, the revival of the 1920s hit that had played the Ohio Theatre in its original national tour. Forty-six years later, it conquered Broadway anew, and the Hanna hosted the revival tour for a three-week stand over the Christmas holidays. A near-capacity audience gave ovations for the raising of the curtain and the first appearances of stars June Allyson, Dennis Day, and Judy Canova. "The show is a pleasant reminder of more graceful times when boys and girls danced together to lilting music instead of writhing to tuneless rock 'n' roll," wrote Bellamy, possibly making mental comparisons with the previous season's *Hair*. Many Clevelanders evidently agreed, as they awarded the Hanna a record box office take of $90,749 for the first week of the run. According to Krantz, the Hanna had been the only legitimate theater in the nation to sell out the house for its New Year's Day matinee.[39]

Far less gratifying were the fates of two shows Krantz booked to fill holes in his subscription lineup caused by cancellations. Both were pre-Broadway tryouts, the first *The Big Show of 1928*, an obvious attempt to exploit nostalgia for the Roaring Twenties with two stars from the era, Sally Rand and Rudy Vallee. The other was described as "a hilarious new comedy," *Keep Off the Grass*, starring Julie Newmar. As Krantz subsequently explained in an apology to subscribers, he had had to book the shows long before they were in rehearsal and consequently had "no way of viewing and appraising these attractions, both of which turned out to be abominable flops." On the basis of scathing reviews, many subscribers hadn't bothered to use their tickets for *Keep Off the Grass*. "Let me assure you it was never our intention to present a bad play," Krantz wrote them, "but an honest attempt to bring to Cleveland a brilliant new comedy prior to Broadway."[40] That "brilliant new comedy" folded at the end of its week in Cleveland.

To lessen chances of having to schedule similar "fiascos" in the future, Krantz announced that he planned to pare the following season's subscription list from ten down to eight shows. Like a politician with his voter base, Krantz always cultivated his subscription base. Later in the decade, he announced a plan to reward subscribers by allowing them to purchase extra tickets for two upcoming hits, equal to the number of their subscription seats, before they went on public sale. "Cleveland subscribers to the Hanna have been so loyal and patient that I feel a definite moral obligation to them, and this is the most effective means I can think of to show the Hanna's appreciation," explained the manager. He hoped to achieve a record seven thousand subscribers that season, which would fill in advance 60 percent of the theater's seats for the first week of each subscription show.[41]

Krantz was finding it harder to obtain shows than subscribers. Nonmusical plays and comedies, once the lifeblood of the road, were becoming scarce on Broadway, squeezed out by the increasing popularity of musicals. Moreover, musicals were increasingly dominated by huge, long-running hits in the mold of *My Fair Lady* and *Fiddler the Roof*, which tied up theaters for years and left little chance for fresh and innovative musicals to gain a foothold. "So the problem at the Hanna is not getting an audience, but in getting product," said Krantz. By 1977, the Hanna's subscription season had been reduced to six shows.[42]

Another sign of the straitened times was the increased frequency of one- and two-character plays. Theater legends Henry Fonda, Julie Harris, and James Earl Jones all came to the Hanna for solo performances in the seventies, each playing an iconic American figure. In his third and final call at the Hanna, Fonda came as lawyer Clarence Darrow, defender of unpopular causes. He made Bellamy feel like a member of the jury and earned a standing ovation before they became obligatory. Harris made her Hanna farewell as the reclusive poet Emily Dickenson in *The Belle of Amherst*. Backstage one evening came Audrey Watts and Vincent Dowling from the Great Lakes Shakespeare Festival in Lakewood to present the actress with a tiny gold bell to commemorate her election to the festival's board of directors. Much later, the Great Lakes festival would be back at the Hanna. Jones made his Hanna debut as *Paul Robeson*, who three decades earlier had appeared on the same stage as *Othello*. "Jones strode toward the colossal, and at moments touched it," wrote Bill Doll in the *Plain Dealer*, while admitting in the next breath, "This one-man play format is getting to be something of a bore."[43]

Anything but boring was opening night at the two-character play *The Gin Game*, with Hume Cronyn and Jessica Tandy. "On opening night they were so good, the fact that a truckload of scenery was missing could be completely overlooked," said the *Plain Dealer*'s Michael Ward. A February snowstorm had driven the truck off the turnpike, but the show went on anyway, with no more than the veteran acting team, a table, two chairs, and a deck of cards against a black velvet backdrop. "Afterward the audience cheered and raved," recalled Krantz. "I went back to Cronyn and told him, 'It's a great idea. Why don't you do it again?'" Unfortunately the scenery arrived, and the performance remained a memorable one-of-a-kind theatrical experience.[44]

Though not as frequently as in former days, musicals and comedies still appeared on the Hanna's boards. One musical became even bigger than *Hair*. This was *Godspell*, a joyful retelling of the Gospel of St. Matthew originally conceived by Clevelander John-Michael Tebelak and set to a score by Stephen Schwartz.[45] It gave the Hanna a six-week run in 1973, one week less than *Hair*, but would return three more times during the decade for a total of thirteen weeks. Two big musicals came in 1978: *A Chorus Line* for a five-week run, and *The Wiz* for three. *Chicago* also came that year with Jerry Orbach as lawyer Billy Flynn. Critic Jackie Demaline said it succeeded "without a sympathetic character, a strong score, a literate book. What makes it succeed is pizzazz."[46] A musical reimagination of Homer's *Odyssey* could have used some of that pizzazz for its world premiere at the Hanna. Despite Yul Brynner's charisma, the show would endure endless revisions before opening and closing on Broadway in one night.

Straight comedies continued to make their rounds on the road, thanks largely to the writing of Neil Simon and the presence of name stars such as Jack Weston in *Last of the Red Hot Lovers*, Nancy Kelly in *The Gingerbread Lady*, and Don Murray in *California Suite*. One notable revival was Kaufman and Ferber's *The Royal Family*, which had originally played the Hanna in 1929. Sam Levene and theater legend Eva Le Gallienne starred this time in a comedy loosely patterned on the Barrymore clan. "Miss Le Gallienne is nearing 80 and it is a life spent almost entirely in the theater," noted Mastroianni. "Like [her character] Fanny Cavandish, she obviously has no qualms about taking to the road and touring in a play." Though some critics thought her voice had lost some of its carrying power, Mastroianni pointed out that the cast was performing "without the aid of microphones and amplifiers, a rarity in touring shows."[47]

New genres and audiences also kept the Hanna's lights twinkling. In the seventies, Black plays and musicals with predominantly Black casts enjoyed a long overdue vogue. Among the plays that showed up at the Hanna was *River Niger*, in which Bellamy saw a universality that would apply equally to all viewers, regardless of race. "The first act is one of the strongest and most engrossing this viewer has seen in years," he wrote. Black-themed musicals at the Hanna included *The Wiz, Bubbling Brown Sugar, Ain't Misbehavin',* and *Timbuktu!* with Eartha Kitt. To promote the last five days of the two-week run of *Eubie!* Krantz took a full page ad in the *Plain Dealer*. The Hanna manager observed that in their first week Black-themed shows played to a 95 percent white subscription audience, but audiences the second week were 60 percent Black. Overall, the Black share of the Hanna audience had increased from 2 to 20 percent in the 1970s. Krantz attributed it to the rising prosperity of Cleveland's Black community. "I realize the financial and cultural impact on the Hanna when I see more and more Blacks paying for tickets with credit cards or by check," he said.[48]

Another newly tapped audience for the Hanna was that for classical ballet. Searchlights pierced the sky over East Fourteenth

Street to herald the debut of Cleveland Ballet on November 19, 1976. Dancer-choreographers Ian Horvath and Dennis Nahat had nursed and rehearsed the company from its beginning as School of Cleveland Ballet to this professional premiere before a capacity audience. The program opened with "Suite Characteristique," danced to Tchaikovsky's Orchestra Suite No. 2, and ended with a standing ovation. By the end of the decade, Cleveland Ballet was presenting four programs a season at the Hanna.[49]

How Goes the Neighborhood?

"Light by light, Playhouse Square is coming on strong again," observed the *Plain Dealer* in November 1973. After holding the fort alone since 1969, the Hanna had now been joined by the Playhouse Square Cabaret in the State, and the Palace was set to reopen with its Cole Porter revue. All three theaters were offering various combinations of drinks, refreshments, and/or dinner. A new restaurant and bar had opened nearby, and a pedestrian mall was nearing completion on Huron Road. "The revitalization that is taking place in Playhouse Square has something to do with nostalgia but more to do with the practical recognition that downtown had possibilities for being something more than a parking lot."[50]

Two years later, Playhouse Square Associates updated the neighborhood transformation:

> Entertainment and cultural activities are returning both in the theaters and nearby. The Cleveland Dance Center and Ballet Guild are now headquartered in the Stouffer Building. Bickoff's Art Gallery and the New Organization for the Visual Arts (responsible for the giant and colorful "city canvas" paintings on the otherwise drab walls of several downtown buildings) are in the 1240 Huron Building. Other space in this building is developed for working artists' studios. New restaurants are on the scene, beginning with Ham Biggar's Last Moving Picture Company, and followed more recently by the Parthenon, Rusty Scupper and 'til forbid. The Huron Road Mall, with its wide pedestrian walkways and tree plantings, keynotes a continuing emphasis on people, their needs, convenience and pleasure.[51]

Restaurants were seen as a bellwether of neighborhood vitality. Developments in the downtown Flats appeared to point the way. Older establishments such as Jim's Steak House and the Harbor

Inn were joined in the 1960s by Fagan's Beacon House, Diamond Jim's, and Pickle Bill's. "I am all for the dreamers who would like to see the Flats given a new lease on life and turned into a colorful and picturesque entertainment area that would bring no end of glamour to the banks of the twisting and murky Cuyahoga River," wrote *Press* columnist Winsor French in 1968, when the Cleveland Convention and Visitors Bureau began touting the Flats as an entertainment destination. [52]

The opening of the Last Moving Picture Co. in the spring of 1973, therefore, was seen as a significant step in the Playhouse Square comeback. Hamilton F. Biggar III already operated a night club on East Eighteenth Street and another in Atlanta, Georgia. Symbolically, perhaps, his new venture was located in the recently vacated quarters of the Stouffer's Playhouse Square restaurant. "All the over-50s in town told us Playhouse Square was dead," said Biggar. "Everybody in our group is under 28. When the over-50s say something can't be done, we go ahead and try it." Biggar was twenty-six. Their restaurant's theme was nostalgia for old movies, appropriate for a location adjacent to four former first-run movie houses. Its walls were plastered with classic movie posters, and reproductions of old movie cards served for placemats. Screens in the front window, bar, and restaurant ran highlights from bygone feature films. Entrees and small dishes were named for such stars as Fred Astaire, Ginger Rogers, Bob Hope, Buster Keaton, and Harold Lloyd.[53]

It proved to have a wide appeal. "Imagine, a line of waiting people in Playhouse Square!" marveled a *Plain Dealer* writer of a Friday evening crowd three months after the opening. Guests queued up for entrance to the restaurant's upstairs nightclub. Downstairs was the main dining room, and in between on an old balcony was a game room catering to eighteen- to twenty-year-olds. The encouraging reception had Biggar thinking about opening on Sundays and even looking for a second location in Playhouse Square. Construction of the thousand-unit Park Centre apartments at East Thirteenth Street and Chester Avenue fueled his optimism, which saw the proximity of the Hanna and the State Theatre Cabaret as similarly helpful for business. "He foresees the day when Clevelanders and visitors will be able to find drinks, dining and entertainment in six or seven different spots in Playhouse Square," observed the *Plain Dealer.*[54]

That vision soon appeared on the verge of fulfillment. Jim Swingo had taken over the Downtown Motor Inn at Eighteenth and Euclid, rechristened it the Keg & Quarter Motor Inn, and was planning to open an all-night restaurant in addition to his regular dining room. On the corner of East Fourteenth and Huron Road, a California chain opened the Rusty Scupper restaurant, while the Elegant Hog Saloon took up quarters in the Point Building on Euclid Avenue. At the end of 1977, there were plans to open a futuristically styled rock-disco club in the former domicile of Herman Pirchner's Alpine Village. Modeled after New York's Studio 54, the Cleveland version would be called Night Moves.[55]

Nearly a decade after the closing of the Korner & Woods bookstore, food for thought also returned to Playhouse Square, with the relocation of the Publix Book Mart, evicted in March 1972 from its former location on the corner of Prospect Avenue and East Ninth Street to accommodate a new parking garage for the Cleveland Trust Co. More than half a year passed before owners Ann and Bob Levine found a suitable new home for their sixty thousand old and new volumes. They reopened on November 1, in time for Christmas shopping, in the old Milgrim's ladies shop at the intersection of Huron Road and Euclid Avenue. "The art books are back where the Milgrim's hats were (look closely behind them and you will see yourself staring back)," wrote Frank Hruby in the *Press*, "and where the furs once hung there are the over-sized books, where you can reach them, not up under the ceiling someplace as before."[56]

Hidden away from all the newcomers to Playhouse Square, the Hermit Club remained unperturbed in its half-timbered lodgings on Dodge Court. Its 360 members celebrated their diamond jubilee with an anniversary ball in 1979. With the participation of women auxiliaries, the male bastion maintained a symphony orchestra, jazz concert band, and Dixie band. "Hermits maintain they have a lot more fun than those persons at the Morgue—one of their numerous names for the Union Club," reported Marge Alge in the *Press*. Their 1928 clubhouse, or "abbey," was nominated for Cleveland landmark status in 1976, described as "in the Jacobethan style, built to resemble an old English Tavern."[57]

Despite such examples of stability and renewal, Playhouse Square continued to show signs of loss. Decline may continue on its own momentum, even as revival takes tentative steps toward an opposing momentum. A year after the opening of the Last Moving Picture Co., the F. W. Woolworth store in the same block closed its doors after forty-nine years. District manager R. J. Shoemaker, having returned to Cleveland after a six-year absence, expressed amazement at how rundown the district had become. What really hurt, thought employee William H. Simmons, was the move of the Navy Finance Center from East Thirteenth to the new Federal Building on East Ninth Street. Employees from the center used to fill the now nearly empty Woolworth lunch counter. Speaking for Playhouse Square Associates, Osborne Dodson noted that while ten businesses had left the neighborhood in as many years, most had been replaced by new ones.[58]

Not all the new businesses could make a go of it, however. Five years after opening his Last Moving Picture Co., Hamilton Biggar closed it down, along with his Mad Hatter on East Eighteenth Street. "All this publicity about how downtown Cleveland is making a comeback isn't being realistic," he said. "No matter what they say, people are still afraid to go downtown at night." He cited the recent closing of the Cleveland Arena at East Thirty-Sixth and Euclid in favor of the new Coliseum in the exurbs as a major factor in downtown's lack of excitement. He placed most of the blame on city officials for lack of support, saying that "at least more police, better lighting and parking would give [people] some feeling of security" and claiming he received better cooperation for his restaurant ventures in Milwaukee, Boston, Cincinnati, and Orlando than in Cleveland. While applauding the Playhouse Square Association for saving the theaters, he didn't think it had been much help to others in the area. After the shows, people jumped into their cars and sped back to the suburbs.[59]

"Free Theater"

Meanwhile, Shepardson continued in his campaign to prove the naysayers wrong. After the disappointments in the last months of 1975, the following year brought him another hit. *The All Night Strut* opened in the State on February 18, 1976. The same production had been playing at Pickle Bill's in the Flats for half a year; the only question, thought *Press* critic Frank Hruby, was whether the four-member cast would make the adjustment from the "intimate confines of Pickle Bill's . . . to the broad expanses of the State Theater in Playhouse Square." He concluded, "Quite clearly, they are warming to their task." The show, a revue of popular songs from the 1930s and 1940s, certainly must have felt at home in the old movie and vaudeville palace. Doll of the *Plain Dealer* singled out Laura Robinson, an East Tech High School graduate and former downtown department store model, for her "sultry, Eartha Kitt Styleishness."[60]

On July 24, while *All Night Strut* held forth in the State, Shepardson opened an intimate revue called *City Lights* in Kennedy's, a year after its namesake's death. It was a New York import consisting of three male vocalists backed by a small instrumental combo in pop songs from the past four decades. Hruby called it "another major step forward in the progression of Playhouse Square's renaissance."[61] Shepardson, however, evidently felt the need for a more dramatic step—a game-changer. In September, he announced the beginning of a two-week experiment in "free theater."

"We were doing free or one-dollar theater because Ray wanted to get as many people as possible into the theater so they could see what we were trying to do," explained Hartman. All one needed to do for tickets to *Strut* or *City Lights* was clip a coupon from the *Cleveland Press* and submit it with a self-addressed stamped envelope and a fifty-cent-per-ticket handling charge. "Food and beverage revenue, Ray presumed, would pay for it which gives you a glimpse into his business acumen," said Oliver Henkel. Never one to ignore opportunity, Shepardson also placed contribution envelopes on the tables and, in a "rumpled grey suit," made a pre-show pitch explaining that contributions would go toward the restoration of the theaters. "Where did you get him? He's good!" said one attendee to a staff member, thinking Shepardson must have been part of the act.[62]

Response to the experiment justified its extension into the fall. When the fifty-thousandth request for tickets came in a few weeks later, Shepardson made an occasion of it. A chauffeured limousine picked up seventy-year-old Emaline Harmon and three family members in Parma, drove them to a pre-theater dinner at Jim Swingo's Celebrity Hotel, then delivered them to the State Theatre for *The All Night Strut*. The icing on the cake was the revelation that Harmon and her deceased husband had been vaudeville performers and had even played the State themselves. After meeting the performers backstage, she was introduced to a capacity audience. "I was in the prime of my dancing career when these songs were popular," she said. "I loved the show. The music brought back so many memories."[63]

By the end of 1976 Shepardson decided to raise the stakes with a "Stars Return to the State" format. His free theater "almost broke even," while bringing in $40,000 in contributions. Now he proposed bringing in name stars for $2 on weeknights and $3 on Saturdays. Opening the series was Della Reese, who generated a record $12,000 advance for the PSF. For $2, noted Tony Mastroianni in the *Press,* Shepardson was "offering an amazing bargain in entertainment;

> At that, he has seated himself out at the end of a long limb . . .
>
> Not only does he have to cover operating costs, he has to come up with enough money to bid for talent.
>
> Shepardson has said that he wants to maintain a flow of traffic. If the flow is big enough, he might succeed. If it isn't, then Clevelanders don't know a bargain when one is dumped in their laps.[64]

Clevelanders recognized a bargain when they saw it, and the flow was maintained through the spring. Reese was followed by Mary Travers, Mel Tormé, Chita Rivera, and Nancy Wilson. "The Stars Return to the State Theatre for a Song," said the ad for Rivera, who responded with "a raging red-hot revue that is probably the best song-and-dance production the old town has seen in years," according to *Plain Dealer* reviewer Paul John Mooney. Out of her Broadway credits, Rivera reprised "America" from *West Side Story* and "All That Jazz" from *Chicago.* Travers was making the rounds minus her former partners, Peter Yarrow and Paul Stookey, but still tossing her long, straight, flaxen hair. "The new Mary Travers never sounded better or looked better," said Dick Wootten in the *Press.* "The hall's beautiful, you're beautiful, what more could you ask?" Travers told her audience.[65]

As with *Jacques Brel* four years earlier, word of mouth spread the benefits of (almost) free theater. "This venture is bringing thousands of people downtown at night," stated a letter to the editor to the *Plain Dealer* from Lorain. "Playhouse Square is helping make downtown Cleveland have a remarkable comeback." A letter to the *Press* from suburban Lyndhurst described the writer's seeing Euclid Avenue at Playhouse Square "all tied up with traffic. And this wasn't rush hour. This was 9:30 on a Saturday night in downtown Cleveland. Thousands of people were pouring out of the early performance of Sarah Vaughn, while thousands more entered for the late show."[66]

Word of the downtown activity spread well beyond Greater Cleveland. In April the *Wall Street Journal* reported an increase from ten to eighteen thousand in the State's weekly crowds: "Many of the people going to Playhouse Square are precisely the kind of people who used to go there frequently—middle-class residents who later fled to the suburbs." In the recent past, a local retailer told the reporter, "you could walk down the middle of Euclid Avenue on Tuesday night and not get hit by a car." With the debut of free theater, however, restauranteurs like Jim Swingo found the effect "unbelievable." His Keg & Quarter was "jammed" at 6:00 P.M., followed by "a full house" at 11:30.[67]

Even the stars were impressed with the crowds, the city, and the venue. "The young people [in Cleveland] are doing something fantastic to save the theater and bring people back to the core," commented Della Reese. Ray Charles, Leslie Gare, and John Byner all expressed appreciation at their reception. Singer Paul Williams promised never to tell any more Cleveland jokes. "The theater is the real star of this performance," he remarked. "Be grateful they didn't turn this into another parking lot." All were amazed, according to the *Plain Dealer*'s Robert Ulas, to hear that some of the proceeds from their concerts went back into the restoration.[68]

As they had since *El Grande de Coca-Cola*, audiences not only saw a show on stage but the emerging renewal of the original grandeur of the State auditorium. "The multiple colors, craftsmanship and minute detail under the direction of Rich Trela have made the State Theater a showplace and a restoration model of note," wrote Ulas. Trela, who acquired the in-house sobriquet "Playhouse Square's Michelangelo," possessed all the requisites of a background in art history, artistic competence, knowledge of organic chemistry, and, in his words, the overwhelming need for "patience!" Starting at the bottom, to accustom himself gradually to greater heights, he worked his way up to the lightheaded heights of the vast ceiling. Once there, he had to work in cramped conditions under less than ideal lighting, often a single bulb.[69]

Before applying a single brush stroke, Trela scraped away peeling paint, replastered damaged surfaces, and cleaned areas to be repainted. The auditorium had been repainted about six times, most recently by a spray painting of the walls and of the ceiling other than the dome, obscuring all the original decorative work in monochromatic drabness. As far as could be determined, most of the original surfaces had been painted ivory, with little contrast between background walls and decorative panels. Now it was decided to bring out the decorative panels in a rusty brown against beige walls. Decorative plasterwork within the panels, a nearly lost art, would be highlighted in ivory and gold. In place of the oils of the 1920s, Trela painted with synthetics such as acrylics. Not only would they have longer lifespans than oils, but they would be less subject to yellowing or peeling.[70]

Seeing the work in progress, some of the stars were moved to do more than just admire. Travers was particularly impressed. "I've traveled all over the world and I've seen nothing like this," she said. "It reminds me of the restoration work they are doing in museums in Rome." Reviewing her act in the *Plain Dealer*, Doll noted the peeling plaster and water-gouged ceiling overhead. "Through a spotlight's smoky mist, Mary Travers jerked her head reflexively and looked up at a particularly gangrenous gouge." he wrote. "What she'd like to do, she told them all, was climb right up there and paint that ceiling herself." Sometime that week she did just that. A few weeks later Chita Rivera did the same.[71]

Change in Plan

The much-anticipated Halprin plan, Concept for Cleveland, was unveiled with great fanfare in August 1975. In a front-page editorial, the *Plain Dealer* praised its "color, pizzazz, magnetism, lift." As the paper's former executive editor, Phil Porter, would later recall, however, "at once the fragmentation, skepticism, and doubt so characteristic of Cleveland, the argumentative seesaw city, began." It had taken only a few months for a columnist from the paper to pan the plan. "The curious thing about Cleveland is that the more plans are devised to make it more interesting, the more it stays the same," wrote George Condon. "No city in America has undergone such close scrutiny by so many planners for so many dollars for so few results."[72]

Although historian Mark Souther dismissed Halprin's concepts as "unremarkable and highly derivative of past plans," they contained the germs of some eventual developments. As noted, work began on turning Huron Road from Prospect to East Thirteenth Street into a pedestrian-friendly mall. Euclid Avenue never became a pedestrian mall with a trolley line, but eventually automobile traffic was restricted in favor of exclusive bus lanes in the middle of the roadway. Even Halprin's radical Public Square makeover was partially realized—four decades later!—with the closure of Ontario Street and restriction of Superior Avenue through traffic to buses only.[73]

Some of Halprin's recommendations would bear fruit in Playhouse Square. "The Halprin master plan recognizes lower Euclid Avenue as the central corridor anchored at one end by Public Square

Peter van Dijk's plan demonstrating how the four Euclid Avenue theater lobbies might be interconnected was instrumental in the decision to restore Playhouse Square into a performing arts center. (Courtesy of Cleveland Public Library Photograph Collection)

Facing page: While Ray Shepardson experimented with various entertainments to keep the theaters open, architect Peter van Dijk created a model of his vision for the entire Playhouse Square district. It caught the eye of the Cleveland Foundation and the support of the city's business and political establishment. (Courtesy of *Cleveland Press* Collection, Michael Schwartz Library, Cleveland State University)

and at the other by Playhouse Square," noted the Red Book. Within the latter anchor, Halprin proposed a major new retail space and a new office building at Euclid and Thirteenth Street. For the conjunction of Huron, Euclid, and Fourteenth Street he envisioned a hotel and an active urban square. He also saw Playhouse Square as the logical site for an urban history museum.[74]

Another planner working in Playhouse Square was thinking along the same lines. Peter van Dijk's model of the district had been on display there since 1974. From the beginning he was impressed by downtown Cleveland's system of arcades and passages to provide shelter from "a somewhat hostile climate." He thought I. M. Pei's major mistake in Erieview was a failure to provide covered passageways along East Ninth Street. His Playhouse Square plan provided for interconnected passageways between the theaters. He also proposed raising a plexiglass shield over Euclid Avenue by the Hanna Building. In place of the drab Point Building, he envisioned a dramatic Museum of Light honoring Cleveland's contributions to the development of lighting. Van Dijk also had plans for the alleys behind the theaters, imagining Dodge Court developed with restaurants and shops. He thought the old Seltzer Building, originally home to the Cleveland Athletic Club and later C. A. Selzer's antiques emporium, might be converted into an atrium filled with cafes and boutiques. Numerous groups would drop in to view the model, many brought by Oliver Henkel. Van Dijk would make presentations on the plan, but he didn't seem to ignite much response.[75]

Though they came to Cleveland from widely different backgrounds, Peter van Dijk and Ray Shepardson had a lot in common.

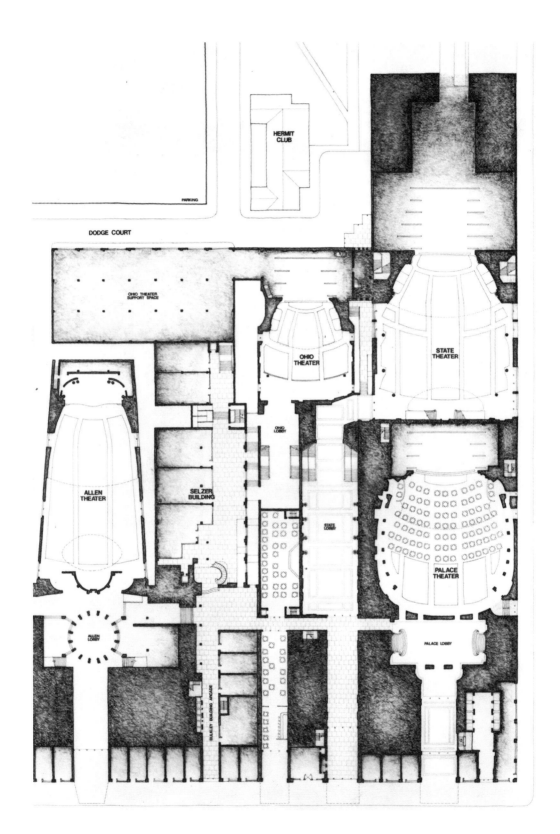

Raised on three different continents—Asia, Europe, and South America—van Dijk was tall, slim, well groomed, and cosmopolitan in attitude. Shepardson, the self-described Washington farm boy, was also tall but thicker in build, shaggier in appearance, and frequently undiplomatic in approach. Both were educated on the West Coast—van Dijk in Oregon, Shepardson in Washington—and both came under the influence of Buckminster Fuller: "Do something big enough to make a difference."[76]

Playhouse Square engaged van Dijk as a planner around the time Shepardson was launching the run of *Jacques Brel*. The architect couldn't remember how many times he had seen *Brel* but did recall that he and his wife once sat in the fireplace. Both men shared the goal of saving the theaters of Playhouse Square, but they had serious differences about what they were to be saved for. "They tolerated each other; they were courteous but not buddies," is how Ceil Hartman recalled their relationship. Van Dijk saw Playhouse Square as a potential Cleveland version of New York's Lincoln Center, driving redevelopment of the entire district. Shepardson, too, had originally touted Playhouse Square as another Lincoln or Kennedy Center, but experience had prompted him to lower his vision. His principal successes had come with cabaret shows in smaller venues.[77]

In 1975, Shepardson and Playhouse Square Associates were negotiating a $1 million loan to purchase the Loew's Building and convert the State Theatre into a restaurant to be leased to the Old Spaghetti Factory chain of Portland, Oregon. According to Shepardson, the plan would save the theaters, and shows could still continue in the State lobby. "Ray was marvelous, but his vision was very limited. He and I battled over this," recalled van Dijk. "I thought we could have a Lincoln Center; he wanted to put a Spaghetti Factory in the State." All other theaters in the complex were landlocked, noted the architect, leaving only the State with the potential for a state-of-the-art stage addition.[78]

Happily for van Dijk, the Spaghetti Factory deal fell through; even more welcome was a call from someone who had been impressed with his model and wanted to help realize his vision. Evidently, the caller had passed almost unnoticed among the delegations that had filed past van Dijk's model. Homer C. Wadsworth was far from just a face in the crowd, however. Though Wadsworth was a newcomer to Cleveland, his position as the new director of the Cleveland Foundation made him ipso facto one of the city's movers and shakers. Wadsworth came from Kansas City, where he had been director of the Kansas City Association of Trusts and Foundations for a quarter of a century. He brought with him Patricia Doyle, former manager of a Kansas City public television station, to fill the new position of the Cleveland Foundation's program officer for cultural affairs.[79]

Wadsworth, a folksy man of sixty with white, somewhat untamed hair and dark-rimmed glasses over a rather small nose in the middle of his round face, was a pragmatist. "You are heavily black in the city and have virtually no in-city middle class population," he observed of his new hometown, "and if you're not very careful and don't do something about it you can close the town down at six P.M. daily." He was impressed with Cleveland's world-class cultural institutions and encouraged the foundation's Distribution Committee to allot a greater share of its disbursements to cultural affairs. He and his wife, Alice, made regular appearances at the Cleveland Museum of Art, Severance Hall, the Play House, and Great Lakes Shakespeare Festival. He saw Playhouse Square, along with the proposed redevelopment of the Terminal Tower Group, as the city's best chances for downtown revitalization.[80]

When the PSF applied to the Cleveland Foundation for a $189,000 operations grant, however, the Distribution Committee decided it wanted more information before making a commitment. It brought in James Cortin, head of the University of Missouri at Kansas City's performing arts center, for an outside evaluation of PSF. "A decision must be made," reported Cortin: "Are the theaters to be used as rentable spaces for any enterprise that will not destroy their restored interiors, or, are they to be used as performance spaces? If space is to be committed to performance . . . one obvious approach would be to examine the possibilities of establishing a multi-theater performing arts center."[81] It was a polite restatement of the Shepardson–van Dijk disagreement: Spaghetti Factory versus Lincoln Center. Cortin's conclusion seemed to lean in van Dijk's direction.

As Diana Tittle pointed out in her study of the Cleveland Foundation, the foundation was beginning to consider the role Playhouse Square might play in the revival of downtown Cleveland. As the foundation's staff saw it, Playhouse Square "has more immediacy than any of the other two major downtown redevelopment plans" (Settler's Landing and Tower City). At the same time, the foundation was giving thought to the long-range needs of the city's major performing arts organizations. While downtown Cleveland had been in decline, it had otherwise been a period of remarkable cultural creativity. Cleveland Ballet had made its professional debut in the Hanna Theatre; Cleveland Opera had made its debut in a junior high auditorium in 1976 and was poised to move into the Hanna. The Great Lakes Shakespeare Festival had been performing at Lakewood High School since 1962 but was looking for a more central location.[82]

At the Cleveland Foundation's invitation, the three newcomers joined the Cleveland Orchestra, Cleveland Play House, Karamu House, and the PSF to attend a meeting with Lawrence Reger, a former director of planning and development with the National Endowment for the Arts. While the orchestra, Play House, and Karamu possessed their own performance facilities, they were open to expanding their presences via alternative sites. The Play House, in particular, had been thinking of integrating its isolated East Seventy-Ninth Street stage with its East Eighty-Fifth Street plant. Karamu, a nationally recognized pioneer in Black theater and nontraditional casting, operated as not only a theater but a neighborhood settlement in its east side location. As for the newcomers, the opera and ballet wanted larger venues than the Hanna, and Great Lakes wanted to move eastward. Following the meeting, according to Pat Doyle, Reger had commented, "We have six organizations looking for performance space and one organization with a surplus of performance space." Playhouse Square, of course, possessed the potential surplus. People were beginning to connect the dots. Peter van Dijk was engaged along with an acoustician and theater lighting designer by the Cleveland Foundation to study turning the Playhouse Square theaters into performance facilities for opera, theater, and ballet.[83]

John F. Lewis, who joined the PSF board around this time, would later observe, "Very little happens in this community unless the Cleveland Foundation is involved." A partner in Squire, Sanders & Dempsey, Lewis had been in charge of the firm's recruiting and recalled potential lawyers asking "What's there to do in Cleveland?" In 1977, as a member of the PSF board, he joined Oliver Henkel and three other trustees to vote to create a performing arts center in the State, Palace, and Ohio theaters. "I never dreamed it would become an arts center," Shepardson would recall nearly twenty years later. "I thought it would be an entertainment center where arts would be welcome; instead, it's an arts center where entertainment is welcome."[84] Before it could become anything, however, the theaters still needed to be secured.

Wrecking Ball Redux

"Time is running out," wrote James M. Wood in the January 1977 issue of *Cleveland Magazine:*

> Setting aside grander plans, there is less than a year left for the Playhouse Square Associates to find a way to buy the Loew's Building, on which they hold a five-year option. If they cannot come up with the $475,000 purchase price by December 31, 1977—and it doesn't seem likely that they can—the building and its two lovely theaters will be razed and replaced with a parking lot. "And you can quote me on that," says the building's owner Mike Miller. This fate is, ironically, a rerun of the first crisis that showed an indifferent Cleveland how important Playhouse Square was to the city's health.[85]

It was nearly five years since William Miller's *Plain Dealer* story had announced the imminent destruction of the State and Ohio Theatres. That had prompted the intervention of the Junior League and formation of the PSF. By the end of 1972, the preservationists had bought five years in which they had rented the theaters while searching for a plan to save them. Less than a year of grace remained, and they weren't much closer to their goal than when they started. In April, Shepardson reported the receipt of a letter from the owners asking for a ninety-day notice if Playhouse Square wasn't planning on buying the building. "They want to line up the wrecking crew," he said. "I don't think it will ever happen—that the building will be torn down, but it is a very real fear."[86]

It appeared to be a challenge beyond the capacity of either Shepardson or the PSF, however, to save the theaters. Shepardson's management style had raised serious doubts among Cleveland's business community. There had been cost overruns in the creation of the Kennedy's cabaret and too many money-losing shows, though Ceil Hartman was credited with keeping the losses relatively small as business manager. "I am the first to admit I am not an administrator," said her husband with commendable candor, "I am a producer." It was a conceit that helped sink a plan that might have saved the Ohio Theatre as a stage for Cleveland State University's drama department. When the cost of remodeling the theater was estimated at $3.6 million, Shepardson protested that students were unlikely to ever act in such a "dream facility" after graduation. "CSU's proposed theater is not my kind of theater," he said dismissively, and CSU dropped its interest in the project.[87]

PSF and the allied Playhouse Square Associates also came in for their share of criticism. PSF was responsible for theater restoration and production, while the associates were charged with acquiring neighboring properties to produce income to support the theatrical efforts. To implement the Spaghetti Factory deal, the associates needed to raise $500,000 as equity for a $1 million bank loan. To raise it, they planned to sell limited partnerships at $10,000 apiece but procrastinated with filing a revised prospectus with the Ohio Division of Securities. In the meanwhile, the Spaghetti Factory withdrew from the undertaking.[88]

As Wood summarized it, the PSF's problems were administrative as well as financial. To alleviate the former, the Cleveland Foundation provided PSF with a $20,000 grant to hire a full-time director. Gordon E. Bell, Shepardson's old college roommate, filled the position. "Ray, myself, and one other person were the founding members of the Playhouse Square Association," said Bell. "We were its initial directors." More importantly, Bell had a background in urban planning and, according to Cleveland Foundation's Pat Doyle, "understood how to deal with politicians."[89]

One of Bell's first moves was to dispel the myth that suburbanites avoided downtown Cleveland out of a fear of crime. Based on a survey of free theater patrons of *The All Night Strut*, Bell disclosed that the overwhelming number of respondents (45 percent) cited the lack of interesting things to do downtown as the main reason for staying away. Next (28 percent) came the high cost or inconvenience of coming downtown. Less than a quarter of those surveyed (22 percent) said fear of crime was their main reason for avoiding downtown. Shortly afterward, Mayor Perk announced an increase in police protection for the parking lots on East Seventeenth Street before and after performances at Playhouse Square. In April, in a cost-cutting move, PSF gave up management of the Palace Theatre, saving up to $15,000 yearly on utilities and maintenance. For the next eight months, said Bell, PSF would concentrate on the fight to save the State.[90]

The outcome of that fight would be the measure of success for Bell's directorship. He had to move swiftly, and he did. Using his political acumen, he formed an alliance with Cuyahoga County archivist Roderick Porter, an advocate for historic preservation. Together they approached Robert E. Sweeney, Cuyahoga County commissioner, who was interested in downtown revival, as well as historic preservation. With Sweeney's backing, Bell and Porter worked with county administrator William Gaskill and members of the commissioner's staff to draft a rescue plan. The result was a wide-ranging proposal that included a school for the performing arts, acquisition of the Palace Theatre for CSU, and creation of an urban park between Playhouse Square and CSU. First, however, was a bold recommendation that Cuyahoga County purchase the Loew's Building and its two theaters, lease the State and Ohio back to PSF, and use the building for office space. Citing his old hometown as an example, Bell said that Seattle had been "one of the cow towns of the country" until the 1962 World's Fair gave it "the facilities it needed for support of the arts." Now, all Cleveland needed was "two commissioners to say OK on the Loews Building."[91]

Sweeney, a Democrat, was presumably in favor of the proposal he had godfathered. The other two commissioners, George V. Voinovich and Seth C. Taft, both Republicans, were more cautious about using public funds for the arts, especially in the private sector. There was some resistance from neighborhood groups, such as the Buckeye-Woodland Congress, at the proposal's perceived elitism. Taft said PSF would have to make a pretty persuasive case to sway the commissioners to invest in Playhouse Square. Voinovich, however, while withholding his decision, stated that the use of public funds for such purposes was not "revolutionary," noting that other communities had built civic centers and theaters and even subsidized symphony orchestras with tax dollars. An editorial in the *Press* urged that the proposal receive "serious consideration." "Private money has done much to revitalize Playhouse Square. It is not nearly enough, and private funds are running out," it said. "It would be a shame to let that vital part of downtown start slipping downhill again without seeking—and debating—alternatives."[92]

On July 14, Bell formally made PSF's case for the purchase before the three commissioners. It would provide Cleveland with up to two hundred jobs as well as cultural attractions. It would also serve as a catalyst for further redevelopment in Playhouse Square. Sweeney was passionate in his support. "Where were the elected officials when Nick Mileti took his Coliseum to Summit County?" he inquired. "The county's record on contributing to culture is zero. We have got to burn a new path on use of public funds." While Taft expressed a preference that the county confine its offices to the present government area on Lakeside Avenue and Voinovich expressed a concern about squandering public money, they were generally receptive to the proposal and promised to give it serious consideration.[93]

Two months later, after due deliberation, the three commissioners voted unanimously to purchase the Loew's Building with its

Robert E. Sweeney, Cuyahoga County commissioner, sponsored the plan by which the county in 1977 purchased the Loew's complex, securing the State and Ohio Theatres for Playhouse Square. (Courtesy of Cleveland Public Library Photograph Collection)

two theaters. Of the total appropriation of $681,000, $475,000 would go to Cleveland Downtown Properties, giving Miller and Cappadora a profit of $150,000 over what they had paid for the parcel several years earlier. Most of the balance would go to PSF for improvements made in the interim. As planned, Cuyahoga County would use the four-story building for juvenile court offices and lease the theaters back to PSF. Bell called the transaction "a happy accident of mutual self-interest." Twenty years earlier, Cuyahoga County commissioners had killed the Public Square to Playhouse Square subway; in 1977 they saved Playhouse Square from being killed for a parking lot. In Oliver Henkel's words, it was "the first public-private partnership of significance in Cuyahoga

County." It was engineered in large part by Gordon Bell, whom Shepardson would later extol as "one of the major forgotten people of Playhouse Square."[94]

A year later, as if to validate the county's decision, the US Department of the Interior added Playhouse Square to the National Register of Historic Places. Included were the Bulkley, Loew's, Keith, and Hanna buildings along with the Allen, Ohio, State, Palace, and Hanna theaters. As summarized in the National Register nomination form, "The Playhouse Square Group is significant historically as a representative collection of theaters in the nationally syndicated circuits of the post–World War I period and architecturally as an unusual surviving cluster of legitimate theaters and early motion picture playhouses, four of which are connected."[95] If the listing had come a year earlier, it might have eased the process, but a satisfactory outcome had been reached nonetheless. Listing is no guarantee for preservation but merely corroboration that a site is worth saving. It was now up to the preservationists to find a viable use for what was saved.

Farewell to a Visionary

"This is the story of a white elephant which has been stirring here for five years, and soon may be strong enough to pull Cleveland's decrepit downtown out of its doldrums." So began a column in the *Washington Post* by Wolf Von Eckardt, architecture critic and in the fall of 1978 a visiting professor at Cleveland State University. The white elephant of his story was "four of the most garishly beautiful old vaudeville-and-movie palaces ever built." Eckardt told how after the palaces had gone dark, a young school administrator named Ray K. Shepardson, in search of a meeting place, had entered them and "emerged as dazzled as archeologist Howard Carter when he first broke into the tomb of Tutankhamen." He described the concert of the Budapest Symphony in the drafty Allen and the phenomenon of *Jacques Brel* in the State lobby. He recounted the cliffhanger of a rescue from destruction and the young artists and volunteers painting and repairing the baroque ceilings and details "as though they were redoing the Sistine Chapel." Now, he observed in conclusion, "Playhouse Square was placed on the national historic landmarks list." Eckardt's column was reprinted in the *Plain Dealer* and widely circulated by Playhouse Square as kind of a victory lap celebrating the success of the crusade to save the theaters.[96]

Earlier that year, Playhouse Square had announced plans for the renovation of the State and Ohio theaters, scheduled to begin in the summer. Most of the work would consist of such basics as new heating, plumbing, roofing, and seating. Restoration of interior artwork and decor would continue. The money would come from a $3.1 million grant from the federal government's Economic Development Administration. That grant originally had been earmarked for a proposed Gateway project at the foot of East Ninth Street, to consist of offices, apartments, and a hotel. Cleveland's new youthful mayor, Dennis J. Kucinich, had pushed for the transfer of the money from the lakefront in the belief that Playhouse Square's economic health depended on the growth of the theater complex.[97]

With the State and the Ohio secure and soon to be under renovation, PSF brought the Palace back into play by securing a long-term lease from its owners. To fill it with name entertainers, Shepardson solicited the sponsorship of Sid Dworkin, head of the Revco drugstore chain, sealing the deal with a promise to have a bust of Dworkin modeled by noted Cleveland sculptor William McVey for display in the Palace. The resulting series, called the Revco Festival of Stars, brought such performers as Ella Fitzgerald, Liza Minelli, Tina Turner, Engelbert Humperdinck, and Lena Horne to Playhouse Square. Besides whatever underwriting it supplied, Revco also offered one-dollar ticket discounts. As for the McVey bust, Henkel recalled seeing it on opening night, after which it apparently did a disappearing act.[98]

Besides star entertainment, the reopening of the Palace also reinjected excitement into Playhouse Square. To *Plain Dealer* entertainment editor Emerson Batdorff, however, the glass seemed half empty. He took note in the spring of 1979 of a confluence of activity in Playhouse Square, with Liza Minelli and Ben Vereen playing the Palace on successive weeks and Cleveland Ballet holding forth at the Hanna. While the entrances of these theaters were kept clean, the Allen's marquee had been smashed and newspapers and wine bottles sometimes collected in the doorways of empty storefronts. He confessed that when attending a performance in Playhouse Square he felt like he was "performing a civic duty," like not littering or contributing to the Cleveland Orchestra. "No one can be forced to come down town; people can only be lured," he concluded. "They don't ordinarily come in large numbers, yet we can't give up on one of the few remaining gracious baubles of Cleveland."[99]

The *Plain Dealer*'s William Miller, who had been covering Playhouse Square for nearly a decade, saw the glass as half full. "I have found that all victories there must be won an inch at a time," he wrote in covering another of those inches in May 1979. The occasion was a pops concert by no less than the Cleveland Orchestra at the Palace Theatre. Doc Severinsen was the trumpet soloist, under the baton of Erich Kunzel of the Cincinnati Pops. One of the happiest concertgoers was Zoltan Gombos, who had underwritten Shepardson's first PSA event, the Budapest Symphony concert in the Allen Theatre. Miller foresaw the day when Playhouse Square would be as well known worldwide as was the Cleveland Orchestra.[100]

Before the concert, there had been a civic dinner in the State Theatre lobby, at which Miller pointedly noted Mayor Kucinich seated at a table across from Brock Weir, president of the Cleveland Trust Co. The animosity between the two during the previous year had brought Cleveland to the nadir of its fortunes and reputation in the postwar era. The brash, confrontational "boy mayor" had swept into office on a populist, antiestablishment wave. He hadn't been in office a year before facing a recall election he survived by only 236 votes out of 120,300. Four months later, the city owed six local banks $14 million for short-term loans. When Kucinich refused to sell the city's municipal lighting plant as an economy measure, the banks, led by Weir, refused to roll over the loans, making Cleveland America's first major city since the Depression to go into default.[101]

It was not the sort of publicity the embattled city needed. An editorial cartoon in the *Denver Post* depicted the mayor as a little boy (uncannily similar to "Dennis the Menace") seated on the floor amid the broken pieces of a model city, addressing a letter: "Dere Santa, Pleeze send me a new city . . . I broke my old one. Yours trooly, Dennis Kucinich." More bad news would come with the results of the 1980 US Census, which showed Cleveland slipping from twelfth to nineteenth place among American cities, with a population decline from 750,879 in 1970 to 573,822. Shepardson's struggles to get Clevelanders back downtown had been taking place in the face of a population loss of 177,057 residents. Most of them had fled to the suburbs, which now outnumbered the mother city by two to one.[102]

One thing the city still had going for it, in the opinion of both Clevelanders and non-Clevelanders, was the reputation of its cultural institutions. In the very month of default, the Cleveland Foundation organized a consortium of six arts organizations to apply for a $2 million challenge grant from the National Endowment for the Arts. These were six of the seven that had met the previous month with the NEA's Lawrence Reger: Cleveland Ballet, Cleveland Opera, Great Lakes Festival, the Play House, Karamu, and Playhouse Square. A year later, the NEA awarded a $1.75 million challenge grant to the Cleveland Consortium of the Performing Arts. It was augmented by corporate gifts and fund-raising from the participants. Playhouse Square's share amounted to $500,000, part of which was applied to reducing debt.[103]

By the end of the pivotal 1970s, then, Playhouse Square was on its way to becoming a downtown arts center, a direction that tended to shunt Shepardson off the main right-of-way. For some time, there had been signs of a growing rift between Shepardson and the two foundations, the Cleveland and the Playhouse Square. PSF in particular had supplanted the original Playhouse Square Association in calling the shots for the theater complex. Shepardson's PSA apparently never much exceeded the five hundred members it reported at the time of *Jacques Brel,* and Hartman thought they had stopped selling them around that time. Much more was needed by then than could be raised by selling $120 lifetime memberships, and PSF had been founded specifically to solicit larger donations and gifts. By 1982, Ohio's secretary of state cancelled the PSA's registration for failure to file a statement of continued existence.[104]

The divergence between Shepardson and foundation types was exacerbated by a clash of personalities. At the onset of his crusade to save the theaters, downtown businessmen had dismissed Shepardson as "a romantic idealist," according to William Miller. Shepardson characteristically put it more bluntly: among the developers, the visionaries like him were seen as "broke f——ing idiots." Ceil Hartman remembered that in the theaters Shepardson started wearing sweat pants and became very casual. "He grew a beard, which [PSF director] John Lewis didn't like." He was also "starting to get a little chip on his shoulder—he was having great success." Joe Garry recalled people asking him, "When did Raymond become so difficult?" to which he would reply, "Become? He was always difficult."[105]

"When the establishment began getting behind the project, Shepardson began losing influence and power," wrote Miller. Seeing the handwriting on the wall, Shepardson had been preparing a fallback position. "I'd been there [Playhouse Square] long enough," he said. "I was getting involved nationally and became a sort of fanatical preservationist." He became a consultant for theater restorations in Cincinnati, Louisville, St. Louis, and other cities. He moved to Columbus, where he was working on the Palace Theater. His wife had resigned as the business manager of PSF and became general manager of Shepardson's new company, Playhouse Management, Inc., to book shows in several cities besides Playhouse Square. "Saving Playhouse Square allowed me to do world-class entertainment," he said. "I had credibility in the industry."[106]

Nevertheless, the final break with Playhouse Square left open wounds. In December 1979 Charles W. Raison, executive director of PSF, announced that Virginia Pfaff would assume the general manager position. Shepardson would be a consultant to book the spring season at the Cleveland Palace. It fell to Oliver Henkel, one of Shepardson's original supporters, to inform him of the board's action. "He was the visionary who was able to imagine what [the theaters] could be, and not only that, but what they could mean for the rest of downtown," Henkel would later reflect. Visionaries, however, were not always great executors. "Ray had the dream, but we needed the practicality, not just on the business things, but also the organizational things that needed to be put in place."[107]

There was also the underlying clash between PSF's commitment to building an arts center and Shepardson's penchant for popular entertainment. Cleveland Foundation director Homer Wadsworth commented at the time of Shepardson's departure that the foundation couldn't afford the entertainment that he only wanted to bring in. "Given the size of the theaters and the needs of opera, ballet, etc., the Cleveland Foundation thought we had too small a vision," said Gordon Bell. "The feeling was they wanted people with performing arts credentials." Pfaff, the new general manager, was formerly associate program director for the Wolf Trap, the Washington, DC, version of Blossom Music Center. Raison had served as director of planning and development of Buffalo's Studio Arena Theater.[108]

Though disclaiming any bitterness, Shepardson couldn't take his leave without a parting shot at the city's establishment. "The negative atmosphere of Cleveland is very depressing. There is an aura of defeatism over the entire city," he told Miller. "It is as if people want others to fail, and if someone has some success there are so many that wish them ill. I've never been able to understand it."[109] On that negative note Ray Shepardson took his leave of Cleveland. He left behind two irreplaceable theaters that without his intervention would have been lost forever.

Timeline of 1971–1979

March 9, 1971
Hair opens at the Hanna Theatre

August 6, 1973
Playhouse Square Foundation incorporated

November 5, 1973
First-night gala for *Ben Bagley's Decline and Fall . . .* in Palace Theatre's Grand Lobby

July 1975
Playhouse Square, Cleveland, Ohio (the "Red Book") is published

Fall 1975
Playhouse Square retains architect Peter van Dijk to draw up a master district redevelopment plan

February 18, 1976
All Night Strut opens at the State Theatre

November 19, 1976
Cleveland Ballet's professional debut at the Hanna Theatre

September 26, 1977
Cuyahoga County Commissioners vote to purchase Loew's Building and its two theaters for Playhouse Square

October 1978
Playhouse Square theaters listed on US Interior Department's National Register of Historic Places

November 23, 1978
Plain Dealer prints Wolf Von Eckardt's "Hope for Playhouse Square"

December 14, 1978
Cleveland goes into default

December 3, 1979
Playhouse Square announces the departure of Ray Shepardson

Widening the Vision

"Last-Chance Opportunity"

Harry Blackstone Jr. was appearing at the Palace as part of the Revco Festival of Stars in the first week of March 1980. He followed in the footsteps of his father, who had played the Hanna Theatre as Blackstone the Magician half a dozen times in the decade after World War II. Before beginning his own engagement, however, the younger Blackstone performed a little magic from the sidewalk in front of the Euclid Avenue theaters. Next door to the Palace, a rebuilt marquee canopied over the entrance to the State Theatre. Arching gracefully upward in the center of its street facade, it awaited its crowning moment from the hand of the visiting magician. Blackstone compliantly waved his baton . . . and voilà! After years of darkness, the marquee of the State was lit once again.[1]

Behind the magic act and the relit marquee lay a more serious purpose. It was the occasion for the Playhouse Square Foundation (PSF) to formally launch an $18 million capital campaign, described as a last-chance opportunity to place the theater complex on a firm business footing. "They were built as palaces for the people . . . so they shall remain," stated PSF president Oliver Henkel. The three theaters, their lobbies interconnected, would be operated as a single multipurpose entertainment center capable of seating seventy-five hundred patrons. The city's cultural organizations would occupy the State, popular entertainment acts the

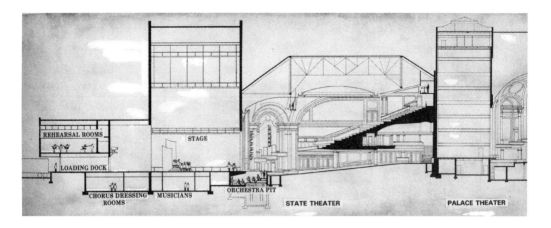

REHEARSAL ROOMS

STAGE

LOADING DOCK

CHORUS DRESSING ROOMS · MUSICIANS

ORCHESTRA PIT

STATE THEATER

PALACE THEATER

A cutaway view depicts plans to prepare the State Theatre for opera and ballet productions. A "bustle" with loading docks and rehearsal rooms was added behind the stage house, and an enlarged orchestra pit was constructed below the stage. (Courtesy of *Cleveland Press* Collection, Michael Schwartz Library, Cleveland State University)

Palace, and community and university theater and dance groups the Ohio. All three theaters needed extensive work. To accommodate opera and ballet, the State's stage had to be deepened from its original twenty-eight to sixty-five feet. Both the State and Palace, with their lobbies, hopefully would be ready in eighteen to twenty-four months, the more heavily damaged Ohio a year later.[2]

"This is not a pie-in-the-sky program, it can work and must work if Cleveland is to have a night life after 5:15 P.M.," said Charles Raison, PSF executive director. "This is more than a theater project," he elaborated. "It is an urban redevelopment project and we're one piece of a larger puzzle." He saw Playhouse Square as an imagemaker for the city. "This could be Cleveland's Broadway," he asserted. "I'd like to see that happen." So, too, thought Cuyahoga County Commissioner Robert E. Sweeney, who had been instrumental in securing ownership of the once threatened theaters for the county. "Cleveland will have a recovery of its national standing," he predicted.[3]

Well-wishers looked on the campaign with a mixture of hope and trepidation. Wolf von Eckardt, the Washington architecture critic who had celebrated Playhouse Square's rescue from destruction and its addition to the National Register, returned two years later to the subject of "our . . . grand old movie palaces," which he deemed "among America's greatest gifts to Western civilization." Some of the last survivors were still on the endangered species list, he warned, naming New York's Radio City Music Hall, the eponymous Chicago, and the four theaters of Cleveland's Playhouse Square. Others were struggling to survive through "adaptive reuse." Pittsburgh's Heinz Hall, Atlanta's Fox, Omaha's Orpheum, Columbus's Ohio, and St. Louis's Powell Hall had been restored for concerts and stage shows. What was really needed, implored von

Eckardt, was "a new kind of entertainment, as gaudy, glittering, glorious, gorgeous and grand as the movie-vaudeville combination that created them in the first place. It ought to be invented."[4] (As if in answer to his prayer, *Cats* was only two years away.)

Closer to home, Thomas E. Bier, a planner with the Northeast Ohio Areawide Coordinating Agency, thought what was needed was a revival of the farsightedness that had brought Cleveland the Ohio & Erie Canal and the region's first major railroad. "Redevelopment of Playhouse Square is not an ordinary opportunity," he wrote in an op-ed piece for the *Plain Dealer*. "It is, I suggest, in the category of those relatively few make-or-break points that come along in a city's evolution." Specifically, he was calling on the city's corporate community to supply $2 million in private funds needed for another Urban Development Action Grant (UDAG). Public funds could only go so far; public-private partnerships could work for projects that would benefit the whole community. An attractive city center with entertainment, culture, and housing would help attract educated young adults to join the staffs of local corporations and law firms. "Playhouse Square, compared to most central city projects," concluded Bier, "is a piece of cake just waiting to be knocked off."[5]

For a piece of cake, considering the total goal of $18 million, it was still a tall order. Directing the campaign was Joseph H. Keller, CEO of the Cleveland-based accounting firm Ernst & Whitney. Within six months, more than $2 million had been committed. The Cleveland Foundation anted up with a leadership grant of $710,000, up to that time its largest single disbursement from unrestricted funds. Cleveland's second-largest foundation, the Gund, chipped in $500,000, which Standard Oil of Ohio matched. Other major donations included $300,000 from TRW (Thompson Ramo Wooldridge) and $200,000 from Eaton Corporation. Unforeseen expenses largely due to the fast-tracking of the Ohio Theatre restoration necessitated a second phase of the capital drive in 1983, raising the target to $27 million. Leading the way again was the Cleveland Foundation, with a $500,000 grant. By the following year, $23 million had been raised, putting the new goal within reach. "I told you if I left town you guys would get the money" was the tongue-in-cheek reaction of Ray Shepardson.[6]

In the meantime, the leadership of Playhouse Square had passed into new hands. John F. Lewis, a member of the board for several years, stepped in 1980 into the office of PSF president, still a voluntary position. Two years later PSF decided to hire a president to assume the duties of Raison, who was resigning as executive director. Lawrence J. Wilker, a director of properties for New York's theatrical Shubert Organization, became the first paid PSF president, supplanting the position of executive director. Prior to working for Shubert, Wilker had been executive director of the Grand Opera House, a restored 1871 theater in Wilmington, Delaware. "I'm fascinated by the scope and magnitude of the Playhouse Square project," said the new president. "It's one of a few, if not the only one, of its kind in the country. It runs the gamut from urban renewal to theatrical productions to fundraising to organization to management." He would serve as chief operating officer, while Lewis remained on the board as chief executive officer.[7]

Downtown Doldrums

If he didn't notice it from the beginning, Wilker would soon see the symbiotic relationship between downtown Cleveland and Playhouse Square. If downtown continued to decline, Playhouse Square's revival was probably doomed in the long run. A revitalized theater district, however, might be a catalyst for a downtown comeback. Whether both could hold out while waiting for a turnaround seemed at times a delicate balancing act. At the beginning of the 1980s, as Playhouse Square appeared to be on the rise with its capital campaign, downtown displayed further signs of decline.

On April 30, 1980, the Hippodrome, oldest of the great downtown movie houses, became the last to close. During the previous decade, while Playhouse Square's darkened movie houses struggled to reinvent themselves, the Hipp had been subsisting largely on martial arts and horror films. In an effort to save the building, Cleveland's landmarks commissioner, John Cimperman, made a lastditch appeal to place it on the National Register. Common Pleas Judge Alvin Krenzler, owner of the theater with its attached eleven-story office tower, countered that he couldn't see a workable plan to reduce the largely vacant building's losses. "I'm not running a philanthropic organization," he said, and both theater and office building were demolished the following winter, to be replaced by a 173-car parking lot—a fate the State and the Ohio had so narrowly escaped.[8]

Another sign of decline, closer to Playhouse Square and a far graver loss, was the closing of the venerable Halle's department store. Uneasy portents had plagued the retailer since its merger with Chicago's Marshall Field's in 1970. Halle's promised seat on the Marshall Field's board of directors never materialized, and within a year Chisholm Halle was ordered to fire twenty-three managers. Under Field's, the store lowered the quality of its goods, and losses amounted to $1 million a year. In 1981, Field's finally sold all fifteen downtown and suburban stores to Jerome Schottenstein of Columbus, Ohio. A couple of months later, an employee in the downtown store's book department approached what appeared to be a customer only to learn that he was a liquidator. On January 26, 1982, Schottenstein announced that he would close all fifteen stores, and the downtown flagship stilled its revolving doors three days later. In the words of Halle's historian James Wood, "The historic rivalry between the Playhouse Square retailer and its Public Square competitor [Higbee's] was finally over."[9]

As if such conspicuous closures weren't bad enough, the specter of crime continued to haunt downtown's image. Early in his tenure as PSF executive director, Raison addressed the subject as a problem of perception, elevated by sensational accounts in the media. "Also suburbanites who haven't been downtown for years come down and see street people," he added, "and they don't know how to react." Raison said that he took regular downtown walks at night or early morning without incident. Still, foot patrols as opposed to squad cars would be helpful, as well as street and building lights. His call for streetlights was seconded by the Downtown Organization of Residents (DOOR),which called on the city's Municipal Light Plant to replace or fix 195 darkened lights it had found while patrolling downtown streets.[10]

DOOR's census of downtown lighting had found thirty-six nonfunctioning lights

The oldest and largest of the Euclid Avenue movie palaces, the Hippodrome finally succumbed to the wrecking ball in 1981. It was replaced by a parking lot—a fate some of the Playhouse Square theaters narrowly avoided. (Author's collection)

in the Cleveland State University area, a few minutes' walk from Playhouse Square. Whether the lighting had improved, a couple of years later three homicides in seven months rocked the urban campus. Having taken place in the Main Classroom Building, two couldn't be blamed on street lighting, but the third occurred in a bus shelter on Euclid Avenue at East Twenty-Fourth Street. They were the university's first killings in thirteen years, shattering the campus's image as an oasis of safety in a high crime area.[11]

Even amid such dark portents, however, not all was unrelieved gloom. Probably the most striking facade on Playhouse Square was that of the original Lindner women's apparel store, clad in five and a half stories of white terracotta. After Lindner's moved down the street to become part of the Sterling-Lindner-Davis department store, Bonwit Teller moved in and modified the first two floors with a limestone covering. After Bonwit closed in 1972, the building was vacant for nearly a decade, until the brokerage house Prescott Ball & Turben purchased the building for offices and restored the exterior to its original beauty. Having paid $1.5 million for the property, it invested an additional $3.5 million on restoration and conversion. With the original terracotta matched by a similar architectural concrete, Prescott Ball & Turben opened its new headquarters on November 20, 1981.[12]

Positive signs also came from City Hall with George V. Voinovich's election as mayor in 1979. Former mayor Dennis Kucinich had secured an Economic Development Administration grant of $3.5 million from the Carter administration which, together with a matching grant from Cuyahoga County, was to be applied to construction of the new State Theatre stagehouse. In 1981, however, the federal funds were held back by budget cuts under the incoming Reagan administration. Mayor Voinovich, though, like Reagan, a Republican, threatened to support filing a lawsuit to force the Reagan administration to release the funds. "There was a commitment and contracts were made and they should be kept," said the mayor. In the end the funds were reinstated without a lawsuit.[13]

Voinovich had been one of the three county commissioners who had voted to purchase the State and Ohio theaters for the benefit of the Playhouse Square Foundation. As a Republican he almost automatically enjoyed the confidence of Cleveland's business community, especially after he reorganized city government and made arrangements to bring Cleveland out of default. His efforts soon gained national recognition when Cleveland became one of ten cities designated as an All-American City by the National Municipal League in 1982. Cleveland was celebrated as a "turn-around city" largely on the basis of three points: its recovery from financial default, extension of terms for mayor and council from two to four years, and cooperation of business and government in restoring Playhouse Square.[14]

Theaters' potential roles in civic revival was addressed at CSU by the man who had pioneered the concept. Ray Shepardson returned to Cleveland in 1985 to speak at the national Back to the City Conference in Mather Mansion, one of the last remnants of

Millionaires' Row. "Cities have no small problems and no simple solutions," he said. "To make cities a better place to live, you have to choose your urban tools. My favorite urban tool is theater." Theaters were instrumental in getting taxpayers and voters to return to declining areas. Theaters could also be a more effective tool for renewal in large cities than in smaller communities. Shepardson, whose mantra was Buckminster Fuller's "Do something big enough to make a difference," was about to undertake the renewal of a five-block theater district in Detroit.[15]

Grand Reopenings

Throughout most of 1980, Playhouse Square appeared dark and quiet. Appearances were deceiving, however. While the capital campaign continued outside, workers inside were busy renovating and reconstructing three theaters for their prospective tenants. To concentrate on the fundraising and renovations, the PSF originally had decided to avoid the distraction of presenting any shows. At the end of the year, it relented, deciding that some entertainment would demonstrate that Playhouse Square was still alive and kicking. *Stompin' at the State,* a 1940s nightclub revue, opened on weekends only in the State Theatre lobby. During its sixteen-month run, it played to forty-five thousand.[16]

Planners were busy scheduling tenants for their respective performing spaces. Because it was the most damaged of the three theaters, dating back to the 1964 fire that had destroyed most of its surviving decor, the Ohio had been placed last in line for reopening. By 1981, however, it had been moved from the back burner. The list of arts organizations knocking at the Ohio's door included Ohio Ballet, the Cleveland Modern Dance Company, and the Cleveland International Film Festival. One company in particular, however, had enough clout to move the Ohio's reopening up to the summer of 1982. This was the Great Lakes Shakespeare Festival (GLSF), which would become the theater's resident company.[17]

GLSF wasn't really a touring company, though it might have seemed that way during its salad days. Actor-director Arthur Lithgow had founded it in 1951 as Shakespeare under the Stars at Antioch College in Yellow Springs, Ohio, where in its first seven seasons it went through Shakespeare's entire canon. Then began the company's peregrinations. It played the Toledo Zoo amphitheater in 1958; then, following a year's hiatus, Stan Hywet Hall in Akron in 1960. The following summer found it in the Ohio Theater in Cuyahoga Falls, called the Akron Shakespeare Festival. The company's travels finally came to a halt in Lakewood, Ohio, where it found a home as the Great Lakes Shakespeare Festival in the Lakewood Civic Auditorium at Lakewood High School.[18]

The GLSF flourished in Lakewood for twenty years, until it strained the confines of its high school facilities. Actors grew tired of limited rehearsal space and hallway dressing rooms with no showers, according to GLSF director Vincent Dowling. Scheduling was also a problem; since the high school needed the auditorium during the academic year, Festival seasons were confined largely to July and August. GLSF officials in the late 1970s began to consider securing their own theater, preferably one in a location more accessible to culturally attuned audiences from the east side. A consensus was forming in support of building a new theater on the shore of Lake Erie in Cleveland's Edgewater Park, still on the west side but closer to downtown. State representative Patrick Sweeney threw his support behind the idea, securing a $1.5 million appropriation from Ohio toward construction of an estimated $4 million theater in the state park. Opposition to the plan came mainly from environmentalists such as the Sierra Club.[19]

Economics rather than ecology derailed the Edgewater idea. Estimates for the facility soon skyrocketed from $4 million to more than $15 million. The financially strapped festival paled at the thought of mounting a major capital campaign, especially one in competition with the ongoing Playhouse Square campaign. At this point, Pat Doyle of the Cleveland Foundation suggested to GLSF president Natalie Epstein that Playhouse Square's Ohio Theatre might hold the answer to the festival's dreams. Epstein went downtown to survey the premises. "The Ohio Theatre was in such shambles, but I fell madly in love with it," she recalled. "The relationship between actor and audience was so wonderful—I just felt like we were home." By April 1981 the GLSF was committed to become the first resident company of Playhouse Square.[20]

Before the opening date in July 1982, Epstein's "shambles" had to be restored to a state-of-the-art legitimate theater such as the Ohio had been at its 1921 opening. Workers replaced the auditorium's leaky roof and installed a smoke vent on the stagehouse. Inside, they installed new electrical, ventilation, air-conditioning, and plumbing systems. Others repaired the plaster walls and ceiling of the auditorium and installed new carpeting and about a thousand new seats. In place of the original chandelier, either sold or stolen, was one salvaged from the recently demolished Hippodrome. The only discernible intrusion into the original interior were two modern steel light bridges suspended from the ceiling above the balcony. To preserve sight lines from the balcony, GLSF opted against replacing the original proscenium stage with a Shakespearean-style thrust stage.[21]

On the evening of July 9, 1982, first-nighters entered through the State's outer lobby, the Ohio's being reserved for restaurant space. At the end of the State's outer lobby, a crossover corridor led to the Ohio's inner lobby, also accessible from the Bulkley Building arcade. Too damaged for restoration, the Ohio's inner lobby was simply tidied up and given a utilitarian paint job. Inside the restored auditorium, the curtain rose on *As You Like It*, one of Shakespeare's most popular comedies. This marked the first time live actors had appeared on those boards in forty-eight years. "It is worth every cent," Michael Ward wrote of the Ohio for the *Plain Dealer*. As for the play, "It is 'As You Like It' as Shakespeare would have loved it."[22]

GLSF followed the Bard with John Millington Synge's *The Playboy of the Western World* and the one-woman show *PIAF: La Vie! l'Amour!* with Gay Marshall. All these were warm-up acts for the season's pièce de résistance: *The Life and Adventures of Nicholas Nickleby*. Based on the Dickens novel, the production was a truly gargantuan undertaking, running eight and a half hours in two parts. It had originated at London's Royal Shakespeare Company, which took it to New York, where it won a Tony for best play along with other awards. Dowling had begun negotiating for the rights to the play even before it reached New York, and Great Lakes would be the first company after the RSC to stage it. Calling for forty-six actors in three hundred roles, with three hundred costumes in ninety-six scenes, the production would strain the company's resources. The payoff was the early sale of 71 percent of its available season subscriptions, with orders coming in from as far as Indianapolis and Minneapolis. Playgoers had the option of viewing *Nicholas Nickleby* over two days or in one marathon session.[23]

Emerson Batdorff of the *Plain Dealer* saw it in a single day. Admitting that even short plays sometimes put him to sleep, he found *Nicholas Nickleby*'s staging "so vivid that I could not sleep. . . . There are villains to be hissed and heroes to be cheered, and furthermore every once in a while someone is chased up one aisle and down the other." Reviewing for *Northern Ohio Live*, Marianne Evett was similarly swept away by "the sheer theatricality of it all." It was "as if the move to the Ohio has suddenly pushed the ensemble into its own." Clive Barnes had seen it in New York, where he had wondered whether *Nickleby* was "really a play—or simply a performance?" Coming to Cleveland for another look, he was convinced by the GLSF production that it really was a play. He also informed his *New York Post* readers that "the new theaters being developed [at Playhouse Square] will make Cleveland one of the nation's theatrical showplaces." Following its stint in the Ohio, the cast went on to a thirteen-week run in Chicago, while GLSF president Epstein addressed a note to Mayor Voinovich. "Over 70,000 people have come downtown to the Ohio Theatre this summer—at least 4,000 from outside the Cleveland area," she told him. "We are a tourist attraction."[24]

Though GLSF finished its Cleveland season in October, the Ohio Theatre had numerous bookings through the following spring. As Robert Finn commented, the schedule resembled "the sort of thing" that G. Bernardi's Cleveland Opera Association had brought to Public Music Hall in former years. Visiting artists included Dave Brubeck, pianist Eugene Istomin, the Roger Wagner Chorale, the Duquesne Tamburitzans, and the Paul Taylor Dance Company. Local groups such as Cleveland Opera and the Ohio Chamber Orchestra would also present programs. Heinz Poll's Akron-based Ohio Ballet would establish a solid Cleveland presence through the season with a series of three different programs. "The taut, trim ensemble has never looked so refined on its home stage in Akron's Thomas Hall . . . as it looked last night at the Ohio Theater," wrote the *Plain Dealer*'s Wilma Salisbury of the debut program in October.[25]

Playhouse Square celebrated the reopening of the Ohio with an all-day street festival on Saturday, September 11. Euclid Avenue was closed from East Ninth to East Seventeenth Streets, and Huron Road from Prospect Avenue to Euclid for the festivities, which began with free theater tours in the morning. Except for in the Ohio, visitors on the theater tours that day largely saw works in progress. The State auditorium was the site of PSF's largest construction project, the enlargement of the stage for ballet and opera. Most of the Palace was in a holding pattern, awaiting the reopenings of the Ohio and the State. One observer described its "soiled damask wallcoverings which have pulled away from the walls, crumbling plaster and peeling paint." One exception in 1982 would have been the dressing rooms in the theater's twin towers. Moe Howard of the Three Stooges comedy team had once described them as a shining exception to the "Spartan at best" accommodations of most dressing rooms on the road. "Best of all [at the Palace] were the dressing rooms, heavily carpeted with mirrored walls and makeup tables," he wrote. "They had everything in them, right down to padded coat hangers."[26]

Bringing the dressing rooms back to their 1922 splendor became a joint undertaking of the Diamond Shamrock Corporation and the Junior League of Cleveland. Diamond Shamrock kickstarted the project with a gift of $350,000, covering more than half of the cost. Though the chemical company had moved its headquarters to Dallas two years previously, it still maintained a significant local presence, with sixteen hundred employees in the area. The Junior League's role was to recruit thirty area interior designers and businesses to donate services and goods for the rooms' refurbishments. When all was done, the league opened up the restored towers to the public for the Diamond Shamrock Towers Showcase '82 fundraiser, which attracted some twenty thousand visitors between April 25 and June 5. It was a nostalgic reminder of the league's first designers' showcase ten years earlier, which provided the seed money that saved the theaters. Contrasted to the decaying condition of the rest of the theater, it was also a reminder, that, in the words of a Junior Leaguer, "We still have a long way to go."[27]

A joint project of the Junior League and the Diamond Shamrock Corporation was the restoration of the luxurious Palace Theatre dressing rooms. They were displayed to the public as part of the festivities for the Ohio Theatre's reopening. (Courtesy of *Cleveland Press* Collection, Michael Schwartz Library, Cleveland State University)

At the moment, with the Ohio back in business, emphasis had switched to preparing the State for the 1984 arts openings. A new development had entered to speed up the timetable—nothing less than the Metropolitan Opera. The "Mighty Met" had been appearing in Cleveland's Public Auditorium annually since 1924, and critics had been complaining about the unsuitability of the cavernous space for opera almost as long. A week prior to the Met's 1983 visit, the *Plain Dealer*'s Robert Finn announced that "various people involved with the annual event" had been discussing the possibility of moving the Met's tour from Public Hall into the State Theatre. One of those who raised the idea was John L. Price Jr., executive director of the Northern Ohio Opera Association, the tour's local sponsor, who said Public Hall was becoming too expensive. Met officials inspected the State the following week, and the following October the opera association and PSF announced that the next year's Met tour would appear in the renovated State Theatre.[28] That meant the State had to be ready by June 11, 1984.

While the auditorium renovations were essentially completed, enlarging the State's stage was a $7 million construction job. It would extend the shallow original stage to a depth of sixty-five feet, with a fifty-by-seventy-two-foot resilient dance floor. Behind the main stage would be a bustle—an extension containing three loading docks for scenery. There would also be eighty sets of lines to hang scenery from, up-to-date lighting and sound equipment, plus an orchestra pit for seventy-five musicians. Work proceeded on schedule for the most part, impeded mainly by the discovery of an underground stream on the construction site. Of necessity, pumps were installed, eating into other items in the budget. Six weeks before the scheduled opening, a *Plain Dealer* writer described the final mad dash to completion: "Wilker was standing near the orchestra pit, where workers were hammering away at the flooring. Up on the stage, other workers were sawing and drilling; still others worked up in the boxes and balconies. Sheets of plastic covered the new red seats in the house. Dust filled the air; the rush to finish the State stagehouse created a construction cacophony."[29]

When the dust had settled there was time for not only the Met but for a gala preview two nights before the opening. On a warm Saturday evening, limousines discharged some fifteen hundred guests on Oriental carpets laid from the curb into the State Theatre lobby. John Lewis introduced Ray Shepardson, Lainie Hadden, and William Miller as true believers from the beginning. Inside, the guests dined in the Palace lobby and mezzanine and the Ohio's lobby and stage. A ninety-minute show followed on the State's new stage, headed by host Mike Douglas and singers Diahann Carroll and Roberta Flack. After-show dancing and desserts in all three theaters brought the evening to a close.[30]

On Monday evening the State's curtain rose on the prologue to the Metropolitan Opera's production of Benjamin Britten's *Peter Grimes*, starring the Canadian tenor Jon Vickers. It wasn't the usual Met Week opener but rather a plum for the opera cognoscenti. To Finn, it was "first of all a riveting musical and dramatic experience for the audience—a masterwork superbly performed." Just as important for the *Plain Dealer* critic, it was performed without in-house amplification, and the theater's acoustics met with his approval. "The sound had a wonderful clean naturalness about it from my seat that was most refreshing." The main complaints on opening night came from Opera Week guarantors and subscribers, members of Cleveland society for the most part, who missed the usual operatic chestnuts served up on Met tours. They also missed the past ambiance of the preperformance Metropolitan Opera Pavilion, formerly in Public Hall's lavishly decorated lower exhibition level. Now it took place in the sparsely trimmed Grand Hall of the Palace Theatre, where the *Plain Dealer*'s society editor noted "a disparity between the elegant gowns that paraded through

Ready for its reopening with the Metropolitan Opera on June 11, 1984, was the renovated State Theatre. Cleveland Opera and Cleveland Ballet would be its principal resident companies. (Photo by David M. Thum, author's collection)

the doors and the threadbare carpeting on the stair treads, stuck together in spots with red or gray duct tape, a jarring reminder that $4 million remains in Playhouse Square's campaign to refurbish the Palace and the State's lobby."[31]

A silver-covered Sixtieth Diamond Jubilee Tour program bore the new name and logo of Playhouse Square Center. Later that month, the Cleveland Orchestra tested the State's acoustics. Yoel Levy opened the concert, fittingly, with Beethoven's "The Consecration of the House" overture. "Every sound on stage was audible, from the smallest detail of phrasing and articulation to distracting extraneous noises such as the players' breathing and the clicking of woodwind keys," wrote reviewer Wilma Salisbury. "The sound projected to the loge level with each choir of instruments clearly defined." Metropolitan Opera officials were also pleased with the State, acclaiming it one of the finest opera houses in the country. Sadly, the Met would visit it for only two more seasons, as it terminated annual tours in 1986.[32]

Later in the State's reopening year, its principal resident companies made their debuts on their new stage. Both Cleveland Ballet and Cleveland Opera had been performing in the Hanna Theatre, the ballet since its public debut, in 1976, and the opera since its fourth season, in 1980. While the Hanna was an excellent venue for legitimate plays and most musicals, it was less than ideal for grand opera and classical ballet, especially when compared with the redesigned State. Its forty-foot stage depth was at least twenty feet short of the State's; its orchestra pit had half the capacity of the State's. Furthermore, opera and ballet at the Hanna had to schedule in between the theater's road show commitments, while as resident companies their needs would have more priority at the State. One huge difference between the two venues, that of capacity, might be viewed as either a blessing or a bane. Ceil Hartman recalled talking with Jane Kirkham, a PSF board member, about moving the ballet into the State and pointing out that a full house at the fifteen-hundred-seat Hanna would be only half a house in the three-thousand-seat State. To David Bamberger, Cleveland Opera's general manager, however, the larger house meant he could accommodate as many patrons in two performances as formerly in three or four.[33]

First up at the State was Cleveland Ballet, confronting not only a new stage but financial and leadership challenges as well. Its financial problems seemed fairly contained, as $300,000 profit in its last fiscal year had halved a troublesome accumulated deficit. Its leadership challenge arose with the recent resignation of one of its two founders. Ian "Ernie" Horvath had been plagued by health issues since collapsing onstage during Cleveland Ballet's New York debut in 1981 and by the end of 1983 had finally decided to take a sabbatical. He and cofounder Dennis Nahat together had branded Cleveland Ballet as the "Dennis and Ernie Show," according to *Plain Dealer* dance critic Salisbury. "The choice of repertoire, the training of the dancers and the shaping of the ensemble reflected their shared artistic vision." From now on it would be Nahat's show.[34]

For the company's State Theatre debut, Nahat had prepared a "reach-for-the-stars-work," a choreographed interpretation of two of Beethoven's most popular symphonies. He had presented Beethoven's Seventh four years earlier under the title *Celebrations,* and now he would reprise it as the prelude to nothing less than the majestic Ninth, or "Choral" Symphony. Putting the two works on stage was a $170,000 undertaking, requiring the thirty-six-member dancing company, an augmented Ohio Chamber Orchestra, four vocal soloists, and a sixty-voice choir trained by Robert Page. As Nahat described his vision, "the ballet does not tell a story. It is movement. It celebrates life through the joy of dance." *Celebration and Ode* had its premiere on the State's new dance floor on October 13, 1984. "A project so enormous naturally had some flaws at its first performance," wrote Salisbury. "Overall, though, the performance gave a good idea of the structure and intent of Nahat's grand concept."[35]

For Cleveland Opera's State Theatre debut a few weeks later, Bamberger chose the perennially popular Johann Strauss operetta *Die Fledermaus.* He livened up the second-act party scene by casting actor Werner Klemperer of television's *Hogan's Heroes* as Prince Orlofsky. Cameo appearances were made by Cleveland pianist Eunice Podis and Dennis Nahat, who, in the words of Robert Finn, "danced a Komzak waltz with showmanship that made the ladies onstage swoon." Overall, Finn judged the performance too leisurely paced. Later that season, Cleveland Opera went to the opposite extreme with the grandest of all grand operas, Verdi's *Aida.* "Splendiferous scenery. Colorful ballet sequences. Augmented chorus. Lots of supers. Live animals on stage. Wow!" wrote Finn in a preview article that tried to get readers to look beyond the spectacle and appreciate the fine points of Verdi's score. Bamberger hedged his bets and nevertheless rented an elephant for the Grand March scene.[36]

In a report for *Opera News,* Finn concluded with an optimistic, if guarded, forecast for Playhouse Square Center: "Perhaps the lesson to be learned from Cleveland Opera's success with *Fledermaus* and from a sold-out three-week run of *The King and I* with Yul Brynner at the State or Great Lakes Shakespeare's 1983 *Nicholas Nickleby* at the Ohio, is simply that when something is offered at Playhouse Square that the Cleveland public wants to see, it will come flocking."[37]

Reviving the Road

Finn wrote his positive prognostication a few years before a movie would popularize the expression "If you build it, they will come." Ever since the days of Ray Shepardson, the Playhouse Square mantra seemed to have been "If you restore it, they will return." In Shepardson's day, that meant drawing several hundred Clevelanders to cabaret shows in theater lobbies. Now Playhouse Square had upped the pot to several thousand people for three restored theaters. "Now they have 7,400 seats—how will they fill them?" a *Plain Dealer* headline put the challenge on the eve of the State's reopening.[38]

Lawrence Wilker was fully aware of the problem of filling in the gaps between performances by Playhouse Square's resident companies. But he was also interested in appealing to a broad audience. "I'm paranoid about a sense of elitism about this thing," he confessed to Joanna Connors in the *Plain Dealer*. Taking a cue from Shepardson, he produced a country-western themed musical, *Pump Boys and Dinettes*, in the Palace early in 1984 and followed it with the touring off-Broadway musical, *Little Shop of Horrors*. Broadway was the traditional source of product for the road, but the well had been running dry. One of the attractions scheduled for a week's run in the State during its reopening month was the preBroadway premiere of *Mahalia*, a musical tribute to the original Queen of Gospel, starring the new queen, Aretha Franklin. Like many projected musicals, it never materialized on stage.[39]

Milton Krantz, recently retired general manager of the Hanna Theatre, contrasted forty-week seasons in the 1940s with the scant six shows in the Hanna's current season. He and Wilker agreed that it was hard to sign up subscribers to a season of "To Be Announced." Lack of product was one side of the dilemma; the other was the cost and scale of whatever product came down the line. As far back as 1936, the Hanna had begun booking costly and popular shows such as *The Great Waltz* in Cleveland's three-thousand-seat Music Hall, thereby doubling its potential house. Krantz, "under the auspices" of the Hanna, had used Music Hall for such shows as

South Pacific, My Fair Lady, Hello, Dolly! with Mary Martin, and *Coco* with Katharine Hepburn.[40]

When Rodgers and Hammerstein's *The King and I* first reached Cleveland in 1954, with Yul Brynner, the original King, it had likewise played in Music Hall. Thirty-one years later, after more than four thousand performances in the role, Brynner brought a revival of the musical back to Cleveland, but this time it played the State. As he had when appearing in *Odyssey* at the Hanna, the star insisted that his dressing room be painted brown at his own expense. Thereafter, explained PSC director of theater operations John Hemsath, the room was described as "Brynner brown." Critic Roxanne Mueller found him a somewhat stumbling starter. "But not to fear," she wrote. "By the second act, he was humming like a well-oiled machine, perhaps realizing that if he didn't start stealing a few scenes for himself, his costar, Mary Beth Peil, would take them all." As Finn had observed for *Opera News*, the star sold out the State for a three-week run.[41]

Another larger-than-life star followed Brynner into the State in early 1985, when Anthony Quinn appeared in the title role of *Zorba*, the musical by John Kander and Fred Ebb, based on Nikos Kazantzakis's novel *Zorba the Greek*. Now Quinn was assuming on stage the role he had made famous in the movie version. Three more Broadway shows came to the State that spring. Mickey Rooney and Ann Miller appeared in a two-week run of *Sugar Babies*. Two non-musicals rounded out the season: Neil Simon's *Brighton Beach Memoirs* and *The Real Thing* with Brian Bedford.

All five shows in the State's 1984–85 season had been booked by the Theatre League

of Cleveland. Its president was Samuel l'Hommedieu, a lawyer turned producer who had succeeded Krantz upon the latter's retirement as the Hanna's manager. Unlike Krantz, l'Hommedieu had more than one iron in the fire. Besides Cleveland, he also managed road theaters in Washington, DC; Atlanta; and St. Louis. While Krantz maintained an office in the theater and a visible presence at all Hanna first nights, his successor ran the Hanna from the aloof height of an office on the eighth floor of the Hanna Building. Balding and businesslike, l'Hommedieu saw his challenge as not only lack of product but a shortage of seats. Although *Amadeus*

With Yul Brynner's appearance in *The King and I* at the State Theatre in 1984, Playhouse Square Center became the Cleveland venue for touring Broadway shows. Before long, the Broadway Series would become the premier attraction of Playhouse Square. (Author's collection)

had sold 96 percent of its seats in 1982, the Hanna had lost money due to its producer's demand for a guarantee of $140,000. The solution, thought l'Hommedieu, would be an increased use of the larger Music Hall for the more lavish productions.[42]

A better answer soon appeared right across Euclid Avenue with the reopening of the State—just as large as Music Hall, closer to restaurants and other theaters, and brilliantly renovated. Following *The King and I,* Playhouse Square Center became the permanent venue for offerings of the Theatre League of Cleveland. To the State came the pre-Broadway tryout of a straight comedy with two storied stars. *Legends!* may have been "cotton candy comedy," in the words of Evett, but "Still, Mary Martin, Carol Channing and the rest of the cast spin this floss into golden entertainment." Later in the 1986–87 season came a certified classic musical, *Cabaret,* with Cleveland native Joel Grey reprising his breakthrough Broadway role as the Master of Ceremonies. "Grey is still incredible as the emcee, perhaps scarier now that he is older," wrote Evett. "Toes twinkling, he is outrageous, funny, charming, desperate, horrifying."[43]

Three months later, however, the "new kind of entertainment" that Wolf von Eckardt had called for came to the State. Andrew Lloyd Webber's *Cats* was the harbinger of a spectacular new breed known as "megamusicals." The theater's stage was transformed into a realistic, verging on expressionistic, junkyard in which a cast costumed as characters from T. S. Eliot's *Old Possum's Book of Practical Cats* cavorted, at times even roaming beyond the proscenium to prowl the aisles of the orchestra section. "They are very good at being cats (hissing, arching backs, looking aloof or endearing)," observed Evett. "The singing, too, is very fine." Webber's tuneful score evoked echoes of the British music halls; those who criticized the show's lack of a plot missed the fact that it wasn't a book musical but a topical revue.[44]

"*Cats* was absolutely a game-changer," said Gina Vernaci, who began working for Playhouse Square in 1984, the year of its first Broadway musical. Hired fresh out of the University of Missouri–Kansas City as a three-month intern, she soon found a place in the production department. *Cats* was PSC's first Cameron MacKintosh production, which according to Vernaci established new standards for touring shows. In place of painted drops, getting scenery allowed shows to have a longer life. "What they did was begin to build public trust; they delivered extraordinary quality," she stated. *Cats* in particular would prove to have legs, as it returned to Playhouse

Square ten times for a total of nearly a hundred performances before the turn of the century.[45]

MacKintosh was British, as was Webber, whose *Jesus Christ Superstar, Evita,* and *Cats* might be regarded as the theatrical counterpart of the British Invasion of 1960s rock. MacKintosh's next big production, however, was French in origin: Alain Boubil and Claude-Michel Schönberg's musicalization of Victor Hugo's *Les Miserables. Les Miz* filled the State Theatre's stage for a two-week run in the summer of 1989. "This megamusical is the stage equivalent of a Hollywood epic, scenes sweeping on and off again with cinematic speed," wrote Evett. Its retelling of the seventeen-year pursuit of ex-convict Jean Valjean by the obsessive Inspector Javert was done with sung-through dialogue. "The music is simple and repetitive," in Evett's opinion, "but the seamless flow gets to you emotionally, and the counterpointing of melodies by different groups of characters sometimes produces an operatic thrill."[46] The sensational staging almost stole the show, however, especially the awesome materialization of a barricade in the 1830 Paris uprising, both sides of which are exposed through the rotation of a turntable. And like that revolving stage, *Les Miz* would be back again . . . and again . . .

Coincidental with the revival of the road came the restoration of the Palace Theatre. Relegated to the background during the renovation and reopening of the Ohio and the State, the Palace was far from neglected. Following the run of *Little Shop of Horrors,* PSF presented a nostalgic revue of parochial education under the cutesy title *Do Black Patent Shoes Really Reflect Up?* "But it's pleasant, undemanding entertainment and it'll probably run at the Palace for ages," summed up Evett. Actually, it opened in a stripped-down Palace for a projected three-month run and held on for the better part of a year, drawing a total audience of a hundred thousand.[47]

Then the renovators took over. Probably the biggest part of the $8.5 million undertaking was the reconstruction of the side boxes and proscenium arch that had been removed in the 1950s to make way for the wide screen of Cinerama. The original shallow orchestra pit was not only enlarged and deepened but placed atop a hydraulic lift, enabling it to be raised or lowered to the desired level. Plumbing, heating, and lighting were modernized, and a new sound system capable of amplification installed. Since the Palace stage backed up against the State's auditorium, an acoustic wall was installed to keep musicians playing the Palace from being heard by audiences in the rear of the State's orchestra section. In the Grand Hall, cleaning and buffing brought out the rich veining of Edward Albee's Carrara marble columns and panels.[48]

Outside the street lobby, a red carpet spread across the Euclid Avenue sidewalk welcomed guests to the gala reopening of the Palace on Saturday, April 30, 1988. Cocktails and refreshments were served at 6:00 P.M. while guests enjoyed music ranging from violins and guitars to Motown.

Theater caricaturist Al Hirschfeld produced a special lithograph for the 1984 State Theatre reopening. Recycled twelve years later to mark Playhouse Square's diamond anniversary, it includes some of the brightest stars who appeared there (*clockwise from upper left*): Benny Goodman, Red Skelton, Judy Garland, Bob Hope, and George Burns and Gracie Allen. (Author's collection)

"People can go from place to place to find whatever kind of entertainment they desire," said volunteer Barbara DiCicco. John Hemsath noted that it would now require 225 red-coated volunteer ushers to seat theatergoers when all three PSC stages were going at once, contrasting that with the "days in the 1970s when 225 people were a good audience." Once the preliminaries were out of the way, there was a show on the Palace stage starring Dionne Warwick and Burt Bacharach.[49] A month later, the Palace hosted its first Broadway show, Meredith Willson's *The Music Man* with John Davidson.

Soon after bringing the Palace back to Broadway standards, Playhouse Square took over the booking and sale of road shows from the Theatre League of Cleveland, eliminating the middleman. Though Vernaci remembers l'Hommedieu as "a lovely guy," complaints from subscribers over his management began reaching Playhouse Square in the 1989–90 season. "That year it wasn't being tended to like it should have been," said Vernaci. "Tickets were going out late." Subscribers were being cut out of choice seats by single-ticket buyers. "If we didn't [take over the series], we were afraid it would alienate Clevelanders." It was marketed as the "Broadway Series" when PSC took over, and Vernaci would be extolled by a future critic as "architect of the popular event." National City Bank became a local sponsor.[50]

One of the offerings in the final season of the old regime was Alfred Uhrey's *Driving Miss Daisy*, a straight play starring Julie Harris and Brock Peters. Though Evett lavished high praise on the production, she felt constrained to attach a caveat: "I suspect that this fragile play needs more intimate surroundings than the Palace to be its best, however." More suitable to the ornate grandeur of the theater was *The Secret Garden,* a musical in the second season of the Broadway Series. It wasn't a "simple children's story," concluded Evett, but "it really is the first intelligent family musical."[51] Indeed, musicals became the mainstay of the Broadway Series, and considering the State's opera and ballet commitments, the Palace became the primary venue for musicals. *Cats* would make its next Cleveland visit there, as would *Guys and Dolls* and Robert Goulet in *Camelot.* In time, the Broadway Series would become the Playhouse Square mainstay.

Location, Location

On the eve of Opening Day in 1994, Dick Feagler was dreaming not only of a new baseball season but the opening of a new baseball stadium for the Cleveland Indians. It had been built on the southern edge of downtown in an area formerly known as Greek Town but now rechristened Gateway. To the often cynical Feagler, erstwhile columnist for the defunct *Cleveland Press* now writing for his former paper's rival, the *Plain Dealer,* it represented more than just a new ballpark: it was the culmination of two decades of downtown resurgence. "As a kid I'd been handed a vibrant, marvelous town," he mused. "Somebody's vision and sacrifice had worked for my benefit. What kind of town would this generation pass along?" Cleveland still had serious urban problems, especially out in the neighborhoods. "But we brought Downtown back from the dead anyway. We did that."[52]

Downtown indeed was back from the dead. That was dramatically apparent on Public Square, where two new skyscrapers challenged Terminal Tower's five-decade dominance. One, the elegant, deco-infused Society (now Key) Tower, actually topped the old Terminal by five stories. But new life also stirred beneath and behind the Terminal Tower, where the abandoned Union railroad station had been redeveloped into The Avenue, an urban shopping mall. Underneath that was the Public Square station of the RTA Rapid Transit, from where a passageway led under West Huron Road to the new baseball park as well as a new downtown arena for the Cleveland Cavaliers.[53]

Cleveland had won its fifth All-American City designation in 1993 and was being hailed as a comeback city. Feagler recalled the not-so-long-ago days of the Cleveland jokes:

A dull comic could coax a cheap laugh from a bored audience by merely mentioning our name. They rewrote the old Philadelphia jokes and made them Cleveland jokes. . . .

When the town actually began to come back, who believed it? We had been stung too many times by smoke blown from pipedreams. But little by little, it really appeared. First Playhouse Square. Then the Flats. The Warehouse District. Tower City. More Flats. More Playhouse Square. The jokes began to dry up.[54]

"First Playhouse Square. . . . More Playhouse Square." It was becoming apparent that Playhouse Square was about more than theaters. Early in Wilker's tenure at PSF, a *Plain Dealer* business reporter found him "juggling the work of the foundation's efforts relating to the three-theater entertainment center and the much larger, and eventually more important, work of the area's development." One might argue as to which was more important—theaters or environs—but from the beginning, those involved in the theaters' restoration saw the connection between the two. Wilker would leave after nine years to direct the Kennedy Center for the Arts in Washington, DC. He was succeeded by Art J. Falco, PSF's vice president for finance, who had been hired in 1985 with no prior arts experience. Falco originally thought he might stick around for five years, but his early involvement in *Black Patent Leather Shoes* evidently transfused greasepaint into his veins. More than three decades later, he reflected, "Playhouse Square is a performing arts center *and* a neighborhood. This is one of our unique business models that we've developed." What distinguished the Playhouse Square model from those of other performing arts centers was its direct involvement in real estate. "They try to influence real estate," said Falco of other centers, "but they don't actually own it."[55]

Acquiring and owning property had been a PSF goal almost from its inception in 1973. One of its ancillary offshoots had been the Playhouse Square Associates, a group containing several interlocking PSF directors. Its purpose was "to acquire and develop property in the area with the long-range goal of creating a thriving entertainment, retail and office center." Perhaps its first real property acquisition came as a gift from the Gund Foundation, which in 1981, along with a $500,000 grant for theater restoration, donated to Playhouse Square the former WJW Building across from the Palace Theatre. The building's colonial-style facade disguised its origins as the old Lake Theater dating from 1928. It still housed a 250-seat theater, which PSF development director Jane Kirkham thought might be put to use as a commercial theater to help raise funds for the restoration work. Unfortunately, budget constraints forced the foundation to sell the building the following year to the T. W. Grogan Company for $270,000, which was used to pay off debt.[56]

Jane Pierce Kirkham was involved in numerous civic and charitable causes, from the Free Clinic to the Hitchcock House for women who were recovering alcoholics, but reviving Playhouse Square became the consuming passion of her life. Born with spina bifida and rarely if ever in the best of health, she refused to let her condition limit her life and activities. She was the daughter of activist parents: her father had been a founder of WVIZ, Cleveland's public television station, and her mother a president of the Cleveland Orchestra's Women's Committee. A graduate of Shaker Heights High School, Jane earned a bachelor of arts degree from Wellesley College and a master's degree in literature from Case Western Reserve, and raised three sons.[57]

Her commitment to Playhouse Square undoubtedly stemmed, as it had for Lainie Hadden and Gwinn York, from her tenure as president of the Junior League, from 1974 to 1976. She saw the theaters in the early stages of restoration, before all the leaks were plugged and the peeling paint repaired. "But, according to a Playhouse Square eulogy, "Jane took one look and saw a vision of Cleveland's future. She dedicated herself to the project." Much as Hadden had done with Shepardson, Kirkham took Wilker in hand, introducing him to movers and shakers during PSF's capital campaign. "She was soft-spoken, gentle, even tender in the way she asked about you," said one who knew her. Fey in appearance, with a wide smile, short hairstyle, and large widely spaced eyes behind outsized lenses, she must have been hard to say no to. She would stay involved with PSF for the rest of her life, serving under such titles as director of planning and area development and director of special projects.[58]

Kirkham recognized that Playhouse Square alone couldn't revitalize downtown, however. Seeing downtown living as another vital piece of the puzzle, she became "an urban pioneer," as one of her sons put it. Between the Flats and Public Square, a movement was taking shape to convert old, largely abandoned nineteenth-century buildings into lofts and apartments. It became trendy as the Warehouse District, and Kirkham not only talked it up but demonstrated her commitment by moving in 1985 into the Bradley Building on West Sixth Street, which she eagerly showed off to friends. "She believed in downtown and its resurgence and whatever she got involved in, she

Activist Jane Kirkham saw the connection between downtown living and Playhouse Square. (Photograph by Timothy Culek, Courtesy of *Cleveland Press* Collection, Michael Schwartz Library, Cleveland State University)

had a passion for," commented Falco. Eventually her health broke down, and she died at fifty-eight from cancer in 1995. Probably her most appropriate memorial was raised not long afterward, when a row of six new townhouses at the edge of the Warehouse District on West Tenth Street was christened Kirkham Place.[59]

By that time, Kirkham had had the satisfaction of seeing several signs of downtown revival in Playhouse Square itself. Considering that the movement to save the theaters was undertaken to prevent them from being replaced by a parking lot, there was a hint of irony in the fact that one of PSF's first projects outside the theaters was the construction of a parking garage. With three theaters in full operation by 1988, however,

providing parking for patrons became a priority. A five-level garage with spaces for 750 cars was built on Chester Avenue with an entrance from East Fifteenth Street, across from the Hermit Club. Soon theatergoers could access the theaters from the garage's second floor through an enclosed climate-controlled connector over Dodge Court. "Totally Enclosed—Never Go Outside Once You Leave Your Car," headed an announcement in PSC programs. A few urbanologists noted that what Playhouse Square had gained in convenience it lost in pedestrian traffic outside the theaters. "It's possible to visit Playhouse Square," pointed out *Plain Dealer* architecture critic Steven Litt, "without ever setting foot on a city street."[60]

Having placed a garage in Playhouse Square's backyard, PSF promoted more progressive improvements for the center's front doorstep. In the 1970s a group of trustees and friends of Playhouse Square had purchased a property on the corner of Huron Road and East Fourteenth Street, once the location of the Euclid Hotel and later the site of a couple of restaurants. The parcel was donated to the foundation, which sold it to a developer for $3 million. On the lot, the developer raised a fifteen-story office building, the first major addition to Playhouse Square in nearly seventy years. Originally named the Renaissance, it later became the US Bank Building. Its only drawback was a forbidding dark glass and black granite facade that led Cleveland's planning director, Hunter Morrison, to dub it the "Darth Vader building."[61]

With its profit from the Renaissance deal, PSF turned its attention to the dowdy, two-story Point Building across Huron Road. The land was acquired in the same way for a new 205-room, $27 million Wyndham Hotel, which opened on July 7, 1995. Anchored into the side of the old Halle Building, the structure narrowed to a graceful rounded tower at the junction of Huron and Euclid Avenue. Its off-white facade provided a welcome contrast to the "Darth Vader building." On the ground floor of the tower was a restaurant-bar named Winsor's in honor of Winsor French, the *Press* columnist who had chronicled the doings of the "Jolly Set" in Playhouse Square's early days. With a hotel back in the center of the theater district, casts and crews of visiting shows could stay only steps away from the theaters.[62]

Construction of the Wyndham led to a major change in the Huron Road configuration. Gone was the pedestrian mall envisioned in the Halprin plan, as Huron was reopened to two-way traffic to allow access to the Halle garage for hotel parking. Eastbound traffic on Huron would no longer merge into Euclid Avenue but make a left turn around the Wyndham's tower to cross Euclid into northbound East Thirteenth Street. As for the Halprin plan, it was superseded by a new vision devised by Benjamin Wood and Jane Thompson of Cambridge, Massachusetts, which imagined a "Times Square feel" for Playhouse Square. It included two large billboards over the Ohio and State marquees and a large message board in the district to publicize shows coming to town. Euclid Avenue would be narrowed to four greenery-lined lanes as part of RTA plans for a dedicated bus line to University Circle.[63]

The Shows Go On

Once past the challenge of reopening three theaters, Lawrence Wilker turned to the more quotidian job of keeping their seventy-four hundred upholstered seats warmed by flesh-and-blood seats. Interspersed among the seasons of its resident companies, PSC offered a variegated smorgasbord of shows for all tastes. For the young, there was a Children's Theatre Series with plays ranging from *The Tale of Peter Rabbit* to *The Story of Jackie Robinson*. For pop fans, there was Gladys Knight and the Pips; for classical aficionados, the Royal Philharmonic Orchestra; for crossover tastes, Wynton Marsalis. Ranging over an entire gamut of genres was Cuyahoga Community College's Showtime at High Noon Series. Dr. Lucille Gruber, the college's director of cultural arts, put together a schedule of monthly, free noontime shows, mostly in the Ohio Theatre, aimed at an audience of students, retirees, and downtown workers. Its attractions included the Tziganka Cossack Dancers, the Paragon Ragtime Orchestra, Balé Folclórico de Bahia, Apollo's Fire Baroque Orchestra, Ritmo Tango, and the Riga Dome Boys Choir of Latvia. Some of the programs were repeated in the evening for paid admission.[64]

If one were looking for a specific moment to mark the "arrival" of Playhouse Square, it might have come in 1993 with the announcement that the Front Row Theater would close operation in suburban Highland Heights and move its bookings downtown to Playhouse Square. Sammy Davis Jr. had opened the circular theater with the revolving stage in 1974. Over the next nineteen years, he was followed by such acts as Richard Pryor, Joan Rivers, Johnny Cash, the Jackson Five, James Taylor, and Redd Foxx. When it opened Playhouse Square had been dark except for *Jacques Brel*. Now, however, the thirty-two-hundred-seat theater-in-the-round was facing costly renovations and increased competition from downtown venues. "Downtown deserves a chance to be revitalized," said Front Row president Lawrence S. Dolin in graceful surrender.[65]

Playhouse Square was ready for prime time. Both the State and Ohio theater lobbies bore signs of improvement. The State's street lobby was designated the Founder's Lobby, with names of major PSC donors etched in mahogany-framed glass panes along the walls. In the Margaret A. and R. Livingston Ireland Grand Lobby, the plaster intaglio ceiling had been completely repainted and the James Daugherty murals cleaned. More dramatic changes were apparent at the Ohio, where the original fire-damaged grand lobby had never been restored. In 1991, it was at least replaced by a classically inspired design courtesy of a gift from the Reinberger Foundation. White statues behind balustrades outlined a star-studded blue sky above, while a Mediterranean mural was visible behind a row of columns below. Restoration purists might carp, but it would have to do—at least for the present. Back at the State, between the street lobby and the Grand Lobby was the Customer Service Center Lobby, with eight ticket windows along its west wall serving all three theaters. Behind the windows, in a space formerly occupied by a restaurant, a sales staff operated a computerized ticketing system that could enable customers to select the best available seat in any price range and print their tickets within seconds, eliminating the need for each resident company to handle its own ticket sales.[66]

In the eyes of many Clevelanders, the ultimate success of Playhouse Square Center was tied to the fortunes of its three resident companies—Cleveland Ballet, Cleveland Opera, and the GLSF. Except for the Broadway Series, and until the Front Row merger, Playhouse Square was largely committed to the arts as opposed to entertainment. The main problem with the arts, however, especially in America, was that ticket sales rarely raised more than half of production costs, making arts organizations dependent on charitable gifts and foundation grants to balance their budgets. In PSC's early days, the Great Lakes company was the most financially stressed of its resident companies. Heady with the success of *Nicholas Nickleby*, it took the production to Chicago the following year, where it ran into competition from a free Royal Shakespeare television production and returned deeply in debt.[67]

Cleveland Ballet might provide a case study of the somewhat awkward pas de deux between artistic achievement and financial equilibrium. Under artistic director Dennis Nahat, the fledgling company ran up a string of dazzling successes following its State Theatre debut in 1985. Its celebrated holiday production of *The Nutcracker*, seen at Music Hall since 1979, moved to the State, where the soaring Christmas tree in the act 1 scene change provided the biggest holiday display in Playhouse Square since the days of the Sterling & Welch Christmas tree. In 1986, the company formed a partnership with the city of San Jose in California's Silicon Valley, which became its second home and a source of financial support. Nearly a million dollars from Cleveland's Reinberger Foundation and Apple cofounder Steve Wozniak underwrote productions of *Swan Lake* and *A Midsummer Night's Dream*. Cynthia Gregory, described by the *Plain Dealer*'s Wilma Salisbury as "America's reigning Swan Queen," not only danced that role in the former but joined the company as permanent guest artist.[68]

Success came at a price, however. "Nahat continued throughout the ballet's existence to insist on the biggest productions, the best materials and personnel," summarized Salisbury. By 1991 a Save Cleveland Ballet campaign addressed an accumulated deficit of nearly $3 million. Ballet trustees pledged more than $1 million, the company was reduced by ten members, and the season by a dozen weeks. Filling out the corps de ballet with dancers from Atlanta, *Swan Lake* was revived and performed in Cleveland, San Jose, and Atlanta. The company officially became Cleveland San Jose Ballet in 1997, in recognition of the increasing influence of its West Coast support. Nahat continued to think big, unveiling a $1.2 million Elvis Presley–infused production of *Blue Suede Shoes* and another based on Karl Orff's *Carmina Burana* requiring a chorus as well as orchestra. Though a $4 million grant from the Cleveland Foundation undertook to provide free theater rent for all three resident companies in Playhouse Square, in the meantime the ballet was locked out of its Playhouse Square studios for nonpayment of rent and forced to practice in Masonic Temple.[69]

More stable during this period, if less spectacular, was the Cleveland Opera. General director David Bamberger, in partnership with his wife, Carola, carefully nurtured the company to a budget of $3.3 million and an audience ranked tenth largest in the United States. "David and Carola are business people as well as artists," stated PSC's director of theater operations, John Hemsath. "When they ask for something, it's because they really need it. I have felt for years that they run the best organization in the arts in town." They did it with generally conservative programming, putting together predictable seasons rarely deviating from an audience-pleasing diet of Puccini and Verdi. In the fifteen seasons following its move into the State, Cleveland Opera gave Puccini ten productions, including three each of *Madame Butterfly* and *Tosca*. Verdi and Mozart followed with seven apiece. [70]

Only occasionally did Cleveland Opera venture out of its comfort zone. There were three American operas: Douglas Moore's *The Ballad of Baby Doe*, Virgil Thomson's *The Mother of Us All*, and George Gershwin's *Porgy and Bess*, this last a production first seen ten years earlier at Houston Grand Opera. There was even a major commission, from a rock star no less: Stewart Copeland, the drummer with The Police. Funded with a $300,000 grant from the Reinberger Foundation, *Holy Blood and Crescent Moon* was ballyhooed for its world premiere at the State on October 10, 1989: "The International Music Event of the Year." To the surprise, and maybe disappointment, of many, Copeland turned out a rather conventional score set in the Crusades, with little evidence of rock and roll. "Copeland admits to being an operatic newcomer who barely knew what opera was when he found himself asked to write this one," wrote Robert Finn in the *Plain Dealer*. "So we are left here with a well-intentioned but essentially amateurish work."[71]

Despite its overall conservative management and repertoire, Cleveland Opera habitually ran in the red. In 1992, Bamberger reported the company as having run the largest deficit in its history the previous year and facing one nearly as large for the present year. A planned production of Mussorgsky's *Boris Godunov* the following year was cancelled in favor of a concert of Russian opera excerpts. In 1995, with the aid of another $300,000 Reinberger grant, however, Bamberger was finally able to mount the company's first (after twenty years!) attempt at a music drama of Richard Wagner. He boldly attacked the German composer's four-and-a-half-hour (plus intermissions) comic masterpiece, *Die Meistersinger von Nürnberg,* and pulled off what *Plain Dealer* music critic Donald Rosenberg called "Cleveland Opera's . . . finest achievement."[72]

Early in the 1990s David Bamberger had said, "I want to make sure we get into the 21st Century." Cleveland Opera was still there in 1998, still operating on a $3.1 million budget, but still carrying a deficit of $350,000. At the time, Great Lakes Theatre had a similar $3.1 million budget but, at $140,000, less than half the opera's deficit. In contrast, Cleveland Ballet was running on an $8.1 million budget with a shortfall of $500,000. That was when the Cleveland Foundation pledged funds to provide the three resident companies with free theater rent for ten years. "This is a tremendous benefit to all of us," commented Carola Bamberger. "It takes an incredible amount of effort to raise that amount of money. The opera is doing well if it makes 45 percent to 50 percent of its income at the box office." Now at least they were sure of reaching the next century.[73]

Of the three resident companies, the GLSF experienced the greatest changes. Its triumph in Nicholas Nickleby had turned into tragedy with the low attendance of the revival and aborted tour the following year. Their holiday production of *A Child's Christmas in Wales* had also failed at the box office, contributing to a record deficit of $700,000. On top of these misfortunes came the resignation of the company's flamboyant director, Vincent Dowling. A search committee brought back a replacement from New York, perhaps the city's most significant artistic appointment since the Cleveland Orchestra's hire of George Szell in 1946.[74]

Gerald Freedman was next to a native Clevelander, born in neighboring Lorain, Ohio, to a dentist and history teacher, both emigrants from Czarist Russia. Like Paul Newman and Joel Grey, he cut his theatrical teeth as a Curtain Puller at the Cleveland Play House. He made his reputation as artistic director of Joseph Papp's New York Shakespeare Festival and staging the premiere of *Hair* at Papp's Public Theater in 1967. In his late fifties, with a full head of steel-gray hair, Freedman looked forward to planning entire seasons with full autonomy at Great Lakes Shakespeare. Joanna Connors described his first look inside the Ohio Theatre as artistic director: "'It's beautiful,' Freedman said, turning to survey the green-and-gold jewel of a theater, holding his arms out and smiling so much his eyes nearly shut behind his steel-rimmed glasses. 'And it's mine.'"[75]

Not just the theater but the festival became Freedman's. Reflecting his desire to broaden the repertory, he dropped the Bard from its name and rebranded it the Great Lakes Theatre Festival. He dropped rotating repertory in favor of uninterrupted runs for each show and extended the season from three months to nine. After the Cleveland Play House ceased its holiday attraction of Dickens' *A Christmas Carol*, Freedman directed his own adaptation at the Ohio, where it remains a fixture, thirty-five years and counting. Most impressive to the average theatergoer, perhaps, was his ability to use his Broadway connections to bring well-known names to his casts. In his second season, he directed a star-studded *Arsenic and Old Lace*, headed by Jean Stapleton as Abby Brewster and Tony Roberts as Mortimer. Freedman took that production from Cleveland to Broadway and would take seven more GLTF productions on tour.[76]

When Hal Holbrook came to town for his 1987 *Mark Twain Tonight* performance, Freedman strolled over to the Palace to say hello and heard the Cleveland-raised actor doing a sound check with the "Blow, winds, and crack your cheeks!" monologue from *King Lear*. On the spot, he invited Holbrook to do the whole play for GLTF at the Ohio, which he did three years later. Holbrook then returned in the title roles of Chekhov's *Uncle Vanya* and Miller's *Death of Salesman*. The procession of guest stars continued with Olympia Dukakis in Brecht's *Mother Courage*, Delroy Lindo in Shakespeare's *Othello*, Piper Laurie in Chekhov's *The Cherry Orchard*, David Birney in Shakespeare's *Antony and Cleopatra*, and Tony Randall in Sheridan's *The School for Scandal*.[77]

Freedman's greatest coup was ninety-nine-year-old Broadway legend George Abbott, who came in 1987 to direct his own 1926 hit *Broadway*. (When it had first appeared at the Ohio in summer stock, it had featured a young actor named Spencer Tracy.) As part of an Abbott mini-festival, Freedman directed the Rodgers and Hart musical comedy *The Boys from Syracuse*, which Abbott had cowritten and directed in 1938. Another notable landmark of the Freedman era was the 1992 world premiere of *The Ohio State Murders*, which had been commissioned by GLTF from native Cleveland playwright Adrienne Kennedy. Though not autobiographical, the mystery drew on Kennedy's experiences as a young Black student at Ohio State. Freedman directed a cast headed by former Clevelander Ruby Dee, and Cleveland State University hosted a symposium centered on the Obie-winning playwright's work.[78]

After twelve years, in which he had directed twenty-eight productions, Freedman left the Great Lakes Theatre Festival for academia, as dean of the drama school at the University of North Carolina School of the Arts. "Gerry Freedman was a gift to theater here," summed up Cleveland actor Reuben Silver, who with his wife, Dorothy Silver, had appeared in Freedman's production of S. Ansky's *The Dybbuk*. Remaining behind as a resident director was Victoria Bussert, whom Freedman had recruited from Northwestern University and who would become the nationally recognized head of Baldwin Wallace University's music theater program. The festival was in comparatively healthy financial shape. Under Anne des Rosiers as managing director, the budget had been balanced five years in a row and the deficit reduced to $200,000.[79]

While the PSC resident companies were experiencing a roller-coaster effect—arduous climbs followed by precipitous drops—the Broadway Series seemed on an unbroken upward roll. There was a positive spike on April 28, 1993, when Andrew Lloyd Webber's *The Phantom of the Opera* opened its initial Cleveland run. Coming in the tracks of *Cats* and *Les Miserables*, *Phantom* proved to be the monarch of megamusicals. "In many respects this is the finest work of Lloyd Webber's career, even if many of his most gorgeous melodies are handed down from composers of true operatic persuasion," wrote Rosenberg in the *Plain Dealer*. "In truth," he caviled nonetheless, "'Phantom' is a triumph of stagecraft over artistic substance." It was performed in the State Theatre, where it might avail itself of the enlarged stagehouse. A hole was drilled above the proscenium to accommodate the fabled chandelier that figures so prominently in the melodrama. "The chandelier falls to breathtaking effect," allowed Rosenberg.[80] Whether for the stagecraft or

Actress Ruby Dee* and director Gerald Freedman go over the script of Adrienne Kennedy's *The Ohio State Murders*, which received its world premiere by Great Lakes Theater in the Ohio Theatre. (Courtesy of Great Lakes Theater, photo by Roger Mastroianni.) *Member of Actors' Equality

the substance, Clevelanders were sold on *Phantom*. Its eight-week run was virtually sold out (98 percent of capacity) to nearly two hundred thousand patrons for a gross of just under $9 million. They came from thirty-six states and Canada, including even tour buses from Manhattan. One woman who went into labor during intermission was given replacement tickets so she and her husband could return and see the rest of the show. The reception of that first visit, said Vernaci, "put Cleveland on the map in this business." And the *Phantom* phenomenon was far from over in Cleveland, as four more tours would call over the next sixteen years. Including the first visit, *Phantom* would give 263 performances in Playhouse Square to a projected audience of six hundred thousand.[81]

Most shows in the Broadway Series played the Palace. Robert Goulet appeared there in *Camelot* two weeks before *Phantom*. Chita Rivera, who had helped to paint the State's auditorium, came to the Palace in *Kiss of the Spider Woman*. Rock fans came there for the Greenwich Village musical *Rent*. Even straight plays occasionally played the Palace, notably Julie Harris and Charles Durning in *Gin Game*. One show that was big enough for the State was the revival of Kern and Hammerstein's *Show Boat,* which came for an eight-week run in 1997, seventy years after the original production had previewed for a week at the Ohio Theatre on its way to Broadway. The Tony-winning revival also gave audiences a chance to see a virtually uncut version of the 1927 original.

Show Boat also inaugurated a milestone season for the Broadway Series. With the exception of megahits such as *Les Miserables* and *Phantom*, most shows in the regular subscription series had run for one week with eight performances. But, as PSC put it, "the recent proliferation of massive, high tech extravaganzas like *The Phantom of the Opera* and *Miss Saigon* has had a powerfully magnetic effect on traditional theatergoers, especially in Cleveland." That "magnetic effect" pulled in more subscribers wanting choice guaranteed seats for such shows. In the first half of the 1990s, the Broadway Series subscription base had doubled to fifteen thousand subscribers, who spoke for fully 70 percent of the available seats in a week's run. To satisfy the demands of single show ticket-buyers, therefore, Playhouse Square announced that all shows in its Broadway Series would be given two-week runs with sixteen performances. "As Northeast Ohio's 'home of the performing arts,' Playhouse Square Center has a responsibility to make quality, live theater available to as many patrons as possible," declared PSC president Falco. "By expanding the Broadway Series, twice as many people will now have an opportunity to experience top-notch musicals at prices more affordable than in larger markets like New York and Toronto."[82]

The Final Pieces

With three theaters fully restored and in production by 1990, in the eyes of most Clevelanders, Playhouse Square might have considered its mission accomplished. Still in plain sight, however, remained two exceptions to the general success story. At the western end of the row of former Euclid Avenue movie palaces sat the Allen, the forgotten theater of Playhouse Square. Nearly a block south of the Allen was the Hanna, stepsister of the Euclid Avenue showplaces.

The Hanna had singly kept the lights burning in Playhouse Square when the Euclid Avenue marquees went dark in 1969. It remained lit through the 1970s, while an aggregation of visionaries and volunteers struggled to come up with a plan to revive the darkened theaters. By the 1980s, however, just when Playhouse Square was on the path to recovery, the Hanna was running on life support. By mid-decade, Cleveland Opera and Cleveland Ballet had moved from the Hanna to the State. Samuel l'Hommedieu followed suit, booking not only musicals but even straight plays at Playhouse Square Center. *'Night, Mother* with Mercedes McCambridge in December 1984 may have been the last traditional Broadway road show to play the Hanna.[83]

Over the next few years, the Hanna subsisted on a spotty grab bag of attractions. There was classical theater, such as four performances by the Old Vic in Shakespeare and Shaw and two weeks of *Kabuki Medea.* There was a dark stretch of a year, followed by a year of movies, from *A Boy and His Dog* to a Kurasowa film festival. A Kenley Players production of *Nunsense* ran for thirteen weeks. Finally, in 1989 a group from the recently dismissed resident company of the Cleveland Play House made a stand at the Hanna. Led by Wayne Turney, the Cleveland Actors' Theatre Co. made its debut with a three-week run of *The Last Days of Route 66.* Three more productions followed, and then union problems and the illness of their backer forced Turney to call it quits. The fabled Hanna curtain had collected its last autographs.[84]

At least the Hanna wasn't in imminent danger of destruction, which was more than could be said of the Allen. Here, too, was a note of irony, as Shepardson had begun his campaign to save Playhouse Square with the Budapest Symphony concert at the Allen in 1971. During his struggle to save the State and Ohio from demolition, he continued booking such attractions as Richard Pryor, Dave Brubeck, and Bruce Springsteen there. "Using the Allen keeps interest alive in the area," he told Tony Mastroianni in the *Press.* By 1976, however, admitting he had his hands full with the State, Ohio, and Palace, Shepardson had no further plans for the Allen. A succession of restaurants moved in and out of the theater's lobby and Romanesque rotunda. Inside the auditorium, $200,000 was spent in 1977 to construct a seventy-foot dome for an attraction called "Laserium." Four laser beams danced on the dome to a rock score before the novelty wore off within two years.[85]

In the meantime, Playhouse Square was working to get the State Theatre ready for opera and ballet by 1984. To expand the theater's stagehouse, however, an additional piece of land was needed; this happened to be part of a property anchored by the Bulkley Building. PSF possessed a five-year option to buy the Bulkley complex, including the Allen Theatre, but it was due to expire in 1982 with Playhouse Square too extended to afford the purchase price. Once more into the breach rode the Cleveland Foundation, which made a program-related investment of $3.8 million to acquire the Bulkley complex. The foundation then sold the land needed for the stagehouse to the owner of the State, Cuyahoga County, which leased it to Playhouse Square.[86]

That done, the Cleveland Foundation inadvertently found itself the owner of the remainder of the complex, which included the Bulkley building, arcade, and garage; the Allen Theatre; and the Selzer Building. One CF official had viewed acquisition of such a varied portfolio as a "necessary evil" to get the land needed for PSF's stagehouse. Playhouse Square had hopes of purchasing the entire property from CF, perhaps to implement Peter van Dijk's vision of shops and cafes along Dodge Court. Five years passed, however, with PSF no nearer to meeting the necessary price and CF in need of funds for other programs. In 1987 the Cleveland Foundation sold the Bulkley complex to a syndicate headed by William N. West, chief executive of Ostendorf-Morris real estate brokers.[87]

West had plans for the complex, but unfortunately they didn't include the Allen Theatre. He estimated it would take $3 million just to repair the Allen, a prohibitive cost if there were no profitable use for the theater. PSF officials had told him they had no use for the Allen's nearly three thousand seats. West therefore proposed to raze the Allen to make way for an atrium containing a restaurant and specialty shops.[88]

Clevelanders somewhat belatedly awoke to the plight of the fourth jewel in the Playhouse Square crown. From Detroit, where he was restoring three downtown theaters, Ray Shepardson expressed dismay that the Cleveland Foundation would sell the Allen to someone who wanted to tear it down: "To me, the Allen is just as exciting as it was in 1970—it just needs creativity to find a new use for it." Architect Gerald Payto voiced much the same sentiment when West took his proposal before Cleveland's Fine Arts Advisory Committee. "All the theaters are redeveloped to the point where it would be easy to say, 'Let's turn this one into a parking lot or a garden,'" said Payto. "I hope it won't be torn down before we realize how important it is."[89]

It began to look like the 1972 playbook all over again, with West cast in the unenviable role of Miller and Cappadora, or Millcap. On December 12, the Cleveland Restoration Society called a forum in the Ohio Theatre that included West on a panel with architect van Dijk and Holly Fiala of the National Trust for Historic Preservation. Van Dijk, who had conceived the idea of connecting PSC's three restored theaters, proposed saving the Allen by dividing it into a film theater, a restaurant, and a party center. Eleven days later, Shepardson returned to lead a Save the Allen rally on the Huron Road mall opposite the Allen. "Despite appearances," wrote Tom Andrzejewski in the *Plain Dealer*, "what we have here is not a greedy developer and uncaring institutions but a lot of people seemingly unable to arrive at a solution other than demolition—which a determined but small group of preservationists, under the name of the Allen Theater Redevelopment Coalition, is trying to change."[90]

Preservationists scrambled to throw up hurdles in the bulldozers' path. City councilman Gus Frangos introduced a resolution to declare the entire Playhouse Square theater area a historic district. The Allen Theater Redevelopment Coalition presented a petition with ten thousand signatures in favor of the legislation to the Cleveland Landmarks Commission, which added its approval to the measure. Passed by city council, the designation would forestall demolition or alteration of the Allen by up to a year.[91] West came up with a new plan that would raze the theater but spare its lobby and rotunda. Signatures on the Allen Theater Redevelopment Coalition's petition urging preservation increased to twenty-five thousand, and the group dramatized its cause by parking a bulldozer in front of the Allen a day after the theater's sixty-ninth birthday. "Until people see a bulldozer or a crane in front of a treasured landmark, they don't take action to save it," explained coalition director Ed Small.[92]

The pendulum began to swing in favor of the Allen. In June 1990, the Fine Arts Advisory Committee voted unanimously to oppose West's partial demolition plan. Several weeks later, the Cleveland Planning Commission backed the committee's recommendation by voting 5–0 to deny West permission to raze the theater. "West left the hearing visibly upset," reported the *Plain Dealer*, lamenting the loss of four years of planning. He finally raised the white flag in January 1993, persuaded by the need to make a mortgage payment and what he termed the first decent offer from PSF. He agreed to lease the theater to Playhouse Square for twenty years with an option to buy. Initial plans included a five-hundred-seat cabaret theater and a possible party center. A $400,000 grant from the Cleveland Foundation would go to repair and redevelop the space.[93]

Nearly two years later, the Allen was a "work in progress." There were new bathrooms and polished floors in the front of the house; the theater's capacious auditorium had been downsized to "a cozy cabaret setting" with tableside seating for 350 amid "the theater's paint-chipped, water-stained walls with missing patches of plaster in the background." While ultimate plans were still evolving, PSF decided to keep the theater in the public eye with another page from the Shepardson playbook, namely, putting on a show. Opening on November 9, *Forever Plaid* was a nostalgic tribute to the guy groups of the 1960s. Evett found it "a wonderfully silly, lovable, entertaining show" but saved the main message for last: "The Allen is back in show business." *Plaid* was originally scheduled to play through the holidays but, like *Jacques Brel*, kept on running, for 437 performances—a hundred or so short of *Brel's* record. Playhouse Square followed that with *Shear Madness*, a "comic murder mystery" that kept the Allen in business until 1997.[94]

Then the wrecking ball really did swing, but for constructive rather than destructive purposes. Gone was the original idea of carving the Allen into three different spaces; in was the new $15 million plan to restore the full auditorium into a twenty-five-hundred-seat venue for Broadway musicals. As PSF president Falco explained, the idea was now to emulate Toronto by booking megamusicals such as *The Phantom of the Opera* and *Miss Saigon* for extended runs of six months to a year and drawing customers from a wide circle outside Cleveland. The Allen's shallow stagehouse was demolished to allow for the construction of a state-of-the-art facility with an expanded stage area and orchestra pit. The project also included a complete renovation of the "atmospheric" auditorium originally designed by architect C. Howard Crane in 1921. The sixteen columns of the rotunda were to be stripped of their gray paint and restored to their original black walnut finish, and the old movie marquee on Euclid Avenue would be replaced by a fiberglass green copper-topped canopy. The elliptical opening between the rear of the orchestra section and mezzanine lobby was covered over, shielding playgoers below from distracting noise from above. Uncovered, though, were four monochrome medallions that had originally surrounded the skylight painted on the auditorium ceiling. [95]

On Tuesday, October 6, 1998, the Allen hosted its first Broadway touring show, the biomusical *Jolson*. It starred Mike Burstyn as the legendary Al Jolson, the singer who virtually owned Broadway when the Allen had first opened its doors. "Toot-Toot-Tootsie Goodbye," "Swanee," and "April Showers" were some of the old standards belted out to an older generation of theatergoers. The Allen was indeed back in show business. With the Allen in full operation, Playhouse Square Center could truly call itself "the second largest performing arts center in the nation and the largest theater restoration project in the world." Added to the State, Ohio, and Palace, the Allen gave PSC a total of 9,500 seats, edging out Denver's Center for the Performing Arts by 200 seats for second place after New York's Lincoln Center.[96]

Some, however, might still consider Playhouse Square incomplete. Outside the glitter of the relit marquees on Euclid Avenue sat the venerable Hanna Theatre, dark since 1989. All the houses on Euclid had had their moments, but none, not even the Palace, could match the Hanna's six unbroken decades of storied stars and groundbreaking shows. *Jolson: The Musical* may have reopened

The orchestra section of the Allen Theatre was cleared in 1998 for renovation as a Broadway touring house. (David M. Thum, Cleveland Landmarks Commission)

the Allen, but Jolson the man had trod the Hanna's stage no fewer than six times. What the Hanna needed now was another Ray Shepardson. Incredibly, Shepardson himself showed up on East Fourteenth Street in the mid-1990s.

"I always felt bad that we put the Hanna out of business when we revived the theaters across the street," Shepardson said. Since leaving Playhouse Square, he had formed a company, Majestic Urban Revivals, and done theater restorations in cities from Louisville to his native Seattle. His latest project, Detroit's Gem Theatre, however, had ended in a dispute with his backers and brought him back to Cleveland, scene of his first and greatest success. He and Cecilia Hartman had separated in 1971, and he had followed this with a second marriage and divorce. Planning a third marriage to Nanette Thomas, one of his employees, he hoped to finally settle down. "I've paid my dues in Cleveland and now I'm hoping to reap some rewards," he told a *Plain Dealer* writer.[97]

What Shepardson had in mind for the Hanna was what had worked best in the past: cabaret theater. This meant Shepardson would have to convert the Hanna into a venue suitable for cabaret, which called for a sizable capital outlay. He hoped to raise $3 million from the private sector for renovation and production costs. Most of the total came from half a dozen individual investors, headed by Lainie Hadden, plus a like number of corporate backers. Since he found the Hanna in "the best condition of any theater I've been involved with," most of the renovations consisted of leveling its raked orchestra section with a three-tiered concrete floor and constructing a new stage four feet above the original for enhanced visibility. Spread across the new floor were tables and chairs seating about 750. While Milton Krantz winced at the idea of cabaret shows in the Hanna, he wished Shepardson success nevertheless. "I hate like hell to see that thing down," he said of the theater he had managed for forty-five years."[98]

Shepardson reopened the Hanna on September 30, 1997, with one of his biggest Playhouse Square hits, *The All Night Strut!* Not content to remain behind the scenes, he introduced the show, circulated among the tables during intermission, and thanked guests on their way out of the theater. A month later, he began rotating *Strut!* with a second revue: *A Brief History of White Music* (performed by an all-Black cast). This time, the magic failed to repeat itself. "I can remember when we used to draw more than the Indians," Shepardson said in recalling the glory days of *Jacques Brel.* When the Hanna Cabaret opened, however, the Indians were playing in the World Series and drawing forty-thousand-plus fans to Jacobs Field at the other end of Huron Road. That competition, lack of a cash reserve, and other problems forced Shepardson to close the Hanna Cabaret two months short of its first anniversary.[99]

But the Hanna wouldn't remain dark for long. "You've heard of 'from shirtsleeves to shirtsleeves in three generations?'" reminisced Don Grogan. "That's the Grogans." He was referring ruefully to his children's decision to sell the Hanna Building complex, which he had inherited from his father, who had bought it from Carl Hanna. Grogan had nursed his legacy for more than three decades. While skeptical of the chances of reviving the four Euclid Avenue movie palaces, he had supported Shepardson's efforts out of loyalty to Playhouse Square. His preeminent loyalty, naturally, was to his Hanna Theatre, which he scrupulously maintained even through the dark years. "It cost thirty to forty thousand a year just to keep it heated, otherwise the plaster starts to fall," he observed. "That never happened to the Hanna, as it did to the Allen, the State, and the others."[100]

Fortunately the Hanna fell into equally friendly hands, as the PSF was in a position to add the entire Hanna complex to its growing real estate holdings. At the time it wasn't looking for another theater, said PSF's John Hemsath, but wanted to be able to control the storefronts.[101] Behind those storefronts, nonetheless, was a gem of a theater. No longer a stepsister, the Hanna Theatre had finally been adopted into the Playhouse Square family.

From Bicentennial to Millennium

"The New American City" was the theme crafted by the Cleveland Bicentennial Commission for the city's 200th birthday in 1996. It was certainly a far different city from that of the Supersesquicentennial celebration of a quarter-century earlier. Cleveland was on a downward spiral that would end only in the jarring crash of default in the final days of 1978.[102]

In many respects, Cleveland looked like a new city in 1996. No longer a burning river, the Cuyahoga provided a picturesque backdrop for al fresco diners in the Flats. The Flats had become a nationally recognized entertainment destination, spreading across the river to the West Bank and climbing up the eastern bluff to the fashionable nightspots of the Warehouse District. Downtown presented a modern, dynamic skyline to boaters on a revitalized Lake

Erie. Playhouse Square had three theaters in operation and was working on a fourth. Gateway had kept the Indians in Cleveland and brought the Cavaliers back from the meadows of Richfield. Neighborhoods such as Tremont and Gordon Square were showing signs of new vitality. Cleveland had been named an All-American City five times in the past fifteen years.

It hadn't come about by accident. Federal environmental regulations, prompted partly in reaction to the Cuyahoga fire and Lake Erie's moribund condition, had led to the cleanup of river and lake. Locally, much of the change was also the result of calculated premeditation, as writer Carlo Wolff described it in a Bicentennial commemoration program: "The miraculous transformation of the Indians was carefully orchestrated by a series of quiet decisions that began ten years ago with developer Dick Jacobs' purchase of the team. The rebirth of Playhouse Square—and with it downtown Cleveland—goes back to key moves made by the Cleveland Foundation and others in the mid-seventies, while other exciting new developments long in the works are just now coming into bloom." Mike Marsalino, acting press secretary for Mayor Mike White, gave PSC credit for boosting the city's economy by $50 million a year and helping to increase tourism to Cleveland from 3.6 million visitors in 1990 to 8.5 million in 1996.[103]

During the months leading up to the actual founding date of July 22, work proceeded on several improvements designed to provide the city with a permanent legacy from the bicentennial year. A City of Light project undertook the permanent lighting in colorful designs of eight bridges in the Flats, from the Conrail bridge near the mouth of the Cuyahoga to the Eagle Avenue bridge near Gateway. Ten thousand trees were to be planted throughout the city once known as the Forest City. Three new pocket parks were to be created downtown, at Settlers Landing, North Coast Harbor, and Playhouse Square.[104]

The Playhouse Square park was planted on the triangle of land created by the rerouting of Huron Road into East Thirteenth Street, putting it perhaps as close as possible to the heart of the district. It would be known as Star Plaza in recognition of a $1.35 million contribution from Star Bank, headquartered in the adjacent Renaissance Building. Designed by Thompson & Wood, it featured shade trees, brick walkways, and a space for programs or performances. Under a shower of balloons dropped from the Renaissance Building, Star Plaza was dedicated on September 19, 1996.[105]

Other changes, both in- and outdoors, continued Playhouse Square's transformation. For two decades, the Palace Theatre had gone without a theatrical entrance, the old movie marquee having been dismantled after the 1969 closing and never replaced due to other priorities. The Palace's need was finally addressed in 1996, when a gift from PSF trustee Lois Horvitz provided for the raising of a stylish, fan-shaped metal and glass canopy also designed by Thompson & Wood. Large ten-by-twenty-foot changeable banners touting current attractions were raised at the same time over the facades of other theaters. Two years later, PSC's Founders Club acquired both a new name and new quarters on the second floor of the former Loew's Building. It was now called the RJF President's Club after longtime Playhouse Square supporter Richard J. Fasenmyer. Half a century earlier, its new clubroom had hosted jitterbugging GIs and junior hostesses as the Playhouse Square Stage Door Canteen. Another historic Playhouse Square location was memorialized in 1998, when a plaque commemorating the twenty-fifth anniversary of *Jacques Brel* was embedded into the floor of the State Theatre lobby.[106]

Other evidence of progress could be measured not by bricks and mortar but the more volatile standard of audience appeal. Ever since the theater reopenings of the early 1980s, Playhouse Square had envisioned the day when it would be attracting a million patrons a year. That goal was finally reached in 1996, when PSC announced that in the theatrical year from July 1, 1995, to June 30, 1996, audience records had surpassed the 1 million–patron mark. With a boost from the expanded two-week Broadway Series and another visit from *The Phantom of the Opera*, the 1996–97 season would also bring in more than a million customers. Another audience milestone was achieved on January 23, 1997, when Playhouse Square Center ushered its 10 millionth patron through the Palace Theatre doors. The winner turned out to be Frances Scalise, an English teacher from Hudson, Ohio. Jerry Lewis, appearing at the Palace that week in *Damn Yankees*, congratulated her and Playhouse Square presented her with a gift package that included a Caribbean cruise and a weekend at the Playhouse Square Wyndham Hotel.[107]

In the twentieth century's waning years, Playhouse Square had finally achieved a firm footing. A $25 million capital campaign launched in 1996 hoped not only to raise $15 million for the Allen Theatre restoration but to provide $10 million toward the establishment of a permanent endowment. By that time, Playhouse Square's influence enabled it to take the lead in the formation of Cleveland's first Special Improvement District (SID). Three-quarters of the landowners in the area petitioned the city council to allow them to assess themselves to provide funds for upgrading security, maintenance, improvements, and marketing in the district. The SID was initially expected to raise $330,000 annually for those purposes. Covering an area extending from East Twelfth to East Eighteenth Street, and Chester to Prospect Avenues the Playhouse Square SID was formally designated as the Cleveland Theater District.[108]

Variety observed PSF's increasing clout, not only in its neighborhood but in the city

Cleveland Ballet's production of Tchaikovsky's *The Nutcracker* became a popular Playhouse Square holiday attraction. Its soaring Christmas tree in the first act may have put older Clevelanders in mind of the bygone Sterling & Welch Christmas tree. (Author's collection)

at large. "With 1993 revenues of $16.4 million and a growing appetite for real estate, this Cleveland arts juggernaut is behaving more and more like an acquisitive corporate giant than a genial bastion of culture and largess," reported the nation's show business weekly. The story reviewed the foundation's absorption of the for-profit Front Row Theater, its role in the construction of the Renaissance Office Tower and Wyndham Hotel, its operation of its own Advantix ticket office in competition with the private Ticketmaster, and its ongoing plans for reopening the Allen Theatre. "Unlike most commercial producers, the nonprofit foundation has all kinds of friends in city and state government, allowing it to influence not only its own real estate but the urban infrastructure that surrounds it," stated writer Christopher Jones. "It's a necessity for non-profits to develop ancillary forms of income, because it's impossible to break even from theater presentations," answered Falco for Playhouse Square.[109]

As Falco implied, the purpose of the foundation's property acquisitions was to enable Playhouse Square to put on shows without profit. In the twentieth century's waning months, PSC was amply fulfilling that purpose. At the State, Cleveland Ballet took Clara and her Nutcracker Prince through a waltz of the snowflakes into the realm of the Sugar-Plum Fairy, to the familiar score of Tchaikovsky's *The Nutcracker*. Next door in the Ohio, the spirits of Christmas Past, Present, and Future melted the hardened heart of Ebenezer Scrooge in Great Lakes Theatre's version of Dickens's *A Christmas Carol*. Between Thanksgiving and Christmas, Broadway revivals of *The Sound of Music*, with Richard Chamberlain, and *Finian's Rainbow* brought families to the Palace.

The Allen saw the century out on a special note, or notes, provided by what many in Cleveland and elsewhere regarded as the world's finest orchestra. Due to the closing of its quarters in Severance Hall for a $36.7 million expansion and restoration, the Cleveland Orchestra needed a performance space in the spring and fall of 1999. It found it in the newly restored Allen, where it had once performed light classics between movies in a few Sunday evening concerts in 1933–34. It didn't have to share billing with movies this time, as music director Christoph von Dohnányi led the ensemble in such fare as Mahler's *Das Lied von der Erde* and a concert performance of Bartok's *Bluebeard's Castle*. In a Scottish-themed concert, percussionist Evelyn Glennie made a guest appearance on the bagpipes in one number's finale. As the year and the century drew to a close, the orchestra added its festive Christmas concerts to the holiday offerings of the ballet and Great Lakes Theatre. It closed the Cleveland Orchestra's longest residency outside Severance Hall since 1931.[110]

On the last evening of 1999, celebrants could still mark the passing of the century with *A Christmas Carol* at the Ohio or *The Nutcracker* at the State. For a once-in a-thousand-years-experience, they might enjoy a "Millennium Eve Concert" by Carl Topilow and the Cleveland Pops Orchestra in the Allen Theatre.[111]

Timeline of 1980–1999

March 1980
Playhouse Square Foundation launches $18 million last-chance fundraising drive to restore Ohio, State, and Palace Theatres

April 1982
Junior League opens restored Palace dressing rooms

July 9, 1982
Great Lakes Shakespeare Festival reopens Ohio Theatre

June 11, 1984
Metropolitan Opera reopens State Theatre with *Peter Grimes*

April 30, 1988
Completely restored Palace Theatre reopens

July 3, 1989
Hanna Theatre goes dark

March 7, 1992
Great Lakes Theatre Festival presents world premiere of Adrienne Kennedy's *The Ohio State Murders* at Ohio Theatre

March 3, 1993
Front Row Theater announces it will move its shows in July from Highland Heights to Playhouse Square

April 28, 1993
The Phantom of the Opera opens at State Theatre

September 19, 1996
Dedication of Star Plaza at Euclid Avenue and Huron Road

January 13, 1997
Playhouse Square Center welcomes its 10 millionth guest

September 4, 1997
Work begins on Allen Theatre stagehouse restoration

September 30, 1997
Ray Shepardson's Hanna Theatre Cabaret opens with *The All Night Strut*

October 6, 1998
Allen Theatre reopens with musical *Jolson*

A National Model

Brave New Century

"How fitting that our first show of the 21st century harks back to a pivotal event of the 20th century," wrote programming director Gina Vernaci in the January 18–30, 2000, program notes for the Allen Theatre. The event was the 1912 sinking of the *Titanic,* and the show was named after the ship—but instead of sinking, it had won a Tony Award for Best Musical. Comparing the show to the recent blockbuster movie of the same event and title, Vernaci found "the stage musical even more stirring than the movie, because in some ways the eye-popping Hollywood special effects distracted us from the real story." There wasn't even any climactic gunplay in the musical, just the human emotions of people from different walks facing unforeseen tragedy in different ways. Coming at the end of its century, *Titanic* may have been the last of the traditional book-driven (as opposed to dancedriven) musical plays. Following it into the Allen that winter would be two more fin-de-siècle musical hits, *Miss Saigon* and *Ragtime.*[1]

In her *Titanic* notes, Vernaci had pointed out "an intriguing Cleveland connection": the coincidence that the former Cleveland offices of the White Star Line, owners of the *Titanic,* had been located in the Bulkley Building, the present home of the Playhouse Square Foundation (PSF). Even as she wrote, PSF was negotiating to add the Bulkley to its holdings, which already included the Allen Theatre. As listed in the *Plain Dealer*, PSF's real estate portfolio also contained the Hanna Building and Annex with the Hanna Theatre, the Wyndham Cleveland Hotel, the Chester Avenue parking garage, development sites east of the Hanna complex, and the One Playhouse Square Building.[2]

On the whole, Cleveland entered the new century amid mixed signs of progress. The 2000 census would show that the city was still bleeding residents. Although preliminary estimates had its population remaining just above half a million, the official return set the number at 476,575. From twenty-third place in 1990, Cleveland had slipped to thirty-fourth among American cities. Yet the decline wasn't invariable; west side neighborhoods such as Tremont, Detroit Shoreway, and Ohio City continued to show signs of recovery, in both new and rehabilitated housing. Most of the decline occurred on the east side, where Blacks sought greener pastures in such suburbs as Richmond Heights and Maple Heights. One surprising exception was Hough, where the Lexington Village development had anchored a revival with 277 units of townhouses and garden apartments.[3]

Not so surprisingly, the largest increase in the city's population took place downtown in the Warehouse District, which added 1,700 new residents in the 1990s. Downtown's population had increased by 51 percent, from 5,367 to 8,105. That gave Cleveland the seventh-fastest growing downtown area in the United States and the fastest growing downtown in the Midwest, according to Mark S. Rosentraub, dean of Cleveland State University's (CSU) Levin College of Urban Affairs. Downtown living was breaking out of the Warehouse District and spreading eastward into Gateway and undeveloped areas of Erieview.[4]

One setback in downtown Cleveland was the deterioration of the East Bank of the Flats due to crime and unbridled rowdyism. Fagan's, one of the anchors of the entertainment district, closed around the turn of the new century. Much of its old clientele had drifted up the hill to West Sixth Street in the Warehouse District. Nick Kostis, who had run a bar and comedy club in both the East Bank and the Warehouse District, decided to move east of Public Square for his next venture. In 2002, he opened Pickwick and Frolic, a restaurant and comedy club, on East Fourth Street, up to then populated largely by pawn shops and wig outlets. One former tenant, Otto Moser's theatrical restaurant, had recently moved to Playhouse Square. Pickwick put down roots across the street from the former Moser's on a site once occupied by the legendary Euclid Avenue Opera House.[5]

For Playhouse Square, a memorable example of the good news / bad news bromide played out on the single day of September 7, 2000. First came the bad news, with the demise of Cleveland Ballet. The twenty-four-year-old company's denouement had come on quickly, augured two weeks earlier by its failure to make payroll. When an emergency appeal to raise $1 million to save the 2000–2001 season brought in no more than $60,000, ballet president Bob Jones announced the board's inevitable decision to suspend operations. A newly reorganized Ballet San Jose would employ many of the dancers and purchase some of the company's costumes and scenery. Cleveland Ballet's abbreviated swan song came the following month when members of the company performed the "Bacchanale" in Cleveland Opera's production of Saint-Saens's *Samson et Delila*.[6]

It was all over save the postmortems. To the *Plain Dealer*, the company's failure was the inevitable result of "its amazing penchant for million-dollar performances on wish-and-a-prayer budgets." Instead of reining in its artistic ambitions to fiscal realities, "the Cleveland San Jose Ballet chose to dance to its doom." Also at issue were the failure's implications for Playhouse Square. "We saw Playhouse Square as an economic engine, a revitalization for the city," commented Kathleen Cerveny of the Cleveland Foundation. "We didn't anticipate the cost to artistic organizations of doing business in venues much too large for them." Art Falco saw ten dark weeks on the State Theatre's calendar. "The ballet brings 75,000 patrons to Playhouse Square," he said. "We will see if there is any way to salvage what can be salvaged."[7] There would be no *Nutcracker* downtown that season. Playhouse Square had lost one of its three main resident companies.

So much for the bad news; the good news came with the opening of a new show in the Hanna Theatre the evening of the day Cleveland Ballet had called it quits. It was two years since Ray Shepardson had closed his Hanna Cabaret and a year since Playhouse Square had purchased the Hanna complex from the Grogan family. Although Playhouse Square wasn't looking for another theater, the Hanna Theatre came with the property. "You can feel the vibrations in all those old theaters, but the vibes in the Hanna are particularly good," said programming director Vernaci of her new stage. As it happened, however, she inherited the Hanna in its cabaret setup and needed a compatible show to plant there. She

Hanna Theatre audiences became part of the act as invited guests to *Tony n' Tina's Wedding*, an Italian wedding parody that opened on the evening of the day Cleveland Ballet announced its closure. By the time *Tony n' Tina* closed its run more than two years later, it had established a new record Cleveland run of 801 performances. (Author's collection)

found it in Minneapolis, where an audience-participation property called *Tony n' Tina's Wedding* was finishing a five-year run. It was a parody of an Italian wedding in which the cast played the wedding party and the audience the guests.[8]

Plain Dealer critic Tony Brown reported that he drank "lukewarm 'champagne,'" ate "a really horrible penne-and-meatball dinner," and found himself joining a conga line in Fourteenth Street. "But 'T n' T' is brilliant in doing exactly what it sets out to do," he concluded: "getting the audience hysterically involved with people we didn't know when the evening began." And Clevelanders ate it up, horrible meatballs and all. In three weeks, the show was sold out to the end of the year, its projected closing date. Vernaci extended it another three months and hoped it might run for a year or even two. In fact, it did that and more, pushing past the runs of *Shear Madness* (269 performances) and *Forever Plaid* (437). Tony and Tina kept repeating their vows until the spoof broke *Jacques Brel*'s 522-performance record, an occasion celebrated with three members of the original *Brel* cast. Finally, after serving 304,336 pieces of wedding cake, *Tony n' Tina's Wedding* ended a new record Cleveland run of 801 performances on December 1, 2002.[9]

Days after closing *Tony n' Tina's Wedding*, Playhouse Square announced its intention to open an arts education center in conjunction with Cleveland's public radio and television stations. Plans for the education center had been percolating for more than a year, partially in response to criticism that the arts and entertainment center needed to be more responsive to the community's cultural needs. It would be located next door to the Bulkley Building in One Playhouse

Square, the building donated to PSF in 1998, and the State of Ohio committed $3 million toward the renovation of the center's needed forty thousand square feet. The project expanded when public television and radio stations WVIZ-TV and WCPR-FM expressed a desire to consolidate their operations, under the name Ideastream, in the same building. By sharing a combination studio and black-box theater, the needs of the two stations and the education center might be accommodated within ninety thousand square feet. Total cost of the endeavor, projected to open in 2004, had mushroomed to $31 million, most of which was raised privately.[10]

Radio was no stranger to One Playhouse Square. Station WJW had once had its studios there, where a disc jockey named Alan Freed was said to have coined the term *rock and roll*. Half a century later, in a delicious twist of irony, Ideastream acquired WCLV-FM, bringing Cleveland's classical music radio station into the baptistry of rock.[11]

Legit Again!

"What are we going to do with the Hanna?" rhetorically asked Gina Vernaci in 2005. "That's the conversation we actually have all the time around here." Following the success of *Tony n' Tina's Wedding,* an obvious answer at the time was to use it for more cabaret. Shows such as *I Love·You, You're Perfect, Now Change* and *Love, Janis* kept the lights on at the Hanna through February 2005. Next door, Playhouse Square found an equally suitable cabaret site behind a storefront in the Hanna Building. Dubbed the 14th Street Theatre, it became home for nineteen months to the Second City Cleveland improvisational comedy company, succeeded by an even longer-running revue called *Menopause: The Musical.* Predominantly female audiences kept the 286-seat space filled for a run of 625 performances, giving *Menopause* second-place honors to the record run of *Tony n' Tina.*[12]

Cabaret may have been fine for the 14th Street Theatre, but some saw it as a waste of space in the storied Hanna. "I don't particularly see the idea," longtime Hanna manager Milton Krantz had said when Shepardson was remodeling his old theater for cabaret. "My idea was to make that a resident theater downtown." Ten years later his idea was getting serious consideration. Since the turn of the century, eyes on the north side of Euclid Avenue had been focused on the marquee down Fourteenth Street. They belonged to the directors of the Great Lakes Theater Festival (GLTF), who had become dissatisfied with the fit of the Ohio Theatre for their company; they found it too large for classical theater, which wanted more intimacy between players and audience. Furthermore, it lacked the thrust stage that had become virtually de rigueur for producing Shakespeare, still the backbone of the Great Lakes repertory. So did the Hanna for that matter, but converting it back from its cabaret setup opened the possibility of more fundamental structural changes.[13]

Great Lakes had experienced mixed fortunes since Gerald Freedman's departure. James Bundy, Freedman's successor, set a season attendance record of seventy-eight thousand and lowered the festival's debt to $40,000 but left after only four years to become dean of the Yale School of Drama. Bundy was replaced by Charles Fee, artistic director of the Idaho Shakespeare Festival, who hoped to develop a partnership between the two companies. Fee's position at Great Lakes was somewhat tenuous, as the festival was engaged in talks with the Cleveland Play House about a possible merger. Attendance was down and debts were up in both organizations, but a merger would deprive Cleveland of bragging rights as one of only a dozen or so cities in the country with two members of the League of Resident Theaters. In the end, Fee could breathe more easily; Great Lakes couldn't get the Play House to guarantee it parity on the combined board and a say in major hiring decisions, so it broke off the talks.[14]

Like Bundy, Fee also lobbied quietly for a move into the Hanna. In 2004, not so quietly, *Plain Dealer* drama critic Tony Brown discussed GLTF's need for a smaller home. Its audiences of three to four hundred were lost in the thousand-seat Ohio. Furthermore, "under its contract with Actors' Equity Association, Great Lakes has to pay its actors at a higher rate because of the Ohio's size." By the summer of 2005, discussions between GLTF and Playhouse Square were under way, though Falco said, "We're still in limbo as to what the [Hanna's] final use will be." By fall, however, GLTF and PSF had signed a letter of agreement to undertake a "formal study" of renovating the Hanna for Great Lakes, a move that made "great sense" to Cerveny at the Cleveland Foundation. "We have those magnificent theaters, but they were designed for a past age," she commented. "Most regional theaters around the country perform in much smaller spaces."[15]

In September 2007 Great Lakes and Playhouse Square announced that the festival would open its season the following fall in the renovated Hanna Theatre. "Nothing galvanizes your audience, your community like building a theater," Fee had said. Donors were the first to be galvanized for the estimated $20 million project. Leading the way was a $1.5 million grant from the Parker-Hannifin Corporation, a Mayfield Heights manufacturer of high-tech hydraulic and aerospace components. It was the largest donation the company had ever made to a cultural organization. Close behind was the Cleveland Foundation, which committed a total of $750,000–$500,000 as an outright gift, the remainder in matching funds for outside gifts of $25,000 or more. "The foundation has invested in Playhouse Square for decades as a major partner in the renovation of the other theaters," observed program director Cerveny. "This is the final major theater space in the district. It completes the package."[16] By January, 75 percent of the campaign goal of $19.2 million had been raised. For the remaining quarter, GLTF called in a heavy hitter: movie star Tom Hanks, who had landed his first acting gig and earned his Actors' Equity card at the Great Lakes Shakespeare Festival back in its Lakewood days. Besides addressing an appeal to prospective donors, the actor planned to make a personal appearance at the Hanna.[17]

Designing the changeover would be Peter van Dijk's old firm, now Westlake Reed Leskosky and regarded as a national leader in theater architecture. Its assignment was not merely to renovate the Hanna but to "re-imagine" the entire theatergoing experience. According to a GLTF newsletter, reimagining the Hanna would involve

- A thrust stage, which will bring the audience into close proximity to the actors. In the Hanna, no seat will be further than 11 rows from the stage, close enough to feel like part of the action!
- The concept of a Great Room . . . , where all activity occurs in one place! In the new Hanna, audiences will be able to socialize . . . *inside* the audience chamber.
- A unique opportunity . . . to self-define your theater experience. In addition to traditional theater seats, the new Hanna will have a variety of comfortable seating, including armchairs, table and chairs, boxes, and banquettes. A refreshment area *inside* the audience chamber will encourage audience members to engage with each other as well as enjoy what is happening on stage.[18]

Work on the Hanna's "re-imagination" got under way at the end of 2007, when the Turner Construction Company began ripping out the level concrete floor that had been installed for the Hanna

Cabaret. Architect Paul Westlake explained that this job would differ from the "straight restorations" done on Playhouse Square's other four theaters. The orchestra section would be steeply raked and open to the inner lobby with its bar. The mezzanine would contain one row of conventional seating in front of a bank of club boxes, while the upper balcony was masked off to reduce the auditorium's size. In a bow to preservationists, the classical decor of the walls, side boxes, and coffered ceiling would be not only preserved but meticulously restored. According to Westlake, he and Fee had "built more models and redrawn more plans for this project than our firm has ever done."[19]

For the theater's reopening on September 24, 2008, Fee challenged theatrical superstition with a production of the reputedly "bad luck" play of the Shakespeare canon: the "Scottish play," or *Macbeth,* to those who dare mention its name. It was twenty-four years since the Hanna's last Shakespearean presentation, which coincidentally also was *Macbeth,* in a production by London's Old Vic company. Once again the names of the classical dramatists across the theater's ceiling, especially that of the quaintly spelled "Shakspere," were justified. Milton Krantz had been dead for two years, but his theatrical ghost must have been grinning from the wings that night. The Hanna was legit once again!

Breaking in the Elizabethan thrust stage of the "reimagined" Hanna Theatre were the three witches of Shakespeare's *Macbeth,* played by (*from top*) Cathy Prince,* Laura Welsh Berg,* and Sara M. Bruner.* It was the initial Great Lakes Theater production in its new home. (Courtesy of Great Lakes Theater, photo by Roger Mastroianni.) *Member of Actors' Equity

Brown, in the *Plain Dealer*, described Fee's Kabuki-inspired staging of the "Scottish Play" as "always cohesive, often mesmerizing, and fast-flowing." Dougfred Miller played the Thane of Glamis opposite Laura Perotta's Lady Macbeth. Sara Bruner headed the three witches who, with the aid of crutches concealed beneath their black cloaks, scampered across the thrust stage like foreboding spiders. The reimagined Hanna received rave reviews from Brown and Steven Litt, the *Plain Dealer*'s architecture critic. Brown found the acoustics, both downstairs and up, "far better" than those of the Ohio, "where the actors had to yell." Litt called the new Hanna "one of the finest theatrical spaces I've ever seen. . . . The wraparound scenery that flanks the thrust stage makes it easy to see the action from every viewpoint. The arrangement also makes it possible to see how the audience is reacting, which concentrates and magnifies the intensity of the experience."[20]

The Draw of Downtown

In at least one sense, that aborted merger between GLTF and the Cleveland Play House would be realized not long after GLTF's debut at the Hanna. Back then, Great Lakes had been holding the weaker hand—younger, financially less stable, and playing in an unsuitable theater. The Play House, however, was long-established with a modest endowment and owner of its own three-stage complex. Now the roles appeared to be reversed. GLTF was thriving in the custom-rebuilt Hanna, having paid off its accumulated deficit and even acquired a small endowment as part of its recent capital campaign. The Great Recession of 2008 hit the Play House hard, halving its endowment from $7 million to $3.5 million. Its plant on upper Euclid Avenue, redesigned by nationally acclaimed, Cleveland-born architect Philip Johnson and opened with great fanfare in 1983, was proving to be a high-maintenance albatross. Johnson had designed the new 644-seat Bolton Theater and attached it to the older, smaller Drury and Brooks with a series of grandiose, self-indulgent lobbies and corridors. By the end of the new century's first decade, the Play House's managing director, Kevin Moore, had concluded that the ninety-year-old institution had to find new digs or die.[21]

For half a century, there had been talk of moving the Play House out of its 1926 quarters at Euclid Avenue and East Eighty-Sixth Street—at least partly motivated by the postwar deterioration of

Cleveland's east side. As far back as 1962, Frank Joseph, a trustee of the Greater Cleveland Associated Foundation, had urged that "institutions such as the Aquarium and the Play House, which are looking for new homes, should be encouraged to come downtown." It seemed about to happen three years later, when Play House president Kenyon C. Bolton announced plans to build a new theater complex at Euclid and East Eighteenth Street, between Playhouse Square and the proposed CSU campus, but it never left the prospective stage. A decade later, before committing to the Johnson-designed expansion, the board rejected one more recommendation, by its own Future Planning Committee, to move downtown.[22]

Johnson, who devised such impressive lobbies for its complex, may have done the Play House an unintended favor by giving it such an unsuitable theater in the Bolton, which had poor acoustics, worse sight lines, and an utterly conventional proscenium stage. Other than regret over the loss of its two smaller stages, there was little to hold the Play House directors back from seeking a new location. One possibility lay eastward at Case Western Reserve University, which conducted its MFA program in acting in partnership with the Play House, but discussions over that option broke down in 2008. That left the long-resisted magnet of downtown.[23]

By that time, downtown theater was synonymous with Playhouse Square Center. Not only did it have a near monopoly on theaters, but at the moment it had more than it needed. Not only was Cleveland Ballet gone, but the 2008 recession was threatening Cleveland Opera's survival. That left the State Theatre more available for the Broadway Series, which nullified the original impetus of the Allen restoration. At that point, CSU, having outgrown its forthrightly named Factory Theater, came knocking at the door. Talks began between the university and Art Falco about redesigning the Allen into two or three flexible performance spaces for a consortium of regional college theaters to showcase their work. That's when David Abbott of the Gund Foundation lit a fire under Play House management: "You know, if you want to go to the Allen Theater, you better get going because that train is leaving the station."[24]

In what the *Plain Dealer* described as "a blockbuster arts and real-estate deal," the Play House announced on April 8, 2009, that it would sell its Midtown property and move into the Allen Theatre. To no one's surprise, the unnamed buyer was the Cleveland Clinic, which was swallowing up every acre in Midtown from East 107th to East 86th Street. The price of $13 million would go toward the estimated $30 million cost of adapting the Allen to the needs of the

Play House and CSU's drama department, its future roommate in Playhouse Square. "The time was right to bring Playhouse Square and the Cleveland Play House together," observed Falco. "We had to form the 'Power of Three.' The idea was to have the Play House and CSU share the Allen space."[25]

As designed by Westlake Reed Leskosky, the plan was to downsize the Allen and build two smaller theaters in the Bulkley Building parking lot. The Allen would keep its proscenium stage for an auditorium seating 514, mostly on the orchestra and parterre levels with a shallow balcony in the rear. The old balcony's 800 seats were closed off for future, as yet undetermined, use. While the redesigned Allen kept its traditional proscenium design, a new Second Stage next door, opening off the end of the Bulkley Building Arcade, would be adaptable to several staging styles, equipped with a mechanism allowing seating to be arranged in configurations ranging from traditional end stage to thrust and arena staging, with a maximum of 348 seats. On a lower level behind the Second Stage would be a 150-seat lab theater mostly for CWRU's MFA productions. CSU would have access to all three theaters.[26]

In addition, Westlake Reed Leskosky designed a new inner lobby for the Allen and a new pedestrian bridge from the Chester Avenue parking garage to the theaters of Playhouse Square Center. The connecting passageway from the State and Ohio lobbies would lead past the Second Stage directly into the Play House lobby, formed out of the rear of the Allen's foreshortened orchestra section. The lobby could also be reached directly from Euclid Avenue through the Allen's untouched classical rotunda. All PSC theaters would also be reachable through the new "more user-friendly" enclosed passageway from the garage, leading between the Allen and the Second Stage to the common lobby area. The Play House and state funding through CSU would share the cost of the $30 million project.[27]

In the end, so as not to confine theater architects within a preservationist straitjacket, Playhouse Square declined to pursue federal or state historic preservation tax credits for the Allen makeover. Newly installed overhead reflectors and side panels maximized acoustics. Catwalks stretched across the ceiling to accommodate lighting and sound equipment. Intimacy was achieved by narrowing the stage and keeping the last row closer than the first row on the Allen's old balcony. In Litt's bottom-line opinion, in the *Plain Dealer*, "the new high-tech look at the Allen, which allows the original architecture to peek through here and there, was a fair price to pay for a theater that now works so well." As they had endeavored to do in the Hanna, the architects took pains to make their changes reversible. Building on their work for Playhouse Square, dating from van Dijk's original model for an integrated arts center, by the time it finished the Allen, Westlake Reed had designed forty-four new theaters and eighty-eight theater renovations nationwide.[28] On a corporate scale, the Cleveland firm was fulfilling Ray Shepardson's mission.

On September 16, 2011, a year and a month after its final Broadway show—yet another visit from *The Phantom of the*

the LIFE of GALILEO
SEPTEMBER 16 - OCTOBER 9, 2011

PlayhouseSquare

America's oldest resident professional theater, the Cleveland Play House, took up residence downtown in the remodeled Allen Theatre in 2011. It inaugurated its new digs with a twentieth-century classic, Bertolt Brecht's *The Life of Galileo*. (Author's collection)

Opera—the Allen was ready for its initial Cleveland Play House production, Bertolt Brecht's *The Life of Galileo*. Four months later, the Play House inaugurated its Second Stage with *Ten Chimneys*, a play based on Alfred Lunt and Lynn Fontanne, a legendary acting couple who were no strangers to Playhouse Square. From the 1920s through the 1950s, Lunt and Fontanne had made more than a dozen appearances at the Ohio and the Hanna. Play House artistic director Michael Bloom informed playgoers, "Our Second Stage affords the extraordinary opportunity to fit the theatre to the play rather than adapt the play to the theatre." Before long, the space was named the Outcalt Theatre in honor of benefactors Jon and Jane Outcalt. Behind the Outcalt, the lab theatre was known from the beginning as the Helen Rosenfeld Lewis Bialosky Lab Theatre, or familiarly as simply the "Helen."[29]

When the Play House had announced its decision to move downtown, some patrons registered their disapproval by not renewing their season subscriptions. In its first three downtown productions, however, the Play House saw its revenues doubled. Much of the increase came from the city's west side. "Obviously, we thought this was a good idea coming down here, and the community seems to be agreeing with us," said managing director Moore. Play House historian Jeffrey Ullom concluded that the theater wouldn't have survived the 2008 recession had it remained on East Eighty-Sixth. He viewed its move, however, as not only an act of survival but an expression of faith in the future of Cleveland: "The relocation changed the landscape of Cleveland theatre, creating a more dynamic entertainment center for the city. Cleveland Play House's move downtown made the

[Playhouse Square] arts complex *the* place to go for professional theatre in [the] northeast Ohio region."³⁰

"Advancing the Legacy"

"Cleveland's downtown theater district is growing again," wrote Tony Brown in 2010. "This time by getting smaller." The *Plain Dealer* critic was referring to the Allen Theatre's imminent downsizing for the coming of the Cleveland Play House. "Since when, you might be considering, is littler better?" he asked and proceeded to explain. While nearly two thousand seats would be subtracted from the Allen, five hundred or so would be replaced by the Outcalt and Helen Theatres. With the two new theaters Playhouse Square Center would increase from eight to ten stages: the Palace, State, Ohio, Allen, Hanna, Outcalt, Fourteenth Street Theatre, the Helen, Kennedy's Down Under, and the Idea Center's Westfield Insurance Studio. "So," Brown concluded, "the community gains a larger and wider menu of choices." And, counting those nearly one thousand unused seats in the Allen's masked-off balcony, Falco pointed out that Playhouse Square could still claim to be the nation's second-largest performing arts center.³¹

With the theaters once again settled, Playhouse Square turned its attention to ancillary matters. One such project had been accomplished early in the millennium, when James Daugherty's Four Continents murals in the State lobby were restored. The Intermuseum Conservation Association, on Cleveland's near west side, removed the oxidation from the surfaces, painted on canvas preapplied to the walls. Were it not for the depiction of the fourth mural, *America—The Spirit of Cinema,* on the *Life* magazine cover, the State and Ohio Theatres, with their lobbies and the Loew's Building in front, would have been long gone. Cuyahoga County had purchased the entire property in 1977 to ensure their preservation and in turn leased it to PSF for what Falco called "very little." Thirty-five years later, the county was prepared to sell the parcel outright to Playhouse Square for even less—the largely symbolic price of one dollar. Cuyahoga County thereby achieved a savings of about $1 million a year in upkeep, while PSF gained complete ownership of all theaters except the leased Palace.³²

In 2014, to consolidate, improve, and expand its holdings, PSF embarked on a $100 million capital campaign under the name "Advancing the Legacy." Roughly half that sum was earmarked for immediate expenses and improvements, while the remainder would be applied to increasing the center's endowment from $16 million to a goal of $60 million. Some $35 million had been pledged privately when Falco kicked off the campaign's public phase with the announcement of a $9 million megagift from Chris and Sara Connor. Chris Connor, a PSF trustee, was CEO of the Cleveland-based Sherwin-Williams Company. In recognition of the couple's gift, the largest donation from a family in Playhouse Square's history, the center's most resplendent theater was renamed the Connor Palace.[33]

A large portion of that $100 million campaign—$16 million, or nearly one sixth, would be devoted to brightening the signage and streetscape of the theater district, giving Playhouse Square a bolder identity. "The goal has been to create gateways that say you're now in this special district," said Falco. Four gateway arches of gold-tinted aluminum delivered that message, at East Thirteenth Street and Euclid Avenue, East Seventeenth and Euclid, East Fourteenth and Prospect, and East Twelfth and Huron Road, all proclaiming *PLAYHOUSE SQUARE* overhead in silver capitals. Donny Barnycz, a public space designer from Baltimore, was in charge of the plan, which also included a redesigned Star Plaza and a large *PLAYHOUSE SQUARE* sign in lights atop the Cowell & Hubbard and Woolworth buildings.[34]

For his tour de force Barnycz envisioned a centerpiece consisting of a chandelier overhanging the district's central interchange of Euclid and East Fourteenth Street. The idea struck art critic Litt as "glitsy, audacious, and maybe even a bit surreal," leaning "toward kitschy nostalgia," but also a "a striking piece of pop imagery" with "a quirky and unabashed sense of showbiz, which is what the district is all about." He judged it "the most unorthodox and inspired part of the Barnycz plan . . . evoking the numerous chandeliers inside Playhouse Square's theater lobbies" (and perhaps the perennial visits of *The Phantom of the Opera*). It would weigh eighty-five hundred pounds and extend twenty-four feet top to bottom, leaving a clearance of twenty-two feet for traffic passing below. General Electric, a company with a strong local presence at Nela Park in East Cleveland, sponsored the chandelier and contributed advanced LED lighting fixtures.[35]

"Light it up, light it up!" chanted twenty thousand Clevelanders gathered on Playhouse Square on a cool May evening in 2014. As the *Plain Dealer*'s Andrea Simakis described it, "the crush felt like Times Square on New Year's Eve." Fireworks burst from three steel and aluminum supporting arms, as Broadway's Dee Roscioli entered down a long runway to the tune of "Defying Gravity." Billed as "the world's largest outdoor chandelier," the fixture's forty-two hundred crystals, when illuminated at 9:30, packed "more bling than Cher's entire wardrobe" in Simakis's words. "This defines Playhouse Square as a destination," remarked PSC's Vernaci, "which makes us unlike any performing arts center in the United States."[36]

Seven months after the chandelier lit up the neighborhood, the Richard J. Fasenmyer Foundation brightened up the "Advancing the Legacy" campaign with a gift of $10 million. It was the largest one-time gift in the center's history, exceeding the Connor donation by a million. Fasenmyer, who died in 2002, had been an entrepreneur, patron of the arts, and PSF trustee. Three years later, a $10 million gift from KeyBank brought the $100 million campaign within reach of its goal. Nearly half of the total, $44 million, raised the foundation's endowment to a total of $60 million. Keybank's gift was recognized by the naming of the Keybank Broadway Series.[37]

At the heart of the Playhouse Square legacy, both geographically and historically, were the State and Ohio Theatres. Geographically, their marquees were the middle two of the four Euclid Avenue showplaces. Historically they had been the first to open, and their threatened destruction in 1971 had been the catalyst for the preservation and revival of Playhouse Square. Without the State and the Ohio, whatever survived would hardly have been Playhouse Square. The two former Loew's theaters had been the most heavily damaged, however, and corners had been cut or even ignored in their initial restorations. With $8 million of "Advancing the Legacy" funds, Tom Einhouse, PSF vice president for real estate services, undertook to bring them back to their original state.

Conservationists from EverGreene Architectural Arts of New York and Cleveland's Dependable Painting Company mounted scaffolding in the State's auditorium in the summer of 2015. The brown and beige colors of the 1970s renovation were brightened with hues of butternut squash, pale blue and plum, and eggshell white. Imitation gold leaf was applied to highlight the central dome, indistinguishable from the real thing when seen from below. Crews then moved into the huge Ireland Lobby for similar restoration and painting of ceilings, there and in the ticket lobby. They also restored eight decorative urns atop the lobby's Ionic columns, replicating six missing ones from the two surviving models.[38]

Even before starting on the State, work had begun on an even bigger project: the complete replication of the 1921 Ohio Theatre lobby. Barely 1 percent of the original, a section of the entablature bordering the ceiling, had survived the 1964 fire. Bringing it completely back had been a long deferred dream, sidetracked by the press of more urgent needs. While the Ohio's auditorium had been the first area to be restored, its lobby would be the last. It would cost nearly $6 million, half of which was covered by a $3 million gift from the Gund Foundation to "Advancing the Legacy." Struc-

Playhouse Square's revival came full circle with the recreation of the fire-destroyed Ohio Theatre lobby. Working largely from old photographs, restoration experts finished the job in 2016. (Author's collection)

Free Backstage Tours

Playhouse Square

tural work would be supervised by Westlake Reed Leskosky and decorative details by EverGreene Architectural Arts.[39]

They began by raising scaffolding along the ceiling and walls, leaving a passageway for theatergoers to reach the auditorium during construction. The barrel-vaulted 1921 ceiling was duplicated out of drywall-covered sheet metal. Using original photographs, historical research, and their own know-how, EverGreene curators reconstructed it and decorated it with plaster garlands, urns, leafage, and bordering. The elongated ceiling was divided into five shallow, octagonal saucer domes with light green outer panels and dark-blue circular centers. Suspended from the middle and outer domes were three crystal chandeliers salvaged from Philadelphia's Erlanger Theater. These had found an appropriate home: the Ohio was originally the Cleveland outlet for shows on the Klaw-Erlanger circuit. On the walls, even the original Sampitrotti paintings of imagined mythological scenes from the legend of Venus were reproduced.[40]

In all its historical splendor, the Ohio lobby was reopened on June 1, 2016. The following year, EverGreene Architectural Arts and the PSF were corecipients of a State Historic Preservation Office Award from the Ohio History Connection.[41] The legacy was complete.

From Holbrook to *Hamilton*

In 2004, fifty years and more than two thousand performances since his first appearance as author Mark Twain, actor Hal Holbrook was back in Cleveland for another engagement of *Mark Twain Tonight* at the Palace Theatre. He regarded it as a homecoming of sorts, having been born in Cleveland seventy-nine years ago. He was raised largely by his grandparents in Lakewood and South Weymouth, Massachusetts. After breaking into acting at Cain Park in Cleveland Heights, Holbrook went on to a prolific career on Broadway and in television and movies—but Mark Twain became his career-long calling card. He first performed it in Cleveland in 1960 at John Carroll University, for lack of a more "suitable place for it." He didn't return with it until 1979, at the Palace, where he was thrilled to appear "for the first time . . . where I saw so many films and show business stars as a young boy."[42]

For his 2004 engagement, the Palace prepared a program listing about seventy selections, ranging from "A Cyclopedia of Sin" to "Corn Pone Opinions," but warned that "Mr. Twain" couldn't be pinned down as to which he would actually do. "However, he has generously conceded to a printed program for the benefit of those who are in distress and wish to fan themselves." A further caveat announced, "A trombone player was engaged, but is unreliable and should not be expected." Twain didn't need the trombonist, and in early March the Cleveland audience didn't need to fan themselves. Holbrook would return twice more as Twain, the last time at ninety to what had become the Connor Palace. "The Palace is just a beautiful theatre," he observed. "It's just the right size."[43]

Other one-night stands at the Palace ranged from the Grenadier Guards and Scots Highlanders to Tango Buenos Aires to Cab Calloway's Orchestra. The Chieftains played their Irish tunes for an evening at the State. *Flanagan's Wake,* another Irish-themed entertainment, opted for longer runs in the more intimate Kennedy's, while *Girls Night: The Musical* held forth at the Forteenth Street Theatre. Both the State and the Palace hosted musicals in the Broadway Series, such as revivals of *Jesus Christ Superstar, Oklahoma!,* and *South Pacific,* as well as the more recent *Hairspray* and *The Light in the Piazza.* The biggest hit of the new century was the megamusical *The Lion King,* which made its Cleveland debut with an eight-week run in 2003 and returned in 2007 and 2013, when it was still good for four weeks. Visiting ballet companies occasionally called, to compensate local dance fans to some degree for the loss of Cleveland Ballet.[44]

For a decade, Cleveland Opera maintained its residency in the State Theatre. General manager David Bamberger had generally avoided the artistic overreach that had brought Cleveland Ballet down. "[T]he time has perhaps come for us to accept what Cleveland Opera is, instead of what it isn't," one critic had written at the end of the previous century. "Sometimes solid, workmanlike productions are preferable to those mounted in the name of innovation." Early in the following century, *Plain Dealer* critic Donald Rosenberg printed a list of twenty "essential opera composers" that the Cleveland Opera had never touched, including such names as Smetana, Tchaikovsky, Massenet, and Richard Strauss. Opera America regarded Cleveland Opera as a Level 2 company, he reported.[45]

With Bamberger's retirement in 2004, the appointment as general manager of Robert Chumbley, a North Carolina arts administrator, raised hopes for an expanded repertory. While the company produced its first complete Russian opera, Tchaikovsky's *Eugene Onegin,* Chumbley resigned after eighteen months for personal reasons. A succession of revolving executives and artistic directors followed. The company finally got around to Richard Strauss with a production of *Salomé*, but the 2008 recession ate into its small endowment, caused staff layoffs, and reduced the season from four to three productions. Rosenberg saw "a sea of empty seats for many performances," including that of the perennial chestnut *Pagliacci*, and the company canceled productions for 2011.[46] They were never resumed.

That left the two theater troupes as Playhouse Square's major surviving resident companies, both of them comparatively thriving in their new homes. At the Hanna, Great Lakes Theater streamlined its name by dropping the word *Festival*, changing the word *Theater* from adjective to noun. Since the company had already switched its format from a summer repertory schedule to a seasonal fall to spring calendar, said artistic director Fee, the term *festival* had become outmoded and even misleading. The company originally known as the Great Lakes Shakespeare Festival still remained faithful to the Bard, however, averaging two Shakespearean productions a season. Alongside such repertory standards as *Othello* and *The Tempest*, it introduced *Love's Labour's Lost* and *The Comedy of Errors* to the Hanna. Outside the Shakespearean canon was such fare as Chekov's *The Seagull* and Kander and Ebbs's *Cabaret*.[47]

Contemporary repertoire was generally available on the other side of Euclid Avenue, where the Cleveland Play House performed recent works like *Luna Gale* at the Allen and *Mr. Wolf* in the Outcalt. It continued to promote the works of local playwrights, giving the world premiere of Eric Coble's *Fairfield* in 2015. That was the year

In its centennial season, the Cleveland Play House received the 2015 Regional Theatre Tony Award. Productions were performed on the Allen's proscenium stage and in the more flexible Outcalt Theatre. (Author's collection)

of the Play House's centennial, which was highlighted by the news that the company was to receive the 2015 Regional Theatre Tony Award. The same year, Fodor's Travel guide ranked the Play House, in such company as Chicago's Steppenwolf Theatre and Cambridge's American Repertory Theatre, as one of the "10 Best Regional Theaters in the U.S."[48]

With the demise of its prestigious opera and ballet companies, however, the Broadway Series had become the face of Playhouse Square. *Jersey Boys*, a musical about the Four Seasons doo-wop quartet, set several records at the State Theatre in

2008. A one-week gross of $1.9 million was its largest anywhere; its one-week attendance of 24,466 broke a PSC record formerly held by *The Phantom of the Opera;* and its five-week Cleveland run brought in a total box office of $7.7 million. Even straight plays such as the World War I drama *War Horse* were good for at least two-week runs. The Broadway Series clearly was primed to advance to the next level. "It's clear when you're at capacity, you need to do something about it," said executive producer Vernaci.[49]

What PSC did about it was to announce the expansion of what had become the KeyBank Broadway Series from two to three weeks beginning with the 2016–17 season. Cleveland would join a select few theaters in cities such as Washington, Seattle, San Francisco, and Los Angeles to host touring runs of three weeks or more. During the twenty years since Playhouse Square had expanded the series from one week to two, subscriptions had increased from 69 to 76 percent of capacity. With the three-week expansion, the Broadway Series hoped to boost its total season attendance from its present 330,000 to a potential audience of 453,000. Longer runs might boost attendance by allowing word of mouth to spread about popular shows. They also benefitted touring casts and crews by giving them more time to catch their breaths between tour stops. Broadway producer Michael David recalled the dramatic change in Cleveland's downtown over the past thirty-five years. "I remember we'd have to travel in groups," he said. "It's pretty remarkable and as compelling an example of how art and culture can stimulate urban revival as I've seen."[50]

Three-week runs would also make Cleveland a likelier place to launch touring productions. David pointed out that the extra week gave creative teams and casts more time to fine-tune shows before having to move on. In the second season of the three-week expansion, Cleveland inaugurated the tour of the hit musical *Waitress.* "You want the right venue so your show looks good, because after all, the word gets out," said producer Barry Weissler. "Cleveland is the lead city and everyone is gonna be watching us." Speaking for Playhouse Square, Vernaci elaborated: "Whenever you launch tours like that, there's a couple of things you have to bring to the table. You have to create an environment safe for artists to work in. You need an audience that is going to show up, because when you're launching a tour the eyes of the nation are watching you. That may not be the case for week 25 or 30 on a tour, but week number 1 speaks to the important role your community plays in the national arena." At that time Cleveland's KeyBank Broadway

Series claimed, at approximately thirty two thousand, the largest number of season ticket subscribers in the country. "And it does say something," noted Vernaci. "When I go to NY, people tell me 'What is going on in Cleveland? Your results are impressive.'"[51] Vernaci visited New York regularly, not only to line up shows for the Broadway Series but also as a director of the Broadway League.

Cleveland audiences continued to turn out for both the tried and the new. More than six hundred thousand people had turned out for five visits of *The Phantom of the Opera*, and still the mad, masked lover was due for a sixth stop of more than three weeks in 2016. Something new and revolutionary came down the road two years later. Lin-Manuel Miranda's sensational hip-hop musical based on the career of founding father Alexander Hamilton was booked to conclude the 2017–18 Broadway Series season. One of *Hamilton*'s novelties was nontraditional casting (e.g., Blacks playing traditionally white roles), but that was nothing new in the city where Karamu Theatre had pioneered the practice. Clevelanders rushed to purchase Broadway Series subscriptions to ensure getting tickets. Playhouse Square's office staff members were told to conduct business on their cell phones to free up the lines for ticket requests. When the smoke cleared, the subscription list had increased by ten thousand to a total of approximately forty-one thousand. And the *Hamilton* bump didn't subside; indeed, PSC actually gained subscriptions afterward.[52] Small wonder that everyone was looking forward to a return visit in 2020!

Coming Back

For Clevelanders convinced that their city was definitely on the way back to its former prestige, the 2010 census might have served as a reality check. Instead of nudging back up from 476,575 to half a million once again, the city's population continued its downward slide to below 400,000—396,815, to be exact. The nation's one-time Fifth City now ranked a middling forty-fifth. Cleveland had been among the hardest hit cities in the housing slump of the early 2000s, especially in older neighborhoods. According to the *New York Times*, however, it was among the first cities to show signs of recovery from the crisis.[53]

In fact, one might find increasing signs of renewal in neighborhoods across the city. On the west side, Tremont continued its comeback with a mix of new and renovated housing, high cuisine, and comfort food. Ohio City acquired a night life along West Twenty-Fifth Street and Lorain Avenue, where a head-spinning assemblage of brew pubs followed in the wake of the pioneering Great Lakes Brewing Company on Market Square. At the heart of Detroit Shoreway was the Gordon Square Arts District, which offered three theaters and several trendy eating spots within half a dozen blocks.[54] Between Detroit Shoreway and Ohio City sprang up a new neighborhood appropriately dubbed "Hingetown." Cleveland's oldest surviving church building, St. John's Episcopal, was the neighborhood's longtime anchor, but an abandoned transformer station of the Cleveland Railway Company was the catalyst for its resurgence. Art patrons Fred and Laura Bidwell in partnership with the Cleveland Museum of Art arranged to maintain it as a contemporary art gallery.[55]

On the other side of town, the isolated cultural oasis of University Circle was once again acquiring a neighborhood. Project Uptown filled in a long-empty stretch of Euclid Avenue between the striking new Museum of Contemporary Art Cleveland and the converted Model T factory home of the Cleveland Institute of Art, with mixed apartments and retail for both students and residents. Most dramatically, in 2017, on part of the old streetcar turnaround that gave the area its name, rose a twenty-story, 267-unit apartment tower named for its address—One University Circle.[56]

The once celebrated "Millionaires' Row" was long gone, but Euclid Avenue had been reinventing itself as Midtown. From University Circle to Public Square, the Euclid Corridor was streamlined in 2008 with the completion of a $200 million HealthLine by the Regional Transit System. It wasn't a subway, but special buses-only lanes around a center median for bus stops cut the trip on the former No. 6 bus from forty minutes to under a half-hour. More importantly, it added an estimated $9.5 billion in development and thousands of jobs around the Euclid Corridor. Symbolic of the Midtown reawakening was the announcement in 2020 that the Cleveland Foundation was planning to move from downtown's Hanna Building to a new headquarters to be built at East Sixty-Sixth Street and Euclid, next door to the Dunham Tavern Museum. The foundation's relocation might be seen as indicative of an intention to do more for the revitalization of inner-city neighborhoods such as Hough.[57]

Downtown seemed to be flourishing on its own. Public Square, Cleveland's front parlor for two centuries, was slated for a $30 million makeover by 2016, when the city was to host the Republican

National Convention.[58] It would be Cleveland's first major political convention since the glory days of the 1920s and '30s.

For urban authenticity, conventioneers might head to East Fourth Street. In the fourteen years since Nick Kostis opened his Pickwick and Frolic on the foundations of the Euclid Avenue Opera House, East Fourth Street had gone from downtown backwater to a Cleveland destination. Most of the transformation was due to father-and-son developers Rick and Ari Maron, who acquired the properties lining the street, rehabbed their upper floors for tenants, and attracted mid- to upscale restaurants for their ground floors. Kostis welcomed the company, visualizing East Fourth as a reincarnation of Cleveland's defunct Short Vincent nightlife mecca north of Euclid Avenue. Short Vincent had been closed off once a year for a charity bazaar; East Fourth was closed to through traffic permanently and lined from Euclid to Prospect by restaurants with seasonal outdoor seating.[59]

Five blocks east of Fourth Street, brothers Fred and Greg Geis revived the Euclid to Prospect block of East Ninth Street. They built the new Cuyahoga County headquarters on the Prospect corner; in the middle they converted the brutalist former Ameritrust building into The 9, a combination hotel and residence tower. On the Euclid corner, traditionally Cleveland's busiest, they enticed the Heinen brothers to open a downtown supermarket in the historic Cleveland Trust main banking building. Downtown residents could do their grocery and ready-to-eat shopping under a majestic rotunda lined with scenes of the early Western Reserve by noted muralist Francis Millet.[60]

Housing had become the springboard of downtown recovery. "But if Playhouse Square, as seems more than likely, attracts large numbers of people downtown," Wolf Von Eckardt wrote in 1978, "a good many of them will decide to settle there." Cleveland was lagging behind such cities as Baltimore and Philadelphia in luring middle-class urban pioneers to restore downtown townhouses, "simply because there are no townhouses [in Cleveland] to restore."[61] True enough, but Cleveland had plenty of warehouses, and when they ran out of warehouses west of Public Square, rehabbers turned their attentions to the older office buildings to the east. Among them were the Park Building on Public Square, the Standard Building on St. Clair Avenue, and the former East Ohio Building on Superior and East Ninth Street.

With the aid of historic tax credits, residential conversions marched up Euclid Avenue. On the fringe of Playhouse Square the fifteen-story Cleveland Athletic Club became The Athlon, with 163 new apartments and an old, shallower CAC swimming pool. The market for downtown housing began to outstrip the supply of old buildings. Atop an eight-level parking garage at Euclid and East Sixth Street rose the nineteen floors of The Beacon, downtown's first high-rise apartment in more than forty years. By 2019, downtown Cleveland had an estimated population of nineteen thousand, and one study projected a potential thirty thousand downtown residents by 2030.[62]

Playhouse Square was watching downtown's residential renaissance with more than casual interest. In 2011, PSF became indirectly involved in the movement when it sold the Hanna Building Annex to the K & D Group of Willoughby for an undisclosed sum. K & D, the region's largest privately held apartment owner, planned to convert the annex into residential units. The Hanna Theatre would remain under the control of Playhouse Square, which would also lease the annex's ground-floor retail space from K & D. Until then, Playhouse Square hadn't been on the radar screen as a residential area, admitted Art Falco. "This project, I think, is going to start changing that impression." Once the economy recovered from the recession, according to the *Plain Dealer,* "Playhouse Square wished to see new residential construction, atop historic buildings at East 13th and Euclid and in place of a parking lot across from the Palace Theatre."[63]

Economic Driver . . . Speed Bump

In 1994, *Variety* had called it an "arts juggernaut." To the *Wall Street Journal* seventeen years later, Playhouse Square was "a unique business model in downtown Cleveland." It was a model others were emulating. "It's no longer enough for performing arts centers to focus on what's on stage," observed Lawrence Goldman, founder and president of the New Jersey Performing Arts Center. "This model [Playhouse Square] is not only right but smart because it secures the urban environment around the arts center, which is good for the city and generates revenue." In pursuance of that outcome, Goldman and his Newark arts center were planning to go into the real estate business.[64]

"The real estate business is a working endowment for the theaters," explained Playhouse Square's Gina Vernaci. "The stages feed the neighborhood's excitement and vice-versa." As listed in the *Journal,* Playhouse Square Real Estate Services owned five buildings accommodating three thousand workers in 1.6 million square feet of office and retail space. "The hallmark of Playhouse Square is that they realized a successful theater district could only work if there was a successful neighborhood," commented Joe Roman, president of the Greater Cleveland Partnership.[65]

To gain widespread political and popular support, however, Playhouse Square had to do more than revive its own neighborhood; it had to provide a boost for the entire local economy. As PSF was closing its "Last Chance Opportunity" capital campaign in 1985, a study estimated that the arts center's economic impact on the area amounted to $15 million. Twenty years later, a CSU study put the center's annual economic impact at $43 million. More recently, Playhouse Square set a figure of $100 million as its annual contribution to the region's economy. According to a travel-focused research firm, visitors to Cleveland increased from 13.7 million in 2007 to 19.6 million in 2019, leaving behind an estimated $6.4 billion in the latter year. "From arts venues such as Playhouse Square to a lone painter in her Cleveland studio," editorialized the *Plain Dealer,* "arts groups are quietly proving their worth."[66]

Forbes magazine weighed in with a feature article in 2016 calling Cleveland "America's Hottest City Right Now." It was more than the Cavaliers' NBA championship, the Indians making the World Series, and East Fourth Street on Saturday night looking more like SoHo than the "Rust Belt," posited the article. David Gilbert, director of Destination Cleveland, pointed out that the Cleveland Clinic was ranked the second-best hospital in the country, the Cleveland Museum of Art and the Cleveland Orchestra were two of the nation's finest, and Playhouse Square was the largest US theater district outside of Lincoln Center. Fifty years earlier, only the art museum, orchestra, and the Clinic might have been considered world-class; Playhouse Square had now joined the ranks of Cleveland's world-class institutions. (Stylistic note: In the *Journal* article, *PlayhouseSquare* was spelled without a space; *Forbes* went back to the traditional two-word style. The single-word spelling, instituted in 2008, was quietly dropped after 2014.)[67]

The *Journal* noted, "The enterprise keeps growing." Playhouse Square added the large Middough Building at East Thirteenth and Dodge Court to its holdings. Opposite the terminus of Thirteenth Street into Huron Road, PSF converted its Wyndham Hotel into a Crowne Plaza Hotel. Among other amenities, the new affiliation provided access to the International Hotels Group's Rewards

Playhouse Square

Club, the world's largest hotel loyalty program. Included in a $6 million renovation were thirty-six chandelier suites in the hotel's cylindrical eastern façade, overlooking Playhouse Square's iconic GE Chandelier, which hung over Euclid Avenue. A new Ghost Light restaurant (formerly Winsor's, then the Encore) occupied the base of the cylinder. The new name alluded to the stage tradition of burning a light all night to keep away any theater ghosts.[68]

Other restaurants made their debuts on Playhouse Square. In the Bulkley Building, the Driftwood Group, which already operated Cibreo in the Hanna Building, opened Republic Food in the space formerly occupied by Otto Moser's. Undoubtedly the liveliest gathering spot in the Square was the Hofbrauhaus, which opened in 2014 between Dodge Court and Chester Avenue. It occupied a new building built in a land-sharing agreement around the Tudoresque quarters of the Hermit Club. The Bavarian-styled Hofbrauhaus included Playhouse Square's first brewery, seating for six hundred inside, and hundreds more in an outdoor beer garden on Chester. "It activates the north campus, where in the past Chester was our back door," said Falco. He envisioned Playhouse Square eventually expanding north into the parking lots surrounding the Greyhound bus station.[69]

Most of Falco's vision for the future would be left for other hands, as PSF's president and CEO announced his retirement in the summer of 2019. He had been with Playhouse Square for thirty-four years and in charge for twenty-eight, during which he had grown the center from five to eleven stages, increased its staff from 100 to 425, and maintained its attendance at 1 million patrons annually. A headhunter had originally recruited Falco for the center, but his replacement was promoted from the ranks. Gina Vernaci, who had cultivated the KeyBank Broadway Series from something of an afterthought to "an economic driver for downtown Cleveland and for cultural tourism," moved up from chief operating officer to chief executive officer. She had arrived in Cleveland fresh out of college around the time of Falco's hiring. "I loved the city. There was so much to do, with an arts scene you couldn't imagine," she recalled. Now she was one of the most influential movers on that scene.[70]

In retirement, Falco remained involved as special adviser to one project that had been on his wish list for nearly a decade. In the spring of 2018, they broke ground in the parking lot across from the Palace Theatre for the Lumen, a 34-floor, 318-unit apartment tower. At 396 feet, it would be the tallest building in Playhouse Square and one of Cleveland's half-dozen highest. Bank loans, state, county, and city grants and loans, foundation gifts, and the PSF provided financing for the $136 million project, downtown's largest residential development in forty years. "If you think about it, we've come full circle from the days when the theaters almost became parking lots," reflected Falco. "Now we are turning what is already a parking lot into something much more beneficial for our neighborhood and for downtown Cleveland." Pictures from Great Lakes Theater and Cleveland Play House productions would lend a theatrical flair to the apartment's hallways and common areas.[71]

Vernaci was embarking on a new direction in Playhouse Square programming—or maybe not so new, considering the theaters' history. It came out of a lunch with Marcie Goodman, executive director of the Cleveland International Film Festival. Goodman began describing the uncertainty hanging over the film festival's thirty-year residency in Tower City, which was about to embark on a $110 million reinvention. "What about Playhouse Square?" suggested Vernaci. A year later, in January 2020, CIFF announced that in 2021 the film festival would be moving up Euclid Avenue, from Tower City to Playhouse Square. The move would bring a hundred thousand patrons to Playhouse Square Center for up to six hundred screenings. "We're looking into every nook and cranny right now," said Vernaci concerning screening venues.[72] That unused Allen Theatre balcony possibly could harbor moviegoers again, just as in the old days.

Goodman and Vernaci viewed Playhouse Square as a permanent home for the film festival. "I think that as we as a center now think about what the future of this district is, it redefines Playhouse Square from a theater district to an entertainment and media center," stated Vernaci. "And the notion that it [the festival] is going to remain in downtown Cleveland is also big."[73]

As the Scottish poet Robert Burns postulated, even the best laid plans were often thwarted, and not necessarily through any fault of the planners. Two months after announcing the film festival's projected move, Vernaci opened a touring production of *Jesus Christ Superstar* in the State Theatre. Though the show had appeared many times at Playhouse Square, she was particularly excited about this visit, which would feature a live theatrical surround-sound experience exclusive to the Cleveland run. It had barely gotten started, however, before it was forced to close, not by poor reviews but the COVID-19 pandemic, which on March 13, 2020, prompted a ban of all mass gatherings in Ohio. "Not knowing how long the shutdown might continue, we debated whether or not to leave the set on stage," commented Vernaci. "We decided it would be best for the show to pack everything up, and it turned out that was the right call."[74]

It definitely was the right call, as the ban continued in Ohio and elsewhere through the end of the year. Playhouse Square in April extended its shutdown through May 31 but held out hope that *Superstar* might return in August and *Hamilton* in the fall. Those hopes were dashed, as even Broadway announced it would remain dark through May 2021. By the fall of 2020, Playhouse Square had cancelled or postponed 680 performances. Great Lakes Theater cancelled its annual production of *A Christmas Carol* for the holiday season. And the Cleveland International Film Festival wouldn't be going anywhere soon. Its 2020 festival, which was to be its last in Tower City, went virtual. The film festival then announced that its 2021 event would also be virtual, serving as a bridge toward the inauguration of its new home in Playhouse Square in the spring of 2022.[75]

As hard as the shutdown was for Cleveland theatergoers, its costs to unemployed theater artists and workers were devastating. Out of a total of 8,250 workers employed by 65 county arts and cultural organizations, 3,157 were laid off, furloughed, or placed on reduced hours in 2020. Some 6,500 events had been cancelled, costing their sponsors more than $119 million in earned and donated revenue. As of early May, Playhouse Square had laid off or furloughed 193 mostly part-time employees. "We must take the necessary measures to overcome the impact caused by the crisis so that Playhouse Square can return to a place of strength, continue our not-for-profit mission and welcome our audiences back safely," announced Vernaci.[76]

As if COVID-19 wasn't enough, Cleveland was one of the many cities hit by civil unrest following the killing of George Floyd in Minneapolis that May. Looters headed from the Justice Center near Public Square to Euclid Avenue, where they broke into Heinen's and other establishments. Playhouse Square's theaters came out unscathed, and most of the vandalized businesses reopened by September. Pandemic closings took an even greater toll on restaurants, downtown and elsewhere. Fire in Shaker Square and Sokolowski's in Tremont were among those announcing that they had served their last meals. Probably the greatest shock came from news in November that Michael Symon's signature Lola bistro on East Fourth Street was planning to close.[77]

A few glimmers of hope relieved the bleakness of pandemic-induced isolation. On December 5, Shaker Heights singer/songwriter Jim Brickman performed a virtual version of his holiday show from a downtown studio, a portion of the profits benefitting Playhouse Square. Ideastream enabled the Great Lakes Theater to deliver *A Christmas Carol* after all, in a radio version over stations WCLV and WCPN. In October, the Lumen had been completed, with close to a third of its units already spoken for. At the end of 2020, Vernaci announced that thirty-four thousand subscribers were committed for the return of the KeyBank Broadway Series.[78]

With the ringing in of New Year 2021 came the arrival of the eagerly anticipated COVID vaccine. Masking and social distancing kept the theaters dark through spring, while Clevelanders underwent immunization. By summer, Vernaci was ready to test the waters. It would be a small show in a small theater, with a limited audience, but Playhouse Square would be back! Opening-night buzz, as described by *Plain Dealer* critic Joey Morona, returned to Playhouse Square on June 11, 2021, for *The Choir of Man* in the Mimi Ohio Theatre. An all-male cast of thirteen singers and dancers transported a socially distanced audience of 248 through an evening in an Irish pub.

"We're season-ticket holders," commented first-nighter Suzanne Fernee. "We always had hope. I told Cindy, 'that first night, we will be there.'" "I'm just so happy for the theater district to be able to welcome everybody back," added her sister Cindy Reitz. "People don't realize how strong the theater community here is. We have one of the best in the country." Following the performance inside, cast members reveled with theatergoers under the GE Chandelier on Euclid Avenue.[79]

Playhouse Square definitely entered the post-pandemic stage that fall, when *The Lion King* heralded the return of the Broadway Series. Health protocols such as face masks remained in place, but Morona reported "near-capacity crowds" and "sidewalks, restaurant patios and the [State] theater lobby . . . brimming with activity. " Closure of sorts came a few months later with the return of *Jesus Christ Superstar*, the musical that the COVID pandemic had literally shut dawn in Playhouse Square two years earlier. It came just as originally planned, with twenty-two local string players in the balcony complementing the eleven-member rock band in the pit to provide a surround-sound experience heard in only the Cleveland appearance.[80]

Another pandemic postponement was redeemed that spring with the long-anticipated Playhouse Square debut of the Cleveland International Film Festival. Nearly thirty thousand filmgoers turned out to view 146 feature pictures and 182 short subjects in six venues including the Westfield Studio Theater and the Upper Allen. Nearly fifty thousand more viewed them online. "I think of the history of Playhouse Square and how these theaters were almost torn down in the 1970s," remarked the festival's associate director Patrick Shepherd. "They were built as movie palaces and vaudeville stages in the 1920s. The fact that we're repurposing those theaters back to what they were originally built for is such an honor and a thrill."[81]

With Playhouse Square in full swing again, Gina Vernaci announced plans to retire early in 2023. Her legacy, the Broadway Series, had rebounded to nearly its pre-COVID level with forty thousand subscribers—still the largest base for touring shows in the country. She would pass on to her successor eleven stages and an array of resident companies headed by two Equity theaters, a resuscitated Cleveland Ballet, Dance Cleveland, CSU's Arts Campus, the Cleveland International Film Festival , and the Tri-C Jazz Fest. Craig Hassall, formerly head of Opera Sydney and chief executive of

London's Royal Albert Hall, was Vernaci's successor. "I've never seen such a concentration of quality venues in one place, in the world," Hassall said of his new assignment. "Seeing the venues . . . clinched it. I thought: 'This is extraordinary.'"[82]

Preservation and Adaptation

However the COVID-19 pandemic fallout finally settles, the theaters of Playhouse Square at least are still there to share in the outcome. "To imagine what would have happened to the city if the Playhouse Square theaters had been bulldozed in 1969 is to shudder," wrote Steven Litt in 2012.[83]

They weren't destroyed, of course, for which Clevelanders might feel eternally grateful. There appears to be a pretty general consensus that the preservation and revival of Playhouse Square provided the spark that relit downtown Cleveland and the city in general. "The creation of Playhouse Square Center gave demoralized Clevelanders the first tangible sign in decades that their city's physical decline could be reversed," stated Diana Tittle in her study of the Cleveland Foundation. "While certainly not the most critical factor, this psychological boost played a part in breaking the 50-year moratorium on downtown development that had been ushered in by the Depression." Arthur Ziegler, president of the Pittsburgh History and Landmarks Foundation, gave the theater revival the place of honor in the Cleveland renaissance. "The Warehouse District, the Tower City project, Gateway, the Flats, the East Fourth Street district—they all followed Playhouse Square," he said. Hunter Morrison, Cleveland's planning director in the 1990s, gives dual credit to Playhouse Square and Gateway. When the downtown department stores closed, he said, "there was no great wringing of hands; because of the investment in Playhouse Square and Gateway, we had a viable model for downtown. Theater and sports created enough of a market to support restaurants, and so on."[84]

But Playhouse Square still came first. According to Tom Yablonsky, director of both the Historic Warehouse District and the Historic Gateway Neighborhood, Playhouse Square was the place where Cleveland philanthropy first came in to save old buildings. It proved the city's capacity to raise money and became a prime mover in the management of buildings. Having formed the city's first Special Improvement District in 1996, Playhouse Square worked with three other groups—the Warehouse District, Gateway Neighborhood, and the Downtown Cleveland Partnership—to expand it into the Downtown Cleveland Improvement District in 2005.[85]

What would the consequences have been for downtown if the theaters had been demolished in the 1970s? "It would be a totally different downtown," said Yablonsky. "It would have been very demoralizing," elaborated Kathleen Crowther of the Cleveland Restoration Society, who thought it might have set back the effort to bring people downtown for decades: "The effort to preserve the theater district came early in Cleveland's preservation movement. It wasn't just about the theaters but also about the role it played in reviving a whole downtown neighborhood. . . . It brought people downtown for performing arts programs. Now Cleveland is a 'foodie' place, and some of that has to be attributed to Playhouse Square. I don't know how you can overestimate its impact."[86]

Due to its position in the vanguard of local preservation and revival, Playhouse Square not only became an inspiration but provided a model for what was to come, downtown and beyond. Detroit Shoreway was one of the first neighborhoods to follow the Playhouse Square example, not only in real estate but in its use of theater as, in Ray Shepardson's words, an "urban tool" to attract urban pioneers back to the central city.[87] Under its founding director, Ray Pianka, and his successor, Jeff Ramsey, the Detroit Shoreway Community Development Organization's first big campaign was to stave off demolition of the Gordon Square Building, a block-long complex containing apartments, storefronts, an arcade, and the Capitol Theatre. It purchased the building in 1979 and ran the Capitol, despite a lack of air-conditioning, on a program of second-run and foreign films until fire shut down the theater in 1984.[88]

By then, however, a lawyer with theatrical proclivities had turned up in the neighborhood. James Levin had been doing "Shakespeare at the Zoo" and special shows at the Capitol, but he recalled, "People told me, 'If you're trying to start a theater, talk to Ray Shepardson.' He was larger than life," Levin said of Shepardson. "Ray was very emphatic," advising Levin, "You need your own space to establish a brand." Levin was encouraged to lease a dance hall at West Sixty-Fifth Street and Detroit Avenue for his Cleveland Public Theatre. In coming years, the derelict Gordon Square Theater and a former Russian Orthodox church and hall were added to the public theater complex.[89]

"Ray absolutely wanted the Capitol to remain as a theater and was encouraged when Cleveland Public Theatre began," said Pianka's widow, Karen. "He understood that two theaters could actually draw more people to the area he so desperately wanted revive." By 2005, a newly formed Gordon Square Cultural Arts District undertook to bolster the area with not two but three theaters. First on its agenda was the reopening of a renovated Capitol Theatre, followed by construction of a new home for the Near West Theatre, a youth theater that had outgrown makeshift quarters in Ohio City. Also included in its $30 million capital campaign were Cleveland Public Theatre renovations and streetscape improvements. "I think the success of Playhouse Square showed donors that the Arts can be a driver for economic development," said Ramsey.[90]

Other neighborhood development groups displayed Playhouse Square influences. "I was certainly aware of the steps Playhouse Square took to get started," said Tom McNair, executive director of the Ohio City Near West Development Corporation. The corporation emulated Playhouse Square by getting grants to own and operate commercial buildings including three co-owned with Detroit Shoreway. Further west, redevelopment of the Variety Theater, a onetime movie and vaudeville house, figured in the plans of Westown Community Development. On the far east side, the LaSalle Theater is a centerpiece for the Collinwood neighborhood's revival. "We want to use it as the spark to reinvigorate 185th Street," said venue manager Lauren Calevish.[91]

Neighborhoods across the city took inspiration from the preservation and resurrection of the theaters of Playhouse Square.

Out of hundreds who contributed to saving the theaters, three individuals stand out. First came Joseph Laronge, the "Father of Playhouse Square." Laronge's determination to build two theaters in the district and squeeze their entrances through a narrow bottleneck to Euclid Avenue gave Playhouse Square its unique concentration of marquees—and two of the world's longest theater lobbies.

The key individual was Ray Shepardson, the school employee from Seattle who stumbled on the theaters after they had gone dark and dedicated himself to saving and relighting them. He originally thought he could restore the State and Ohio for $2 million and hoped to raise the money by attracting twenty-four thousand Playhouse Square Association subscribers at $120 apiece. Two years later, his estimated cost had grown to $7 million, while PSA subscriptions had stalled at only five hundred. Nonetheless, through donations from the Junior League and others, and the profits from *Jacques Brel* and cabaret, he kept the show going on a shoestring for five years, until Cuyahoga County stepped in to secure the future of the theaters. Were it not for Shepardson, the State and Ohio almost certainly would have been destroyed, and with them the uniqueness of Playhouse Square. Morrison believes that probably only the Palace would have been saved. "Most cities kept one," he observes. "The Palace would have been like the Benedum in Pittsburgh—a place but not a district. We would have lost the ability to bring in CSU and the Play House."[92]

So, all the theaters being saved, the question became what to do with them. Architect Peter van Dijk became the third individual instrumental in the revival of Playhouse Square by coming up with the plan to integrate the four Euclid Avenue theaters into the nation's largest arts district outside of Lincoln Center. Van Dijk's vision of a downtown arts center finally captured the establishment support that had eluded Shepardson throughout the 1970s. As Crowther put it, "Ray Shepardson started the vision, then people took over who could make sense of it."[93]

With the backing of the city's foundations and corporations, plans—and costs—for the center grew exponentially. From Shepardson's $120 PSA membership plan, the ante was revised in 1980 to an $18 million capital campaign (the "Last Chance Opportunity"), soon boosted to $27 million. Other campaigns followed to renovate the Allen Theatre and adapt the Hanna for Great Lakes Theater, culminating in the $100 million "Advancing the Legacy" drive. Along the way an ancillary real estate operation materialized to maintain and revitalize the neighborhood and to serve as an endowment for the theaters.

Shepardson had had the support of volunteer visionaries and nascent preservationists all along. It has taken Americans two centuries to discover the romance of the past and to set about preserving and restoring surviving pieces of it. World War II may have been a turning point, as Americans both in service and at home became aware of the tragic destruction of Europe's architectural heritage. The years immediately afterward saw the efforts of its cities to repair, rebuild, and even replicate what they valued the most. Given the desire and the resources, as Playhouse Square has itself demonstrated, even such a total loss as the Ohio Theatre's lobby could be reconstructed.

One of the underlying considerations of preservation is whether there is a use for the thing to be preserved. "Most landmarks must be adapted to other uses than a public exhibition place if they are to be preserved," wrote the local preservationist John Pyke.[94] Public Square's Soldiers' and Sailors' Monument survives as a public exhibition space with the additional purpose of serving as a teaching tool on the Civil War.

While Playhouse Square was preserved primarily for theater use, it has had to adapt to the evolution of theater. The Palace was built exclusively for vaudeville, the State for vaudeville and movies, the Allen primarily for movies, and the Ohio and Hanna for "legitimate" theater. By the end of World War II vaudeville was dead, and all were first-run movie houses except the Hanna, which remained as a venue for touring Broadway shows. Exclusive first-run films left downtown for suburban theater chains by the 1960s, however, and for economic reasons, Broadway's "road" was sending out fewer but bigger shows to the Hanna, which was often too small to profitably house some of the largest megamusicals.

Since its rescue and reopening of the theaters, therefore, PSC has had to become a master of adaptation. Preserving its auditorium and lobby, PSC enlarged the State's stage to accommodate opera and ballet. The Ohio was returned to its original condition to provide a residence for the Great Lakes Shakespeare Festival. The Palace became home to popular music acts and touring Broadway shows. With the popularity and growth of its Broadway Series, PSC even took the Allen out of mothballs and expanded its stage for extended runs of such megamusicals as *The Phantom of the Opera*.

Changing theatrical fashions have necessitated further adaptation in the twenty-first century. The demise of Cleveland Ballet and Cleveland Opera freed the State for more broadways shows, but the decline of the megamusical made the Allen somewhat superfluous. Audiences for legitimate theater were becoming smaller, however, and the Allen was downsized to provide a downtown home for the Cleveland Play House, a move that also involved construction of two smaller theaters in an empty lot next door. Meanwhile, Great Lakes Theater's desire for a more intimate stage brought back the Hanna as a legitimate house.

And so it goes. Retaining its original layout, the Ohio serves various uses ranging from chamber operas such as Opera Circle's *Die tote Stadt* to a reading by Pulitzer Prize–winning poet Mary Oliver. The center also had several smaller stages on hand for cabaret theater and for its extensive educational programs. The return of movies with the Cleveland International Film Festival opened other unexpected spaces, including the unused Allen balcony. "The point is that Playhouse Square is remarkable because they keep figuring things out, they've always been enterprising in trying to accommodate Cleveland's arts groups," observed Crowther.

"They're continuously problem-solving and pulling rabbits out of their hat."[95]

Remaining unchanged through changing fashions and tastes are those awesome Euclid Avenue lobbies, which can serve not only as theater entrances but for public exhibition spaces and ceremonial chambers in themselves.

A recurring regret of Cleveland historians has been the nearly total disappearance of Millionaires' Row. Lauren DeMarco expressed one of the most recent lamentations in the *Plain Dealer:* "There is no bigger loss in Cleveland cultural history than that of Millionaires' Row." One might argue, however, that the loss of Playhouse Square would have represented an even greater deprivation. Lobbying for the listing of Playhouse Square on the National Register, Tom Fisher echoed Archie Bell's laudatory "Little Journey to B. F. Keith Palace." Edward F. Albee, wrote Fisher, "commissioned the Chicago firm of Rapp and Rapp to design the 'finest theater in America,' a palace for people unable to afford the luxuries of marble, chrystal [*sic*], and brocade in their own homes." Entry to most palaces, as Bell had written, was by invitation only; but all were invited to enjoy the luxuries of Keith's Palace, "First come, first admitted."[96]

If a few Euclid Avenue mansions had been saved, they would likely have been scattered—and rarely visited by most Clevelanders. The Playhouse Square theaters are remarkably concentrated and open to every Clevelander and visitor who attends one of their shows. Ceil Hartman took her son, Bill Shepardson, to the Palace in 1990 to see Cathy Rigby in *Peter Pan.* Like those opening-nighters of 1922, she gave as much attention to the surroundings as to the show. "Looking around, I was overcome and very proud of what we had done," she recalled. "That moment kind of solidified the thought that it had been worth it."[97]

Timeline of 2000–2021

September 7, 2000
Cleveland Ballet announces suspension of operations; *Tony n' Tina's Wedding* opens in the Hanna Cabaret

December 1, 2002
Tony n' Tina's Wedding closes record Cleveland run of 801 performances

February 26, 2006
Menopause: The Musical ends its 625-performance run in the 14th Street Theatre

September 24, 2008
Great Lakes Theater opens the "reimagined" Hanna Theatre with Shakespeare's *Macbeth*

September 16, 2011
Cleveland Play House inaugurates the re-renovated Allen Theatre with Brecht's *The Life of Galileo*

May 2, 2014
"World's largest outdoor chandelier" lights up Playhouse Square

June 20, 2014
Playhouse Square kicks off $100 million capital endowment campaign

August 5, 2015
Playhouse Square announces expansion of KeyBank Broadway Series to three-week runs

June 1, 2016
Restored 1921 Ohio Theatre lobby reopened

March 13, 2020
Governor's ban on mass gatherings due to COVID-19 pandemic closes theaters of Playhouse Square

October 2020
Lumen completed

June 11, 2021
The Choir of Man reopens Playhouse Square after pandemic

Remembering a "Forgotten Man"

On an early spring Tuesday night in 2014, the marquees of Playhouse Square were dimmed for the first time since being relighted in the 1980s. Clevelanders learned why the following morning, in their *Plain Dealer:* Ray Shepardson, the man responsible for having turned those lights back on, had died the previous Monday in Wheaton, Illinois. A month later, a long background story by Joanna Connors revealed that the cause of Shepardson's death was a likely suicide.[1]

He had reached the age of seventy and had already seen the passing of some of his early supporters. William Miller, whose *Plain Dealer* stories had publicized Shepardson's early efforts to save the theaters, died at seventy-three in 2009. Providence Hollander, one of the four *Jacques Brel* cast members, had reached the age of eighty-four when she died in 2010. Upon hearing the news, Shepardson had broken into tears. After Shepardson's death, more figures in the rejuvenation of Cleveland's theatre scene departed. Another *Brel* singer, David Frazier, died at seventy-six in 2016. In 2019, architect Peter van Dijk, whose vision of an arts center won the support of the Cleveland Foundation, passed at ninety. Two weeks later came the death, at eighty-eight, of Elaine Hadden, who had marshaled the power of the Junior League behind Shepardson.[2]

No one had believed in Shepardson more than Lainie Hadden. She backed her belief with continued support long after he left

Playhouse Square and Cleveland. When he returned after seventeen years in search of a remunerative occupation, doing what he loved in his adopted hometown, she became the chief backer of his Hanna Theatre Cabaret. Its failure depressed him as much on her account as his own.

For a while Shepardson worked out of Cleveland as a theater restoration consultant. Then he and his third wife, Nanette, moved to Waukegan, Illinois, north of Chicago, where they became actively involved in restoring the Genesee Theatre. There had been varying

Ray Shepardson's memorial service was held on June 14, 2014, at the State Theatre. (Author's collection)

A CELEBRATION
of THE LIFE *of*
RAY SHEPARDSON
(1944–2014)

FOUNDER. LEGEND. VISIONARY. FRIEND.

His vision and dedication helped to chart a course for PlayhouseSquare and saved our historic theaters for the residents of Northeast Ohio. We will all be forever grateful.

degrees of friction in all of Shepardson's restoration projects, from Playhouse Square to the Gem Theatre in Detroit, but in three grueling years the Genesee became the project from hell. The restoration ran over budget and over schedule. Personality clashes arose among Shepardson, the theater's board, and city officials. He had hoped to stay and manage the Genesee after its restoration, but he couldn't win the support of one of the theater's major backers.[3]

The Shepardsons moved on across Chicago to a former farmhouse in the suburb of Wheaton. Their final restoration project was the Wheaton Grand Theatre, which, due to chronic funding problems, they never finished. They subsisted on sporadic consulting assignments, and Shepardson was plagued by a heart condition and other health issues. He began spending time in nearby Aurora, where a former protégé was successfully running the restored Paramount Theatre. His mind was still fixated on the Genesee in Waukegan, however—on his frustrated plans to manage it and his inability to obtain a hearing with his would-be angel.[4]

He also began meeting with a friend named Jeff Baas, who wanted to make a video about Shepardson's theatrical experiences. Baas envisioned it as a chronicle of theater restoration and show business through the life of an insider; Shepardson had his own motives. Early in the filming, he led Baas to a parking garage in Aurora, across the street from the Paramount. He had Baas film him spreadeagled on the sidewalk, looking up at the camera and addressing the backer he had been courting: "Did I really have to do this to get your attention?" Heightening the drama, Shepardson left Baas on the sidewalk and went up to the roof of the garage, telling the videographer he was going to fake a jump. Several times, he leaned further and further over the edge, repeating his accusatory question to the elusive backer, while an increasingly fearful Baas pleaded with him to come down. He did, but only after the Aurora police arrived to investigate.[5]

Two mornings later, Aurora police called Nanette with the news that Shepardson had actually carried out his filmed fantasy. Showman that he was, he had staged his own exit. He had left Nanette a long farewell letter and an equally long list of instructions, including where to find his life insurance policy. One of his standing jokes in recent years was that he was worth more dead than alive.[6]

As Joe Garry recalled, Shepardson had always been difficult. Frank Dutton, who had worked for him for a decade, remembers mood swings from "often laid back" to "a bit hyper when the pressure was on" before an opening. His language could be "colorful at times. . . . Sure, when you deal with IATSE 27 [the stagehands' union] you need to speak the language they understand. I think it just carried over." He could be verbally abusive, as when a worker dropped an urn that broke into pieces. "Ray called him 's——t for brains' for two weeks until he quit and joined the Air Force." Yet most of the faithful remained. "He wasn't always difficult; he was usually laid back," reiterates Dutton. "The idea of helping Cleveland turn around, while saving some significant buildings was also part of the appeal. . . . There was a lot of comradery, especially early on. There was a real sense of 'us against the world' or at least us against Millcap." Garry likened Shepardson's charisma to that of the Pied Piper.[7]

There was a time following Shepardson's departure when some regarded him as "The Forgotten Man of Playhouse Square." That was the head over a commentary by the *Plain Dealer*'s Robert Finn after the success of the NEA's Challenge Grant fund drive in 1982. In a congratulatory program at the State Theatre, Finn had listened in vain for someone to "at least pronounce the name of Ray K. Shepardson in public." That silence, on top of the record of Shepardson's clashes with the city's establishment, led Finn to conclude, "Since his departure, Shepardson has been more or less written out of the history of Playhouse Square."[8]

At times it may have seemed that way, especially in the 1980s, when Playhouse Square was moving in a direction different from Shepardson's vision. Regardless of what form Playhouse Square took, however, Shepardson never became a nonperson in the center's annals. Even when things began to slip out of his control in the late 1970s, Don Robertson extolled him in his *Cleveland Press* column. "He was a believer when none of us believed," wrote Robertson. "He was a worker when we all were apathetic." Eventually Playhouse Square permanently memorialized Shepardson, Hadden, Miller, Garry, and Frazier as "Visionaries" on a plaque in the State Theatre's outer lobby. At his death, even the staid Cleveland Foundation, the very embodiment of the establishment, gave credit where credit was due. "Clearly there were a lot of people who were critical to the success of Playhouse Square," stated the foundation's executive vice president, Richard Eckardt, "but Ray was the person who watered the first seed."[9]

Perhaps the most impressive testimonial had come a few years earlier in the form of an honorary Doctor of Humane Letters degree from Case Western Reserve University. The citation is worth quoting in full:

During the 1970s, Raymond Shepardson mobilized and led a grass-roots campaign to save Cleveland's historic downtown theatres. By staging 200 to 300 productions a year, he succeeded in calling attention to the need for renovating the theatres and prevented their demolition. With the theatres saved from the wrecking ball, other community leaders were able to raise funds to support the restoration. Eventually public and private efforts united to raise $40 million to preserve the historic venues, and one by one they reopened—the Ohio Theatre in 1982, followed by the State and Palace in the late 1980s, and finally the Allen in 1997. The work spearheaded by Shepardson has been hailed by civic leaders as one of the top ten successes in Cleveland history.[10]

Lainie Hadden gave a reception afterward in Shepardson's honor. White-haired and bearded, he seemed quietly pleased but tired. Shepardson valued recognition for his achievements but was reluctant to appear to be reaching for compliments. The idea of him as a "forgotten man" may have gone back to the publication of Play-house Square's "Red Book" in 1975, whose sixty-eight pages did not contain the name Ray K. Shepardson. According to Lainie Hadden, however, its absence was by his own direction. Editor Kathleen Kennedy wanted to put his name in, said Hadden, but Shepardson demurred. "No," he told Kennedy. "If it works, they'll know."[11]

Notes

Abbreviations

In citing works in the notes, short titles have generally been used. Works frequently cited have been identified by the following abbreviations:

CM	*Cleveland Magazine*
CN	*Cleveland News*
CP	*Cleveland Press*
CPD	*Cleveland Plain Dealer*
CPDF	*Cleveland Plain Dealer Friday*
CPDSM	*Cleveland Plain Dealer Sunday Magazine*
CPDWMAS	*Cleveland Plain Dealer Women's Magazine and Amusement Section*
CPS	*Cleveland Press Showtime*
DCB	David D. Van Tassel and John J. Grabowski, eds., *The Dictionary of Cleveland Biography* (Bloomington: Indiana Univ. Press, 1996).
ECH	David D. Van Tassel and John J. Grabowski, eds., *The Encyclopedia of Cleveland History*, 2nd ed. (Bloomington: Indiana Univ. Press, 1996).
FBC	John Vacha, *From Broadway to Cleveland: A History of the Hanna Theatre* (Kent, OH: Kent State Univ. Press, 2007).
HMFDS	James M. Wood, *Halle's: Memoir of a Family Department Store, 1891–1987* (Cleveland: Geranium Press, 1987).
PSCEH	Kathleen Kennedy and Jean Emser Schultz, *Playhouse Square Cleveland: An Entertaining History* (Cleveland: Playhouse Square Foundation and Joseph-Beth Booksellers, c. 2000).
PSCO	Kathleen Kennedy, *Playhouse Square, Cleveland, Ohio* (Cleveland: Playhouse Square Foundation, 1975).
SC	John Vacha, *Showtime in Cleveland: The Rise of a Regional Theater Center* (Kent, OH: Kent State Univ. Press, 2001).
WRHS	Western Reserve Historical Society

Preface and Acknowledgments

1. Kathleen Kennedy, *PSCO*.
2. Dick Feagler, "How We've Changed," *CM* 17 (Aug. 1988): 28.
3. *CPD*, June 2, 1980, 31A.

1. Another Op'nin'

1. *CPD*, Feb. 6, 1921, 4B.
2. *CP*, Feb. 4, 1921, 14.
3. *CPD*, Feb. 5, 1921, Loew's State Theater Section, 7.
4. *CN*, Feb. 5, 1921, State Theater Section, 1.
5. *CPD*, Feb. 4, 1921, 14; *CN*, Feb. 5, 1921, 3.
6. *CN*, Feb. 5, 1921, 1.

7. *CPD*, Feb. 4, 1921, 10.

8. *CN*, Feb. 5, 1921, 3.

9. *CPD*, Feb. 6, 1921, 4B.

10. *CP*, Feb. 7, 1921, 10.

11. Darcy Tell, *Times Square Spectacular: Lighting Up Broadway* (New York: Harper Collins for Smithsonian Books, 2007), 68.

12. William Morrison, *Broadway Theatres: History and Architecture* (Mineola, NY: Dover, 1999).

13. *CPD*, Feb. 15, 1921, 1.

14. Ohio Theatre Opening Night Souvenir Program, Feb. 14, 1921, CPL literature department.

15. Ohio Theatre Opening Night Souvenir Program; *CPD*, Feb. 15, 1921, 1.

16. *CN*, Feb. 2, 1921, 10.

17. *CN*, Feb. 15, 1921, 16.

18. Morrison, *Broadway Theatres*, 113–23.

19. Hanna Theatre Opening Night Souvenir Program, Mar. 28, 1921, CPL literature department; *CPD*, Mar 29, 1921, 12; *FBC*, 1–8.

20. *CN*, Mar. 29, 1921, 1.

21. *Cleveland Free Times*, Jan. 30–Feb. 5, 2008, 20.

22. *CN*, Mar. 29, 1921, 14.

23. *CN*, Mar. 29, 1921, 14.

24. *CPD*, Apr. 3, 1921, Playhouse Square Section, 3A; Apr. 2, 1921, 12.

25. *CPD*, Apr. 3, 1921, Playhouse Square Section, 3A; Apr. 2, 1921, 12.

26. *CPD*, Apr. 2, 1921, 12.

27. Charles S. Brooks, "A Million in 1930," in *Like Summer's Cloud: A Book of Essays* (New York: Harcourt, Brace & Company, 1925), 178. Alas, Cleveland never fulfilled that dream, reaching its highest population of 914,808 in 1950.

28. "Euclid Ave.," in *ECH*, 401.

29. Edward P. Hingston, *The Genial Showman: Being the Reminiscences of the Life of Artemus Ward* (1870; repr., Barre, MA: The Imprint Society, 1971), 60.

30. Jan Cigliano, *Showplace of America: Cleveland's Euclid Avenue, 1850–1910* (Kent, OH: Kent State Univ. Press, 1991), 2.

31. Cigliano, *Showplace of America*.

32. Cigliano, *Showplace of America*.

33. Clay Herrick Jr., *Cleveland Landmarks* (Cleveland: Cleveland Restoration Society and the Early Settlers Association of the Western Reserve, 1986), 92–93, 164–65.

34. *CPD*, Apr. 3, 1921; Herrick, *Cleveland Land-marks*, 140–41.

35. "Cowell and Hubbard," in *ECH*, 317.

36. *SC*, 43–98.

37. *CPD*, Oct. 11, 1964, 1.

38. *CN*, Feb. 5, 1921, 2; *CPD*, Dec. 8, 1963, 17D.

39. *CN*, Sept. 3, 1953, 17.

40. *CN*, Feb. 5, 1921, 2.

41. *CN*, Sept. 3, 1953, 17.

42. *CN*, Feb. 5, 1921, 2.

43. *CN*, Feb. 5, 1921, 2.

44. *CN*, Feb. 5, 1921, 1.

45. *CN*, Feb. 5, 1921, 2.

46. *CPD*, Nov. 5, 1922, Keith's Palace Theater Building Section, 7; *CP*, Nov. 30, 1956, 53; *CPD*, Oct. 11, 1964, 1.

47. *CPD*, Apr. 3, 1921, 2A.

48. *CPD*, Nov. 5, 1922, 3.

49. *CPD*, Nov. 5, 1922, 3.

50. *CPD*, Mar. 18, 1937, 8; Aug. 9, 1938, 6.

51. *SC*, 94–95.

52. *CPD*, Apr. 3, 1921, 6A; Nov. 5, 1922, 5.

53. *CPD*, Nov. 5, 1922, 4; Archie Bell, *A Little Journey to B. F. Keith Palace, Cleveland* (Privately printed, n.d.), 18, 25.

54. Herrick, *Cleveland Landmarks*, 114; *CPD*, Apr. 3, 1921, 6A.

55. Morrison, *Broadway Theatres*, 91–93; *CPD*, Nov. 5, 1922, 4; Oct. 27, 1922.

56. *CPD*, Nov. 7, 1922, 6; *CP*, Nov. 7, 1922, 20.

57. Bell, *Little Journey*, 12–13.

58. See preface, ix.

59. *CPD*, Apr. 3, 1921, 6A; Bell, *Little Journey*.

60. Bell, *Little Journey*, 38–41, *PSCEH*, 32–33.

61. *CPD*, Apr. 3, 1921, 6A.

62. B. K. Keith Palace Theatre, Opening Night Souvenir Program, Nov. 6, 1922, author's collection.

63. B. K. Keith Palace Theatre, Opening Night Souvenir Program.

64. *CP*, Nov. 7, 1922, 20; Palace Theatre Opening Night Program.

65. Bell, *Little Journey*, 6–7.

2. High Times, Hard Times

1. "Sterling-Lindner Co.," in *ECH*, 957–58.

2. Clay Herrick Jr., *Cleveland Landmarks* (Cleveland: Cleveland Restoration Society and the Early Settlers Association of the Western Reserve, 1986), 92–93; James M. Wood, *Halle's: Memoir of a Family Department Store, 1891–1982* (Cleveland: Geranium Press, 1987), 98.

3. *PSCEH*, 35.

4. "Cowell and Hubbard Co.," in *ECH*, 317; Herrick, *Cleveland Landmarks*, 28–29.

5. William Ganson Rose, *Cleveland: The Making of a City* (Cleveland: World, 1950), 469–70, 525, 704.

6. *CPD*, Oct. 29, 1931, 4; *CP*, Oct. 29, 1931, 5.

7. *CPD*, Dec. 7, 1932, 7.

8. B. K. Keith Palace Theatre, Opening Night Souvenir Program, Nov. 6, 1922, author's collection.

9. *CPD*, Nov. 5, 1922, 7; Herrick, *Cleveland Landmarks*, 114.

10. Palace Theatre Opening Night Program.

11. "Korner & Wood" in *ECH,* 617.

12. Herrick, *Cleveland Landmarks*, 94–95; Palace Theatre Opening Night Program.

13. *Cleveland City Directory, 1921* (Cleveland: Cleveland Directory Company, 1921), 397.

14. Palace Theatre Opening Night Program; Herrick, *Cleveland Landmarks*, 74.

15. "Grays Armory" and "Wigmore Coliseum," both in *ECH*, 494, 1086.

16. *CPD*, Apr. 3, 1921, 6B.

17. *CPD*, Oct. 17, 1921, 12.

18. *Motion Picture News*, Aug. 20, 27, Nov. 19, 1921.

19. Pictures of many of these Allen stagings may be seen in the Photograph Collection of the Cleveland Public Library's Louis Stokes Wing.

20. *CPD*, Aug. 7, 1921, Amusement and Auto News, 5.

21. *CPD*, Aug. 8, 1921, 10.

22. *Variety*, June 3, 1921.

23. *Variety*, June 30, 1921.

24. *CN*, Feb. 5, 1921, 3.

25. *CPD*, Oct. 2, 1921, Amusement and Auto News, 4.

26. *CP*, Nov. 28, 1921, 16.

27. *Variety*, Sept. 22, 1922; *CPD*, Nov. 17, 1925, 19.

28. *CPD*, Mar. 9, 1927, 1; John Vacha, "He Saved Nome . . . Cleveland Saves Balto," *Timeline* 22, no.1 (Jan.–Mar. 2005): 54–69.

29. *Exhibitors Trade Review*, Oct. 4, 1924.

30. Scott Smith, *The Film 100: A Ranking of the Most Influential People in the History of the Movies* (Secaucus, NJ: Citadel Press, 1998), 135–36.

31. *CPD*, Apr. 3, 1921, 6A; Nov. 5, 1922, Keith's Palace Theater Section, 2.

32. "Keith's East 105th St. Theater," in *ECH*, 609.

33. *CPD*, Nov. 9, 1947, 17D.

34. *CPD*, May 11, 1926, 18; Mar. 4, 1925, 14; Sept. 30, 1924, 20.

35. *CPD*, Feb. 15, 1978, 7E.

36. Yet the story has persisted nearly to the present day. See "Palace Theatre/1922," *CM* 40, no. 12 (Dec. 2011): 104.

37. Application No. 208442, Probate Court Marriage Records, Cuyahoga County Archives; George Burns, *The Third Time Around* (New York: G. P. Putnam's Sons, 1980), 63–65; *CP*, Mar. 22, 1926, 12.

38. *CPD*, June 28, 1925, Dramatic-Feature Section, 1; Nov. 9, 1947, 17D.

39. *SC*, 131.

40. "Robert H. McLaughlin," in *DCB*, 299.

41. *SC*, 87, 95–97.

42. *CN*, Sept. 11, 1928, 18.

43. *CN*, Nov. 2, 1926, 16.

44. *CPD*, Nov. 3, 1926, 22.

45. *FBC*, 19–29.

46. *FBC*, 31–47.

47. *CPD*, Feb. 24, 1925, 16; Nov. 10, 1926, 20.

48. *CN*, Nov. 12, 1929, 18.

49. *CPD*, Nov. 30, 1927, 21; *CP*, Nov. 29, 1927, 22.

50. Howard Taubman, *The Making of the American Theatre* (New York: Coward McCann, Inc., 1965), 206.

51. *SC*, 110–19.

52. *CPD*, Oct. 14, 1928, Women's and Dramatic Feature Section, 16; Jan. 1, 1929, 27.

53. *CPDWMAS*, Dec. 21, 1930, 9; *CP*, Dec. 24, 1930.

54. *CPDWMAS*, Dec. 21, 1930, 12; *CPD*, Dec. 24, 1930, 16.

55. *CP*, Dec. 24, 1930, 10.

56. "Hermit Club," in *ECH*, 517; Rose, *Cleveland*, 640; Hermit Club, "Fireside Chat," Jan. 25, 1983 (newsletter, author's collection).

57. Eric Johannesen, Ohio Historic Inventory: "The Hermit Club" (Nov. 1975); Cleveland Landmarks Commission Nomination Form, Hermit Club, May 21, 1976, File No. 197; Herrick, *Cleveland Landmarks*, 98–99.

58. "An Emblem of Public Service" (Cleveland: The Ohio Bell Telephone Company, c. 1927); Rose, *Cleveland*. 848.

59. Rose, *Cleveland*, 885–86; "Cleveland Union Terminal" and "Shaker Heights Rapid Transit" in *ECH*, 297–98, 916–17.

60. "Cleveland Mirrors Progress in New Rail Project," *CPD*, June 29, 1930, Union Terminal Section, 7.

61. Philip W. Porter, *Cleveland: Confused City on a Seesaw* (Columbus; Ohio State Univ. Press, 1976), 122; "Euclid Ave. Assn.," in *ECH*, 497.

62. *CPDWMAS*, Sept. 30, 1934, 11.

63. *CPD*, Jan. 11, 1930, 19.

64. *CPDWMAS*, Apr. 3, 1932, 9.

65. *CPDWMAS*, Sept. 24, 1933, 9–10.

66. See John Vacha, *Meet Me on Lake Erie, Dearie! Cleveland's Great Lakes Exposition, 1936–1937* (Kent, OH: Kent State Univ. Press, 2011), 22–26.

67. *CP*, Dec. 9, 1932, 8.

68. *CP*, Oct. 16, 1934, 1.

69. *FBC*, 30–31.

70. Ann Douglas, *Terrible Honesty: Mongrel Manhattan in the 1920s* (New York: Farrar, Straus & Giroux, 1995), 60, 467.

71. *SC*, 131–34.

72. *SC*, 148–49.

73. *CP*, Oct. 23, 1934, 18.

74. *CPD*, Oct. 24, 1934, 17.

75. *CPDWMAS*, Oct. 20, 1935, 9.

76. *SC*, 151–52; *FBC*, 55–56.

77. James M. Wood, *Out and About with Winsor French* (Kent, OH: Kent State Univ. Press, 2011), 2–12; *CP*, Jan. 3, 1933, 18; *CPD*, Jan. 3, 1933, 4.

78. Wood, *Out and About with Winsor French*; *CN*, Jan. 3, 1933, 7; *CPD*, Jan. 3, 1933, 4, 23.

79. See chap. 1, 19.

80. *CPD*, Oct. 23, 1935, 1.

81. *CP*, Oct. 21, 1935, 20.

82. *CP*, Oct. 23, 1935, 16.

83. Morrison, *Broadway Theatres*, 125–27; *CP*, Oct. 21, 1935, 20.

84. *CP*, Oct. 23, 1935, 16; *CPD*, Oct. 23, 1935, 1.

85. *CPD*, Oct. 23, 1935, 1.

86. *CPD*, Oct. 23, 1935, 1.

87. *CPD*, Apr. 3, 1936, 21.

88. *CPD*, July 10, 1936, 10; *CP*, Oct. 13, 1936, 18; Nov. 18, 1936, 14.

89. *CN*, Dec. 4, 1936, 12; *CP*, Nov. 25, 1935, 9; Donald T. Grogan to John D. Cimperman, Feb. 2, 1988, in Cleveland Landmarks Commission files, Cleveland City Hall.

90. See Vacha, *Meet Me on Lake Erie, Dearie!*, 163–66.

91. Vacha, *Meet Me on Lake Erie, Dearie!*, 163–66; *CP*, Feb. 27, 1936, 20.

92. "Stouffer Foods," in *ECH*, 958; *CPD*, Nov. 22, 1935, 28; May 8, 1936, 16.

93. *CPD*, July 13, 1936, 11; *CP*, July 20, 1936, 6; Herrick, *Cleveland Landmarks*, 74.

94. *CPD*, Feb. 5, 1928, Dramatic and Feature Section, 4; Mar. 4, 1928, Dramatic and Feature Section, 4.

95. *CPD*, Jan. 6, 1929, Women's and Dramatic Feature Section, 6; Dec. 21, 1928, 23; Dec. 30, 1928, Women's and Dramatic Feature Section, 9.

96. See above, 42.

97. *CPD*, Mar. 3, 1934, 16; Alan F. Dutka, *Historic Movie Theaters of Downtown Cleveland* (Charleston, SC: History Press, 2016), 53, 149.

98. *CP*, Oct. 6, 1932, 6.

99. *CPD*, Apr. 22, 1939, 14; Dec. 4, 1941, 16; Oct. 10, 1941, 18; *Motion Picture Herald*, Mar. 19, 1938.

100. *CP*, July 17, 1937, 16.

101. *CPD*, May 20, 1939, 7; May 13, 1939, 9; Joel Grey with Rebecca Poley, *Master of Ceremonies: A Memoir* (New York: Flatiron Books, 2016), 15.

102. Dutka, *Historic Movie Theaters of Downtown Cleveland*, 181.

103. *CPD*, Oct. 27, 1934, 18; *CPDWMAS*, Feb. 25, 1934, 9.

104. *CPD*, June 9, 1939, 12; Mar. 2, 1939, 19; Aug. 19, 1939, 8; Dec. 1, 1939, 18.

105. *CPD*, Jan. 26, 1940, 9.

106. *CPD*, Jan. 26, 1940, 9; Sept. 27, 1941, 14.

107. Hallie Flanagan, *Arena: The Story of the Federal Theatre* (New York: Limelight Editions, 1985), 12–14.

108. *FBC*, 53–54; Herrick, *Cleveland Landmarks*, 95.

109. Alexander Woollcott, "Miss Kitty Takes to the Road," *Saturday Evening Post*, Aug. 18, 1934.

110. *CN*, Jan. 30, 1931, 17.

111. *CP*, Dec. 11, 1934, 22.

112. *CN*, Mar. 16, 1937, 18.

113. *CP*, Oct. 30, 1934, 18.

114. *CPD*, June 8, 1936, 15.

115. *CPD*, Oct. 25, 1938, 18.

116. *CPDWMAS*, Nov. 13, 1938, 13B; *CPD*, Nov. 14, 1938, 11; Nov. 15, 1938, 10.

117. *CP*, Oct. 1, 1940, 16.

118. *CP*, Dec. 30, 1936, 9; Dec. 31, 1936, 6; *CN*, Dec. 31, 1936, 12.

119. *CP*, Sept. 2, 1941, 1; Milton Krantz, interview with author, Dec. 14, 1995.

120. Don Grogan, interview with author, Dec. 28, 2004.

3. Backing the Home Front

1. *CPDWMAS*, Dec. 7, 1941, 15B.

2. *CPD*, Dec. 8, 1941, 4.

3. *CPD*, Dec. 9, 1941, 1; *CN*, Dec. 9, 1941, 13.

4. "Fireside Chat on the Entrance of the United States into the War," Dec. 9, 1941, in *Noth-*

ing to Fear: The Selected Addresses of Franklin Delano Roosevelt, 1932–1945, ed. B. D. Zevin (Cambridge, MA: Houghton Mifflin, 1946), 305–6.

5. *CP,* Dec. 10, 1941, 12; *Time,* Dec. 22, 1941.

6. *CN,* Dec. 15, 1941, 15; Dec. 17, 1941, 20.

7. Milton Krantz, interview with author, Dec. 14, 1995.

8. "World War II," in *ECH,* 1107–9; *CN,* Sept. 24, 1942, 1.

9. *CP,* Sept. 24, 25, 1942, 8; *CPD,* Sept. 25, 1942, 8.

10. Richard R. Lingeman, *Don't You Know There's a War On? The American Home Front, 1941–1945* (New York: G. P. Putnam's Sons, 1970), 170, 175.

11. Lingeman, *Don't You Know There's a War On?,* 206; *CPDWMAS,* June 28, 1942, 11B; *CPD,* Oct. 2, 1942, 10.

12. *CPD,* Apr. 29, 1943, 15.

13. *CPDWMAS,* Dec. 31, 1944, 5C.

14. Lingeman, *Don't You Know There's a War On?,* 206.

15. *CN,* Aug. 29, 1942, 14.

16. *CPD,* July 7, 1944, 13.

17. *CPD,* July 20, 1944, 6.

18. Douglas Gomery, *Shared Pleasures: History of Movie Presentation in the United States* (Madison: Univ. of Wisconsin Press, 1992), 82.

19. "World War II," in *ECH,* 1107–9; *Variety,* Sept. 14, 1943.

20. *Variety,* Feb. 7, Oct. 30, 1940.

21. *CP,* Sept. 23, 1943, 14; *CPD,* Sept. 22, 1943, 9–10.

22. *CPD,* Oct. 3, 1942, 8; *CN,* Sept. 23, 1943, 17.

23. *CPD,* Sept. 1, 1942, 16; Sept. 2, 1942, 17.

24. Lingeman, *Don't You Know There's a War On?,* 175; *CPD,* Sept. 14, 1942, 2.

25. *CPD,* July 20, 1944, 6; *Motion Picture Herald,* Jan. 6, 1945; William F. Miller, "The Perils of Herman Pirchner," *CPDSM,* Dec. 4, 1983, 17; Alan F. Dutka, *Historic Movie Theaters of Downtown Cleveland* (Charleston, SC: History Press, 2016), 110–11; *Motion Picture Herald,* Apr. 1, 1944.

26. *CP,* Jan. 25, 1943, 1; Feb. 6, 1943, 13.

27. *CPD,* Feb. 14, 1944, 11; Dutka, *Historic Movie Theaters of Downtown Cleveland,* 75.

28. *CPD,* Sept. 2, 1942, 17.

29. William Morrison, *Broadway Theatres: History and Architecture* (Mineola, NY: Dover, 1999), 80–81; Richard Goldstein, *Helluva Town: The Story of New York City during World War II* (New York: Free Press, 2010), 139.

30. *CPD,* Sept. 2, 1942, 17.

31. *CPD,* Sept. 2, 1942, 17.

32. *CP,* Sept. 2, 1942, 17; *CP,* Oct. 31, 1942, 18.

33. *CP,* Sept. 2. 1942, 17; *CPD,* Dec. 29, 1942, 11; Elaine Fasciano et al., eds., *Here's Looking at Ya!* (Cleveland: American Theatre Wing / Stage Door Canteen of Cleveland, n.d.).

34. *CPD,* Dec. 29, 1942, 11; *CP,* Nov. 21, 1942, 7; *CPD,* Nov. 22, 1942, 17A.

35. *CPD,* Jan. 15, 1943, 1; *CP,* Jan. 14, 1943, 24.

36. Lawrence J. Quirk, *Bob Hope: The Road Well Traveled* (New York: Applause Books, 1998), 4–5, 19–22; Bob Hope as told to Pete Martin, *Have Tux, Will Travel* (New York: Simon & Schuster, 1954), 5, 40.

37. Quirk, *Road Well Traveled.*

38. *CPD,* June 14, 1943, 14; *CP,* June 14, 1943, 10.

39. Dorothy Renker, "Canteen Was Full of Laughter, Warmth, Help," *CPD,* Oct. 26, 1995, 10E; *CP,* July 22, 1943; Jan. 14, 1944.

40. Ann Carroll, telephone interviews with author, Apr. 6, May 3, 2018.

41. Undated draft by canteen volunteer Betty Whitty for "War Chest Speech," WRHS.

42. Carroll interviews.

43. Renker, "Canteen Was Full of Laughter"; *CP,* Aug. 28, 1943, 2; *CPD,* Oct. 25, 1945, 14.

44. Cleveland Stage Door Canteen *Callboard,* June 1944); *CPD,* Nov. 25, 1943, 42.

45. *CPD,* Nov. 25, 1943, 42.

46. Renker, "Canteen Was Full of Laughter"; *CPD,* Jan. 15, 1944, 3.

47. *CPD,* June 24, 1943; Renker, "Canteen Was Full of Laughter"; *CPD,* Sept. 4, 1944, 26; Jan. 15, 1943, 1.

48. *Variety,* June 14, 1944; *CPD,* Aug. 3, 1944, 13; Stage Door Canteen of Cleveland letterhead, WRHS.

49. *CPD,* Oct. 27, 1945, 14; Oct. 25, 1945, 14; *CP,* Oct. 27, 1945, 6..

50. Krantz interview.

51. See *FBC,* 140–44.

52. Krantz interview.

53. *FBC,* 72; *CP,* Dec. 8, 1942, 22.

54. *CPD,* Feb. 14, 1944, 11.

55. *CP,* Nov. 22, 1943, 18; Mar. 6, 1945, 10; *CPD,* Dec. 4, 1983, 13D

56. *CPD,* Dec. 24, 1942, 6; Mar. 24, 1943, 10; Dec. 28, 1943, 15.

57. *CP,* Oct. 4, 1943, 12.

58. *CPD,* Sept. 19, 1944, 13; May 4, 1943, 13; *CPDWMAS,* May 9, 1943, 13B.

59. *CN*, Oct. 31, 1944, 12.

60. Krantz interview; Myrna Katz Frommer and Harvey Frommer, *It Happened on Broadway* (New York: Harcourt Brace, 1998), 100.

61. *CPD*, Nov. 4, 1943, 11; Krantz interview; *CP*, Nov. 9, 1943, 10.

62. *CN*, Nov. 25, 1942, 14; *CPD*, Mar. 20, 1945, 11; *CP*, May 22, 1945, 16.

63. *CPDWMAS*, Dec. 31, 1944, 5C.

64. *CPD*, Feb. 2, 1945, 1; Feb. 5, 1945, 17; Feb. 12, 1945, 11.

65. *CPD*, Apr. 14, 1943, 5, 11.

66. Clay Herrick Jr., *Cleveland Landmarks* (Cleveland: Cleveland Restoration Society and the Early Settlers Association of the Western Reserve, 1986), 164; *CPD*, Nov. 13, 1942, 6.

67. *CPD*, May 9, 1945, 1.

68. *CPD*, Aug. 15, 1945, 1.

4. Postwar Peak to Pits

1. *CPD*, Jan. 1, 1946, 1.

2. *CPD*, Dec. 31, 1945, 4–5.

3. *CPD*, Dec. 31, 1945.

4. "World War II," in *ECH*, 1107–9.

5. *CPD Pictorial Magazine*, Jan. 1, 1950, 29.

6. "Cleveland: A Bicentennial Timeline," in *ECH*, xii–xxvii.

7. William Ganson Rose, *Cleveland: The Making of a City* (Cleveland: World, 1950), 950; *CP*, Mar. 18, 1937, 1.

8. Clay Herrick Jr., *Cleveland Landmarks* (Cleveland: Cleveland Restoration Society and the Early Settlers Association of the Western Reserve, 1986), 164–65.

9. *HMFDS*, 178–79.

10. *HMFDS*, 176, 180.

11. Herrick, *Cleveland Landmarks*, 141; *FBC*, 110–15.

12. *CN*, Feb. 18, 1954, 17; *CPD*, Dec. 14, 1948, 7; May 15, 1954, 3.

13. "WEWS" in *ECH*, 1058.

14. *CP*, Nov. 7, 1947, 18; *CPDWMAS*, Nov. 9, 1947, 17D.

15. *CPD*, Nov. 14, 1947, 25.

16. Ann Carroll, interview with author, May 3, 2018.

17. *CPD*, June 8, 1951, 14; *CPD*, June 12, 1951, 20.

18. Alan F. Dutka, *Historic Movie Theaters of Downtown Cleveland* (Charleston, SC: History Press, 2016), 170–71.

19. Douglas Gomery, *Shared Pleasures: A History of Movie Presentation in the United States* (Madison: Univ. of Wisconsin Press, 1992), 82.

20. *Life*, Sept. 24, 1943, 60–75.

21. *CPD*, Jan. 10, 1957, 8.

22. *CPD*, Jan. 10, 1957, 8; "Nike Missile Bases" in *ECH*, 738–39.

23. *CP*, June 27, 1952, 1, 21; June 28, 1952, 14.

24. *CPD*, Dec. 22, 1948, 13.

25. *CPD*, Nov. 30, 1956, 22.

26. *CP*, June 14, 1957, 28.

27. Dutka, *Historic Movie Theaters of Downtown Cleveland*, 149–51.

28. *FBC*, 78–110.

29. *CPD*, Dec. 19, 1947, 20.

30. Richard Rodgers, *Musical Stages: An Autobiography* (New York: Random House, 1975), 243.

31. *CP*, Mar. 15, 1949, 14; *CPD*, May 31, 1949, 13.

32. *CPD*, Mar. 12, 1946, 18; *CP*, Mar. 12, 1946, 20.

33. *CPDWMAS*, Sept. 21, 1947, 15-B; *CPD*, Sept. 23, 1947, 17.

34. Tallulah Bankhead, "It's Not 'The Road'—It's Detours," in *The Passionate Playgoer: A Personal Scrapbook*, ed. George Oppenheimer (New York: Viking, 1958), 213. As owner of the Cleveland Indians, Veeck brought droves of baseball fans into Cleveland Stadium.

35. *CP*, Oct. 18, 1952, 14.

36. *CN*, Apr. 14, 1953, 18; *CPD*, Apr. 5, 1953, 41D.

37. *CPD*, Apr. 19, 1953, 58D.

38. Frederick Nolan, *The Sound of Their Music: The Story of Rodgers and Hammerstein* (London: Unwin, 1979), 188; *CP*, Apr. 22, 1953, 24; Rodgers, *Musical Stages*, 283.

39. *CP*, Apr. 21, 1953, 20; *CPD*, Apr. 21, 1953, 18.

40. Dutka, *Historic Movie Theaters of Downtown Cleveland*, 182; *CN*, Dec. 23, 1948.

41. *CPD*, Dec. 22, 1948, 20; Dutka, *Historic Movie Theaters of Downtown Cleveland*.

42. *CPD*, Jan. 23, 1947, 10; Oct. 23, 1949, 25D; Dutka, *Historic Movie Theaters of Downtown Cleveland*.

43. Gomery, *Shared Pleasures*, 56–57, 67.

44. Neal Gabler, *An Empire of Their Own: How the Jews Invented Hollywood* (New York: Doubleday Anchor, 1989), 408; *CPD*, Dec. 20, 1964, 2H; *CP*, July 4, 1964, 17.

45. James Agee, "Prize Day," *Nation*, Dec. 25, 1943, reprinted in *James Agee: Film Writing and Selected Journalism* (New York: Library of America, 2005), 81–82; US Bureau of the Census, *The*

Statistical History of the United States from Colonial Times to the Present, ser. R90–98 (Stamford, CT: Fairfield, 1965), 491.

46. US Bureau of the Census, *Statistical History of the United States*, 491; *CP*, June 28, 1952, 12.

47. *CPD*, Jan. 22, 1953, 19; Jan. 23, 1953, 14.

48. *CPD*, Apr. 22, 1953, 30; Dutka, *Historic Movie Theaters of Downtown Cleveland*, 150; Gomery, *Shared Pleasures*, 240.

49. Dutka *Historic Movie Theaters of Downtown Cleveland;* Gomery, *Shared Pleasures*, 241–43.

50. *CPD*, Apr. 5, 1953, 41D.

51. *CPD*, Oct. 5, 1956, 20; *CN*, Oct. 23, 1956, 17; *CPD*, Nov. 2, 1956, 42.

52. *CPD*, Nov. 30, 1956, 23; Dutka, *Historic Movie Theaters of Downtown Cleveland*, 173.

53. *CP*, Nov. 14, 1957, 58; *New York Times,* Jan. 19, 2018, 1C.

54. *CP*, June 21, 1960, 14.

55. *CP*, June 20, 1960, 1; "Cleveland: A Bicentennial Timeline," in *ECH*, xii–xxvii.

56. "World War II," in *ECH*, 1107–9.

57. Dick Feagler, "How We've Changed," *CM* 17 (Aug. 1988): 76.

58. *CP*, Sept. 22, 1960, 26.

59. J. Mark Souther, *Believing in Cleveland: Managing Decline in "The Best Location in the Nation"* (Philadelphia: Temple Univ. Press, 2017), 20–21.

60. Souther, *Believing in Cleveland*, 21–22; *CPD*, July 12, 1953, 16A.

61. *CP*, Aug. 1, 1953, 2.

62. *CP*, Apr. 7, 1957, 1; Souther, *Believing in Cleveland*, 23–24.

63. *CPD*, Dec. 19, 1959, 24; Souther, *Believing in Cleveland*, 26; *CPD*, Dec. 16, 1959, 15; *CP*, Dec. 21, 1959, 1.

64. *CP*, Dec. 22, 1959, 1; Don Grogan oral history in Jeff Heydrich, "How We've Changed," *CM* 17 (Aug. 1988): 35.

65. *CP*, Dec. 22, 1959, 1.

66. "Erieview" in *ECH*, 396; Souther, *Believing in Cleveland*, 20, 33.

67. Souther, *Believing in Cleveland*, 33–34; Philip W. Porter, *Cleveland: Confused City on a Seesaw* (Columbus; Ohio State Univ. Press, 1976), 181.

68. Souther, *Believing in Cleveland*, 41–42.

69. Porter, *Cleveland*, 180–82.

70. Grogan oral history in Hedrich, "How We've Changed," 35.

71. *CPD*, Nov. 1, 1964, 3H.

72. *SC*, 217–18.

73. Milton Krantz, interview with author, Dec. 14, 1995; Bill Doll, "What happened to Theater Guild?," *CPD*, Mar. 7, 1976, Section 6, 1.

74. Krantz interview.

75. Don Grogan, interview with author, Dec. 28, 2004; Krantz interview.

76. Grogan interview.

77. Krantz interview.

78. *CPD*, Oct. 16, 1960, 1H.

79. John Lithgow, *Drama: An Actor's Education* (New York: HarperCollins, 2011), 15.

80. *CP*, Oct. 25, 1960, 20.

81. *FBC*, 163–77.

82. *CPD*, Dec. 9, 1958, 28; *CP*, Feb. 2, 1969, 24.

83. *CPD*, May 14, 1963, 24; Joel Grey with Rebecca Poley, *Master of Ceremonies: A Memoir* (New York: Flatiron Books, 2016), 33.

84. *CPD*, May 14, 1963, 24; *CP*, May 14, 1963, C5.

85. *CPD*, Dec. 13, 1967, 22, *CP*, Jan. 30, 1969, C6.

86. *CPD*, Feb. 9, 1965, 27.

87. *CPD*, Jan. 21, 23, 1968.

88. Jan Cigliano, *Showplace of America: Cleveland's Euclid Avenue, 1850–1910* (Kent, OH: Kent State Univ. Press, 1991), 309, 317–20, 337–38; "William Taylor Son & Co.," in *ECH*, 1089.

89. Herrick, *Cleveland Landmarks*, 112; *CPD*, Aug. 14, 1965, 18; "Cleveland State University," in *ECH*, 292.

90. Dutka, *Historic Movie Theaters of Downtown Cleveland*, 113, 140, 150; *CPD*, Dec. 9, 1957, 1.

91. "Hough Riots," in *ECH*, 548; Porter, *Cleveland*, 259; *CPD*, Sept. 6, 1966, 1.

92. *CPD*, Jan. 21, 1968, 1F.

93. Dutka, *Historic Movie Theaters of Downtown Cleveland*, 129.

94. Dutka, *Historic Movie Theaters of Downtown Cleveland*, 113, 151, 174.

95. *CPD*, Nov. 1, 1964, 3H; Jan. 21, 1968.

96. *CPD*, Oct. 11, 1964, 1; *CP*, Nov. 30, 1956, 53.

97. *CN*, Feb. 5, 1921, 2; "Stillman Theater," in *ECH*, 958.

98. Porter, *Cleveland*, 258; "Korner & Wood" and "Sterling-Lindner Co.," both in *ECH*, 617, 957–58.

99. *CPD*, July 6, 1964, 1; *CP*, July 6, 1964, C2.

100. *CP*, Jan. 25, 1969, 1; Nov. 12, 1957, 34.

101. *CPD*, Mar. 10, 1968, 4H; *CPD*, May 4, 1968, 56.

102. *CP*, Jan. 25, 1969, 1; *CPD*, Feb. 9, 1969, 4G.

103. *CP*, Aug. 1, 1967, A8.

104. Dutka, *Historic Movie Theaters of Downtown Cleveland*, 175.

105. *CPD*, Aug. 8, 1971, 1H.

5. "It Was Those Murals"

1. *Life*, Feb. 27, 1970, 39; *CPD*, Feb. 5, 2010.

2. Elaine Hadden, telephone interview with author, Aug. 31, 2012.

3. See chapter 1, 5; "A Shy Artist Paints Bold Murals: James Daugherty's favorite subject is America," *Life*, Oct. 25, 1937, 48.

4. *PSCEH*, 24.

5. *CPD*, May 8, 2011, A2; Ray Shepardson, telephone interview with author, Sept. 12, 2012.

6. David Naylor and Joan Dillon, *American Theaters: Performance Halls of the Nineteenth Century*, rev. 2nd ed. (Atglen, PA: Schiffer, 2006), 193–94; A. J. P. Taylor, *From Sarajevo to Potsdam* (London: Thames & Hudson, 1966), 97; Ray Shepardson, telephone interview with author, Sept. 12. 2012.

7. *CPD*, Apr. 24, 1969, 1A, 6A; *CP*, July 19, 1969, A3.

8. *CP*, June 1, 1970, D3; Shepardson interview, Sept. 12, 2012.

9. *CPD*, June 11, 1995, 6; Shepardson interview, Sept. 12, 2012.

10. *CP*, June 1, 1970, D3; *Parma Sun-Post*, June 4, 1970.

11. *CPD*, Aug. 1, 1993, 1B.

12. Shepardson interview; Mrs. John A. [Elaine] Hadden Jr., oral interview, Jan. 17, 1984, 29, Cleveland Families Oral History Project, WRHS; "Intown Club," in *ECH*, 576.

13. *CP*, Apr. 6, 1971, B4.

14. *CPD*, July 25, 1971, 18A; Shepardson interview with author, Nov. 8, 1996.

15. *CPD*, July 25, 1971, 18A.

16. *CPD*, July 23, 1971.

17. "Cuyahoga River Fire" and "Glenville Shootout," both in *ECH*, 338–39, 479.

18. *CPD*, Aug. 20, 1971, 28C.

19. Douglas Gomery, *Shared Pleasures: A History of Movie Presentation in the United States* (Madison: Univ. of Wisconsin Press, 1992), 93; Hadden interview, Aug. 31, 2012; Shepardson interview, Sept. 12, 2012.

20. Cecilia Hartman, email interview with author, Dec. 4, 2018.

21. Hartman interview, Dec. 4, 2018; Oliver Henkel, "A Tribute to Ray Shepardson," remarks at *A Celebration of the Life of Ray Shepardson*, State Theatre, June 24, 2014; Cecilia Hartman, interview with author, Jan. 9, 2019.

22. Hartman interview, Jan. 9, 2019; Hartman, email correspondence to author, Dec. 6, 2018.

23. *CPD*, Nov. 27, 1984, 16A; *CPD Pictorial Magazine*, June 28, 1959, 12; *CP*, May 17, 1960, 10A; *CPD*, Oct. 17, 1971, 47D.

24. Hartman interview, Jan. 9, 2019.

25. *CPD*, Feb. 7, 1972, 10A; Mar. 19, 1972, 1AA.

26. *CPD*, Oct. 17, 1971, 47D; *CP*, Nov. 9, 1971, 4A.

27. *CP*, Nov. 22, 1971, 2E.

28. *CP*, Nov. 22, 1971; Hartman interview, Jan. 9, 2019, *CPD*, Nov. 28, 1971, 13F.

29. *CPD*, Feb. 7, 1972, 10A.

30. *CPD*, Mar 19, 1972, 1AA.

31. Frank Dutton, email interview with author, Nov. 26, 2018; *CP*, Apr. 15, 1971, 9C.

32. Dutton interview, Nov. 26, 2018

33. *CPD*, Mar. 27, 1972, 7D.

34. *CPD*, Apr. 5, 1972, B1.

35. *CP*, Apr. 5, 1972, B4.

36. *CPD*, Apr. 4, 1972, B2; Dutton interview, Nov. 26, 2018.

37. Alan F. Dutka, *Historic Movie Theaters of Downtown Cleveland* (Charleston, SC: History Press, 2016), 152–53; Hartman interview, Jan. 9, 2019.

38. Hartman interview, Jan. 9, 2019; Peter van Dijk, Remarks at Allen Theatre Forum, Dec. 12, 1987, in George V. Voinovich Papers, WRHS.

39. *CPD*, May 25, 1972, 1A.

40. *CPD*, May 25, 1972; *HMFDS*, 198–207.

41. *CPD*, May 25, 1972, 1A.

42. *CP*, July 21, 1972, 3.

43. Dutton interview, Nov. 26, 2018.

44. *CPD*, May 28, 1972, 6AA; June 4, 1972, 7AA.

45. *CPD*, May 28, 1972, 1B; June 4, 1972, 7AA.

46. *CPD*, June 3, 1972, 1A; May 26, 1972, 11C.

47. *CPD*, June 3, 1972, 1A

48. "Junior League of Cleveland, Inc.," in *ECH*, 605.

49. Hadden oral history interview, 30; *CPD*, June 3, 1972, 1A.

50. *CPD*, Oct 5, 1975, Section 5, 1; Hadden interview, Aug. 31, 2012.

51. *CPD*, June 3, 1975, 1A; Rebecca Meiser, "Lainie Hadden, Philanthropist," *CM* 40 (Sept. 2011): 22; "John A. Hadden, Jr.," in *DCB*, 197–98; Hadden, oral history interview, 29–30.

52. Hartman interview, Jan. 9, 2019; *CPD*, June 3, 1972, 1A.

53. *CPS*, July 21, 1972, 3–4.

54. *CP*, July 25, 1972, A6.

55. *CP* special edition, Aug. 7–13, 1972, 1–2; *CPD*, July 11, 1972, 6B.

56. Frank Dutton, "A Cleveland Classic Party in a Classic Cleveland Theatre," *Frank's Place* (blog), Aug. 12, 2017, http://frank-dutton.blog spotcom /2017/08/a-cleveland-classic-party-in-classic.html; *CP* special edition, Aug. 7–13, 1972, 2.

57. *CP*, Aug. 14, 1972, B2; *CPD*, Aug. 14, 1972, 3C; Dutton, "Cleveland Classic Party."

58. *CP*, Aug. 10, 1972, D3; *CPD*, Aug. 22, 1972, 1.

59. *HMFDS*, 198; Hadden oral history interview, 19; *CPD*, July 28, 2013, G1; Elaine Hadden, telephone interview with author, Apr. 16, 2019.

60. *CPD*, Sept. 9, 1972, 14B.

61. Dutton, email correspondence with author, Mar. 26, 2019; Hadden interviews, Aug. 31, 2012, Apr. 16, 2019.

62. *CPD*, Apr. 24, 1969, 1A; Aug. 14, 2005, 5B; Hadden interview, Apr. 16, 2019; Hartman interview, Jan. 9, 2019.

63. *CP*, Dec. 22, 1972, A7; *CPD*, Dec. 23, 1972, 6C.

64. *CPD*, Sept. 2, 1972, 11A.

65. Joseph Garry, telephone interview with author, Oct. 17, 2012; *CPD*, Mar. 20, 2016, 3D; Hartman interview, Jan. 9, 2019.

66. Hadden, interview of Aug. 31, 2012; Hartman interview, Jan. 9, 2019.

67. *CPD*, June 9, 1985, 42P; Frank Dutton, "Jacques Brel Is Alive and Well and Living in Paris," *Frank's Place* (blog), Apr. 18, 2017, http://frank-dut ton.blogspot.com/2017/04/jacques-brel-is-alive-and-well-and.html; *CPD*, Apr. 19, 1973, 14A.

68. Dutton, "Jacques Brel Is Alive and Well"; *CPD*, Apr. 19, 1973, 14A.

69. Dutton, "Jacques Brel Is Alive and Well"; Frank Dutton, email interview with author, Nov. 26, 2018.

70. Dutton, "Jacques Brel Is Alive and Well."

71. Hartman, email correspondence with author, Jan. 16, 2019; Hartman interview, Jan. 9, 2019; *CP*, Apr. 14, 1973, 5B.

72. *CPD*, Apr. 19, 1973, 14A.

73. *CP*, Apr. 21, 1973, 5B; *CPD*, Apr. 23, 1973, 1F.

74. *CP*, Apr. 21, 1973, 5B; *CPD*, Apr. 23, 1973, 1F.

75. *CP*, Apr. 21, 1973, 5B; *CPD*, Apr. 23, 1973, 1F.

76. *CP*, Apr. 21, 1973, 5B; *CPD*, Apr. 23, 1973, 1F.

77. Dutton, "Jacques Brel Is Alive and Well"; Hartman interview, Jan. 9, 2019; *CPD*, Apr. 19, 1973, 14A.

78. *CP*, Apr. 26, 1973.

79. Henkel, "Tribute to Ray Shepardson"; *CPD Action Tab*, June 1, 1973, 3; *CP*, June 23, 1973, B4; *CPD*, July 2, 1973, 26E.

80. Henkel, "Tribute to Ray Shepardson"; *CPD Action Tab*, June 1, 1973, 3; Hadden interview, Aug. 31, 2012; Hartman interview, Jan. 9, 2019.

81. Garry interview; *CPD*, Oct. 24, 1993, 2I; *CP*, June 15, 1973, 7B; Dutton interview.

82. Garry interview; *CPD*, Aug. 5, 1973, 7F.

83. *CPD*, Aug. 5, 1973, 7F.

84. *CPD*, Aug. 5, 1973, 7F; *CPD*, Apr. 27, 1977, 1B

85. *CPD*, Aug. 5, 1973, 7F; Hadden, oral history interview, 31–32.

86. *CPD*, Apr. 27, 1977, 1B.

87. Joe Garry, remarks to Ohioana Library Association, Palace Theatre, Sept. 8, 2012; James M. Wood, "Can the Curtain Stay Up on Playhouse Square?," *CM* 6 (Jan. 1977): 85; SC, 131–34.

88. *CPD*, Oct.7, 1973; Henkel, "Tribute to Ray Shepardson"; Frederik N. Smith, "Playing the Palace Again," *CM* 2 (Nov. 1973): 95–96; Hadden interview, Aug. 31, 2019.

6. In Search of a Plan

1. James M. Wood, "Can the Curtain Stay Up on Playhouse Square?," *CM* 6 (Jan. 1977): 84; Kathleen Kennedy, *PSCO* insert.

2. CP Showtime, July 21, 1972, 3; Playhouse Square Foundation (PSF) website, https://www .playhousesquare.org; Kennedy, *PSCO* insert.

3. PSF website; *PSCO* insert.

4. *PSCO* insert.

5. Russell W. Kane, "Flats Project/Now and Future," *CPDSM*, Mar. 3, 1974, 24, 31.

6. *CPD*, Feb. 13, 1973, 10A.

7. J. Mark Souther, *Believing in Cleveland: Managing Decline in "The Best Location in the Nation"* (Philadelphia: Temple Univ. Press, 2017), 131–36.

8. John S. Pyke Jr., *Landmark Preservation*, 2nd ed. (New York: Citizens Union Research Foundation, Inc. of the City of New York, 1972), 9; "Cleveland Landmark Structures," in *ECH*, 257–59.

9. Pyke, *Landmark Preservation*, 1.

10. John Pyke, interview with author, July 18, 2019.

11. Andrea Velis, "Back to the Bijou," *Opera News* 36 (Sept. 1971): 12–14.

12. "Peter van Dijk interview, 31 August 2006," Cleveland Regional Oral History Collection,

EngagedScholarship @ Cleveland State University, interview 951011, https://engagedscholarship csuohio.edu/crohc000/224/; Cecilia Hartman, interview with author, Jan. 9, 2019.

13. Frederik N. Smith, "Playing the Palace Again," *CM* 2 (Nov. 1973): 96; *CPS*, July 20, 1973, 16; Oliver Henkel, "A Tribute to Ray Shepardson," remarks at *A Celebration of the Life of Ray Shepardson*, State Theatre, June 24, 2014.

14. Henkel, "Tribute to Ray Shepardson." One story about how Exit 85 acquired its name asserts it was so designated to commemorate the retirement of a foundation president in 1985.

15. *CPD*, Nov. 4, 1973, 3H; Oct. 17, 1973, 1C; *CP*, Nov. 6, 1973, B3; *CPD*, Dec. 30, 1973, 2E.

16. *CPD Action Tab*, Dec. 28, 1973, 1, 3.

17. *CPD Action Tab*, Mar. 8, 1974, 1, 3.

18. *CPD*, Feb. 5, 2010, A1; May 8, 2011, A2; John Hemsath, telephone interview with author, Aug. 24, 2019.

19. *CPD*, Oct. 4, 1974, 8D; *CPS*, Oct. 4, 1974, 6.

20. Joe Garry, remarks to Ohio Library Association, Palace Theatre, Sept. 8, 2012; Elaine Hadden, telephone interview with author, Aug. 31, 2014; Cecilia Hartman, interview with author, Jan. 9, 2019.

21. *CPD Action Tab*, May 9, 1975, 2; *CP*, May 10, 1975, B1; Hartman interview, Jan. 9, 2019.

22. *CPS*, July 18, 1975, 3.

23. *CPS*, July 18, 1975, 3

24. *CPS*, July 18, 1975, 3; Hemsath interview; Cecilia Hartman, email correspondence with author, Aug. 26, 2019.

25. *CPD*, July 28, 1975, 4A; Hartman, email correspondence.

26. Kennedy, *PSCO*.

27. *CPD*, July 13, 1975, Section 9, 4; *CP*, July 21, 1975, C6; *CPD*, July 21, 1975, 13A.

28. Hartman interview, Jan. 9, 2019; *CPD*, July 28, 1975, 4A.

29. *CP*, July 28, 1975, 3D; Hemsath interview.

30. *CP*, May 20, 1976, 9C; *CPD*, Mar. 20, 2016, 3D; Diana Tittle, *Rebuilding Cleveland: The Cleveland Foundation and Its Evolving Urban Strategy* (Columbus: Ohio State Univ. Press, 1992), 243–44.

31. *CPD*, July 14, 1975, 1C.

32. *CPD*, Mar. 1, 1971, 2B. See also *FBC*, 116–36.

33. *CPD*, Mar. 1, 2B; Feb. 28, 1971, 1H; Mar. 10, 1971, 1A, 4A; *CP*, Mar. 1971, 1A.

34. *CP*, Mar. 10, 1971, 1A, 10E; *CPD*, Mar. 10, 1971, 1A.

35. *CPD*, Apr. 14, 1971, 1A; *CP*, Apr. 14, 1971, 1A; *CPD*, Apr. 15, 1971, 4B.

36. *CPD*, Apr. 26, 1971, 6A.

37. *CPD*, Jan. 5, 1971, 7B.

38. *CPD*, Aug. 8, 1971, 1H.

39. *CPD*, Dec. 28, 1971, 1A; Jan. 4, 1972, 8A.

40. Milton Krantz, letter to Hanna Theatre subscribers (c. May 1972), author's collection; *CP*, May 15, 1972, 9C.

41. *CPD*, Aug. 7, 1977, Section 5, 1.

42. *CPD*, May 8, 1977, Section 5, 1.

43. *CPD*, Mar. 13, 1974, 6F; *Lakewood Sun Post*, Mar. 24, 1977, [14A]; *CPD*, Nov. 2, 1977, 11B.

44. *CPD*, Feb. 15, 1976, 7E; Milton Krantz, interview with author, Dec. 14, 1995.

45. *CPD*, Jan. 9, 1973, 12A.

46. *Heights Sun Messenger*, Jan. 5, 1978, 8A.

47. *CP*, Dec. 7, 1976, 6B.

48. *CPD*, Sept. 11, 1974, 6G; Jan. 28, 1979, Section 5, 3; Oct. 14, 1979, 1D.

49. *CPD*, Nov. 20, 1976, 1B, 4B; "Cleveland Ballet," in *ECH*, 201–2.

50. *CPD*, Nov. 4, 1973, 6B.

51. *PSCO* insert.

52. Souther,·*Believing in Cleveland*, 103, 134; *CP*, May 3, 1968, 6C.

53. *CPD*, Jan. 6, 1973, 5A; *CPS*, Apr. 13, 1973, 16; *CPD*, June 17, 1973, 1E.

54. *CPD*, June 17, 1973, 1E.

55. *CPD*, July 11, 1972, 2A; Jan. 14, 1974, 22C; Jan. 12, 1976, 4C; *CPD Action Tab*, Dec. 16, 1977, 30.

56. *CP*, Nov. 1, 1972, 10E.

57. *CP*, Feb. 15, 1979, 1B; Cleveland Landmarks Commission Nomination Form, Nom. No. 197, May 21, 1976, CLC Office, City Hall.

58. *CPD*, Jan. 13, 1974, A25.

59. *CPS*, Oct. 12, 1977, 13D.

60. *CP*, Feb. 19, 1976, 5B; *CPD Action Tab*, Feb. 20, 1976, 6; Feb. 27, 1976, 7.

61. *CPD*, July 26, 1976, 1B; *CP*, July 26, 1976, 4B.

62. Hartman interview, Jan. 9, 2019; Henkel, "Tribute to Ray Shepardson"; *CPD*, Nov. 21, 1976, Section 5, 2.

63. *CP*, Oct. 6, 1976, 8C.

64. *CP*, Jan. 22, 1977, 2B.

65. *CPD*, Mar. 23, 1977, 6B; Mar. 19, 1977, 20A; Feb. 17, 1977, 5B; *CP*, Feb. 9, 1977, 4F.

66. *CPD*, Feb. 6, 1977, Section 6, 6; *CP*, Mar. 21, 1977, 10A.

67. *Wall Street Journal*, Apr. 13, 1977, 48.

68. *CPD Action Tab*, June 3, 1977, 18.

69. Kathleen Kennedy, *Playhouse Square Center*, 2nd ed. (Cleveland: Playhouse Square Foundation, 1984), referred to as the "Blue Book."

70. Kennedy, "Blue Book."

71. *CPD Action Tab*, June 3, 1977, 18; *CPD*, Feb. 17, 1977, 5B.

72. Philip W. Porter, *Cleveland: Confused City on a Seesaw* (Columbus: Ohio State Univ. Press, 1976), 286–87; *CPD*, Mar. 17, 1977, A13.

73. Souther, *Believing in Cleveland*, 136.

74. Kennedy, *PSCO* insert; *The Playhouse Square Redevelopment Area Briefing Book* (Cleveland: Playhouse Square Foundation & Cleveland City Planning Commission, 1981).

75. *Briefing Book; CPD*, July 8, 1976, 10B; Tittle, *Rebuilding Cleveland*, 242–43.

76. Van Dijk interview; *CPD*, Oct. 27, 2019, 1D; Ray Shepardson, interview with author, Sept. 12, 2012.

77. Van Dijk interview; Cecilia Hartman, interview with author, Sept. 16, 2019; Tittle, *Rebuilding Cleveland*, 243.

78. *CPD*, May 25, 1976, 1A; van Dijk interview.

79. Van Dijk interview; Tittle, *Rebuilding Cleveland*, 207–8, 210.

80. *CP*, June 2, 1980, 1B; Souther, *Believing in Cleveland*, 144–45; Tittle, *Rebuilding Cleveland*, 211, 232.

81. Tittle, *Rebuilding Cleveland*, 244.

82. Tittle, *Rebuilding Cleveland*, 241–42; "Cleveland Ballet," "Cleveland Opera," and "Great Lakes Theater Festival," all in *ECH*, 201, 270–71, 496.

83. Tittle, *Rebuilding Cleveland*, 245–46.

84. Tittle, *Rebuilding Cleveland*, 38; *CPD*, Dec. 31, 2009, 1B; Playhouse Square News, http://playhousesquare.org, Nov. 14, 2012; Shepardson, telephone interview with author, Nov. 8, 1996.

85. Wood, "Can the Curtain Stay Up on Playhouse Square?," 84.

86. *CPS*, Apr. 22, 1977, 16.

87. Wood, "Can the Curtain Stay Up on Playhouse Square?," 86, 89.

88. Wood, "Can the Curtain Stay Up on Playhouse Square?," 84, 86–88.

89. Wood, "Can the Curtain Stay Up on Playhouse Square?," 84; Gordon Bell, telephone interview with author, Oct. 23, 2012; Tittle, *Rebuilding Cleveland*, 244.

90. *CPD*, Dec. 13, 1976, 1A; Mar. 2, 1977, 22A; Apr. 30, 1977, 8A.

91. Bell interview; *CPD*, June 20, 1977, 1A.

92. *CP*, June 21, 1977, 3A; July 2, 1977, 4A.

93. *CP*, July 14, 1977, 3A; *CPD*, July 15, 1977, 9A.

94. *CPD*, Sept. 27, 1977, 8A; *CP*, Sept. 27, 1977, 5D; *CPD*, Sept. 17, 1977, 1A; Henkel, "Tribute to Ray Shepardson"; Ray Shepardson interview with author, Sept. 12, 2012.

95. Tom Fisher, National Register of Historic Places—Nomination Form: Playhouse Square Group, Apr. 1977, CLC office.

96. *CPD*, Nov. 23, 1978, 3B.

97. *CPD*, Mar. 24, 1978, 1A; June 30, 1978, 8A.

98. Kennedy, "Blue Book"; Henkel, "Tribute to Ray Shepardson"; *CPD*, Apr. 16, 1978; *CPS*, Apr. 27, 1979, 14; May 25, 1979, 15.

99. *CPD*, Apr. 22, 1979, Section 7, 1; Apr. 16, 1978, Section 5, 8.

100. *CPD*, May 28, 1979, 3D.

101. *CPD*, May 28, 1979, 3D; "Recall Election of 1978," "Default," and "Mayoral Administration of Dennis J. Kucinich," all in *ECH*, 848, 352, 686.

102. *Denver Post*, Dec. 22, 1978, 20; Bicentennial timeline, in *ECH*, xxvii.

103. Tittle, *Rebuilding Cleveland*, 246–47.

104. Hartman, email correspondence; Playhouse Square Foundation website.

105. *CPD*, Dec. 24, 1979, 1A; Shepardson interview, Sept. 12, 2012; Hartman interview, Sept. 16, 2019; Joanna Connors, "Ray Shepardson: Death of a Salesman," *CPD*, Special Report, May 25, 2014, 20A.

106. Shepardson interview, Sept. 12, 2012; *CPD*, Dec. 24, 1979, 1A; Feb. 20, 1979, 5A.

107. *CP*, Dec. 4, 1979, 2B; Connors, "Ray Shepardson."

108. *CPD*, Dec. 24, 1979, 1A; Bell interview.

109. *CPD*, Dec. 24, 1979, 1A.

7. Widening the Vision

1. *CP*, Mar. 5, 1980, 5B.

2. *CP*, Mar. 5, 1980, 5B; *CPD*, Mar. 3, 1980, 1A; *CP*, Mar. 3, 1980, 5B.

3. *CPD*, Mar. 3, 1980, 1A; *CP*, Mar. 19, 1980, 1B; Mar. 5, 1980, 5B.

4. *CPD*, June 2, 1980, 31A.

5. *CPD*, May 28, 1981, 25A.

6. Diana Tittle, *Rebuilding Cleveland: The Cleveland Foundation and Its Evolving Urban Strategy* (Columbus: Ohio State Univ. Press, 1992), 247–48; Kathleen Kennedy, *Playhouse Square Center*, 2nd ed. (Cleveland: Playhouse Square Foundation, 1984), referred to as the "Blue Book."

7. *CPD*, Nov. 16, 1980, 1A; *CP*, Feb. 26, 1982, 6A.

8. Alan F. Dutka, *Historic Movie Theaters of Downtown Cleveland* (Charleston, SC: History Press, 2016), 60; *CP*, Mar. 3, 1980, 6B; *CPD*, Jan. 29, 1981, 4C.

9. *HMFDS*, 199–209.

10. *CP*, Mar. 19, 1980, 1B; Mar. 18, 1980, 4A.

11. *CPD*, Sept. 5, 1982, 1A.

12. Clay Herrick Jr., *Cleveland Landmarks* (Cleveland: Cleveland Restoration Society and the Early Settlers Association of the Western Reserve, 1986), 140–41; *CPD*, Nov. 16, 1980, 1A.

13. *CPD*, Mar. 5, 1981, 3D; *CP*, Mar. 12, 1981, A4; Kennedy, "Blue Book."

14. *CPD*, Mar. 12, 1982,1A; *CP*, Mar. 12, 1982, 1A.

15. *CPD*, June 9, 1985, 22A.

16. Kennedy, "Blue Book."

17. *CPD*, Nov. 29, 1981, 1D.

18. John Lithgow, *Drama: An Actor's Education* (New York: HarperCollins, 2011), 8–60.

19. *CPD*, Apr. 19, 1981, 25A; Margaret Lynch, *The Making of a Theater: The Story of the Great Lakes Theater Festival* (Cleveland: Great Lakes Theater Festival, c. 1987); *CPD*, May 18, 1977, 6D; Oct. 4, 1979, 24A.

20. Tittle, *Rebuilding Cleveland*, 247–48; Lynch, *Making of a Theater*.

21. *CP*, June 26, 1981, 12A; *PSCEH*, 64–65; *CPDF*, July 2, 1982, 7.

22. *CPD*, July 8, 1982, Special Advertising Supplement, 4; July 10, 1982, 1B.

23. *CPDF*, July 2, 1982, 6; *New York Post*, Oct. 9, 1982; Lynch, *Making of a Theater*.

24. *CPD*, Sept. 5, 1982, 1D; "Nickleby Triumphant," *Northern Ohio Live* 3, (Oct. 1982): 22; *New York Post*, Oct. 9, 1982; Natalie Epstein to Hon. George Voinovich, Oct. 11, 1982, in George Voinovich Papers, WRHS.

25. *CPD*, July 8, 1982, Supplement, 3; *CPDF*, July 16, 1982, 4; *CPD*, Oct. 22, 1982, 2B; Lynch, *Making of a Theater*.

26. *CPDF*, Sept. 10, 1982, 16; *CPD*, Apr. 26, 1982, 1D; *PSCEH*, 112.

27. *CPD*, May 28, 1981, 1A; *PSCEH*, 65–66; *CPD*, Apr. 26, 1982, 1D.

28. *CPDF*, May 27, 1983, 4; *CPD*, June 8, 1983, 8C; Oct. 21, 1983, 17B.

29. Playhouse Square Center *Revue*, Summer 1984, 1; Robert Finn, "News From: Cleveland," *Opera News*, Feb. 2, 1985, 33; Joanna Connors, "It's the Talk of the Town," *Plain Dealer Magazine*, June 3, 1984, 20.

30. *CPD*, June 10, 1984, 1A, 6A; Playhouse Square Center *Revue*, Summer 1984, 2.

31. *CPD*, June 12, 1984, 5D; June 12, 1984, 2D.

32. Playhouse Square Center Metropolitan Opera program, June 11–16, 1984; *CPD*, June 28, 1984, 12C; Playhouse Square Center Metropolitan Opera program, 1986.

33. Finn, "News From"; Cecilia Hartman, interview with author, Sept. 16, 2019.

34. *CPD*, Dec. 23, 1983, 1B; Jan. 1, 1984, 1D.

35. Wilma Salisbury, "Grand Jeté," *Plain Dealer Magazine*, Oct. 7, 1984, 8–15; *CPD*, Oct. 14, 1984, 19A.

36. *CPD*, Nov. 17, 1984, 6C; Feb. 17, 1984, 11P.

37. Finn, "News From."

38. *CPD*, June 10, 1984, 1D.

39. *CPD*, June 10, 1984, 1D; Feb. 13, 1984, 1B; *CPDF*, June 8, 1984, 15.

40. *CPD*, June 10, 1984, 1D; *FBC*.

41. *CPD*, May 8, 2011, 2A; Oct. 25, 1984, 10C.

42. *FBC*, 137–38; *CPD*, Dec. 14, 1983, 11F.

43. *CPD*, Oct. 2, 1986, 10E; Mar. 4, 1987, 9F.

44. *CPD*, June 3, 1987, 8G.

45. Gina Vernaci, telephone interview with author, Apr. 8, 2020.

46. *CPD*, Aug. 3, 1989, 10E.

47. *CPDF*, Oct. 11, 1985, 5; "Art Falco," interviewed by Leo McKinstry, *CM* 48 (July 2019): 68.

48. *PSCEH*, 82–83; "The Palace Restoration," Cleveland Opera program, Feb. 6–8, 1998, 44–45.

49. *PSCEH*, 82–83; *CPDSM*, Apr. 24, 1988, 7–27.

50. *CPD*, Aug. 5, 2015, A1; Vernaci interview.

51. *CPD*, Dec. 6, 1989, 9-F; Apr. 29, 1982, 8-F.

52. *CPD*, Apr. 4, 1994, 2-A.

53. "Society Corp.," "Tower City Center," and "Gateway Economic Development Corp.," all in *ECH*, 937–38, 1004–5, 462–63.

54. *CPD*, Apr. 4, 1994, 2A.

55. *CPD*, Sept. 26, 1982, 4E; Art Falco, WCLV radio interview, June 26, 2019; "Art Falco," 68.

56. James M. Wood, "Can the Curtain Stay Up on Playhouse Square?," *CM* 6 (Jan. 1977): 84; *CPD*, Mar. 11, 1981, 1A; July 19, 1982, 2C.

57. *CPD*, Aug. 20, 1995, 12B.

58. *CPD*, Aug. 20, 1995, 12B; PSC *Marquee*, Winter–Spring, 1996, 2; Dennis Dooley, "What Jane Knew," *Northern Ohio Live* 16 (Oct. 1995): 112.

59. *CPD*, Aug. 20, 1995, 12B; Dooley, "What Jane Knew"; *CPD*, Dec. 20, 1998, 8F.

60. PSC programs, Aug. 1–13, 1989, July 16–21, 1991; *CPD*, Dec. 18, 1993, 2E.

61. John Vacha, "The Kick-Start to Cleveland's Comeback," *Northern Ohio Live* 18 (Dec. 1997): special section, 6; Falco WCLV interview; Art Falco, telephone interview with author, May 11, 2020; *CPD*, Mar. 15, 2020, 1D.

62. Vacha, "Kick-Start to Cleveland's Comeback"; Falco interview, May 11, 2020; "Winsor French" in *DCB*, 162–63.

63. Memorandum from Andis Udris to Mayor Voinovich, Aug. 19, 1988, in Voinovich Papers, WRHS; *CPD*, Dec. 18, 1993, 2E; Art Falco, telephone interview with author, Nov. 12, 1996.

64. PSC *Revue*, Summer 1985, 3; Showtime at High Noon programs, various dates, 1993–2000.

65. *CPD*, Mar. 4, 1993, 1A, 1B; June 26, 1993, 1E.

66. *CPD*, Sept. 15, 1987; Oct. 20, 1991, 1H; June 10, 1984, 1E.

67. *CPD*, May 19, 1996, 18A.

68. "History of Cleveland Ballet," leaflet, Cleveland Ballet, c. 1997, author's collection; *CPD*, Sept. 8, 2000, 20A; Mar. 26, 1990, 1C.

69. "History of Cleveland Ballet"; *CPD*, Sept. 8, 2000, 20A; Oct. 26, 1999, 3E.

70. *CPD*, Dec. 1, 1991, 1H.

71. *CPD*, Sept. 17, 1989, 5I; Oct. 11, 1989, 8F.

72. David Bamberger, letter to supporters, May 18, 1992, author's collection; *CPD*, Nov. 21, 1992, 6E; May 15, 1995, 3E.

73. *CPD*, Dec. 1, 1991, 1H; Jan. 16, 1998, 1A.

74. Eleanor Mallet, "Lifetime Devotion," *Reserve*, May, 1991, 10–12.

75. *CPD*, Mar. 22, 2020, 19A; *New York Times*, Apr. 6, 2020, 6D; *CPD*, Dec. 2, 1984, 1P.

76. *CPD*, Apr. 12, 2012, 1E; Mallet, "Lifetime Devotion."

77. *CPD*, Mar. 22, 2020, 1D; PSC programs, 1990, 1991, 1992, 1993, 1994, 1997.

78. Marianne Evett, "Broadway's Living Legend," *Plain Dealer Magazine*, May 17, 1987, 6; *CPD*, Mar. 1, 1992, 1H.

79. *CPD*, Mar. 22, 2020, 19A, 1D; *SC*, 213; *CPD*, Mar. 18, 1997, 5B.

80. *CPD*, Apr. 29, 1993, 12F.

81. *CPD*, July 25, 2010, 1E; *PSCEH*, 97–98.

82. PSC news release, Apr. 8, 1996; *CPD*, Apr. 6, 1996, 8E.

83. *FBC*, 137–38.

84. *FBC*, 138–40.

85. *CPS*, July 21, 1972, 3; Dutka, *Historic Movie Theaters of Downtown Cleveland*, 153.

86. Tittle, *Rebuilding Cleveland*, 248–50.

87. Tittle, *Rebuilding Cleveland*, 82–83, 248–56.

88. *CPD*, Aug. 7, 1987, 4B; Aug. 20, 1987, 4B.

89. *Habitat*, Oct. 30–Nov. 5, 1987, 12; *CPD*, Aug. 7, 1987, 4B.

90. *CPD*, Dec. 11, 1987, 8D; Dec. 13, 1987, 1B; Dec. 23, 1987, 2B.

91. *CPD*, Aug. 7, 1987, 4B; *Habitat; CPD*, Nov. 27, 1987, 1C; Feb. 8, 1988, 1B.

92. *CPD*, Apr. 16, 1988, 2B; *CPD*, Apr. 30, 1988, 2B; *Cleveland Edition* 5 (Mar. 29–Apr. 4, 1990): 21; *CPD*, Apr. 3, 1990, 1B.

93. *CPD*, June 15, 1990, 6B; July 22, 1991, 1B; Jan. 27, 1993, 1F.

94. *CPD*, Dec. 2, 1994, 1E; Nov. 11, 1994, 9B; *PSCEH*, 106.

95. *CPD*, Jan. 18, 1997, 8E; Sept. 5, 1997, 1C; PSC *Marquee*, Winter, 1998, 1; "Wrecking Ball Signals Constructive Demolition of Allen Theatre," *Avenues* 10 (Sept. 1998): 48.

96. *Jolson: The Musical* program, Cleveland: PSC Allen Theatre, Oct. 6–18, 1988; *CPD*, Oct. 4, 1988, 1I.

97. Ray Shepardson, telephone interviews with author, Nov. 8, 1996, Sept. 12, 2012; Connors, "It's the Talk of the Town," *CPDSM*, June 11, 1995, 6.

98. Program: "The Hanna Cabaret Presents *The All Night Strut!*"; *FBC*, 146–50; Milton Krantz, interview with author, Dec. 14, 1995.

99. *FBC*, 149–50; Ray Shepardson, telephone interview with author, Oct. 22, 1997.

100. Don Grogan, telephone interview with author, Dec. 28, 2004; *CPD*, Aug. 19, 2005, 5B.

101. John Hemsath, telephone interview with author, July 14, 2005.

102. *Bicentennial News*, Sept. 1994, newsletter, author's collection.

103. Carlos Wolff, "Toasting the Past, Charting the Future," *Celebration 200! The Official Commemoration Program of Cleveland's Bicentennial Celebration* (Cleveland: Live Publishing, 1996), 13–14; Mike Marsalino, telephone interview with author, Oct. 23, 1997.

104. *Bicentennial News*, c. Jan. 1996; *CPD*, July 22, 1994, 9B; Ross De Alessi Lighting Design, fax to author, Mar. 6, 1996.

105. *CPD*, Nov. 11, 1995, 1C; PSC *Marquee*, Fall, 1996, 1.

106. PSC *Marquee*, Fall, 1996, 1; *PSCEH*, 104–5, 113–15.

107. PSC *Marquee*, Fall, 1996, 1; *CPD*, Jan. 28, 1977, 5B.

108. *PSCEH*, pp. 102–3, 107; Vacha, "Kick-Start to

Cleveland's Comeback," 7; PSC *Marquee,* Spring–Summer, 1995, 1; *CPD,* Mar. 17, 1996, 1I.

109. *Variety,* Nov. 7–13, 1994, 53.

110. Donald Rosenberg, *The Cleveland Orchestra Story: "Second to None"* (Cleveland: Gray & Company, 2000), 11, 142–43; Cleveland Orchestra/Allen Theatre programs, Spring 1999.

111. *CPD,* Dec. 21, 1999, 6E.

8. A National Model

1. PSC program for *Titanic,* Allen Theatre, Jan. 18–30, 2000, 20.

2. *Titanic* program; *CPD,* Jan. 16, 2000, 1H.

3. *CPD,* Aug. 30, 2000, 1A; Mar. 18, 2001, 1A; Oct. 1, 2000, 1E.

4. *CPD,* Mar. 18, 2001, 1A; Oct. 21, 2002, 7B; July 19, 2008, 1E.

5. *CPD,* Oct. 13, 2013, 1D.

6. *CPD,* Sept. 8, 2000, 1A; Sept. 14, 2000, 1E; Sept. 21, 2000, 1E; Oct. 15, 2000, 1I.

7. *CPD,* Sept. 10, 2000, 2G; Oct. 15, 2000, 1I; Sept. 9, 2000, 1E.

8. Gina Vernaci, telephone interview with author, Aug. 25, 2005; *CPD,* Aug. 29, 2000, 7E.

9. *CPDF,* Sept. 8, 2000, 16; *CPD,* Sept. 21, 2000, 1E; Jan. 27, 2002, 5J; *FBC,* 151–52; *CPD,* Dec. 2, 2002, 5C.

10. *CPD,* July 1, 2001, 1B; Dec. 10, 2002, B3; Art Falco, interview with author, Aug. 25, 2020.

11. *CPD,* Dec. 10, 2002, 3B; Falco interview.

12. Vernaci interview, Aug. 25, 2005; *CPD,* Apr. 21, 2004, 1E; Feb. 27, 2006, 1D.

13. Milton Krantz interview with author, Dec. 14, 1995; *CPD,* July 24, 2005, 1J.

14. *CPD,* Oct. 3, 2001, 1E; June 6, 2002, 1J; *CPD,* Aug. 25, 2002, 1A; Iryna V. Lendel et al., *Staging Cleveland: A Theater Industry Study* (Cleveland: Community Partnership for Arts and Culture, 2017), 36–37; *CPD,* Dec. 9, 2002, 1A.

15. *CPD,* July 24, 2005, 1J; July 30, 2004, 3E; Art Falco, telephone interview with author, Sept. 8, 2005; *CPD,* Sept. 16, 2005, 1E.

16. *CPD,* Sept. 22, 2007, 1A; Sept. 16, 2005, 1E; Nov. 15, 2007, 1E; Dec. 19, 2007, 1E.

17. *CPD,* Jan. 18, 2008, 1A; Aug. 13, 2008, 1A.

18. *CPD,* Nov. 15, 2007, 1E; GLTF *Progress,* May 2007.

19. *CPD,* Dec. 19, 2007, 1E; Jan. 18, 2008, 1A; *CPD,* June 20, 2008, 6E.

20. *CPD,* Sept. 28, 2008, 5E; Oct. 26, 2008, 1E.

21. *Cleveland Free Times,* Mar. 1–7, 2006, 43; *CPD,* Jan. 18, 2008, 1A; Jeff Ullom, *America's First Regional Theatre: The Cleveland Play House and Its Search for a Home* (New York: Palgrave Macmillan, 2014), xiii, 182; "Cleveland Play House," in *ECH,* 273–274; *Cleveland Scene,* Apr. 29–May 5, 2007.

22. Diana Tittle, *Rebuilding Cleveland: The Cleveland Foundation and Its Evolving Urban Strategy* (Columbus: Ohio State Univ. Press, 1992), 113; *CPD,* May 21, 1965, 1; Ullom, *America's First Regional Theatre,* 152.

23. Ullom, *America's First Regional Theatre,* 182.

24. Falco interview; *CPD,* July 3, 2008, 1A; Ullom, *America's First Regional Theatre,* 183.

25. *CPD,* Apr. 8, 2009, 1A; July 23, 2009, 1C; Falco interview.

26. Falco interview; *CPD,* May 15, 2011, 5E; Aug. 19, 2012, 1E; Jan. 8, 2012, 1E.

27. *CPD,* Aug. 19, 2012, 1E; July 17, 2011, 5E; Sept. 4, 2011, 1E.

28. *CPD,* Aug. 19, 2012, 1E; Cleveland Play House program for *The Life of Galileo,* Sept. 16, 2011, 4.

29. *CPD,* Sept. 4, 2010, 1E; Cleveland Play House program for *Ten Chimneys,* Jan. 13, 2012, 4.

30. *CPD,* Jan. 7, 2012, 1A; Ullom, *America's First Regional Theatre,* 190–91.

31. *CPD,* June 6, 2010, 1E; Falco interview, Aug. 25, 2020.

32. Tom Einhouse, telephone interview with author, Nov. 5, 2020; Falco interview; *CPD,* Feb. 26, 2014, 4A.

33. *CPD,* June 21, 2014, 1A.

34. *CPD,* June 21, 2014, 1A; Apr. 8, 2013, 1A.

35. *CPD,* June 2, 2013, 1E; Apr. 27, 2014, 1D.

36. *CPD,* May 3, 2014, 3A.

37. *CPD,* Dec. 3, 2014, 2A; June 18, 2017, 1B; Falco interview, Aug. 25, 2020.

38. *CPD,* July 26, 2015, 2D; Feb. 14, 2016, 1D; Einhouse interview.

39. *CPD,* Mar. 15, 2015, 1A.

40. *CPD, CPD,* Mar. 15, 2015, 2A; Feb. 14, 2016, D1; Einhouse interview.

41. Ohio History Connection *Echoes* 57 (Jan.–Feb. 2018): 2–3.

42. *CPD,* Mar. 4, 2004, 1F; Hal Holbrook, *Harold: The Boy Who Became Mark Twain* (New York: Farrar, Straus & Giroux, 2011), 26–27, 69; *CPS,* May 10, 1979, 2D; *CPD,* May 19, 1979, 1C.

43. PSC program for *Mark Twain Tonight!,* Mar. 5, 2004, 19–20; *CPD,* Feb. 15, 2015, 1D.

44. PSC programs, various dates (2003–12); *CPD,* Aug. 9, 2013, 2T.

45. Rice Hersey, "Bizet Body," *Northern Ohio Live* 19 (Oct. 1998): 75; *CPD*, May 18, 2003, 6J.

46. *CPD*, Jan. 23, 2004, 1E; Nov. 3, 2005, 1F; Aug. 6, 2010, 1A; Aug. 15, 2010, 1E.

47. *CPD*, July 14, 2011, 2B.

48. *CPD*, Apr. 25, 2015, 1A.

49. *CPD*, July 22, 2008, 1A; Apr. 15, 2008, 1A; Aug. 5, 2015, 1A.

50. *CPD*, Aug. 5, 2015, 1A.

51. *CPD*, Aug. 5, 2015, 1A; *CPD*, Apr. 27, 2016, 1P; Lendel et al., *Staging Cleveland*, 36, 68.

52. *CPDF*, June 10, 2016, 6T; Gina Vernaci, telephone interview with author, Apr. 8, 2020; *CPD*, July 16, 2017, 1D.

53. *CPD*, May 20, 2010, 1B; *New York Times*, Aug. 26, 2009, 1B.

54. *CPD*, Mar. 18, 2012, 1A; *Gordon Square Print* 13 (Nov.–Dec. 2016): 6; *CPD*, Sept. 3, 2014, 1A.

55. *CPD*, Sept. 16, 2011, 1A; Jan. 29, 2013, 1A.

56. *CPD*, Oct. 15, 2017, 1A; Jan. 1, 2014, 11A.

57. *CPD*, Oct. 31, 1993, 3I; Jan. 25, 2017, 4A; Nov. 4, 2018, 1F; Oct. 25, 2020, 20A.

58. *CPD*, Dec. 13, 2009, 1G; Apr. 18, 2014, 1A.

59. *CPD*, Apr. 10, 2016, 1A.

60. *CPD*, Oct. 9, 2016, 1F; Mar. 5, 2017, 2D.

61. *CPD*, Nov. 23, 1978, 3B.

62. *CPD*, Oct. 27, 2019, 1D; Jan. 19, 2020, 1D; Sept. 29, 2018, 1A; Nov. 9, 2019, 1A.

63. *CPD*, Dec. 30, 2011, 8A.

64. *Wall Street Journal*, May 4, 2011, 5D.

65. *Wall Street Journal*, May 4, 2011, 5D.

66. *CPD*, Oct. 17, 2004, 1B; Sept. 23, 2018, 3D; Oct. 28, 2020, 13A; Dec. 16, 2015, 2E.

67. Peter Lane Taylor, "Why Cleveland Is America's Hottest City Right Now," *Forbes*, Oct. 27, 2016, https://www.forbes.com/sites/peter taylor/2016/10/27/why-cleveland-is-americas -hottest-city-right-now/?sh=16a4a0696488; *CPD*, Mar. 30, 2014, 5A.

68. *Wall Street Journal*, May 4, 2011, D5; *CPD*, Aug. 25, 2017, 14A; Apr. 29, 2018, 1F.

69. *CPD*, Oct. 12, 2018, 11A; Feb. 6, 2019, 2C; July 24, 2013, 1A; Falco interview.

70. *CPD*, Mar. 12, 2019, 1A; Art Falco, WCLV radio interview, June 26, 2019; *CPD*, Sept. 23, 2018, 3D; Vernaci interview, Apr. 8, 2020.

71. *CPD*, Apr. 6, 2018, 11A; Sept. 14, 2018, 1A; Oct. 9, 2020, 11A; Gina Vernaci, telephone interview with author, Dec. 10, 2020.

72. *CPD*, Jan. 24, 2020, 1A; Vernaci interview, Dec. 10, 2020.

73. *CPD*, Jan. 24, 2020, 1A.

74. "Playhouse Square Faces Pandemic Challenges Head On with 'BWY in CLE' Expected to Return Fall 2021," news release, Playhouse Square website, Nov. 30, 2020, https://www.play housesquare.org/news/detail/playhouse-square -faces-pandemic-challenges-head-on-with-bwy -in-cle-expected-to-return-fall-2021.

75. *CPD*, Apr. 19, 2020, 5D; May 3, 2020, 6D; Oct. 10, 2020, 7B; Nov. 8, 2020, 2D.

76. *CPD*, Sept. 20, 2020, 1D; May 29, 2020, 12A.

77. *CPD*, Oct. 2, 2020, $2; Nov. 21, 2020, 12A.

78. *CPD*, Sept. 12, 2020, 2A; Oct. 9, 2020, 11A; Falco interview, Aug. 25, 2020; "Playhouse Square Faces Pandemic Challenges Head On."

79. *CPD*, June 13, 2021, 8A.

80. *CPD*, Mar. 12, 2021, 2A; "Jesus Christ Superstar, Keybank Broadway Series," Playhouse Square website, https://www.playhousesquare .org/events/detail/jesus-christ-superstar-3.

81. *CPD*, Mar. 12, 2021, 2A; Aug. 20, 2021, 2A; Apr. 4, 2021, 6D.

82. *CPD*, July 25, 2021, 3D; Aug. 1, 2021, D4; Apr. 23, 2021, 7; Aug. 18, 2021, 1A.

83. *CPD*, Aug. 19, 2012, 9E.

84. Tittle, *Rebuilding Cleveland*, 14–15; *CPD*, Feb. 5, 2010, 1A; Hunter Morrison, telephone interview with author, Sept. 3, 2020.

85. Thomas Yablonsky, telephone interview with author, June 7, 2021.

86. Yablonsky interview; Kathleen Crowther, telephone interview with author, July 8, 2021.

87. See above, 204–205.

88. Karen Pianka, email interview with author, July 13, 2021; Jeff Ramsey, email interview with author, May 21, 2021.

89. James Levin, interview with author, May 4, 2021.

90. Karen Pianka, email interview with author, July 7, 2021; Jeff Ramsey, email interview with author, May 7, 2021.

91. Tom McNair, telephone interview of Apr. 30, 2021; Jennifer Polanz, "Rejuvenating Collinwood," *City Life*, 2020–21, 10, 61.

92. Morrison interview.

93. Crowther interview

94. John S. Pyke Jr., *Landmark Preservation*, 2nd ed. (New York: Citizens Union Research Foundation, Inc. of the City of New York, 1972), 2.

95. Crowther interview.

96. *CPD*, Nov. 10, 2019, 1D; Tom Fisher, National Register of Historic Places—Nomination Form: Playhouse Square Group, Apr. 1977,

Cleveland Landmarks Commission office, City Hall; Archie Bell, *A Little Journey to the B. F. Keith Palace, Cleveland* (N.p.: privately printed, [c. 1922]), 6–7.

97. Cecilia Hartman, interview with author, Jan. 9, 2019.

Epilogue

1. *CPD*, Apr. 16, 2014, 1A; Joanna Connors, "Ray Shepardson: Death of a Salesman," *CPD*, May 25, 2014, 19–22A.

2. *CPD*, Aug. 5, 2009, 1B; Sept. 11, 2010, 3B; Mar. 20, 2016, 3D; Oct. 13, 2019, 2D; Sept. 27, 2019, 8A.

3. Connors, "Ray Shepardson," 20A.

4. Connors, "Ray Shepardson," 20A.

5. Connors, "Ray Shepardson," 21–22A.

6. Connors, "Ray Shepardson," 21–22A.

7. Connors, "Ray Shepardson," 20A, 22A; Frank Dutton, email to author, Aug. 7, 2020.

8. *CPD*, July 4, 1982, 6D.

9. *CP*, Sept. 29, 1977, B5; Connors, "Ray Shepardson," 22A; *CPD*, Apr. 16, 2014, 1A.

10. Case Western Reserve University Honorary Degrees (May 2008), list in author's collection.

11. Elaine Hadden, telephone interview with author, Aug. 31, 2012.

Selected Bibliography

Bell, Archie. *A Little Journey to B. F. Keith Palace, Cleveland.* N.p.: Privately printed, [c. 1922].

Cigliano, Jan. *Showplace of America: Cleveland's Euclid Avenue, 1850–1910.* Kent, OH: Kent State Univ. Press, 1991.

Dutka, Alan F. *Historic Movie Theaters of Downtown Cleveland.* Charleston, SC: History Press, 2016.

Gomery, Douglas. *Shared Pleasures: A History of Movie Presentation in the United States.* Madison: University of Wisconsin Press, 1992.

Herrick, Clay, Jr. *Cleveland Landmarks.* Cleveland: Cleveland Restoration Society and the Early Settlers Association of the Western Reserve, 1986.

Kennedy, Kathleen. *Playhouse Square, Cleveland, Ohio.* Cleveland: Playhouse Square Foundation, 1975.

Kennedy, Kathleen, and Jean Emser Schultz. *Playhouse Square Cleveland: An Entertaining History.* Cleveland: Playhouse Square Foundation and Joseph-Beth Booksellers, c. 2000.

Lendel, Iryna V. et al. Staging Cleveland: A Theater Industry Study. Cleveland: Community Partnership for Arts and Culture, 2017.

Lingeman, Richard R. *Don't You Know There's a War On? The American Home Front, 1941–1945.* New York: G. P. Putnam's Sons, 1970.

Lithgow, John. *Drama: An Actor's Education.* New York: HarperCollins, 2011.

Lynch, Margaret. *The Making of a Theater: The Story of the Great Lakes Theater Festival.* Cleveland: Great Lakes Theater Festival, c. 1987.

Morrison, William. *Broadway Theatres: History and Architecture.* Mineola, NY: Dover, 1999.

Porter, Philip W. *Cleveland: Confused City on a Seesaw.* Columbus: Ohio State Univ. Press, 1976.

Pyke, John S. Jr. *Landmark Preservation,* 2nd ed. New York: Citizens Union Research Foundation, Inc., of the City of New York, 1972.

Souther, J. Mark. *Believing in Cleveland: Managing Decline in "The Best Location in the Nation."* Philadelphia: Temple Univ. Press, 2017.

Tittle, Diana. *Rebuilding Cleveland: The Cleveland Foundation and Its Evolving Urban Strategy.* Columbus: Ohio State Univ. Press, 1992.

Ullom, Jeffrey. *America's First Regional Theatre: The Cleveland Play House and Its Search for a Home.* New York: Palgrave Macmillan, 2014.

Vacha, J[ohn]. E. "The Kick-Start to Cleveland's Comeback," *Northern Ohio Live* 18 (Dec.: 1997): special section, 1–14.

Vacha, John. *From Broadway to Cleveland: A History of the Hanna Theatre.* Kent, OH: Kent State Univ. Press, 2007.

———. *Meet Me on Lake Erie, Dearie! Cleveland's Great Lakes Exposition, 1936–1937.* Kent, OH: Kent State Univ. Press, 2011.

——. *Showtime in Cleveland: The Rise of a Regional Theater Center.* Kent, OH: Kent State Univ. Press, 2001.

Van Tassel, David D. and John J. Grabowski, eds. *The Encyclopedia of Cleveland History,* 2nd ed. Bloomington: Indiana Univ. Press, 1996.

——. *The Dictionary of Cleveland Biography.* Bloomington: Indiana University Press, 1996.

Wood, James M. "Can the Curtain Stay Up on Playhouse Square?" *Cleveland Magazine* 6, (January 1977): 82–89.

——. *Halle's: Memoir of a Family Department Store, 1891–1987.* Cleveland: Geranium Press, 1987.

Index

Page numbers in *italics* refer to illustrations.

Ameritrust, 265

Anderson, Judith, 40, 82

Anderson, Maxwell, 39, 60–61, 82

Anderson, Stan, 97, 113–15, 120–21

Andorn, Sidney, 42

Andrzejewski, Tom, 233

Annie Get Your Gun (Berlin), 99

Ansky, S., 229

Antioch College, 205

Anti-Trust Act, 102

Antony and Cleopatra (Shakespeare), 228

Apollo's Fire Baroque Orchestra, 224

Applause, 172

Apple, 225

Aquarium, 252

Arliss, George, 44, 48, 51

Armington, Ray, 146, 166

Armstrong, Louis, 76

Around the World in 80 Days, 97, 121

Arsenic and Old Lace (Kesselring), 67, 81, 228

Arthur, Julia, 22

Arthur Murray Dance Studio, 138

Ashcraft, Peggy, 60

Associated Inns & Restaurants Corp. of America, 140

Associated Press, 49

Astaire, Adele, 37

Astaire, Fred, 37, 67, 70, 177

As You Like It (Shakespeare), 207

Athlon, The, 266

Awake and Sing, 59

Baas, Jeff, 283

Bab, 38

Bacharach, Burt, 172, 218

Bacon, Faith, 52

Bacon, Henry, 27

Bailey, Henry Turner, 5, 126

Baker, Dick, 146

Baker, Josephine, 94

Baker, Newton D., 25

Baldwin Wallace College, 154

Baldwin Wallace University, 229

Balé Folclórico de Bahia, 224

Ball, Lucille, 95

Ballad of Baby Doe, The (Moore), 226

Ballet Guild, 176

Ballet San Jose, 245

Balto, 34–35

Bamberger, Carola, 226–27

Bamberger, David, 212–13, 226–27, 260

Bampton, Rose, 130

Band Box Theater, 75

Bankhead, Tallulah, 60, 79, 99, 114

Bara, Theda, 33

Barnes, Cliff, 64

Barnes, Clive, 208

Barnycz, Donny, 256

Barrett, Lawrence, 11

Barretts of Wimpole Street, The, 58

Barrie, James, 35

Barrymore, Ethel, 35, 38, 44, 48, 51, 59

Barrymore, John, 39, 44, 48, 51

Barrymore, Lionel, 95

Barthelmess, Richard, 42

Barton, John, 81

Basie, Count, 76

Batdorff, Emerson, 115, 117–18, 193–94, 207

Bay Village, 111

Beacon, The, 266

Beattie jewelers, 143

Beau Geste, 57

Beck, Jeff, 137

Beck, Martin, 22

Bedford, Brian, 215

Beethoven, Ludwig van, 213–14

Behan, Brendan, 166, 168–69

Behrman, S. N., 58, 60

Belasco, David, 8

Belkin, Jules, 160

Belkin Productions, 137

Bell, Archie, 8, 11, 21–23, 25, 37–38, 40, 58, 278

Bell, Gordon, 136, 190, 191, 196

Bellamy, Peter, 67, 83, 114–16, 122, 136–37, 147, 149–51, 156, 170–73, 175

Belle of Amherst, The, 174

Bemis, Cliff, 147–50, 154

Ben Bagley's Decline and Fall of the Entire World as Seen through the Eyes of Cole Porter, 163–65, 176

Benedum, the, 276

Ben-Hur, 37, 118

Benny, Jack, 35, 94

Berea Summer Theater, 147

Berg, Gertrude, 113

Berg, Laura Welsh, *250*

Bergman, Bernard, 154

Bergman, Ingrid, 69

Bergman, Sally, 154

Berlin, Irving, 9, 66–67, 99

Berlin to Broadway, 169

Bernardi, G., 208

Bernhardt, Sarah, 20

Bernstein, Leonard, 98, 114

Bevan, Yolande, 165

B. F. Keith Building, 29–30, 43, 63, 116, 192; electric sign, *20, 21*; lobby, 21

B. F. Keith Palace Theatre, 21–25, 29, 35, 55, 93, 278. *See also* Palace Theatre

Bickoff's Art Gallery, 176

Bidwell, Fred, 264

Bidwell, Laura, 264

Bier, Thomas E., 201

Big Broadcast of 1938, The, 75

Biggar, Hamilton F., III, "Ham," 176, 177, 179

Big Parade, The, 38

Big Show of 1928, The, 173

Billy Rose, the, 9

Birnbaum (Burns), Nathan, 36

Birney, David, 228

Birth of a Nation, 69

Bizet, Georges, 35, 84

Loew, Marcus, 3, 6–7, 17–18, 22, 33–35, 57, 95–97
Loewe, Frederick, 98
Loew's Building, 74, 127, 138–39, 147, 186, 189, 191–92, 239, 255
Loew's Theaters, 3–4, 6–8, 17, 29, 33–35, 50, 54, 66, 68, 76, 85, 95–96, 102–3, 117, 120–21, 125–26, 139, 145, 257
Loew's West, 103
Lola, 271
Lombardo, Guy, 76
Loos, Anita, 3
Love, Montagu, 3
Love, Janis, 247
Loveland, Roelif, 86
Lovers and Friends, 76
Love's Labour Lost (Shakespeare), 261
Lumen, the, 269, 271
Luna Gale, 261
Lundoff-Bicknell Company, 21
Lunt, Alfred, 37, 49, 58–59, 65, 79, 114, 254
Lutheran West High School, 165
Lyon & Healy, 53
Lyric, the, 16
Lytell, Bert, 3

Macbeth (Shakespeare), 250–51
MacDonald, Jeanette, 39, 40
MacKintosh, Cameron, 216–17
MacLaine, Shirley, 100, 101
Madame Butterfly (Puccini), 35
Mad Hatter, 179
Magnificent Obsession, 94
Mahalia, 214
Majestic Urban Revivals, 236
Majority of One, A, 113
Mall Theater, 17–18, 33
Maltese Falcon, The, 63
Mamoulian, Rouben, 98
Manhattan Cocktail, 54
Mantell, Robert, 37, 96
Marco Millions (O'Neill), 39
Mark Twain Tonight, 228, 259–60
Marlowe, Julia, 39
Maron, Ari, 265
Maron, Rick, 265
Marsalis, Wynton, 223
Marsh, W. Ward, 3, 6, 35, 55–57, 59, 66–67, 69, 93, 96–97, 101–3, 105, 110, 118, 121
Marshall, Gay, 207
Martha, 35
Martin, Mary, 84, 215–16
Marx, Groucho, 45
Marx Brothers, 38
Marshall Field & Co., 139, 202–3
Marsalino, Mike, 238
Mary of Scotland, 59
Mason, Dave, 137
Masonic Temple, 226
Massey, Ilona, 70
Massey, Raymond, 60, 76

Mastbaum, the, 162
Masters of Men, 54
Mastroianni, Tony, 115, 121, 139, 143, 149–51, 165, 170, 175, 180–81, 231
Mather, William G., 10
Mather Mansion, 204–5
Maugham, Somerset, 38, 59
May Company, 107, 109
Mayer, Louis B., 35, 95
Mayfair Casino, 50–53, 64, 68, 128
Mayland, the, 110
McCambridge, Mercedes, 231
McCormick, S. Barret, 32–33
McCoy, Kid, 29
McDermott, William, 21, 34–35, 38–39, 41, 44–45, 47–49, 54, 59–60, 82–83, 96, 98, 100–101
McFarlane, Willis M., 140, 146, 159, 161
McGuire, Dorothy, 74, 75
McLaughlin, Dick, 143
McLaughlin, Robert, 7, 37, 47, 50
McNair, Tom, 275
McNeil, Claudia, 113
McVey, William, 193
Meade, Frank Bell, 42–43
Means, Russell, 131
Meet Me in St. Louis, 67, 85
Me and Juliet (Rodgers and Hammerstein), 99–101
Mellott, Lowell, 65
Memphis, the, 103
Menjou, Adolphe, 34
Me Nobody Knows, The, 172
Menopause: The Musical, 247
Meredith, Burgess, 60
Merman, Ethel, 75
Merry Wives of Windsor, The, 37
Metro Films, 3
Metro-Goldwyn-Meyer (MGM), 35, 54, 57, 94–95, 102
Metro Pictures, 35
Metropolitan Opera, 16, 130, 210–12
Metropolitan Opera Pavilion, 211
Metropolitan Parks, 65
Metropolitan Theater, 37
Middough Building, 267
Midland, the, 162
Midsummer Night's Dream (Shakespeare), 60, 113, 225
Mikado, The, 64
Miles, Nadine, 74
Mileti, Nick, 191
Millcap Corporation, 133, 137–39, 143, 145–46, 233, 284
Millennium Eve Concert, 241
Miller, Ann, 215
Miller, Arthur, 115, 228
Miller, Dougfred, 251
Miller, Michael L., 133, 138, 145–47, 189, 192, 233
Miller, William F., 138, 141, 153, 164, 189, 194–97, 210, 281
Millet, Francis, 265
Mimi Ohio Theatre, 271
Minelli, Liza, 193, 194
Mink, Max, 93